National Review
Politically Incorrect
Reference Guide

Your Handbook for the
Right
Information Sources

COMPILED BY

Russell Jenkins
John J. Virtes
Frederick W. Campano

A National Review Book

To
William and Dorothy Jenkins,
John and Anne Virtes,
and
Fred and Brigitte Campano.

And,
of course,
Dorothy McCartney.

With an eye towards future editions or reprintings of this book, we invite readers and organizations to address suggestions and information updates of the material published in **The National Review Politically Incorrect Reference Guide** to National Review, Books Division, 150 East 35th Street, New York, N.Y. 10016.

Jacket design by John Dernbach

Library of Congress Catalog Card Number 93-85244

ISBN: 0-9627841-1-7

PRINTED IN THE UNITED STATES OF AMERICA

TABLE OF CONTENTS

Acknowledgments .... *iv*

A Few Words On Using this Book .... *v*

Foreword -- **Rush Limbaugh**.. *vii*

Introduction -- **William F. Buckley, Jr.** .... *ix*

Index of Topics .... *xi*

Topics .... *1 - 302*

Appendix A (State Governor and Tourism Offices)............ *303*

Appendix B (Conservative Publications)............................. *308*

Acknowledgments

The idea for **The National Review Politically Incorrect Reference Guide** started with a comment from Robert McFadden, a Washington lobbyist (and son of *National Review's* former Associate Publisher Jim McFadden), who mentioned in passing that he had just purchased the New York Public Library's 1991 information reference guide, **The Book of How and Where to Look It Up**, and found that the sources it suggested were typically liberal and politically correct. Curious, we purchased the book and found Robert's assessment to be dead-on. And then the idea struck us: why not have *National Review* publish a similar topic-by-topic reference book, but one that points to conservative information sources, the very ones *NR's* research staff turn to when they are searching for the *right* data?

Before undertaking the book, we asked a sample of *NR* readers if they would want a conservative, topical, information reference guide. Their response was an overwhelming *yes*. And so, armed with our readers' endorsement, the project commenced.

This book is the product of the thoughts and efforts of many people. At *National Review,* those who provided advice on which topics the book should include were Senior Editor Priscilla Buckley, Articles Editor Mark Cunningham, and Assistant to the Editor-at-Large Tony Savage. The first round of fact-checking and proofreading was directed by Editorial Associate Rich Lowry, who was ably assisted by his colleague, Richard Samuelson, along with Paul Marra, Bill Bolan and Elizabeth Capano. Karen Stevens performed the bulk of second-round proofreading duties. She performed the same duties on the third go-round, as did Bob Tobin and *NR* Publishing Assistant Julie Crane. As ever, Cate Moraetis was of endless help tying up loose ends. And you would not be holding this book now were it not for the guidance of Publisher Edward A. Capano.

But this book is really the product of the trio of gentlemen who make up *National Review's* research staff. Who better than they to compile an authoritative conservative reference guide? Librarian *extraordinaire* John J. Virtes, now in his 18th year at *NR*, and Research Assistants Frederick W. Campano, now on the verge of graduating from Fordham University Law School, and Russell Jenkins, the industrious soul who spearheaded this book project, spent many an evening and weekend burrowed away in the *National Review* library researching and assembling the best conservative and politically *in*correct information sources available on hundreds of topics.

We conclude with special thanks to Jeanne Gough of Gale Research, Inc., who gave permission to use organization descriptions from the *Encyclopedia of Associations*, a most-useful work which we heartily recommend. For information about this fine book write Gale Research at 835 Penobscot Building, Detroit, MI 48226-4094.

Jack Fowler
Assistant Publisher

A Few Words On Using this Book

The National Review Politically Incorrect Reference Guide is an information-source handbook covering hundreds of topics of both general interest and of particular interest to conservatives.

The book is easy to use. Topics are 1) listed alphabetically, 2) cross-referenced where possible, and 3) composed of either one or (usually) two categories: "Books and Articles" -- a thorough bibliography of the most seminal writings on that topic -- and "Organizations" -- which provides the names, addresses, phone numbers, publications, and (in most cases) brief descriptions of conservative organizations active on that issue.

The typical Books and Articles section lists 1) books which, in our judgement, are either seminal, informative, and/or admired by conservatives for their excellence and insight into a particular subject, and 2) articles which have been culled from the nation's leading conservative journals, such as *National Review, Policy Review, Commentary, The American Spectator, Crisis, Modern Age, Chronicles, The Cato Journal, The American Enterprise* and *Reason*. Regarding the listing of articles first published in these journals, the time frames used by the compilers of this book are as follows: for *National Review*, articles published from 1982 through June, 1993; for the other conservative journals, from 1988 through 1992.

Included in the book are general interest topics that are non-ideological. We do not, in those cases, provide "conservative" information sources, as there are none. We do, however, list whatever reputable information sources exist on those topics.

You will also find in *The National Review Politically Incorrect Reference Guide* numerous topics that other "popular" and politically correct reference guides fail or refuse to list (due, no doubt, to these topics' natural appeal to conservatives), such as Reaganism, Stalinism, Pornography, Gold Standard, Media Bias, Conservatism, Leftism, Welfare, Tobacco, Home Schooling, and many, many more. Naturally, there *are* topics which both this book and other reference books list. However, there is a major difference in our presentations: we provide the authoritative conservative information sources that the other books just flat out *won't*.

Two notes of caution for purists. The first: not every organization listed in this book is conservative. For example, on certain topics government agencies are listed. We do this to assist those of you who, for whatever reason, need to obtain "official" data and information. The second, related note: often listed are groups which, for one reason or another (such as having narrow goals), cannot be described accurately as "conservative." However, by virtue of their advancing a conservative principle or position, they can be fairly regarded as being part of the wider conservative movement. Hence their inclusion in this book.

Foreword

Rush Limbaugh

At last. From the magazine that has spent nearly four decades debunking the inanities and calamities of the Left comes a take-home debunking kit, a do-it-yourself guide to disassembling the dissemblings of the PC clergy from Nina Totenberg to Dan Rather.

NR's research library -- an Excellence in Researching Network unto itself -- has gathered hundreds of articles from conservative publications and books from conservative minds, forging them into a reference book that even my formerly nicotine-stained fingers can flip through with ease. The topics range from the Hot Button -- abortion and capital punishment -- to the Fun -- baseball and sailing. Uniting them all is a cliché-exploding perspective that can be found nowhere else, except perhaps on a certain growing radio and T.V. show.

With catchphrases like "Decade of Greed" and factoids purporting to show everything from the poor getting poorer to an imminent breakout of AIDS into the general population, the liberal elite media controls America's public debate. It helped put Billary in the White House. Now, with the information that can be culled from this book, you can fight back and -- even with one hand tied behind your back -- win. Consider the facts herein a hidden rocket under the GM Truck of the media establishment.

And it comes just in time. Americans' passivity has ended. Whether it was tax-evading Zöe Baird and her illegal nannies or Lani Guinier and her quota-mongering vision of an America balkanized, ordinary Americans have effectively raised their voices in opposition to threats to the country's ideals. At a time when your opinion matters more than ever, this book is a way to ensure it's an informed one.

Inside is the side of the story you've likely missed -- no matter how many newspapers you read. Did you know the rich got richer under Reagan because *more* people got rich? Or that some of the most effective public school systems in the nation are those that spend the *least*? Or that not so long ago scientists were warning about global *cooling*? With the reference guide and a trip to the library these facts -- often hidden beneath the bluster of our Pat Schroeders and Paul Wellstones -- are within grasp.

There's nothing a liberal hates more than the inconvenient fact. This is a guided tour of a bevy of them. It's a first step to loosening the bonds of an America held hostage.

June 24, 1993

Introduction

William F. Buckley, Jr.

This *Reference Guide* is wonderfully useful, and I devoutly hope that everybody who has written to me or to another editor of *National Review* asking for a little help in researching this point or that will acquire a copy and consult it. During the past twenty or thirty years several efforts have been made to bring together what one might call a conservative bibliography, and these have varied in form. Some have included portraits of leading conservative figures and writers, others accounts of what it is that appears between the covers of this or that critically important book. One or two have given brief histories of a conservative organization or lobby; all of this, as I say, very useful.

What this *Guide* attempts is a measure of comprehensiveness. A "measure" is here if not the operative word, a very important qualifier. By this I mean that many readers will discover a title unaccountably missing under "Astronomy" or "Chile." For instance -- me. In 1970 I travelled with Alistair Horne, the distinguished British historian, in South America, spending considerable time in Chile, which had inaugurated the awful Salvador Allende and was beginning the brutal years that would in 1973 see the overthrow of Allende by Pinochet who also brought brutal years, but did so headed for liberal democracy rather than Gulag: so that the stars look down differently on the two men. Anyway: Mr. Horne wrote a book, "Small Earthquake in Chile" published by Viking Press in 1973 and lo! it was dedicated to me, and lo! it is not included under "Chile." I labor this point in order to mollify those readers who find missing in our *Guide* a book or an article or an organization that nestles in their memory as critical to their memory of this or of that.

But this is pettifoggery. In this book under "Baseball" one will find the reference to the wonderful exchange between George Will and Donald Kagan. There are 302 pages, carefully culled, an extraordinary labor by John Virtes, Russell Jenkins and Frederick Campano which cost them thousands of hours of work, which will translate into saving readers of their *Guide* hundreds of thousands of hours of searching, often to no avail, because the skills of the trained librarian and researcher are of the essence of philanthropy. It is because of their industry that we are spared great pains, spared, in many cases, exercises in futility; because although we know that such and such a volume or article must exist, to find it may call for the use of skills we have not developed. For this reason I am grateful, as I am sure you will be, to the compilers of this *Guide*, and to those who midwived this important enterprise.

June 29, 1993

Index of Topics

Abortion	1	Balance of Payments	37
Academia	5	Balanced Budget Amendment	37
AIDS	5	Ballet	37
Adoption	7	Banking/Banks	38
Advertising	8	Baseball	40
Affirmative Action	8	Bible	40
AFL-CIO	10	Bilingual Education	41
Africa	10	Bio-Medical Ethics	41
Afro-Centric Curriculum	12	Biology	42
Agriculture	12	Birth Control	44
Air Pollution	14	Black Capitalism	44
Airlines	14	Black Conservatives	46
Alcohol	15	Black Education	47
Alcoholism	17	Black Islam	47
American Civil Liberties		Black Leaders	48
Union	17	Blacks	48
American Government	18	Boating	50
American History	20	Bonds	51
American Indians	22	British Commonwealth	51
American Revolution	23	Broadcasting	52
Anthropology	23	Cable TV	52
Animal Cruelty	23	Cambodia	52
Anti-Communist Groups	24	Campaign Financing	53
Anti-Semitism	24	Canada	53
Anti-Trust	25	Cancer	54
Arab League	26	Capital Punishment	55
Arab States	26	Capitalism	55
Archaeology	26	Catholic Church	60
Architecture	27	Catholic Education	63
Artificial Intelligence	28	Catholic Schools	63
Arms Control	28	Catholics	64
Arms Sales	29	Celebrities	65
Army	30	Censorship	66
Art/Artists	30	Central Intelligence Agency	66
Asia	32	Charities	67
Asian-Americans	33	Chemical-Biological Warfare	67
Astronomy	34	Chemistry	67
Authors	34	Chess	67
Auto Industry	36	Child Care	68
Auto Insurance	37	Children	68

Chile 69
China 69
Christianity 70
Church/State 72
Cigarettes 73
Cities 73
Citizenship 73
Civil Rights 73
Civil War 75
Cold War 75
Colleges 75
Commonwealth of Independent
    States 75
Communications 78
Communism 78
Communitarianism 80
Competitiveness 80
Computers 80
Condoms 81
Congress 81
Conservatism 83
Conspiracy Theories 92
Constitution 92
Consumer Issues 94
Contraception 95
Copyrights 95
Corporations 95
Courts 96
Crime 97
Crime/Punishment 98
Criminal Law 99
Cuba 100
Cults 101
Day Care 101
Death 102
Death Penalty 102
Deficit 102
Democracy 102
Democratic Party 103
Desegregation 104
Détente 104
Disabled 104
Disarmament 104
Disease 105
District Attorneys 105

Divorce 105
Doctors 105
Domestic Violence 105
Drama 105
Drugs 106
Eastern Europe 106
Economic Planning 107
Economic Theories 107
Economics 109
Ecology 110
Education, Higher 110
Education, Lower 113
Elderly 117
Election Reform 117
Elections 117
Electoral Reform 117
Electorate 118
Employment 118
Endangered Species 119
Energy 119
Energy Alternatives 120
Environment 120
Equal Rights Amendment 124
Espionage 124
Ethics 124
Ethnic Groups 125
Etiquette 125
Europe 125
European Community 125
Euthanasia 126
Evolution 126
Family 126
Family Planning 128
Far East 128
Federal Budget 129
Federal Bureau of
    Investigation 130
Federal Bureaucracy 131
Federal Deficit 131
Federal Reserve 131
Federalism 131
Fetal Tissue Research 132
Fiber Optics 132
Fiction 132
Film 132

First Amendment 132
Flags 133
Food Stamps 133
Foreign Aid 134
Foreign Investment 134
Foreign Languages 135
Foreign Policy 135
Foster Care 135
Foundations 135
France 135
Freedom of Information 135
Genealogy 136
Genetics 136
Genocide 136
Geography 137
Germany 137
Gold/Gold Standard 138
Government Agencies 138
Government and the Arts 138
Governors 139
Grammar 139
Gun Control 140
Handicapped 141
Health Care 141
Health Insurance 143
Highways 143
Hispanics 143
Historiography 144
History 144
History, Ancient 145
History, Dark Ages 146
History, Medieval 147
History, 16th Century 150
History, 17th Century 150
History, 18th Century 150
History, 19th Century 151
Home Schooling 152
Homelessness 152
Homosexuals 154
Hong Kong 155
House of Representatives
    (U.S.) 155
Housing 155
Human Rights 156
Humor 157

Hunger 157
Hydro-Electric Power 157
Illegal Aliens 158
Immigration 158
Independent Counsel 160
Industrial Policy 160
Insurance 160
Intelligence 161
Intelligence Quotient 163
Internal Revenue Service 163
International Economy 163
International Relations 164
International Trade 165
Inventions 167
Ireland 167
Islam 167
Israel 168
Japan 169
Jerusalem 170
Jobs 170
Journalism 170
Judaism 171
Judges 173
Jurisprudence 173
Jury System 174
Just War 175
Juvenile Crime 175
Labor Unions 175
Language 176
Latin America 177
Law 179
Law of the Sea 180
Lawyers 181
Leftism/Leftists 182
Liberalism 184
Libertarianism 186
Liquor 186
Literacy 187
Literature 187
Lobbyists 191
Local Government 191
Love 191
Mafia 191
Manners 191
Marijuana 192

Marine Corps 192
Maritime Issues 192
Mathematics 193
Media Bias 194
Medicaid/Medicare 196
Medicine 196
Mental Health 196
Mexico 196
Middle East 197
Military (U.S.) 198
Military Spending 200
Minorities 201
Modernism 201
Movies 202
Multiculturalism 203
Multinational Corporations 203
Municipal Government 204
Music 204
Narcotics 206
National Parks 207
National Security 208
National Service 210
National Socialism 210
Natural Law 210
Navy 211
Nazism 211
Nicaragua 211
NATO 212
Nuclear Energy 212
Nuclear Proliferation 213
Nuclear War 213
Nuclear Weapons 214
Oil Industry 214
Old Age 215
Opera 215
Organizations 215
Organized Crime 215
Patents 216
Peace Corps 217
Pentagon 217
Performing Arts 217
Pharmaceuticals 217
Philanthropy 217
Philosophy 218
Physics 219

Plays 220
Poetry 220
Poland 220
Police 220
Political Correctness 221
Politics 222
Pollution 223
Population 223
Pornography 224
Postal Service 225
Poverty 225
POW/MIA 226
Presidency 227
Primaries 227
Prison 227
Privacy 228
Private Schools 228
Privatization 228
Property Rights 229
Protectionism 229
Protestantism 230
Psychiatry 232
Psychology 232
Public Relations 233
Public Schools 233
Publishing 233
Quotas 233
Racism 234
Radio 234
Railroads 234
Reaganism 235
Reapportionment 237
Recession 238
Redistricting 238
Refugees 238
Regulation 238
Religion 240
Republican Party 242
Research and Development 242
Revenue Sharing 243
Revolutionary War 243
Right to Work 243
Sanitation 244
School Choice 244
Science 245

Second Amendment Rights 246
Selective Service 246
Senate 246
Sexual Revolution 246
Sexually Transmitted
    Diseases 247
Shakespeare 247
Slavery 248
Smoking 248
Social Science 249
Social Security 249
Social Work 249
Socialism 249
The South 250
South Africa 252
South America 252
Soviet Military 252
Soviet Union 253
Space Exploration 253
Spain 254
Special Prosecutor 254
Sports 254
Stalinism 255
State/Regional Conservatism 256
Stock Market 260
Strategic Defense Initiative 260
Supreme Court 261
Taxation 262
Teachers 263
Technology 264
Telecommunications 265
Television 265
Term Limits 266
Terrorism 267
Test-Ban Treaty 268
Textbooks 268
Theater 269
Third World 269
Tobacco 270

Tourism 271
Toxic Waste 271
Transportation 271
Travel 272
Treaties 273
Trucking Industry 273
Unemployment 273
Union of Soviet Socialist
    Republics 273
Unions 274
United Kingdom 274
United Nations 274
U.S. Civil War 275
U.S. Foreign Policy 277
Universities 282
Urban Affairs 283
Utilities 284
Veterans 284
Vietnam 284
Vietnam War 285
Vouchers 286
Volunteerism 286
Wall Street 286
War 287
War of Independence 289
Water Projects 290
Welfare 290
The West 291
Western Civilization/
    Heritage 292
Western Europe 293
Women 293
Workforce 296
World Bank 296
World War I 297
World War II 298
Writing 300
Yachting 300
Youth 301

ABORTION
(see also **Fetal Tissue Research**)

Books and Articles

Allen, Charlotte Low, "The Mysteries of RU-486," *The American Spectator*, Volume 22 (October, 1989), pp. 17-20.

Andrews, Joan, *You Reject Them, You Reject Me: The Prison Letters of Joan Andrews*, Richard Cowden-Guido, ed. (Manassas, VA: Trinity Communications, 1988).

Arkes, Hadley, "How to Roll Back *Roe*," *National Review*, Volume XL (October 28, 1988), pp. 30-35, 59.

Coursen, Kimberly, "The Profits of Pro-Choice: How Abortion Makes Some People Rich," *Crisis*, Volume 10 (March, 1992), pp. 16-19.

Cowden-Guido, Richard, "The Post-*Webster* Press," *National Review*, Volume XLII (November 19, 1990), pp. 36-39.

Craycraft, Kenneth, Jr., "Fact and Fiction: What Americans Really Think About Abortion," *Crisis*, Volume 9 (May, 1991), pp. 21-23.

Cunningham, Mark, "The Abortion War," *National Review*, Volume XLIV (November 2, 1992), pp. 42-48.

Davis, John Jefferson, *Abortion and the Christian: What Every Believer Should Know* (Philipsburg, NJ: Presbyterian and Reformed Publishing Company, 1984).

Eastland, Terry, "Who Put the Wrong in 'Wrongful Births?,'" *This World*, Number 5 (Spring/Summer, 1983), pp. 84-93.

Feder, Don, "Abortion, Judaism, and Jews," *National Review*, Volume XLIII (July 8, 1991), pp. 37, 50-53.

Fowler, Jack, "The War Within the States," *National Review*, Volume XLI (August 4, 1989), pp. 35-36.

Glendon, Mary Ann, *Abortion and Divorce in Western Laws* (Cambridge, MA: Harvard University Press, 1987).

Heaphy, Michael R., M.D., "Dismemberment and Choice," *National Review*, Volume XLIV (November 2, 1992), pp. 44-45.

Horan, Dennis J., et al., eds., *Infanticide and the Handicapped Newborn* (Provo, UT: Brigham Young University Press, 1982).

Koop, C. Everett, *The Right to Live, the Right to Die* (Wheaton, IL: Tyndale House, 1976).

Krason, Stephen, *Abortion: Politics, Morality, and the Constitution* (Lanham, MD: University Press of America, 1984).

McConnell, Margaret Liu, "Living with *Roe v. Wade*," *Commentary*, Volume 90 (November, 1990), pp. 34-38.

McGurn, William, "Abortion and the GOP," *National Review*, VolumeXLV (March 15, 1993), pp. 51-54.

Marshall, Robert and Donovan, Charles, *Blessed Are the Barren: The Social Policy of Planned Parenthood* (San Francisco, CA: Ignatius, 1991).

Mathewes-Green, Frederica, "Unplanned Parenthood: Easing the Pain of Crisis Pregnancy," *Policy Review*, Number 57 (Summer, 1991), pp. 28-36.

Morgan, Anne Marie, "Alone Among Strangers: Abortion and Parental Consent," *Chronicles*, Volume 14 (October, 1990), pp. 54-56.

Myers, Bishop John J., "The Limits of Dissent: Abortion and Catholic Obligation," *Crisis*, Volume 8 (June, 1990), pp. 14-21.

Nathanson, Bernard N. and Ostling, Richard N., *Aborting America* (Garden City, NY: Doubleday and Company, 1979).

Neuhaus, Richard John, "After *Roe*," *National Review*, Volume XLI (April 7, 1989) pp. 38-42.

Noonan, John T., *A Private Choice: Abortion in America in the Seventies* (New York: The Free Press, 1979).

Noonan, John T., ed., *The Morality of Abortion: Legal and Historical Perspectives* (Cambridge, MA: Harvard University Press, 1970).

Olasky, Marvin, "Victorian Secret: Pro-Life Victories in 19th Century America," *Policy Review*, Number 56 (Spring, 1992), pp. 30-37.

Reagan, Ronald, *Abortion and the Conscience of The Nation* (Nashville, TN: Thomas Nelson Publishers, 1984).

Reardon, David C., *Aborted Women - Silent No More* (Chicago, IL: Loyola University Press, 1987).

Rees, Grover Joseph, "Scourge or Plot?," *National Review*, Volume XLI (August 4, 1989), pp. 34-35.

Scheidler, Joseph M., *Closed: 99 Ways to Stop Abortion* (Washington, DC: Regnery Gateway, 1984).

Sherlock, Richard, "Supreme Court Challenge: Inside the Making of the Utah Abortion Law," *Policy Review*, Number 56 (Spring, 1991), pp. 85-87.

Smith, Janet E., "The Health of Nations: What America Can Learn from Other Countries About Abortion and Divorce," *Crisis*, Volume 8 (April, 1990), pp. 20-24.

Sobran, Joseph, *Single Issues: Essays on the Crucial Social Questions* (New York: The Human Life Press, 1983).

Sobran, Joseph, "What Now? The New Politics of Abortion," *Crisis*, Volume 8 (January, 1990), pp. 12-16.

Zappia, Andrew, "Unplanned Parenthood: Why Do Corporations Support the Nation's Largest Abortion Group?," *Crisis*, Volume 8 (November, 1990), pp. 26-29.

Organizations

Ad Hoc Committee in Defense of Life 1187 National Press Building, Washington, DC 20045, (202)-347-8686. Seeks to have *Roe v. Wade* decision repealed.

Alliance for Life B1-90 Garry Street, Winnipeg, Manitoba R3C 4H1, Canada, (204)-942-4772. Performs pro-life educational work in Canada.

Alternatives to Abortion International 4680 Lake Underhill, Orlando, FL 32807, (407)-277-1942. Publication: *Heartbeat Magazine.* Affiliates are service groups offering alternatives to abortion.

American Association of Pro-Life Obstetricians and Gynecologists 4701 N. Federal Highway, Fort Lauderdale, FL 33308, (305)-771-9242. Publication: *Directory Newsletter.* Obstetricians and gynecologists who oppose abortion.

American Life League P.O. Box 1350, Stafford, VA 22554, (703)-659-4171. Publications: *All About Issues, Levers of Power, Secular Humanism, Population Primer, Population Report, Choice in Matters of Life and Death, The Living Will.* Pro-life educational organization.

Americans United for Life 343 S. Dearborn, Suite 1804, Chicago, IL 60604, (312)-786-9494. Publications: *Lex Vitae: A Reporter on Life and Death Issues in the Law, Studies in Law and Medicine.* Educational and legal pro-life group.

Birthright, United States of America 686 N. Broad Street, Woodbury, NJ 08096, (609)-848-1819. Publication: *The Life-Guardian.* Helps pregnant women find alternatives to abortion.

Doctors For Life 11511 Tivoli Lane, St. Louis, MO 63146, (314)-567-3446. Educational work; many members do free obstetrical work for needy pregnant women.

Feminists for Life of America Route 3, Box 23, Monticello, FL 32605, (904)-997-2722. Publications: *Sisterlife, Prolife Feminism: Different Voices.* Individuals united to secure the right to life from conception to natural death.

Free Speech Advocates New Hope, KY 40052, (502)-549-5454. Provides legal defense for pro-life activists.

Human Life Center Franciscan University of Steubenville, Steubenville, OH 43952, (614)-282-9953. Publications: *Human Life Issues, International Review.* Seeks to promote the sanctity of human life from conception to natural death.

Human Life Foundation 150 E. 35th Street, Room 840, New York, NY 10016, (212)-685-5210. Publication: *Human Life Review.* A charitable and educational foundation providing funding for baby-saving groups and crisis pregnancy centers.

Human Life International 7845-E Airpark Road, Gaithersburg, MD 20879, (301)-670-7884. Serves as a research, educational, and service program offering positive alternatives to what the group calls the anti-life/anti-family movement.

International Life Services 2606 1/2 West 8th Street, Los Angeles, CA 90057, (213)-382-2156. Comprehensive pro-life directory of U.S. and Canadian pregnancy aid centers and pro-life groups.

Lawyers for Life P.O. Box 217, Lakeville, CT 06039, (203)-229-0252. Advice on defending activists against police brutality or other violations of civil rights.

Libertarians for Life 13424 Hathaway Drive, Wheaton, MD 20906, (301)-460-4141. Uses nonreligious arguments to show why abortion is homicide and why it violates individual rights.

Life Decisions International P.O. Box 419, Amherst, NY 14226, (716)-839-4420. Encourages boycotts of corporations supporting Planned Parenthood.

Life Fund c/o Respect Life Office, Archdiocese of St. Paul and Minneapolis, 328 West Kellogg Boulevard, St. Paul, MN 55102, (612)-291-4515. Provides advice on establishing fund to aid women with crisis pregnancies.

Lutherans for Life 275 N. Syndicate, St. Paul, MN 55104, (612)-645-5444. Publications: *Life Date, Living.* Pro-life educational/outreach organization.

March for Life P.O. Box 90300, Washington, DC 20090, (202)-LIFE-377. Organizes the annual pro-life march in Washington.

National Association of Pro-Life Nurses P.O. Box 82, Elysian, MN 56028. Educational work; also defends the conscience rights of nurses.

National Conference of Catholic Bishops Secretariat for Pro-Life Activities, 3211 Fourth Street, NE, Washington, DC 20017, (202)-541-3070. Educational work; runs Respect Life Program for Catholic parishes.

National Federation of Officers for Life P.O. Box 892, Corpus Christi, TX 78403, (512)-992-1296. Police, judges, court officers, and lawmakers who oppose abortion.

National Organization of Episcopalians for Life 10523 Main Street, Fairfax, VA 22030, (703)-591-NOEL. Publications: *The NOEL News, Abortion and the Early Christians.* Episcopalians organized to reaffirm their faith and reestablish moral responsibilty in the Christian response to human life issues.

National Right to Life Committee 419 Seventh Street, NW, Suite 500, Washington, DC 20004, (202)-626-8800. Publication: *National Right to Life News.* Pro-life lobbying organization that opposes abortion, euthanasia, and infanticide.

National Youth Pro-Life Coalition P.O. Box 34693, Washington, DC 20043, (202)-736-9752. Runs intern program for young pro-lifers in Washington each summer, including lobbying on Capitol Hill and research.

Operation Rescue P.O. Box 1180, Binghamton, NY 13902, (607)-723-4012. Organizes rescues/sit-ins at abortion clinics.

Pro-Life Action League 6160 N. Cicero, #210, Chicago, IL 60646, (312)-777-2900. Publications: *Bulletin, Pro-Life Action News.* Pro-life activist organization.

Pro Vita Advisors P.O. Box 292813, Dayton, OH 45429, (513)-298-8125. Advises on fighting corporate support of pro-abortion organizations.

Professional Women's Network P.O. Box 146842, Chicago, IL 60614, (312)-362-1620. Professional women who speak out on behalf of unborn life.

Stop Planned Parenthood P.O. Box 8, La Grange, NY 12540, (914)-473-3316. Helps parents fight Planned Parenthood in the schools.

Susan B. Anthony List 811 East 47th Street, Kansas City, MO 64110, (816)-561-4117. Raises money for pro-life women candidates.

University Faculty for Life Box 2273, Georgetown University, Washington, DC 20057, (202)-687-4208. Pro-life educational work and witness in the academic community.

Value of Life Committee 637 Cambridge Street, Brighton, MA 02135, (617)-787-4400. Pro-life educational organization.

Women Affirming Life P.O. Box 35532, Brighton, MA 02135, (617)-254-1558. Catholic women who speak out for life; emphasis on prayer and public witness.

ACADEMIA
(see **Education (Higher), Universities**)

ACQUIRED IMMUNE DEFICIENCY SYNDROME (AIDS)

Books and Articles

Antonio, Gene, *The AIDS Cover-Up? The Real and Alarming Facts About AIDS* (San Francisco, CA: Ignatius, 1987).

Bethell, Tom, "The Cure that Failed," *National Review*, Volume XLV (May 10, 1993), pp. 33-36.

Bethell, Tom, "Could Duesberg Be Right?," *National Review*, Volume XLIV (August 17, 1992), pp. 22-23.

Bethell, Tom, "Heretic," *The American Spectator*, Volume 25 (May, 1992), pp. 18-19.

Dannemeyer, William E. and Franc, Michael G., "The Failure of AIDS-Prevention Education," *The Public Interest*, Number 96 (Summer, 1989), pp. 47-60.

Duesberg, Peter H. and Ellison, Bryan J., "Is the AIDS Virus a Science Fiction? Immunosuppressive Behavior, Not HIV, May Be the Cause of AIDS," *Policy Review*, Number 53 (Summer, 1990), pp. 40-51.

Duesberg, Peter H. and Ellison, Bryan J., "Is HIV the Cause of AIDS? Peter H. Duesberg and Bryan J. Ellison Respond to Their Critics," *Policy Review*, Number 54 (Fall, 1990), 70-83.

Fumento, Michael, "Are We Spending Too Much on AIDS?," *Commentary*, Volume 90 (October, 1990), pp. 51-53.

Fumento, Michael, "The AIDS Numbers Racket: Chapter 37," *National Review*, Volume XL (October 14, 1988), pp. 45, 60.

Fumento, Michael, "Chicken Little With a Hypodermic: Mandatory Testing Won't Keep the Sky From Falling In," *Reason*, Volume 20 (November, 1988), pp. 31-34.

Fumento, Michael, "Do You Believe in Magic?," *The American Spectator*, Volume 25 (February, 1992), pp. 16-21.

Fumento, Michael, "The Incredible Shrinking AIDS," *The American Spectator*, Volume 22 (May, 1989), pp. 21-26.

Fumento, Michael, "The Magic's Gone," *National Review*, Volume XLIV (October 19, 1992), pp. 49-52.

Fumento, Michael, *The Myth of Heterosexual AIDS* (New York: New Republic Books, 1989).

Fumento, Michael, "Put to the Test," *Reason*, Volume 24 (May, 1992), pp. 44-46.

Grutsch, James F. and Robertson, A. D. J., "The Coming of AIDS," *The American Spectator*, Volume 19 (March, 1986), pp. 12-15.

Grutsch, James F. and Robertson, A. D. J., "The Coming of Aids II: A Viral Update," *The American Spectator*, Volume 19 (September, 1986), pp. 18-20.

Horowitz, Irving Louis, "The Politics of AIDS Research," *Chronicles*, Volume 12 (March, 1988), pp. 20-24.

Kirp, David L., "The AIDS Perplex," *The Public Interest*, Number 96 (Summer, 1989), pp. 61-72.

Lutton, Wayne, et al., *AIDS: Acquired Immune Deficiency Syndrome* (Manitou Springs, CO: Summit Ministries Research Center, 1986).

McConnell, Margaret Liu, "What Children Shouldn't Know," *National Review*, Volume XLIV (December 14, 1992), pp. 45-46.

McNamee, Lawrence J. and Brian F., *AIDS: The Nation's First Politically Protected Disease* (La Habra, CA: National Medical Legal Publishing House, 1988).

Rosen, Stephen Peter, "Strategic Implications of AIDS," *The National Interest*, Number 9 (Fall, 1987), pp. 64-73.

Sobran, Joseph, "The Politics of AIDS," *National Review*, Volume XXXVIII (May 23, 1986), pp. 22-26, 51-52.

Szasz, Thomas, "Psychiatry in the Age of AIDS," *Reason*, Volume 21 (December, 1989), pp. 31-34.

Vogel, David, "AIDS and the Politics of Drug Lag," *The Public Interest*, Number 96 (Summer, 1989), pp. 73-85.

Organizations

Americans for a Sound AIDS Policy P.O. Box 17433, Washington, DC 20041, (703)-471-7350. Broad-based conservative citizens' organization dedicated to education on AIDS issues.

Centers for Disease Control Office of Public Affairs, 1600 Clifton Road, NE, Building 1, Room 2167, Atlanta, GA 30333, (404)-639-3286. Administers AIDS research which is being conducted at four agencies within the Department of Health and Human Services.

ADOPTION

Books and Articles

McFadden, Maria, "The Choice That Pro-Choicers Aren't Pro," *National Review*, Volume XLV (June 7, 1993), pp. 42-43.

Olasky, Marvin, "The War on Adoption," *National Review*, Volume XLV (June 7, 1993), pp. 38-44.

Organizations

National Committee for Adoption, 1930 17th Street, NW, Washington, DC 20009-6207, (202)-328-1200. Publications: *Legal Notes, Memo, National Adoption Reports, NCFA Directory of Member Agencies, Unmarried Parents Today*. Works to protect the institution of adoption and ensure the confidentiality of all involved in the adoption process. Serves as information clearinghouse; represents voluntary agencies, adoptive parents, adoptees, and birthparents.

ADVERTISING

Books and Articles

Arlen, Michael J., *Thirty Seconds* (New York: Farrar, Straus & Giroux, 1980).
Schmertz, Herbert and Novak, William, *Goodbye to the Low Profile: The Art of Creative Confrontation* (Boston, MA: Little, Brown, 1986).

Organizations

American Association of Advertising Agencies Member Information Service, 666 3rd Avenue, New York, NY 10017, (212)-682-2500. Publications: *Bulletin, 401(K) News, Media Newsletter, New York and Washington, DC Newsletter, Roster.* Seeks to promote and implement improvements in the advertising industry.

Catholic Major Markets Newspaper Association 675 North Court, Suite 360, Palatine, IL 60067, (312)-934-6004. Seeks to educate advertisers about the benefits of appealing to a Catholic audience and to promote increased advertising in Catholic newspapers.

Federal Communications Commission Media Bureau, Enforcement Division, Fairness in Political Programming, Room 6008, 2025 M Street, NW, Washington, DC 20554, (202)-632-7586.

Federal Trade Commission Bureau of Consumer Protection, Advertising Practices, Room 6124A STAR, 6th and Pennsylvania Avenue, NW, Washington, DC 20580, (202)-376-8617.

National Advertising Division c/o Council of Better Business Bureaus, 845 3rd Avenue, New York, NY 10022, (212)-754-1333. Publications: *Do's and Dont's in Advertising Copy, NAD Case Report.* Polices the advertising industry for incidents of false claims, distortions, and misrepresentations.

AFFIRMATIVE ACTION

Books and Articles

Belz, Herman, *Equality Transformed: A Quarter Century of Affirmative Action* (New Brunswick, NJ: Transaction Publishers, 1991).
Blanton, James, "A Limit to Affirmative Action?," *Commentary*, Volume 87 (June, 1989), pp. 28-32.
Bunzel, John H., "Affirmative Action Admissions: How It 'Works' at UC Berkeley," *The Public Interest*, Number 93 (Fall 1988), pp. 111-129.

Bunzel, John H., "Exclusive Opportunities," *The American Enterprise*, Volume 1 (March/April, 1990), pp. 47-51.

Capaldi, Nicholas, *Out of Order: Affirmative Action and the Crisis of Doctrinaire Liberalism* (Buffalo, NY: Prometheus Books, 1985).

Daniels, Edmund D. and Weiss, Michael David, "'Equality' Over Quality," *Reason*, Volume 23 (July, 1991), pp. 44-45.

Eastland, Terry and Bennett, William J., *Counting by Race: Equality from the Founding Fathers to Bakke* (New York: Basic Books, 1979).

Eastland, Terry, "George Bush's Quota Bill: The Dismaying Impact of *Griggs*," *Policy Review*, Number 57 (Summer, 1991), pp. 45-49.

Eastland, Terry, "Racial Preference in Court (Again)," *Commentary*, Volume 87 (January, 1989), pp. 32-38.

Finn, Chester E., Jr., "Quotas and the Bush Administration," *Commentary*, Volume 92 (November, 1991), pp.17-23.

Glazer, Nathan, *Affirmative Discrimination: Ethnic Inequality and Public Policy* (New York: Basic Books, 1975).

Holland, Robert G., "Big Brother's Test Scores," *National Review*, Volume XLII (September 3, 1990), pp. 35-36.

Holland, Robert G., "Race-Norming By Any Other Name," *National Review*, Volume XLIII (July 29, 1991), pp. 36-37.

Holland, Robert G., "Testscam: A New Grading Curve," *Reason*, Volume 22 (January, 1991), pp. 47-48.

King, Florence, "The Goading of America," *Chronicles*, Volume 15 (May, 1991), pp. 23-27.

Lynch, Frederick R., *Invisible Victims: White Males and the Crisis of Affirmative Action* (Westport, CT: Greenwood Press, 1989).

Lynch, Frederick R., "Surviving Affirmative Action (More or Less)," *Commentary*, Volume 90 (August, 1990), pp. 44-47.

Lynch, Frederick R. and Beer, William R., "'You Ain't the Right Color, Pal': White Resentment of Affirmative Action," *Policy Review*, Number 51 (Winter, 1990), pp. 64-67.

Maguire, Timothy, "My Bout With Affirmative Action," *Commentary*, Volume 93 (April, 1992), pp. 50-52.

Mansfield, Harvey C., Sr., "The Underhandedness of Affirmative Action," *National Review*, Volume XXXVI (May 4, 1984), pp. 26-32, 61.

Nieli, Russell, *Racial Preference and Racial Justice: The New Affirmative Action Controversy* (Washington, DC: Ethics and Public Policy Center, 1991).

Roche, George, *The Balancing Act: Quota Hiring in Higher Education* (La Salle, IL: Open Court, 1974).

Skerry, Peter, "Borders and Quotas: Immigration and the Affirmative Action State," *The Public Interest*, Number 96 (Summer, 1989), pp. 86-102.

Sowell, Thomas, *Affirmative Action Reconsidered: Was It Necessary in Academia?* (Washington, DC: American Enterprise Institute, 1975).

Sowell, Thomas, *Civil Rights: Rhetoric or Reality?* (New York: William Morrow, 1984).

Sowell, Thomas, *The Economics and Politics of Race: An International Perspective* (New York: William Morrow, 1983).

Sowell, Thomas, *Preferential Policies: An International Perspective* (New York: William Morrow, 1990).

Steele, Shelby, *The Content of Our Character* (New York: St. Martin's Press, 1990).

Thernstrom, Abigail M., "On the Scarcity of Black Professors," *Commentary*, Volume 90 (July, 1990), pp. 22-26.

Williams, Walter and Seligman, Daniel, "Race, Scholarship, and Affirmative Action," *National Review*, Volume XLI (May 5, 1989), pp. 36-40.

Organizations

Civil Rights Division Department of Justice, Appellate Section, 10th Street and Constitution Avenue, NW, Washington, DC 20530, (202)-633-2195.

Lincoln Institute for Research and Education 1735 DeSales Street, NW, Suite 500, Washington, DC 20036, (202)-347-0872. Publication: *The Lincoln Review*. Founded to study the social, economic, and political issues affecting black America, and to provide an alternative voice on those issues.

Office of Personnel Management Office of Affirmative Employment Programs, 1900 E Street, NW, Room 7H07, Washington, DC 20415, (202)-632-4420.

AFL-CIO
(see **Labor Unions**)

AFRICA

Books and Articles

Ayittey, George B. N., *Africa Betrayed* (Washington, DC: Cato Institute, 1992).

Ayittey, George B. N., "Beyond Apartheid: What About Human Rights Abuses in the Rest of Africa?," *Crisis*, Volume 8 (July/August, 1990), pp. 18-23.

Bauer, P. T., *Equality, the Third World and Economic Delusion* (Cambridge, MA: Harvard University Press, 1983).

Bienen, Henry S., *Armed Forces, Conflict, and Change in Africa* (Boulder, CO: Westview Press, 1989).

Birley, Robin, "Brave New Order," *National Review*, Volume XLIV (October 19, 1992), pp. 52, 69.

Bridgeland, Fred, *Jonas Savimbi: A Key to Africa* (New York: Paragon House, 1987).

Decalo, Samuel, *Psychoses of Power: African Personal Dictatorships* (Boulder, CO: Westview Press, 1989).

Duignan, Peter and Gann, L. H., *Burden of Empire: An Appraisal of Western Colonialism in Africa South of the Sahara* (Palo Alto, CA: Hoover Institution Press, 1967).

Eberstadt, Nick, "Four Myths About Africa," *The National Interest*, Number 10 (Winter, 1987/8), pp. 61-68.

Harden, Blaine, *Africa: Dispatches from a Fragile Continent* (New York: Norton, 1990).

Horne, Alistair, *A Savage War of Peace: Algeria 1954-1962* (New York: Viking Press, 1977).

Lamb, David, *The Africans* (New York: Vintage Books, 1983).

Maier, Francis X., "Kingdoms of Death: A Reporter's African Journal," *This World*, Number 8 (Spring/Summer, 1984), pp. 27-46.

Moroney, Sean, ed., *Africa* (New York: Facts on File, 1989).

Oliver, Roland and Fage, J. G., *A Short History of Africa* (Harmondsworth, United Kingdom: Penguin Books, 1962).

Organizations

American-African Affairs Association 1001 Connecticut Avenue, NW, Suite 1135, Washington, DC 20036, (202)-223-5110. Publication: *Spotlight on Africa*. Seeks to educate the public on African issues, giving special attention to the threat posed to American national interests by the spread of communism on the continent.

Bureau of African Affairs Public Affairs, Department of State, 2201 C Street, NW, Room 3509, Washington, DC 20520, (202)-632-0362. Regional profiles of sub-Saharan African countries.

Human Rights Watch 485 Fifth Avenue, New York, NY 10017, (212)-8400. Publication: *Africa Watch*. Promotes and monitors human rights worldwide.

International Freedom Foundation 200 G Street, NE, Suite 300, Washington, DC 20002, (202)-546-5788. Publication: *Southern African Freedom Review*. Fosters individual freedom throughout the world by promoting the development of free and open societies based on the principles of free enterprise, while recognizing and respecting the sovereignty and cultural heritage of nations.

National Center for Public Policy Research Free Africa Coalition, 300 I Street, NE, Suite 3, Washington, DC 20002, (202)-543-1286.

World Africa Chamber of Commerce P.O. Box 33144, Washington, DC 20033, (202)-223-3244. Publication: *The African Connection*. Interested in advancing the efficiency of commerce between the U.S. and Africa by promoting trade, industrial development, transportation, communication, agricultural development, tourism, and investment.

AFRO-CENTRIC CURRICULUM
(see **Black Education**)

AGRICULTURE

Books and Articles

Armey, Dick, "Moscow on the Mississippi: America's Soviet-Style Farm Policy," *Policy Review*, Number 51 (Winter,1990), pp. 24-29.

Bovard, James, *The Farm Fiasco* (San Francisco, CA: Institute for Contemporary Studies Press, 1989).

Bovard, James, "The International Agricultural Swamp," *National Review*, Volume XLI (February 10, 1989), pp. 46-48.

Evangelista, Anita, "The (Unexpected) Comeback of the Small Farm," *Chronicles*, Volume 13 (November, 1989), pp. 19-20.

Faulk, Odie, "The Lure of Rural Life," *Chronicles*, Volume 13 (November, 1989), pp. 16-18.

Fumento, Michael, "Some Dare Call Them Robber Barons," *National Review*, Volume XXXIX (March 13, 1987), pp. 32-38.

Gardner, Richard L., *The Governing of Agriculture* (Lawrence, KS: The Regents Press of Kansas, 1981).

Hurst, Blake, "Farming With Uncle Sam: High Finance Comes to Rural Missouri," *Policy Review*, Number 44 (Spring, 1988), pp. 54-56.

Hurst, Blake, "Field of Dreams: Organic Agriculture Doesn't Pay the Seed Bills," *Policy Review*, Number 55 (Winter, 1991), pp. 76-78.

Hyde, Henry, "One and a Half Cheers for David Stockman," *National Review*, XXXVII (June 28, 1985), pp. 26-28.

Isaac, Rael Jean, "Legal Services and the Farmer," *The American Spectator*, Volume 19 (November, 1986), pp. 22-27.

Luttrell, Clifton B., *The High Cost of Farm Welfare* (Washington, D.C.: The Cato Institute, 1989).

Miles, Stephen B., "Old McDonald's Farm: A Call for a National Agricultural Policy," *Chronicles*, Volume 14 (August, 1990), pp. 55-57.

Paarlberg, Philip, *Farm & Food Policy: Issues of the 1980s* (Lincoln, NE: University of Nebraska Press, 1980).

Paarlberg, Philip, *Farmers of Five Continents* (Lincoln, NE: University of Nebraska Press, 1984).

Paarlberg, Philip, *Toward a Well-Fed World*, "Henry A. Wallace Series on Agricultural History & Rural Studies," Volume 6; text ed., (Ames, IA: Iowa State University Press, 1988).

Paarlberg, Philip, foreword to *Food & Agricultural Policy* (Washington, DC: American Enterprise Institute for Public Policy Research, 1977).

Paarlberg, Philip and Chambers, Robert, eds., *Macroeconomics, Agriculture & Exchange Rates,* "Special Studies in International Economics & Business"; (Boulder, CO: Westview, 1988).

Pasour, E. C., *Agriculture and the State: Market Processes and Bureaucracy* (New York: Holmes & Meier, 1990).

Zinsmeister, Karl, "Bitter Harvest: Farmers Pay A High Price for Government Subsidies," *Reason*, Volume 21 (November, 1989), pp. 22-31.

Zinsmeister, Karl, "Cultivating Independence," *Reason*, Volume 21 (January, 1990), pp. 28-36.

Zinsmeister, Karl, "Plowing Under Subsidies," *Reason*, Volume 21 (October, 1989), 30-37.

Zinsmeister, Karl, "Technology, Ecology, and the American Farmer," *Reason*, Volume 21 (December, 1989), pp. 22-31.

Organizations

Agricultural Research Service U.S. Department of Agriculture, 14th Street and Independence Avenue, SW, Washington, DC 20250, (202)-447-3656. Conducts research on crops, livestock, poultry, soil and water conservation, agricultural engineering, and control of insects and other pests; develops new uses for farm commodities.

American Statistical Association 1429 Duke Street, Alexandria, VA 22314, (703)-684-1221. Advises government agencies on statistics and methodology in agency research; promotes development of statistical techniques for use in business, industry, finance, government, agriculture, and scientific fields.

Animal Industry Foundation 1701 North Fort Meyer Drive, Suite 1200, Arlington, VA 22209, (703)-524-0810. Publication: *AIF Newsletter*. Works to dispel misconceptions that a diet of meat, milk and eggs is unhealthy and that conditions under which animal production occurs are inhumane; conducts animal production research and provides information on livestock and poultry production.

Economic Research Service U.S. Department of Agriculture, 1301 New York Avenue, NW, Washington, DC 20005, (202)-786-3300, (202)-786-1504. Analyzes factors affecting farm production and their relation to the environment, prices and income, and the outlook for various commodities, including aquaculture and industrial crops.

National Agricultural Statistics Service U.S. Department of Agriculture, 14th Street and Independence Avenue, SW, Washington, DC 20250, (202)-447-2707. Prepares estimates and reports of production, supply, price, and other items relating to the U.S. agricultural economy.

AIR POLLUTION
(see **Environment**)

AIRLINES

Books and Articles

Bruce, Peter C. and Traynham, David, "Looking Back on Airline Deregulation," *National Review*, Volume XXXII (May 16, 1980), pp. 588-595.

Gattuso, James L., "Clear the Runways: Ending Congestion and Delays," *Reason*, Volume 20 (February, 1989), pp. 31-32.

Kahn, Alfred E., "Surprises, But Few Regrets: A Conversation With Alfred E. Kahn," With Robert W. Poole, Jr., *Reason*, Volume 20 (February, 1989), pp. 35-39.

Person, Lawrence, "Super Saver: $100 Billion and A Whole Lot of Time," *Reason*, Volume 20 (February, 1989), p. 30.

Poole, Robert W., Jr., "Deregulation: Finishing the Job," *National Review*, Volume XLIV (November 2, 1992), pp. 25-29.

Poole, Robert W., Jr., "Onward and Upward: Free the Airports," *Reason*, Volume 20 (February, 1989), pp. 33-35.

Samuel, Peter, "Over and Out: The Drama Behind Airline Deregulation," *Reason*, Volume 20 (February, 1989), pp. 27-29.

Organizations

Airline Data Collection Research and Special Programs Administration, U.S. Department of Transportation, 400 7th Street, SW, Washington, DC 20590, (202)-426-8969. Maintains airline data collection, financial and statistical reporting and serves as liaison for public access to air carrier reports.

Federal Aviation Administration U.S. Department of Transportation, 800 Independence Avenue, SW, Washington, DC 20591, (202)-426-8058. Regulates air commerce in a manner that promotes its development and safety and fulfills the requirements of national defense; controls the use of navigable airspace of the United States; regulates both civil and military operations in such airspace in the interest of safety and efficiency; and promotes, encourages, and develops civil aeronautics.

Federal Aviation Administration Public Inquiry Center, U.S. Department of Transportation, 800 Independence Avenue, SW, Room 907E, Washington, DC 20591, (202)-426-8058. General information concerning subjects covered by the FAA.

Federal Aviation Administration Aviation Statistics, Information Analysis Branch, Management Standards and Statistics Division, Office of Management Systems, U.S. Department of Transportation, 800 Independence Avenue, SW, Room 607, Washington, DC 20591, (202)-426-3791. Historical and current aviation statistics.

ALCOHOL

Books and Articles

Anderson, Will, *From Beer to Eternity: Everything You Always Wanted to Know About Beer* (Lexington, MA: Stephen Greene Press, 1987).

Carson, Gerald, *The Social History of Bourbon: An Unhurried Account of Our Star-Spangled American Drink* (Lexington, KY: University Press of Kentucky, 1984).

Embury, David, *The Fine Art of Mixing Drinks,* (New York: Doubleday, 1952).

Finch, Christopher, *Beer: A Connoisseur's Guide to the World's Best* (New York: Abbeville Press, 1989).

Jackson, Michael, *The Simon & Schuster Pocket Guide to Beer* (New York: Simon and Schuster, 1991).

Jackson, Michael, *The World Guide to Whiskey: A Comprehensive Taste-Guide to Single Malts and the World's Best-Known Blends* (Scranton, PA: Salem House, 1987).

Miller, David, *The Complete Handbook of Home Brewing* (Pownal, VT: Storey Communications, 1988).

Murphy, Tommy, *Elegant Wine Cocktails: 111 Recipes for Delicious Wine Drinks* (New York: Warner Books, 1985).

Powell, Fred, ed., *Bartender's Standard Manual* (New York: Educator Books, 1971).

Schumann, Charles, *Schumann's Tropical Bar Book* (New York: Stewart, Tabori & Chang, 1989).

Watkins, Derek, *Wine and Beer Making* (North Pomfret, VT: David & Charles, 1978).

Organizations

Alcohol Beverage Legislative Council 5101 River Road, Suite 108, Bethesda, MD 20816, (301)-656-1494. Publication: *Status Report.* Association of alcoholic beverage retailers and retail companies.

Association of Brewers Box 287, Boulder, CO 80306, (303)-447-0816. Publications: *Beer and Brewing: National Conference for Quality Beer and Brewing, Brewery Operations: Practical Ideas for Microbrewers, Microbrewers Resource Handbook and Directory, New Brewer, Zymurgy: The Magazine for the Homebrewer and Beer Lover.* Individuals interested in the home brewing of beer; beer retailers, consumers, wholesalers, and manufacturers.

Champagne News and Information Bureau 355 Lexington Avenue, New York, NY 10017, (212)-949-8475. Importers of authentic champagne from northern France. Serves as educational and promotional arm in the U.S. for the French champagne industry.

Distilled Spirits Council of the United States 1250 I Street, NW, Suite 900, Washington, DC 20005, (202)-628-3544. Publication: *Summary of State Laws and Regulations Relating to Distilled Spirits.* National trade association of producers and marketers of beverage distilled spirits sold in the U.S.

International Beer Tasting Society 1800 E. First Street, Santa Ana, CA 92705, (714)-973-1345. For beer lovers who want to enjoy beer in the company of other beer lovers.

National Alcoholic Beverage Control Association 4216 King Street, W., Alexandria, VA 22302, (703)-578-4200. Publications: *Contacts, Statistical Reports, American Experience with Alcohol, A Continuing Commitment to Responsible Moderation, Alcohol Server.* State agencies controlling the purchase, distribution, and sale of alcoholic beverages under the control system.

National Association of Beverage Importers 1025 Vermont Avenue, NW, Suite 1205, Washington, DC 20005, (202)-638-1617. Publications: *Bulletin, National Association of Beverage Importers - Statistical Report.* Represents importers of alcoholic beverages.

National Conference of State Liquor Administrations Liquor Control Commission, 301 Centennial Mall, S., Lincoln, NE 68509, (402)-471-2571. Publications: *National Conference on State Liquor Administrators - Minutes of Annual Meeting, NCSLA Official Directory.* State agencies administering liquor control laws and collecting beverage taxes under a license system rather than a state-controlled monopoly stores system.

ALCOHOLISM

Books and Articles

Dardis, Tom, *The Thirsty Muse: Alcohol and the American Writer* (New York: Ticknor & Fields, 1989).

Fingarette, Herbert, "Alcoholism: The Mythical Disease," *The Public Interest*, Number 91 (Spring, 1988), pp. 3-22.

Fingarette, Herbert, *Heavy Drinking: The Myth of Heavy Drinking as a Disease* (Berkeley, CA: University of California Press, 1988).

O'Brien Robert and Chafetz, Morris, *The Encyclopedia of Alcoholism*, 2nd ed., Glen Evans, ed. (New York: Facts on File, 1991).

Vaillant, George, *The Natural History of Alcoholism: Causes, Patterns, and Paths to Recovery* (Cambridge, MA: Harvard University Press, 1983).

Organizations

Calix Society 7601 Wayzata Blvd., Minneapolis, MN, (612)-546-0544. Publications: *The Chalice, Directory of Calix Units in the U.S. and Canada, Calix and the Twelve Steps, What and Why.* Catholic alcoholics who are maintaining sobriety through affiliation and participation in Alcoholics Anonymous. Non-Catholic alcoholics are welcome.

Children of Alcoholics Foundation P.O. Box 4185, Grand Central Station, New York, NY 10163, (212)-351-2680. Publications: *Directory of National Resources for Children of Alcoholics, Report of Conference on Prevention Research, Children of Alcoholics on the Job.* Seeks to educate the public about children of alcoholics and alcohol abusers and stimulate interest in seeking solutions to their problems.

National Catholic Council on Alcoholism and Related Drug Problems 1200 Varnum Street, NE, Washington, DC 20017, (202)-832-3811. Publications: *The Blue Book, Mustum.* Promotes adequate treatment for all clergy and religious men and women suffering from alcoholism and drug dependency through consultation and supportive services.

AMERICAN CIVIL LIBERTIES UNION

Books and Articles

Decter, Midge, "The ACLU's Next Target," *National Review*, Volume XLIII (June 24, 1991), pp. 29-30.

Donohue, William A., *The Politics of the American Civil Liberties Union* (New Brunswick, NJ: Transaction Books, 1985).

AMERICAN GOVERNMENT
(see also **Congress**)

Books and Articles

Allison, Wick, et al., "*National Review* Special Supplement: Rebuilding America: A Citizen's Guide," *National Review*, Volume XLII (May 28, 1990), pp. 1S-15S.

Anderson, Don, "Reviving Self-Rule: Ward Government in the South," *Chronicles*, Volume 14 (March, 1990), pp.14-17.

Banfield, Edward C., *Here the People Rule: Selected Essays* (New York: Plenum Publishing Corp., 1985).

Berger, Raoul, *Federalism: The Founders' Design* (Norman, OK: University of Oklahoma Press, 1987).

Bryan, Frank and McClaughry, John, *The Vermont Papers: Recreating Democracy on a Human Scale* (Post Mills, VT: Chelsea Green Publishing, 1989).

Buckley, William F., et al., *Dialogues in Americanism* (Chicago, IL: Henry Regnery Co., 1964).

Burnham, James, *Congress and the American Tradition* (Chicago, IL: Henry Regnery Co.), 1965.

Colson, Chuck and Eckerd, Jack, *Why America Doesn't Work* (Irving, TX: Word Publishing, 1991).

De Tocqueville, Alexis, *Democracy in America,* Phillips Bradley, ed., 2 vols. (New York: Knopf, 1944).

De Tocqueville, Alexis, *Democracy in America,* J. P. Mayes and A. P. Kerr, eds. (New York: Doubleday, 1969).

Evans, M. Stanton, *Clear and Present Dangers: A Conservative View of America's Government* (San Diego, CA: Harcourt Brace Jovanovich, 1975).

Fleming, Thomas, "Government of the People," *Chronicles*, Volume 14 (March, 1990), pp. 10-12.

Fleming, Thomas, "Leveraged Buyout," *Chronicles*, Volume 16 (June, 1992), pp. 10-12.

Fleming, Thomas, "The Statecraft of Stooges," *Chronicles*, Volume 12 (March, 1988), pp. 6-7.

Francis, Samuel, "Imperial Conservatives," *National Review*, Volume XLI (August 4, 1989), pp. 37-38.

Francis, Samuel, "Nationalism, Old and New," *Chronicles*, Volume 16 (June, 1992), pp. 18-22.

Francis, Samuel, "Who's In Charge Here?," *Chronicles*, Volume 12 (March, 1988), pp. 12-15.

Horwitz, Robert H., ed., *The Moral Foundations of the American Republic*, 3rd ed. (Charlottesville, VA: University Press of Virginia, 1986).

Jaffa, Harry V., *American Conservatism and the American Founding* (Durham, NC: Carolina Academic Press, 1985).

Kendall, Willmoore and Carey, George, *Basic Symbols of the American Political Tradition* (Baton Rouge, LA: Louisiana State University Press, 1970).

King, Florence, "The Goading of America," *Chronicles*, Volume 15 (May, 1991), pp. 23-27.

Kirk, Russell, *Roots of the American Order* (Los Angeles, CA: Pepperdine University Press, 1974).

Kopff, E. Christian, "The American Crisis Without Alternative," *Chronicles*, Volume 16 (June, 1992), pp. 23-25.

Lindsey, Brink, "System Overload: The Size of Our Government Is Unsafe for Democracy," *Policy Review*, Number 55 (Winter, 1991), pp. 52-56.

McDonald, Forrest, *E Pluribus Unum: The Formation of the American Republic 1776 - 1790* (Boston, MA: Houghton Mifflin, 1965).

McDonald, Forrest, *Novus Ordo Seclorum: The Intellectual Origins of the Constitution* (Lawrence, KS: University Press of Kansas, 1985).

McKenzie, Richard B., "Capital Flight: The Hidden Power of Technology to Shrink Big Government," *Reason*, Volume 20 (March, 1989), 22-26.

Murray, Charles, *In Pursuit of Happiness and Good Government* (New York: Simon & Schuster, 1988).

Murray, John Courtney, *We Hold These Truths* (Kansas City, MO: Sheed & Ward, 1960).

O'Rourke, P. J., *Parliament of Whores: A Lone Humorist Attempts to Explain the Entire US Government* (New York: Atlantic Monthly Press, 1991).

Pangle, Thomas L., *The Spirit of Modern Republicanism: The Moral Vision of the American Founders and the Philosophy of Locke* (Chicago, IL: University of Chicago Press, 1988).

Sandoz, Ellis, *A Government of Laws: Political Theory, Religion, and the American Founding* (Baton Rouge, LA: Louisiana State University Press, 1990).

Utley, Robert L., Jr., ed., *The Promise of American Politics: Principles and Practice After Two Hundred Years* (Lanham, MD: University Press of America, 1988).

Will, George, *Statecraft as Soulcraft: What Government Does* (New York: Simon & Schuster, 1983).

Wilson, Clyde, "Restoring the Republic," *Chronicles*, Volume 16 (June, 1992), pp. 14-17.

Wilson, James Q., *American Government: Institutions and Policies*, 4th ed., (Lexington, MA: Heath, 1988).

AMERICAN HISTORY

Books and Articles

Abel, Lionel, et al., "How Has the United States Met Its Major Challenges Since 1945? A Symposium," *Commentary*, Volume 80 (November, 1985), pp. 25-107.

Amos, Gary T., *Defending the Declaration: How the Bible Influenced the Writing of the Declaration of Independence* (Brentwood, TN: Wolgemuth and Hyatt, 1990).

Barone, Michael, *Our Country: The Shaping of America from Roosevelt to Reagan* (New York: The Free Press, 1990).

Boorstin, Daniel, *The Americans*, 3 vols. Vol. 1: *The Colonial Experience* (New York: Random House, 1958), Vol. 2: *The Democratic Experience* (New York: Random House, 1973), Vol. 3: *The National Experience* (New York: Random House, 1965).

Boorstin Daniel, *The Decline of Radicalism: Reflections on America Today* (New York: Random House, 1969).

Bradford, M. E., *Against the Barbarians and Other Reflections on Familiar Themes* (Columbia, MO: University of Missouri Press, 1992).

Carson, Clarence B., *A Basic History of the United States*, 5 vols. (Wadley, AL: American Textbook Committee, 1983, 1984, 1985, 1986).

Connell, Evan S., *Son of the Morning Star: Custer and the Little Big Horn* (Berkeley, CA: North Point Press, 1984).

Fischer, David Hackett, *Albion's Seed: Four British Folkways in America* (New York: Oxford University Press, 1989).

Folsom, Burton W., Jr., *The Myth of the Robber Barons: A New Look at the Rise of Big Business in America* (Herndon, VA: Young America's Foundation, 1981).

Greene, Jack P., *Pursuits of Happiness: The Social Development of Early Modern British Colonies and the Formation of American Culture* (Chapel Hill, NC: University of North Carolina Press, 1988).

Hart, Jeffrey, *From This Moment On: America in 1940* (New York: Crown, 1987).

Hart, Jeffrey, *When the Going Was Good!: American Life in the Fifties* (New York: Crown, 1982).

Hawke, David Freeman, *Nuts and Bolts of the Past: A History of American Technology 1776 - 1860* (New York: Harper and Row, 1988).

Hodgson, Godfrey, ed., *The United States*, 3 vols. (New York: Facts on File, 1992).

Jaffa, Harry., "Another Look at the Declaration," *National Review*, Volume XXXII (July 11, 1980), pp. 836-840.

Kirk, Russell, *The Roots of American Order,* 3rd ed. (Washington, DC: Regnery Gateway, 1991).

Lukacs, John, *Outgrowing Democracy: A History of the United States in the Twentieth Century* (New York: Doubleday, 1984).

McDonald, Forrest, *E Pluribus Unum: The Formation of the American Republic 1776 - 1790* (Boston, MA: Houghton Mifflin, 1965).

McDonald, Forrest, *The United States in the 20th Century: 1900 - 1920, Vol. I* (Reading, MA: Addison-Wesley Publishing, 1968).

McDonald, Forrest, "Understanding Alexander Hamilton," *National Review*, Volume XXXII (July 11, 1980), pp. 827-833.

Morison, Samuel E., *The Oxford History of the American People,* 3 vols. (New York: New American Library, 1972).

Morris, Richard B., et al., eds., *Encyclopedia of American History,* 6th ed. (New York: Harper & Row, 1982).

Nisbet, Robert, *The Present Age: Progress and Anarchy in Modern America* (New York: Harper & Row, 1988).

Plumb, J. H., *The Collected Essays of J. H. Plumb, Vol. II: The American Experience* (Athens, GA: University of Georgia Press, 1989).

Schlereth, Thomas J., *Victorian America: Transformations in Everyday Life, 1876 - 1915* (New York: Harper Perennial, 1991).

Schlesinger, Arthur M., Jr., ed., *The Almanac of American History* (New York: Putnam, 1983).

Sutherland, Daniel E., *The Expansion of Everyday Life, 1860 - 1876* (New York: Harper Perennial, 1989).

Turner, Frederick Jackson, *The Turner Thesis Concerning the Role of the Frontier in American History* (Boston, MA: D.C. Heath and Co., 1956).

Wilson, Clyde, "The Future of American Nationalism," *Chronicles*, Volume 14 (November, 1990), pp. 16-21.

Organizations

American Antiquarian Society 185 Salisbury Street, Worcester, MA 01609-1634, (508)-755-5221. Publications: *American Antiquarian Society Proceedings, Newsletter of the Program in the History of the Book in American Culture, News-Letter of the American Antiquarian Society.* Gathers, preserves, and promotes serious study of the materials of early American history and life.

American Association for State and Local History 172 Second Avenue, N., Suite 202, Nashville, TN 37201, (615)-255-2971. Publications: *Directory of Historical Societies and Agencies in the U.S. and Canada, History News, History News Dispatch, Bicentennial State Histories Series.* Organization interested in improving the study of state and local history in the U.S. and Canada.

Americans for Historic Preservation 1608 New Hampshire Avenue, NW, Washington, DC 20009, (202)-462-2500. Political action committee.

American Historical Association 400 A Street, SE, Washington, DC 20003 (202)-544-2422. Publications: *Perspectives, American Historical Review, Doctoral Dissertations in History, Grants and Fellowships of Interest to Historians, Guide to Departments of History, Proceedings.* Interested in promoting historical studies and collecting and preserving historical manuscripts.

National Trust for Historic Preservation 1785 Massachusetts Avenue, NW, Washington, DC 20036, (202)-673-4000. Publications: *Historic Preservation, Preservation Forum, Preservation Forum Newsletter, Preservation Law Reporter, Preservation News.* National private organization chartered by the U.S. Congress to facilitate public participation in the preservation of buildings, sites, and objects significant in American history and culture.

Society for Historians of the Early American Republic History Department, Lebanon Valley College, Annville, PA 17003, (717)-867-6355. Publication: *Journal of the Early Republic.* Interested in the study of U.S. history between 1789-1848.

AMERICAN INDIANS

Books and Articles

Connell, Evan S., *Son of the Morning Star: Custer and the Little Big Horn* (Berkeley, CA: North Point Press, 1984).

Edmonds, Margot and Clark, Ella E., *Voices of the Winds: Native American Legends* (New York: Facts on File, 1989).

Frazier, Gregory W., *The American Indian Index* (Denver, CO: Arrowstar Publishing, 1985).

Greenway, John, "Will the Indians Get Whitey?," *National Review*, Volume XXI (March 11, 1969), pp. 223-28, 245.

Hirschfelder, Arlene and Molin, Paulette, *Encyclopedia of Native American Religions* (New York: Facts on File, 1992).

Leitch, Barbara, *A Concise Dictionary of Indian Tribes of North America* (Algonac, MI: Reference Publications, 1979).

Sarf, Wayne Michael, "Russell Means on Custer Hill," *The American Spectator*, Volume 21 (December, 1988), pp. 32-34.

Waldman, Carl, *Atlas of the North American Indian* (New York: Facts on File, 1985).

Waldman, Carl, *Encyclopedia of Native American Tribes* (New York: Facts on File, 1988).

Waldman, Carl, *Who Was Who in Native American History: Indians and Non-Indians From First Contacts Through 1900* (New York: Facts on File, 1990).

Organizations

Bureau of Indian Affairs Information Office, Department of the Interior, Room 4627, Washington, DC 20240, (202)-343-7445. Information is available on Indians.

Huntington Free Library and Reading Room 9 Westchester Square, Bronx, NY, 10461, (212)-829-7770. Formerly the Library of the Museum of the American Indian.

Museum of the American Indian Broadway and 155th Street, New York, NY 10032, (212)-283-2497.

AMERICAN REVOLUTION
(see **War of Independence**)

ANTHROPOLOGY

Books and Articles

Chodes, John, "Mutiny In Paradise," *Chronicles*, Volume 12 (February, 1988), pp. 10-13.
Encyclopedia of Anthropology (New York: Harper & Row, 1976).
Fox, Robin, "Anthropology's Auto-Da-Fe," *Encounter*, Volume LXXIII (September/October 1989), pp. 58-64.
Fox, Robin, *Encounter With Anthropology* (New York: Harcourt Brace Jovanovich, 1973).
Harris, Marvin, *The Rise of Anthropological Theory: A History of Theories of Culture* (New York: Harper & Row, 1968).
Levi-Strauss, Claude, *Anthropology and Myth: Lectures, 1957-1982* (Cambridge, MA: Basil Blackwell, 1987).
Lind, Michael, "The Two Cultures (continued)," *Commentary*, Volume 92 (August, 1991), pp. 31-35.

ANIMAL CRUELTY

Books and Articles

Evangelista, Angela, "Battling for Animal Rights," *Chronicles*, Volume 14 (March, 1990), pp. 50-52.

Hughes, Jane, "Reigning Cats and Dogs," *National Review*, Volume XLII (July 23, 1990), pp. 35-38.

Organizations

American Fur Resources Institute 1825 K Street, NW, Suite 901, Washington, DC 20006, (202)-281-0209. Purpose is to formulate and obtain passage of legislation for the support and regulation of scientific, professional wildlife management, particularly with regard to furbearing animals.

Fur Takers of America Rt. 3, Box 211A1, Aurora, IN 47001, (812)-926-1049. Publications: *The Fur Taker, Is Mother Nature Humane?, Essential Facts on Trapping*. Seeks to educate trappers in humane methods of trapping and conservation ethics.

National Trappers Association P.O. Box 3667, Bloomington, IL 61702, (309)-829-2422. Publication: *American Trapper*. Promotes sound environmental education programs and conservation of natural resources.

ANTI-COMMUNIST GROUPS
(see **Conservatism**)

ANTI-SEMITISM

Books and Articles

Brownfeld, Allan C., "Defining Anti-Semitism: Pat Buchanan and His Critics," *Chronicles*, Volume 15 (January, 1991), pp. 49-51.

Buckley, William F., Jr., et al., "In Pursuit of Anti-Semitism, Chapter II," *National Review*, Volume XLIV (March 16, 1992), pp. S3-S30.

Buckley, William F., Jr., "In Search of Anti-Semitism: What Christians Provoke What Jews? Why? By Doing What? - and Vice Versa," *National Review*, XLII (December 30, 1991), pp. 20-62.

Buckley, William F., Jr., *In Search of Anti-Semitism* (New York: Continuum, 1992).

Himmelfarb, Milton, "Jackson, the Jews, and the Democrats," *National Review*, Volume XL (November 7, 1988), pp. 42-44, 78.

Lewis, Bernard, *Semites and Anti-Semites: An Inquiry Into Conflict and Prejudice* (New York: Norton, 1986).

Meyer, Michael A., "Anti-Semitism and Jewish Identity," *Commentary*, Volume 88 (November, 1989), pp. 35-40.

Muller, Jerry Z., "Communism, Anti-Semitism, and the Jews," *Commentary*,
Volume 86 (August, 1988), pp. 28-39.

Muravchik, Joshua, "Patrick J. Buchanan and the Jews," *Commentary*, Volume
91 (January, 1991), pp. 29-37.

Podhoretz, Norman, "What Is Anti-Semitism?: An Open Letter to William F.
Buckley, Jr.," *Commentary*, Volume 93 (February, 1992), pp. 15-20.

Prager, Dennis and Telushkin, Joseph, *Why the Jews? The Reason for Anti-
Semitism* (New York: Simon & Schuster, 1983).

Sobran, Joseph, "Le Nouveau Canard," *National Review*, Volume XXXIX
(February 13, 1987), pp. 44-45, 62.

ANTITRUST

Books and Articles

Adams, Walter and Brock, James W., *Antitrust Economics on Trial: A
Dialogue on the New Laissez Faire* (Princeton, NJ: Princeton University
Press, 1991).

Armentano, D. T., "Antitrust and Insurance: Should the McCarran Act be
Repealed?," *The Cato Journal*, Volume 8 (Winter, 1989), pp. 729-749.

Armentano, Dominick T., *Antitrust and Monopoly: Anatomy of a Policy Failure*
(New York: John Wiley and Sons, 1982).

Benson, Bruce and Greenhut, M. L., *American Antitrust Laws in Theory and
Practice* (Brookfield, VT: Gower, 1989).

Bork, Robert, *The Anti-trust Paradox: A Policy at War with Itself* (New York:
Basic Books, 1978).

Brozen, Yale, *Concentration, Mergers, and Public Policy* (New York: The Free
Press, 1982).

Brozen, Yale, *Is Government the Source of Monopoly?* (Washington, DC: The
Cato Institute, 1979).

Coll, Steven, *The Deal of the Century: The Breakup of AT&T* (New York:
Atheneum, 1986).

McChesney, Fred, "Antitrust and Regulation: Chicago's Contradictory Views,"
The Cato Journal, Volume 10 (Winter, 1991), pp. 775-798.

Oliver, Daniel, "Lowering the Ante in Antitrust," *The American Enterprise*,
Volume 2 (November/December, 1991), pp. 78-79.

Posner, Richard A., *Antitrust Law: An Economic Perspective* (Chicago, IL:
University of Chicago Press, 1976).

Organizations

Alliance for Fair Competition 7315 Wisconsin Avenue, 13th Floor, Bethesda,
MD 20814, (301)-869-5800. Seeks to protect small businesses from unfair and

anti-competitive trade practices through legislation and litigation; provides case studies for assisting state and local associations.

Consumer Litigation Department of Justice, 666 11th Street, NW, Room 910, Washington, DC 20530, (202)-724-6786.

Legal Procedures Unit Anti-trust Division, Department of Justice, 10th Street and Constitution Avenue, NW, Room 7416, Washington, DC 20530, (202)-633-2481.

ARAB LEAGUE
(see **Middle East**)

ARAB STATES
(see **Middle East**)

ARCHAEOLOGY

Books and Articles

Bray, Warwick and Trump, David, *The Penguin Dictionary of Archaeology* (New York: Penguin, 1982).
Ceram, C.W., *Gods, Graves, and Scholars: The Story of Archaeology* (New York: Knopf, 1986).
Fagan, Brian M., *Archaeology: A Brief Introduction* (Glenview, IL: Scott, Foresman & Co., 1988).
MacIntosh, Jane, *The Practical Archaeologist* (New York: Facts on File, 1986).

Organizations

Archaeological Conservancy 415 Orchard Drive, Santa Fe, NM, 87501, (505)-982-3278. Publications: *Newsletter, Quarterly.* Works with government agencies, universities, and museums to preserve sites from looters, urban sprawl, etc. Largely concerned with American Indian ruins.

Archaeological Institute of America 675 Commonwealth Avenue, Boston, MA 02215, (617)-353-9361. Publications: *American Journal of Archaeology, Archaeology, Bulletin, Archaeology on Film, Archaeological Fieldwork, Opportunities Bulletin.*

Biblical Archaeology Society 3000 Connecticut Avenue, NW, Washington, DC 20008, (202)-483-3423. Publication: *Biblical Archaeology Review.*

ARCHITECTURE

Books and Articles

Bess, Philip H., "Beyond Irony: Can Religion Point the Way to Architectural Renewal?," *This World*, Number 12 (Fall, 1985), pp. 96-107.

Brolin, Brent C., *The Failure of Modern Architecture* (New York: Van Nostrand Reinhold, 1976).

Charles, H. R. H. The Prince of Wales, *A Vision of Britain: A Personal View of Architecture* (New York: Doubleday, 1989).

Gardner, James, "Postmodernist Blues," *Commentary*, Volume 87 (January, 1989), pp. 55-61.

Gibson, Eric, "Waiting for the Resurrection," *National Review*, Volume XLIV (July 6, 1992), pp. 48-49.

Lewis, Michael J., "What Lewis Kahn Built," *Commentary*, Volume 93 (March, 1992), pp. 39-43.

Pevsner, Nikolaus, *Dictionary of Architecture* (New York: Overlook Press, 1976).

Regnery, Henry, "Louis H. Sullivan: Visionary and Architect," *Modern Age*, Volume 33 (Summer, 1991), pp. 356-366.

Scruton, Roger, *The Aesthetics of Architecture* (Princeton, NJ: Princeton University Press, 1979).

Tigerman, Stanley, *The Architecture of Exile* (New York: Rizzoli International Publications, 1988).

Watkin, David, *A History of Western Architecture* (New York: Thames and Hudson, 1986).

Whiffen, Marcus, *American Architecture Since 1780: A Guide to the Styles* (Cambridge, MA: MIT Press, 1992).

Wolfe, Tom, *From Bauhaus to Our House* (New York: Farrar, Straus & Giroux, 1981).

Organizations

American Architectural Foundation 1735 New York Avenue, NW, Washington, DC 20006, (202)-626-7500. Publication: *Forum*. Sponsors exhibitions and educational programs. Administers the Octagon Museum.

Architectural Heritage Foundation Old City Hall, 45 School Street, Boston, MA 02108, (617)-523-8678. Concerned with conservation of environmental assets, with emphasis on architectural preservation and rehabilitation.

National Building Museum Judiciary Square, NW, Washington, DC 20001, (202)-272-2448. Publication: *Blueprints*. Collects and disseminates information on building arts. Encourages the public to take part in the on-going debate over what relationship society should establish between the built and natural environments.

National Trust for Historic Preservation 1785 Massachusetts Avenue, NW, Washington, DC 20036, (202)-673-4000. Publications: *Historic Preservation, Preservation Forum, Preservation Forum Newsletter, Preservation Law Reporter, Preservation News.* National private organization chartered by the U.S. Congress to facilitate public participation in the preservation of buildings, sites, and objects significant in American history and culture.

ARTIFICIAL INTELLIGENCE

Books and Articles

Aleksander, Igor and Burnett, Piers, *Thinking Machines: The Search for Artificial Intelligence* (New York: Knopf, 1987).

Dennett, Daniel and Hofstadter, Douglas, *Godel, Escher, and Bach: An Eternal Golden Braid* (New York: Random House, 1979).

Dennett, Daniel and Hofstadter, Douglas, *The Mind's I: Fantasies and Reflections of Self and Soul* (New York: Basic Books, 1981).

Jackson, Philip, *An Introduction to Artificial Intelligence* (New York: Dover Publications, 1974).

Winston, Patrick, *Artificial Intelligence* (Reading, MA: Addison-Wesley Publishing Co., 1984).

Organizations

American Association for Artificial Intelligence 445 Burgess Drive, Menlo Park, CA 94025, (415)-328-3123. Publication: *AI Magazine.* Intellectual clearinghouse for the field.

ARMS CONTROL

Books and Articles

Adelman, Kenneth, *The Great Universal Embrace: Arms Summitry - A Skeptic's Account* (New York: Simon and Schuster, 1989).

Berkowitz, Bruce D., *Calculated Risks: A Century of Arms Control, Why It Has Failed, and How It Can Be Made to Work* (New York: Simon & Schuster, 1987).

Codevilla, Angelo and Wallop, Malcolm, *The Arms Control Delusion* (San Francisco, CA: Institute for Contemporary Studies, 1987).

Fairbanks, Charles H., "Arms Races: The Metaphor and the Facts," *The National Interest*, Number 1 (Fall, 1985), pp. 75-90.

Foerster, Schuyler, et al., *Defining Stability: Conventional Arms Control in a Changing Europe* (Boulder, CO: Westview, 1989).

Gaffney, Frank J., Jr., "A Policy Abandoned: How the Reagan Administration Formulated, Implemented, and Retreated From Its Arms Control Policy," *The National Interest*, Number 11 (Spring, 1988), pp. 43-52.

Glynn, Patrick, *Closing Pandora's Box: Arms Races, Arms Control, and the History of the Cold War* (New York: Basic Books, 1992).

Glynn, Patrick, "The Sarajevo Fallacy - The Historical and Intellectual Origins of Arms Control Theology," *The National Interest*, Number 9 (Fall, 1987), pp. 3-32.

Hallenbeck, Ralph A. and Shaver, David E., eds., *On Disarmament: The Role of Conventional Arms Control in National Security Strategy* (New York: Praeger, 1991).

Novak, Michael, "Moral Clarity in the Nuclear Age," *National Review*, Volume XXXV (April 1, 1983), pp. 354-92.

Staar, Richard F., ed., *Arms Control: Myth Versus Reality* (Stanford, CA: Hoover Institution Press, 1984).

Tower, John G., et al., eds., *Verification: The Key to Arms Control in the 1990s* (McLean, VA: Brassey's, 1992).

Organizations

Center for Security Policy 1250 24th Street, NW, Suite 600, Washington, DC 20037, (202)-466-0515. Publication: *Newsletter*. Policy information network focusing on international security policy issues. Provides information to members of legislative and executive branches of government, the media, and the general public.

National Institute for Public Policy 3031 Javier, Suite 300, Fairfax, VA 22031, (703)-698-0563. Studies National Security policy with focus on weapons systems, force posture, and arms control.

U.S. Arms Control and Disarmament Agency Public Affairs, 320 21st Street, NW, Room 5840, Washington, DC 20451, (202)-632-9504. Publications: *ACDA Annual Report, World Military Expenditures, Arms Control and Disarmament Agreements*.

ARMS SALES

Books and Articles

Bajusz, William D. and Louscher, David J., *Arms Sales and the U.S. Economy: The Impact of Restricting Military Exports* (Boulder, CO: Westview, 1988).

Organizations

Arms Transfer Division Bureau of Weapons Evaluation and Control, Arms Control and Disarmament Agency, ADGA/NWC/ATD, 320 21st Street, NW, Room 4734, Washington, DC 20451, (202)-632-3469.

ARMY
(see **Military, U.S.**)

ART/ARTISTS
(see also **Government and the Arts**)

Books and Articles

Canaday, John, *The Lives of the Painters,* 4 vols. (New York: Norton, 1969).

Chilvers, Ian, et al., eds., *The Oxford Dictionary of Art* (New York: Oxford University Press, 1988).

Duby, Georges, *Sculpture: The Great Art of the Middle Ages From the 5th to the 15th Century* (New York: Rizzoli, 1990).

Gablik, Suzi, *Has Modernism Failed?* (New York: Thames and Hudson, 1984).

Gardner, James, "Having It All: Uncritical Critics in Today's Art World," *National Review,* Volume XLI (May 19, 1989), pp. 47-50.

Gardner, James, "Nowhere Man," *National Review,* Volume XLV (March 29, 1993), pp. 72-73.

Gardner, James, "Postmodernist Blues," *Commentary,* Volume 87 (January, 1989), pp. 55-61.

Golomstock, Igor, *Totalitarian Art in the Soviet Union, the Third Reich, Fascist Italy, and the People's Republic of China* (London: Collins Harvill, 1990).

Haraszti, Miklos, *The Velvet Prison: Artists Under State Socialism* (New York: Basic Books, 1987).

Horgan, Paul, *A Certain Climate: Essays on History, Arts, and Letters* (Middletown, CT: Wesleyan University Press, 1988).

Hughes, Robert, *Nothing If Not Critical* (New York: Knopf, 1990).

Hughes, Robert, *The Shock of the New: The Life and Death of Modern Art* (New York: Knopf, 1991).

Karetnikova, Inga and Golomstock, Igor, "Totalitarian Culture: The Encounter in Paris," *National Review,* Volume XXXVIII (May 9, 1986), pp. 42-45.

Kramer, Hilton, *Abstract Art: A Cultural History* (New York: Free Press, 1989, 1992).

Kramer, Hilton, *Revenge of the Philistines: Art and Culture, 1972-1984* (New York: Free Press, 1985).

Lind, Michael, "A Map of Modern Art," *Commentary*, Volume 93 (April, 1992), pp. 39-42.

Lucie-Smith, Edward, *The Thames and Hudson Dictionary of Art Terms* (New York: Thames and Hudson, 1984).

Marks, Claude, ed., *World Artists 1980 - 1990* (New York: H.W. Wilson Co., 1991).

Marks, Claude, ed., *World Artists 1950 - 1980* (New York: H.W. Wilson Co., 1984).

Nicolaides, Kimon, *The Natural Way to Draw* (Boston, MA: Houghton Mifflin, 1961).

Perl, Jed, *Paris Without End: On French Art Since World War I* (Berkeley, CA: North Point Press, 1988).

Pieper, Josef, *Only the Lover Sings: Art and Contemplation* (San Francisco, CA: Ignatius Press, 1990).

Read, Herbert and Stangos, Nikos, *The Thames and Hudson Dictionary of Art and Artists* (New York: Thames and Hudson, 1985).

Rewald, John, *Post-Impressionism: From Van Gogh to Gauguin* (Boston, MA: Bullfinch Press, 1979).

Ryan, Richard, "1492 and All That," *Commentary*, Volume 93 (May, 1992), pp. 41-46.

Scruton, Roger and Huffington, Arianna, "The Patron Saint of the Painted Word," *National Review*, Volume XL (December 9, 1988), pp. 46-53.

Simon, John, "Arc Without Covenant," *National Review*, Volume XLI (May 5, 1989), pp. 30-32.

Tomkins, Calvin, *Post to Neo: The Art World of the 1980s* (New York: Henry Holt, 1988).

Watson, George, "The Terror of the Obvious," *Chronicles*, Volume 15 (September, 1991), pp. 16-18.

Who's Who in Art (Detroit, MI: Gale Research, Inc., 1992).

Wolfe, Gregory, "Two Cheers for Modern Art: Despite Traditionalist Concern, Religion Has Nothing to Fear," *Crisis*, Volume 9 (April, 1991), pp. 24-29.

Wolfe, Tom, *The Painted Word* (New York: Farrar, Straus & Giroux, 1975).

Zeri, Federico, *Behind the Image* (New York: St. Martin's, 1990).

Organizations

Art Dealers Association of America 575 Madison Avenue, New York, NY 10022, (212)-940-8590. Publications: *Art Dealers Association of America Directory*, *Art Dealers Association of America - Update*.

Christians in the Arts Networking P.O. Box 1941, Cambridge, MA 02238-1941, (617)-783-5667. Aims to establish Christian presence in the arts.

Metropolitan Museum of Art Thomas J. Watson Library, Fifth Avenue and Eighty-Second Street, New York, NY 10028, (212)-879-5500. 300,000 volumes on art from ancient to modern times.

Paul VI Institute for the Arts 924 G Street, NW, Washington, DC 20001, (202)-347-1450. Publications: *Art and Religion, Cultural Resources for Leisure Clubs, Newsletter*. Promotes the arts as part of the Catholic church's evangelical mission and seeks to reestablish and promote the church's role as sponsor of the arts.

ASIA

Books and Articles

Berger, Peter and Hsiao, Hsin-Huang, eds., *In Search of an East Asian Development Model* (New Brunswick, NJ: Transaction Books, 1985).
Buckley, Priscilla L. and Buckley, William F., Jr., "Pacific Rim: Off and Running," *National Review*, Volume XLIV (August 17, 1992), pp. 29-33.
Elegant, Robert, *Pacific Destiny: Inside Asia Today* (New York: Crown, 1990).
Elegant, Robert, "Where the Action Is," *National Review*, Volume XLV (May 10, 1993), pp. 36-40.
The Far East and Australasia 1992 (Detroit, MI: Gale Research, Inc., 1992).
Fisher, Richard N., et al., *U.S. and Asia Statistical Handbook: 1991 Edition* (Washington, DC: The Heritage Foundation, 1991).
King, Robert D., "Incident at Ayodhya," *National Review*, Volume XLV (March 15, 1993), pp. 24-26.
McCord, William, "Explaining the East Asian 'Miracle,'" *The National Interest*, Number 16 (Summer, 1989), pp. 74-82.
McGurn, William, "Corazon Aquino's Poverty Pimps," *The American Spectator*, Volume 23 (September, 1990), pp. 14-17.
McGurn, William, *Perfidious Albion* (Washington, DC: Ethics and Public Policy Center, 1992).
McGurn, William, "Yankees Go Home," *The American Spectator*, Volume 25 (January, 1992), pp. 42-45.
Neher, Clark D., *Southeast Asia in the New International Era* (Boulder, CO: Westview, 1991).
Palmer, Ronald D. and Reckford, Thomas J., *Building ASEAN: 20 Years of Southeast Asian Cooperation* (New York: Praeger, 1987).
Rostow, W. W., *The United States and the Regional Organization of Asia and the Pacific 1965 - 1985* (Austin, TX: University of Texas Press, 1986).
Taylor, Robert, ed., *Asia and the Pacific* (New York: Facts on File, 1991).
Vogel, Ezra F., *The Four Little Dragons: The Spread of Industrialization in East Asia* (Cambridge, MA: Harvard University Press, 1991).

Organizations

American Council for a Free Asia 214 Massachusetts Avenue, NW, Suite 300, Washington, DC 20002, (202)-547-7150. Publication: *Free Asia Report*. Lobbies for support of non-communist countries in Asia; also calling for re-recognition of Taiwan.

Asian Studies Center The Heritage Foundation, 214 Massachusetts Avenue, NW, Washington, DC 20002, (202)-546-4400.

Association of Asian-American Chambers of Commerce P.O. Box 1933, Washington, DC 20013, (202)-775-1113. Publication: *Asian-American Commerce Newsletter*.

Bureau of East Asia and Pacific Affairs Public Affairs, Department of State, 2201 C Street, NW, Room 5310, Washington, DC 20520, (202)-632-2538.

Free Asia Foundation 214 Massachusetts Avenue, NE, Suite 300, Washington, DC 20002, (202)-547-7150. Publication: *Free Asia Foundation Report*. Seeks to raise public awareness of Asian affairs; concerned with communist expansion and U.S. security issues in the region.

ASIAN-AMERICANS

Books and Articles

Asian Americans Information Directory (Detroit, MI: Gale Research, Inc., 1992).
Norden, Edward, "South-Central Korea: Post-Riot L.A.," *The American Spectator*, Volume 25 (September, 1992), pp. 33-40.
Rothenberg, Stuart, "The Invisible Success Story," *National Review*, Volume XLI (September 15, 1989), pp. 43-46.
Takaki, Ronald, *Strangers from a Different Shore: A History of Asian Americans* (Boston, MA: Little, Brown, 1989).
Tucker, William, "Back to the Streets," *National Review*, Volume XLII (June 25, 1990), p. 39.
Winnick, Louis, "America's 'Model Minority,'" *Commentary*, Volume 90 (August, 1990), pp. 22-29.

Organizations

Asian American Voters Coalition 8837 Sleepy Hollow Lane, Potomac, MD 20854, (301)-299-4859. Seeks to enhance political influence of Asian Americans. Lobbies the U.S. government on immigration and other matters.

ASTRONOMY

Books and Articles

Ferris, Timothy, *The Red Limit: The Search for the Edge of the Universe* (New York: William Morrow, 1983).

Hawking, Stephen, *A Brief History of Time: From the Big Bang to Black Holes* (New York: Bantam Books, 1988).

Jastrow, Robert, *God and the Astronomers* (New York: W.W. Norton, 1978).

Kuhn, Thomas, *The Copernican Revolution: Planetary Astronomy in the Development of Western Thought* (Cambridge, MA: Harvard University Press, 1957).

Lusis, Andy, *Astronomy and Astronautics: An Enthusiasts Guide to Books and Periodicals* (New York: Facts on File, 1986).

Moore, Patrick, ed., *The International Encyclopedia of Astronomy* (New York: Crown, 1987).

Pasachoff, Jay M., *A Field Guide to Stars and Planets* (Boston, MA: Houghton Mifflin, 1992).

Organizations

Amateur Astronomers Association 1010 Park Avenue, New York, NY 10028, (212)-535-2922. Publications: *Eyepiece, Sky and Telescope.* For the layman; has educational program and library.

American Astronomical Society 2000 Florida Avenue, NW, #300, Washington, DC 20009, (202)-328-2010. Publications: *Astronomical Journal, Astrophysical Journal, Bulletin of the American Astronomical Society, AAS Newsletter, Membership Directory.* Professional group; maintains speakers bureau.

American Institute of Aeronautics and Astronautics Technical Information, Service Library, 555 West 57th Street, New York, NY 10019, (212)-247-6500. Provides answers for any questions that public may have regarding the field.

National Aeronautics and Space Administration 400 Maryland Avenue, SW, Washington, DC 20546, (202)-453-1010.

AUTHORS
(see also **Literature**, **Publishing**)

Books and Articles

Author Biography Master Index (Detroit, MI: Gale Research, Inc., 1989).

Colby, Vineta, ed., *World Authors 1980 - 1985* (New York: H.W. Wilson Co., 1991).

Colby, Vineta, ed., *World Authors 1975 - 1980* (New York: H.W. Wilson Co., 1985).

Concise Dictionary of American Literary Biography (Detroit, MI: Gale Research, Inc., 1992).

Concise Dictionary of British Literary Biography (Detroit, MI: Gale Research, Inc., 1992).

Contemporary Authors (Detroit, MI: Gale Research, Inc., 1992).

Dictionary of Literary Biography (Detroit, MI: Gale Research, Inc., 1992).

Grant, Michael, *Greek and Latin Authors 800 B.C. - A.D. 1000* (New York: H.W. Wilson Co., 1980).

Kunitz, Stanley J. and Haycraft, Howard, eds., *American Authors 1600 - 1900: A Biographical Dictionary of American Literature* (New York: H.W. Wilson Co., 1977).

Kunitz, Stanley J. and Haycaraft, Howard, eds., *British Authors Before 1800: A Biographical Dictionary* (New York: H. W. Wilson Co., 1965).

Kunitz, Stanley J. and Haycraft, Howard, eds., *British Authors of the Nineteenth Century* (New York: H. W. Wilson Co., 1973).

Kunitz, Stanley J. and Colby, Vineta, eds., *European Authors 1000 - 1900: A Biographical Dictionary of European Literature* (New York: H. W. Wilson Co., 1968).

Kunitz, Stanley J. and Haycraft, Howard, eds., *Twentieth Century Authors: A Biographical Dictionary of Modern Literature* (New York: H. W. Wilson Co., 1973).

Kunitz, Stanley J., ed., *Twentieth Century Authors: A Biographical Dictionary of Modern Literature: A First Supplement* (New York: H. W. Wilson Co., 1979).

Neff, Glenda, *Writer's Market* (Cincinnati, OH: Writer's Digest Books, Annual).

Polking, Kirk, *Writer's Encyclopedia* (Cincinnati, OH: Writer's Digest Books, 1983).

Redman, Linda, ed., *International Literary Market Place* (New York: R. R. Bowker, Annual).

Torpie, Stephen L., et al., eds., *Literary Market Place: The Directory of American Book Publishing* (New York: R. R. Bowker, Annual).

Wakeman, John, ed., *World Authors 1950 - 1970: A Companion Volume to Twentieth Century Authors* (New York: H. W. Wilson Co., 1975).

Wakeman, John, ed., *World Authors 1970 - 1975: A Biographical Dictionary* (New York: H. W. Wilson Co., 1980).

Organizations

Christian Writers Guild 260 Fern Lane, Hume, CA 93628, (209)-335-2333. Publication: *Quill O' the Wisp.*

AUTO INDUSTRY

Books and Articles

Bruce-Briggs, B., *The War Against the Automobile* (New York: E.P. Dutton, 1977).

Collier, Peter and Horowitz, David, *The Fords: An American Epic* (New York: Summit Books, 1987).

Crandall, Robert W., et al., *Regulating the Automobile* (Washington, DC: Brookings Institution, 1986).

Goodrich, Tucker, "Iacocca Broke," *National Review*, Volume XLII (December 3, 1990), pp. 44-45.

Holt, Thomas Harvey, "Trapped Inside the Safety Belt," *Reason*, Volume 22 (August/September, 1990), pp. 27-31.

May, George S., ed., *The Automobile Industry 1885-1930* (New York: Facts on File, 1989).

May, George S., ed., *The Automobile Industry 1920-1980* (New York: Facts on File, 1989).

Smith, Fred L., "Autonomy: The Liberating Benefits of a Safer, Cleaner, and More Mobile Society," *Reason*, Volume 22 (August/September, 1990), pp. 22-26.

Taub, Eric, *Taurus: The Making of the Car that Saved Ford* (New York: E.P. Dutton, 1991).

Wylie, Jeanie, *Poletown: Community Betrayed* (Champaign, IL: University of Illinois Press, 1989).

Yates, Brock, *The Decline and Fall of the American Automobile Industry* (New York: Random House, 1983).

Organizations

Automotive Hall of Fame P.O. Box 1727, Midland, MI 48641, (517)-631-5760. Publication: *Automotive Hall of Fame - News*. Aims at keeping alive the memory of the giants of the industry.

Automotive Information Council 13505 Dulles Technology Drive, Herndon, VA 22071, (703)-904-0700. Dedicated to improving relations between the industry and consumers.

Insurance Institute for Highway Safety 1005 North Glebe Road, Arlington, VA 22201, (703)-247-1500. Provides data on highway safety; seeks ways to reduce accidents.

National Highway Traffic Safety Administration Department of Transportation, 400 7th Street, SW, Washington, DC 20590, (202)-426-0123, 1-800-424-9393. Enforces laws on recalls and remedies; institutes vehicle safety standards.

AUTO INSURANCE

Books and Articles

Berte, Marjorie, *Hit Me - I Need the Money!: The Politics of Auto Insurance Reform* (San Francisco, CA: Institute for Contemporary Studies, 1991).
Sullum, Jacob, "Totaled! Short-Sighted Interference Has Wrecked the Car-Insurance Market," *Reason*, Volume 22 (November, 1990), pp. 30-35.

Organizations

American Insurance Association 1130 Connecticut Avenue, NW, Washington, DC 20036, (202)-828-7100. Provides information on all facets of the industry.

Consumer Insurance Interest Group 9321 Millbranch Place, Fairfax, VA 22031, (703)-691-2440. Seeks to make the industry more responsive to the needs of the consumer.

BALANCE OF PAYMENTS
(see **International Trade**)

BALANCED BUDGET AMENDMENT
(see **Federal Budget**)

BALLET

Books and Articles

Anderson, Jack, *Ballet and Modern Dance: A Concise History* (Pennington, NJ: Princeton Book Co., 1986).
Balanchine, George and Mason, Francis, *Balanchine's Complete Stories of the Great Ballets* (New York: Doubleday, 1977).
Koegler, Horst, *The Concise Oxford Dictionary of Ballet* (New York: Oxford University Press, 1977).
Villella, Edward and Kaplan, Larry, *Prodigal Son: Dancing for Balanchine in a World of Pain and Magic* (New York: Simon & Schuster, 1992).

BANKING/BANKS

Books and Articles

Adams, James Ring, "The Big Fix," *The American Spectator*, Volume 22 (March, 1989), pp. 21-24.

Adams, James Ring, "How to Win Friends and Influence Regulators," *National Review*, Volume XLII (March 19, 1990), pp. 36-38.

Benston, George J. and Kaufman, George G., "Understanding the Savings and Loan Debacle," *The Public Interest*, Number 99 (Spring, 1990), pp. 79-95.

Brimelow, Peter, "Racism at Work?," *National Review*, Volume XLV (April 12, 1993), p. 42.

Brookes, Warren T., "Have We Seen the End of Banks?," *The American Spectator*, Volume 25 (August, 1992), pp. 33-36.

Coyne, Andrew, "The Vote Standard," *National Review*, Volume XLIII (June 10, 1991), pp. 23-29.

Ely, Bert and Petri, Thomas E., "Real Taxpayer Protection: Sound Deposit Insurance Through Cross-Guarantees," *Policy Review*, Number 60 (Spring, 1992), pp. 25-29.

England, Catherine, *Banking and Monetary Reform: A Conservative Agenda* (Washington, DC: The Heritage Foundation, 1985).

England, Catherine and Huertas, Thomas, eds., *The Financial Services Revolution* (Washington, DC: The Cato Institute, 1988).

England, Catherine and Niskanen, William, "Too Little, Too Late," *National Review*, Volume XLI (May 19, 1989), pp. 38-39.

England, Robert Stowe, "A Run for Our Money," *National Review*, Volume XLII (September 17, 1990), pp. 36-38.

England, Robert Stowe, "Breaking the Banks," *National Review*, Volume XLV (April 12, 1993), pp. 40-44.

Friedman, Milton, *Money Mischief* (New York: Harcourt Brace Jovanovich, 1992).

Glasner, David, *Free Banking and Monetary Reform* (New York: Oxford University Press, 1989).

Hindle, Tim, *The Economist Pocket Banker* (Cambridge, MA: Basil Blackwell, 1985).

Jeffrey, Terence P., "The Man Who Bought Washington," *The American Spectator*, Volume 23 (February, 1990), pp.17-21.

Macey, Jonathan R. and Miller, Geoffrey P., "The Once and Future American Banking Industry: Part I," *The American Enterprise*, Volume 2 (September/October, 1991), pp. 10-12.

Macey, Jonathan R. and Miller, Geoffrey P., "The Once and Future American Banking Industry: Part II," *The American Enterprise*, Volume 2 (November/December, 1991), pp. 12-13.

Selgin, George A., *The Theory of Free Banking: A Study of the Supply of Money*

Under Competitive Note Issue (Lanham, MD: Rowman and Littlefield, 1988).

Thies, Clifford F. and Gerlowski, Daniel A., "Deposit Insurance: A History of Failure," *The Cato Journal*, Volume 8 (Winter, 1989), pp. 677-693.

Thomson, James B. and Todd, Walker F., "Rethinking and Living With the Limits of Bank Regulation," *The Cato Journal*, Volume 9 (Winter, 1990), pp. 579-600.

White, Lawrence H., *Competition and Currency: Essays on Free Banking and Money* (New York: New York University Press, 1989).

Organizations

American Bankers Association 1120 Connecticut Avenue, NW, Washington, DC 20036, (202)-663-5000. Publications: *ABA Bankers Weekly, ABA Banking Journal.* Seeks to enhance the role of commercial banks as preeminent providers of financial services through communications, research, legal action, lobbying of federal legislative and regulatory bodies, and education and training programs.

Association of Bank Holding Companies 730 15th Street, NW, Washington, DC 20005, (202)-393-1158. Provides information on banking and financial issues.

Cato Institute 224 Second Street, SE, Washington, DC 20003, (202)-546-0200. Publications: *Cato Journal: An Interdisciplinary Journal on Public Policy Analysis, Cato Policy Report, Regulation.* A public policy research foundation dedicated to increasing policy debate to allow consideration of more options the institute believes are consistent with traditional American principles of limited government, individual liberty, and peace.

Committee to Abolish the Fed 325 Pennsylvania Avenue, Washington, DC 20335. Publication: *Anti-Fed Report.* Considers the Federal Reserve undemocratic and seeks to force it to become more accountable to the public and Congress; researches and disseminates information on central banking practices.

Federal Deposit Insurance Corporation Hotline 550 Seventeenth Street, NW, Washington, DC 20429, (202)-898-3536, (800)-424-5488. Provides information on consumer banking laws.

Federal Reserve System Research and Statistics Division, Room 3048, 20th Street and Constitution Avenue, NW, Washington, DC 20551, (202)-452-3301.

U.S. League of Savings Institutions 1709 New York Avenue, NW, Washington, DC 20006, (202)-637-8900. Information and statistics regarding issues bearing on savings institutions.

BASEBALL

Books and Articles

Angel, Roger, *The Summer Game* (New York: Ballantine, 1972).

Hall, Donald, *Fathers Playing Catch With Sons: Essays on Sport (Mostly Baseball)* (Berkeley, CA: Northpoint Press, 1985).

James, Bill, *The Bill James Baseball Abstract* (New York: Ballantine, annual).

James, Bill, *The Bill James Historical Abstract* (New York: Random House, 1988).

Kagan, Donald, "George Will's Baseball - A Conservative Critique," *The Public Interest*, Number 101 (Fall, 1990), pp. 3-20.

Reichler, Joseph, ed., *The Baseball Encyclopedia* (New York: St. Martin's Press, 1989).

Sobran, Joseph, "The Republic of Baseball," *National Review*, Volume XLII (June 11, 1990), pp. 36-39.

Will, George, *Men at Work* (New York: Macmillan, 1990).

Will, George, "The Romantic Fallacy in Baseball - A Reply," *The Public Interest*, Number 101 (Fall, 1990), pp. 21-27.

Organizations

National Baseball Hall of Fame P.O. Box 590, Cooperstown, NY 13326, (607)-547-9988.

BIBLE

Books and Articles

Abingdon's Strong's Exhaustive Concordance of the Bible (Nashville, TN, 1980).

Achtemeier, Paul J., et al., eds., *Harper's Bible Dictionary* (San Francisco, CA: Harper Religious Books, 1985).

Brown, Raymond Edward, *The Jerome Biblical Commentary* (Englewood Cliffs, NJ: Prentice-Hall, 1968).

Botterweck, G. Johannes and Ringgren, Helmer, eds., *Theological Dictionary of the Old Testament* 6 vols. (in progress). (Grand Rapids, MI: William B. Eerdmans, 1978).

Eberstadt, Fernanda, "Responding to the Bible," *Commentary*, Volume 85 (January, 1988), pp. 27-35.

Grant, Robert M. and Tracy, David, *A Short History of the Interpretation of the Bible* (Minneapolis, MN: Augsberg Fortress Publications, 1984).

Kass, Leon, "Evolution and the Bible: Genesis I Revisited," *Commentary*, Volume 86 (November, 1988), pp. 29-39.

Kittel, Gerhard and Friedrich, Gerhard, *Theological Dictionary of the New Testament,* 10 vols. (Grand Rapids, MI: William Eerdmans, 1985).

Levine, Mark and Rachlis, Eugene, eds., *The Complete Book of Bible Quotations* (New York: Pocket Books, 1986).

Ratzinger, Joseph Cardinal, "Biblical Interpretation in Crisis: On the Question of the Foundations and Approaches of Exegesis Today," *This World,* Number 22 (Summer, 1988), pp. 3-19.

Saint Jerome, Trans., *Douay-Rheims New Testament* (Rockford, IL: Tan Books, 1977).

Watson, E. Mills, ed., *Mercer Dictionary of the Bible* (Macon, GA: Mercer University Press, 1990).

Organizations

Catholic Biblical Association of America 620 Michigan Avenue, NE, Washington, DC 20064, (202)-635-5519. Publications: *Catholic Biblical Quarterly, Old Testament Abstracts*. Research scholars in the biblical field.

BILINGUAL EDUCATION

Organizations

U.S. English 818 Connecticut Avenue, NW, Suite 200, Washington, DC 20006, (202)-833-0100. Publications: *Congressional Update, Update*. Defends the use of English in public life; seeks the restriction of government funding for bilingual education programs; desires adoption of constitutional amendment making English the official language of the U.S.

BIO-MEDICAL ETHICS

Books and Articles

Beauchamp, Tom L. and Childress, James F., *Principles of Biomedical Ethics* (New York: Oxford University Press, 1986).

Bishop, Jerry E. and Waldholz, Michael, *Genome* (New York: Simon & Schuster, 1990).

Brown, I., and de Cameron, Nigel S., eds., *Medicine in Crisis: A Christian Response* (Edinburgh, United Kingdom: Rutherford House Books, 1988).

Cronin, Archbishop Daniel, *Conserving Human Life* (Braintree, MA: The Pope John XXIII Medical-Moral Research and Educational Center, 1989).

Harris, John, *The Value of Life: An Introduction to Medical Ethics* (New York: Routledge, Chapman & Hall, Inc., 1985).

Kass, Leon, "Death With Dignity and the Sanctity of Life," *Commentary*,
   Volume 89 (March, 1990), pp. 33-43.
Kass, Leon, "Organs for Sale? Propriety, Property, and the Price of Progress,"
   The Public Interest, Number 107 (Spring, 1992), pp. 65-86.
Lasch, Christopher, "Engineering the Good Life: The Search for Perfection,"
   This World, Number 26 (Summer, 1989), pp. 9-17.
Neuhaus, Richard John, "The Return of Eugenics," *Commentary*, Volume 85
   (April, 1988), pp. 15-26.
van den Haag, Ernest and Washington, Lacey, "Baby Jane Doe: Two Views,"
   National Review, Volume XXXVI (February 10, 1984), pp. 36-38.

Organizations

Center for Bioethics Georgetown University, Asian/International Bioethics
Program, Kennedy Institute, 1437 37th Street, Washington DC 20057, (202)-687-
6747. Cross-cultural bioethical issues focusing on Asian and international aspects
of gene manipulation, death and dying, medical and nursing care, patients'
attitudes, holistic medicine, and the environment, including public policy on
human and animal experimentation.

Center for Ethics, Medicine, and Public Issues Baylor College of Medicine,
Houston, TX 77030, (713)-799-6290. Publication: *News Bulletin*. Priorities for
health care services, methods of funding health care services, and social controls
on health care service, including studies on ethics in clinical decision making and
value issues in controlling the cost of medicine.

BIOLOGY

Books and Articles

Augros, Robert and Stanciu, George, *The New Biology: Discovering the Wisdom
   in Nature* (Boston, MA: New Science Library/Shambala, 1988).
Dictionary of Biology (New York: Oxford University Press, 1986).
Dulbecco, Renato, *The Design of Life* (New Haven, CT: Yale University Press,
   1987).
Kass, Leon R., *Toward a More Natural Science: Biology and Human Affairs*
   (New York: The Free Press, 1985).
Medawar, P. B. and Medawar, J. S., *Aristotle to Zoos: A Philosophical
   Dictionary of Biology* (Cambridge, MA: Harvard University Press, 1983).
Toothill, Elizabeth, ed., *The Facts on File Dictionary of Biology* (New York:
   Facts on File, 1988).
Wilson, Edward O., *Biophilia* (Cambridge, MA: Harvard University Press, 1984).
Wilson, Edward O., "Deep History," *Chronicles*, Volume 14 (April, 1990), pp.

16-17.
Wilson, Edward O., *On Human Nature* (Cambridge, MA: Harvard University Press, 1978).

Organizations

American Institute of Biological Sciences 730 11th Street, NW, Washington, DC 20001-4584, (202)-628-1500. Publications: *Public Issues, The Life Sciences and You, Annual Meeting Program, Bioscience.* Promotes unity and effectiveness of effort among persons engaged in biological research, education, and application of biological sciences, including agriculture, environment, and medicine.

American Society for Biochemistry and Molecular Biology 9650 Rockville Pike, Bethesda, MD 20814, (301)-530-7145. Publication: *Journal of Biological Chemistry.* Operates a placement service for biochemists and molecular biologists who have conducted and published original investigations in biological chemistry and/or molecular biology.

American Society for Microbiology 1325 Massachusetts Avenue, NW, Washington, DC 20005, (202)-737-3600. Publications: *Antimicrobial Agents and Chemotherapy, Applied and Environmental Microbiology, ASM Directory of Members, ASM News, Clinical Microbiology Reviews, Infection and Immunity, International Journal of Systematic Bacteriology, Journal of Bacteriology, Journal of Clinical Microbiology, Journal of Virology, Microbiological Reviews, Molecular and Cellular Biology.* Promotes the advancement of scientific knowledge in order to improve education in microbiology. Encourages the highest professional and ethical standards, and the adoption of sound legislative and regulatory policies affecting the discipline of microbiology at all levels.

Biomedical Engineering Society P.O. Box 2399, Culver City, CA 90231, (213)-206-6443. Publications: *Annals of Biomedical Engineering, BMES Bulletin, BMES Membership Directory, Biomedical Engineering Careers.* Encourages the development, dissemination, integration, and utilization of knowledge in biomedical engineering.

Federation of American Societies for Experimental Biology 9650 Rockville Pike, Bethesda, MD 20814, (301)-530-7000. Publications: *FASEB Feature Service, FASEB Journal, FASEB Summary of Legislation, Federation of American Societies for Experimental Biology - Directory of Members, Federation of American Societies for Experimental Biology - Public Affairs Newsletter.* Maintains placement service. Appoints congressional fellows.

International Union of Biochemistry c/o Dr. Robert Hill, Department of Biochemistry, Duke University Medical Center, Durham, NC 27710, (919)-684-

5326. Publications: *Biochemical Education, Biochemical Nomenclature and Related Documents, Biochemistry International, Journal of Biotechnology and Applied Biochemistry.* Promotes international cooperation in the research, discussion, and publication of matters relating to biochemistry. Is working toward standardizing methods, nomenclature, and symbols used in the field.

Society for Industrial Microbiology P.O. Box 12534, Arlington, VA 22209-8534, (703)-941-5373. Publications: *Developments in Industrial Microbiology, Journal of Industrial Microbiology, SIM News, Society for Industrial Microbiology, Actinomycete Taxonomy.* Interested in biolgical processes as applied to industrial materials and processes concerning microorganisms. Serves as liaison between the specialized fields of microbiology.

BIRTH CONTROL
(see **Contraceptives**)

BLACK CAPITALISM

Books and Articles

Green, Shelley and Pryde, Paul, *Black Entrepreneurship in America* (New Brunswick, NJ: Transaction Publishers, 1989).
Hill, George H., *Black Business and Economics: A Selected Annotated Bibliography* (New York: Garland Publishing, 1984).

Organizations

Minority Business Information Institute 130 Fifth Avenue, 10th Floor, New York, NY 10011, (212)-242-8000. Publication: *Index to Black Enterprise.* Purpose is to expand information on minority economic development.

National Business League 4324 Georgia Avenue, NW, Washington, DC 20011, (202)-829-5900. Publications: *Corporate Guide for Minority Vendors, National Memo, President's Briefs.* Promotes the economic development of minorities. Encourages minority ownership and management of small businesses and supports full minority participation within the free enterprise system.

National Minority Business Council 235 E. 42nd Street, New York, NY 10017, (212)-573-2385. Publications: *Better Business, Corporate Minority Vendor Directory, NMBC Business Report.* Seeks to increase profitability by developing marketing, sales, and management skills in minority businesses. Acts as an informational source for the national minority business community.

44

National Minority Business Directories 2105 Central Avenue, NE, Minneapolis, MN 55418, (612)-781-6819. Publications: *Guide to Obtaining Minority Business Directories, Try Us.* Objective is to compile and publish minority business directories to acquaint major corporations and government purchasing agents with the products and services of minority firms.

National Minority Supplier Development Council 15 W. 39th Street, 9th Floor, New York, NY 10018, (212)-944-2430. Publications: *Minority Supplier News, Minority Vendor Directory, National Minority Supplier Development Council-Annual Report, Public Law 95-507 Handbook.* Program provides, exclusively for educational purposes, consultative, advisory, and informational services and technical resources to minority businesses and to regional and local minority purchasing councils.

*The following list of agencies may help
minority entrepreneurs in answering questions:*

Association of Minority Enterprises of New York 250 Fulton Avenue, Suite 505, Hempstead, NY 11550, (516)-489-0120.

Interracial Council for Business Opportunity 51 Madison Avenue, Suite 2212, New York, NY 10010, (800)-252-4226.

Minority Business Enterprise Legal Defense and Education Fund 300 I Street, NE, Suite 200, Washington, DC 20002, (202)-543-0040.

Minority Small Business and Capital Ownership Development Program 409 Third Street, SW, Washington, DC 20416, (202)-205-6629.

National Association of Investment Companies 1111 14th Street, NW, Suite 700, Washington, DC 20005, (202)-289-4336.

National Association of Minority Contractors 1333 F Street, NW, Washington, DC 20004, (202)-347-8259.

National Bankers Association P.O. Box 71440, Washington, DC 20024-1440, (202)-331-1900.

National Business League 1629 K Street, NW, Suite 605, Washington, DC 20006, (202)-466-5483.

National Federation of Independent Business 600 Maryland Avenue, SW, Suite 700, Washington, DC 20024, (202)-554-9000.

National Minority Business Council 235 East 42nd Street, New York, NY 10017, (212)-573-2385.

National Minority Supplier Development Council 15 W. 39th Street, 9th Floor, New York, NY 10018, (212)-944-2430.

National Small Business United 1155 15th Street, NW, Suite 710, Washington, DC 20005, (202)-293-8830.

Small Business Legislative Council 1156 15th Street, NW, Suite 510, Washington, DC 20005, (202)-639-8500.

BLACK CONSERVATIVES

Books and Articles

Lieberman, Adam, "Up from Liberalism," *National Review*, Volume XLV
    (March 1, 1993), pp. 26-28.
Thomas, Clarence, "No Room at the Inn: The Loneliness of the Black
    Conservative," *Policy Review*, Number 58 (Fall, 1991), pp. 72-78.

Organizations

Black PAC P.O. Drawer 6865, McLean, VA 22106, (703)-442-7510. Represents interests of black working- and middle-class Americans; assists like-minded political candidates; supports traditional family values, a growth economy, and a strong national defense.

Black Silent Majority Committee of the U.S.A. Box 5519, 2714 West Avenue, San Antonio, TX 78201, (512)-340-2424. Publication: *The Crusader*. Organizes Americans who do not want to be identified with black radicals and emphasizes the positive gains that blacks have made.

Council for a Black Economic Agenda 1367 Connecticut Avenue, NW, Washington, DC 20036, (202)-331-1103. Seeks black economic self-sufficiency; wants to reverse dependence on the welfare state and increase free enterprise within the black community; supports school choice and tax credits.

Lincoln Institute for Research and Education 1735 DeSales Street, NW, Suite 500, Washington, DC 20036, (202)-223-5112. Publication: *The Lincoln Review*. Studies public policy issues affecting middle-class black Americans. Re-evaluates theories and programs which it feels are harmful to the long-range interests of blacks.

National Black Republican Council 440 First Street, NW, Suite 409, Washington, DC 20001, (202)-662-1335. Works to elect more black Republicans to national, state, and local offices.

National Center for Neighborhood Enterprise 1367 Connecticut Avenue, NW, Washington, DC 20036, (202)-331-1103. Publication: *Policy Dispatch*. Promotes community self-sufficiency through support of effective neighborhood mediating structures in low-income communities.

BLACK EDUCATION

Books and Articles

Armor, David J., "Why Is Black Educational Achievement Rising?," *The Public Interest*, Number 108 (Summer, 1992), pp. 65-80.
Davidson, Nicholas, "Was Socrates a Plagiarist?," *National Review*, Volume XLIII (February 25, 1991), pp. 45-46.
Decter, Midge, "E Pluribus Nihil: Multiculturalism and Black Children," *Commentary*, Volume 92 (September, 1991), pp. 25-29.
Gourevitch, Philip, "The Jeffries Affair," *Commentary*, Volume 93 (March, 1992), pp. 34-38.
Hood, John, "Strength in Diversity," *Reason*, Volume 22 (January, 1991), pp. 28-34.
Lefkowitz, Mary, "Not Out of Africa: The Origins of Greece and the Illusions of Afrocentrists," *New Republic*, Volume 206 (February 10, 1992), pp. 29-36.
Podles, Leon J., "Dead Black Males: The Problem Is Gender, Not Race," *Crisis*, Volume 10 (February, 1992), pp. 19-21.
Sowell, Thomas, *Education: Assumptions Versus History* (Stanford, CA: Hoover Institution Press, 1986).
Sowell, Thomas, *Black Education: Myths and Tragedies* (New York: David McKay, 1972).
Thernstrom, Abigail M., "On the Scarcity of Black Professors," *Commentary*, Volume 90 (July, 1990), pp. 22-26.

BLACK ISLAM

Books and Articles

Ferguson, Andrew, "Jesse's Old Pals," *The American Spectator*, Volume 21 (May, 1988), pp. 27-29.
Himmelfarb, Milton, "Jackson, the Jews, and the Democrats," *National Review*, Volume XL (November 7, 1988), pp. 42-44, 78.

Iannone, Carol, "Bad Rap for Malcolm X," *National Review*, Volume XLIV (December 14, 1993), pp. 47-49.

Reed, Adolph, Jr., "False Prophet I: The Rise of Louis Farrakhan," *The Nation*, Volume 252 (January 21, 1991), pp. 37, 51-56.

Reed, Adolph, Jr., "False Prophet II: All for One and None for All," *The Nation*, Volume 252 (January 28, 1991), pp. 86-92.

BLACK LEADERS

Books and Articles

Gigot, Paul, "The Jackson Package," *The American Spectator*, Volume 21 (June, 1988), pp. 14-16.

Pappas, Theodore, "A Doctor in Spite of Himself: The Strange Career of Martin Luther King, Jr.'s Dissertation," *Chronicles*, Volume 15 (January, 1991), pp. 25-29.

Pitney, John J., Jr., "What Jesse Really Wants: The Rev. Jackson's Dangerous Agenda," *Reason*, Volume 20 (July, 1988), pp. 37-39.

Powell, Scott Steven, "Little Policy Shop of Horrors: Jesse Jackson's Brain Trust," *Policy Review*, Number 45 (Summer, 1988), pp. 64-68.

Puddington, Arch, "Clarence Thomas and the Blacks," *Commentary*, Volume 93 (February, 1992), pp. 28-33.

Puddington, Arch, "The Question of Black Leadership," *Commentary*, Volume 91 (January, 1991), pp. 22-28.

BLACKS

Books and Articles

Alexander, Edward, "Race Fever," *Commentary*, Volume 90 (November, 1990), pp. 45-48.

Anderson, Lorrin, "Cracks in the Mosaic," *National Review*, Volume XLII (June 25, 1990), pp. 36-40.

Anderson, Lorrin, "Crime, Race, and the Fourth Estate," *National Review*, Volume XLII (October 15, 1990), pp. 52-56.

Anderson, Lorrin, "Race, Lies, and Videotape," *National Review*, Volume XLII (January 22, 1990), pp. 40-42.

Bernstein, David, "Exclusionary Rule: Something's Not Kosher About Davis-Bacon," *Reason*, Volume 23 (August/September, 1991), pp. 32-35.

Bigelow, Barbara Carlisle, ed., *Contemporary Black Biography* (Detroit, MI: Gale Research, Inc., 1992).

Blits, Jan H. and Gottfredson, Linda S., "Employment Testing and Job Performance," *The Public Interest*, Number 98 (Winter 1990), pp. 18-25.

Brelin, Christa, ed., *Who's Who Among Black Americans 1992 - 93* (Detroit, MI: Gale Research, Inc., 1992).

Bunzel, John H., "Black and White at Stanford," *The Public Interest*, Number 105 (Fall, 1991), pp. 61-77.

Carlson, Tucker, "That Old-Time Religion: Why Black Men Are Returning to Church," *Policy Review*, Number 61 (Summer, 1992), pp. 13-17.

Colton, Elizabeth, *The Jackson Phenomenon: The Man, the Power, the Message* (New York: Doubleday, 1989).

Crouch, Stanley, *Notes of a Hanging Judge: Essays and Reviews 1979 - 1989* (New York: Oxford University Press, 1990).

Cruse, Harold, *Plural but Equal: Blacks and Minorities in America's Plural Society* (New York: William Morrow, 1988).

Drummond, William J., "About Face: From Alliance to Alienation - Blacks and the News Media," *The American Enterprise*, Volume 1 (July/August, 1990), pp. 23-29.

Epstein, Joseph, "Racial Perversity in Chicago," *Commentary*, Volume 86 (December, 1988), pp. 27-35.

Furtaw, Julia C., ed., *Black Americans' Information Directory 1992-93* (Detroit, MI: Gale Research, Inc., 1991).

Gilder, George, *Visible Man: A True Story of Post-Racist America* (New York: Basic Books, 1978).

Grenier, Richard, "Spike Lee Fever," *Commentary*, Volume 92 (August, 1991), pp. 50-53.

Herrnstein, R. J., "Still an American Dilemma," *The Public Interest*, Number 98 (Winter 1990), pp. 3-17.

Hornsby, Alton, Jr., ed., *Chronology of African-American History: Significant Events and People from 1619 to Present* (Detroit, MI: Gale Research, Inc., 1991).

Horton, Carrell Peterson, ed., *Statistical Record of Black America* (Detroit, MI: Gale Research, Inc., 1990).

Landess, Thomas and Quinn, Richard, *Jesse Jackson and the Politics of Race* (Ottawa, IL: Jameson Books, 1985).

Lester, Julius, *Falling Pieces of the Broken Sky* (Berkeley, CA: Arcade Publishers, 1990).

Morrison, Micah, "The World According to Spike Lee," *National Review*, Volume XLI (August 4, 1989), pp. 24-25.

Moynihan, Daniel Patrick, "How the Great Society 'Destroyed the American Family,'" *The Public Interest*, Number 108 (Summer, 1992), pp. 53-64.

Murray, Charles, "The Legacy of the 60s," *Commentary*, Volume 94 (July, 1992), pp. 23-60.

Perkins, Joseph, "Boom Time for Black America: The Middle Class Is Surging Under Reagan," *Policy Review*, Number 45 (Summer, 1988), pp. 26-28.

Ploski, Harry A. and Williams, James, eds., *The Negro Almanac* (Detroit, MI:

Gale Research, Inc., 1989).

Podles, Leon J., "Dead Black Males: The Problem Is Gender, Not Race," *Crisis*, Volume 10 (February, 1992), pp. 19-21.

Puddington, Arch, "Is White Racism the Problem?," *Commentary*, Volume 94 (July, 1992), pp. 31-36.

Scanlan, James P., "The Perils of Provocative Statistics," *The Public Interest*, Number 102 (Winter, 1991), pp. 3-14.

Short, Thomas, "A 'New Racism' on Campus," *Commentary*, Volume 86 (August, 1988), pp. 46-50.

Skerry, Peter, "On Edge: Blacks and Mexicans in Los Angeles," *The American Spectator*, Volume 21 (May, 1988), pp. 16-18.

Sleeper, Jim, *The Closest of Strangers: Liberalism and the Politics of Race in New York* (New York: Norton, 1990).

Sowell, Thomas, *The Economics and Politics of Race: An International Perspective* (New York: William Morrow, 1985).

Steele, Shelby, "On Being Black and Middle Class," *Commentary*, Volume 85 (January, 1988), pp. 42-47.

Taylor, Jared, *Paved with Good Intentions: The Failure of Race Relations in Contemporary America* (New York: Carroll & Graf, 1992).

Teachout, Terry, "Rap and Racism," *Commentary*, Volume 89 (March, 1990), pp. 60-61.

Tucker, William, "Back to the Streets," *National Review*, Volume XLII (June 25, 1990), p. 39.

Williams, Walter, *The State Against the Blacks* (New York: The New Press, 1982).

Valiunas, Algis, "Black and White Mischief in Chicago," *The American Spectator*, Volume 21 (October, 1988), pp. 21-25.

Organizations

Congress of Racial Equality 1457 Flatbush Avenue, Brooklyn, NY 11210, (718)-434-3580. Publications: *CORE Magazine, The Correspondent, Equal Opportunity Employment Journal, Population Studies, Profiles in Black*. Black nationalist organization that has a philosophy based on the tenets of Marcus Garvey.

BOATING

Books and Articles

Aymar, Brandt, ed., *Men at Sea: The Best Sea Stories of All Time from Homer to William F. Buckley, Jr.* (New York: Crown Books, 1988).

Bestic, A. A., *Kicking Canvas: The Ordeal of the "Denbigh Castle"* (London: Evans Brothers, Ltd., 1957).

Biddlecombe, George, *The Art of Rigging* (Salem, MA: Marine Research Society, 1990).

Buckley, William F., Jr., *Airborne* (New York: Macmillan, 1976).

Buckley, William F., Jr., *Atlantic High* (New York: Doubleday, 1982).

Buckley, William F., Jr., *Racing Through Paradise* (New York: Random House, 1987).

Buckley, William F., Jr., *WindFall: The End of the Affair* (New York: Random House, 1992).

Dear, Ian and Kemp, Peter, *An A-Z of Sailing Terms* (New York: Oxford University Press, 1992).

Goshell, Harpur Allen, *Before the Mast in the Clippers: The Diaries of Charles A. Abbey, 1856 to 1860* (New York: Dover Publications, 1989).

Harlow, Frederick Pease, *The Making of a Sailor or Sea Life Aboard a Yankee Square-Rigger* (Salem, MA: Marine Research Society, 1988).

Kunhardt, C. P., *Small Yachts: Their Design and Construction,* Edited and abridged by the editors of *WoodenBoat* (Brooklin, ME: WoodenBoat Publications, 1985).

Matthews, Frederick C., *American Merchant Ships, 1850 - 1900: Series I* (New York: Dover Publications, 1987).

Matthews, Frederick C., *American Merchant Ships, 1850 - 1900: Series II* (New York: Dover Publications, 1987).

Matthews, Frederick C. and Howe, Octavius T., *American Clipper Ships, 1833 - 1858* Vol. 1. (New York: Dover Publications, 1986).

Matthews, Frederick C. and Howe, Octavius T., *American Clipper Ships, 1833 - 1858* Vol. 2. (New York: Dover Publications, 1986).

McCutchan, Philip, *Tall Ships: The Golden Age of Sail* (New York: Crown Publishers, Inc., 1976).

Whipple, A. B. C., *The Challenge* (New York: William Morrow, 1987).

Organizations

Boat Owners Association of the United States 880 Pickett Street, Alexandria, VA 22304, (703)-823-9550. Publications: *BOAT/U.S. Reports, Boating Equipment Guide.* Offers numerous services to boat owners, including: marine insurance, navigational charts, charter and travel, admiralty law; maintains library on boating subjects.

BONDS
(see **Wall Street**)

BRITISH COMMONWEALTH
(see **United Kingdom**)

BROADCASTING
(see also **Radio, Television**)

Books and Articles

Sidak, J. Gregory, "Broadcast News," *The American Enterprise*, Volume 3 (March/April, 1992), pp. 71-75.

Organizations

National Association of Broadcasters Library and Information Center, 1771 N Street, NW, Washington, DC 20036, (202)-429-5490. Provides information on radio and television broadcasting.

National Religious Broadcasters 7839 Ashton Avenue, Manassas, VA 22110, (703)-330-7000. Publication: *Directory of Religious Broadcasting*. Association of radio and tv producers and station owners interested in religious broadcasting; dedicated to the communication of the Gospel and complete access to broadcast media for religious broadcasting.

CABLE TV

Books and Articles

Armstrong, Richard, "Gutter Politics in the Global Village," *National Review*, Volume XXXVI (April 20, 1984), pp. 30-33, 64.

Organizations

National Cable Television Association 1724 Massachusetts Avenue, NW, Washington, DC 20036, (202)-775-3550. Publications: *Linking Up, Newsletter, Report, TechLine*. Serves as a national medium for exchange of experiences and opinions through research, study, discussion, and publications.

CAMBODIA

Books and Articles

Arostegui, Martin, "Night of the Living Dead," *National Review*, Volume XLV (June 7, 1993), pp. 44-47.
Magstadt, Thomas M., "Marx, Moral Responsibility, and the Cambodian Revolution," *National Review*, Volume XXXIII (July 24, 1981), pp. 831-836.

CAMPAIGN FINANCING

Books and Articles

Barnes, Stephen B., et al., *1987-88 Election Cycle: Business and Association PAC Study* (Springfield, VA: The Leadership Institute, 1990).

England, Robert Stowe, "Coming to Terms With Campaign Reform," *The American Spectator*, Volume 22 (November, 1989), pp. 22-25.

Malbin, Michael J., "Fixing the Race: Dollars and Sense in Campaigns," *The American Enterprise*, Volume 2 (November/December, 1991), pp. 62-69.

Moussalli, Stephanie D., *Campaign Finance Reform: The Case for Deregulation* (Tallahassee, FL: The James Madison Institute of Policy Studies, 1990).

Schwalm, Steven, "Back to the Congress: Campaign Finance Reform in 1992," Heritage Foundation *Backgrounder*, (February 28, 1992).

Organizations

Federal Election Commission Library, 990 E Street, NW, Washington, DC 20463, (202)-219-3440.

Federal Election Commission Public Records Office, 1325 K Street, NW, Washington, DC 20463, (202)-219-4140.

CANADA

Books and Articles

Brimelow, Peter, *The Patriot Game: Canada and the Canadian Question Revisited* (Palo Alto, CA: The Hoover Institution Press, 1986).

Brimelow, Peter, "Oh? Canada?," *National Review*, Volume XLIV (November 30, 1992), pp. 22-24.

Casse, Daniel, "Canada - The Empty Giant," *The National Interest*, Number 8 (Summer, 1987), pp. 94-100.

Gardner, William D., *The Trouble With Canada: A Citizen Speaks Out* (Toronto, Canada: Stoddart Publishing Company, 1991).

Haislmaier, Edmund F., "Northern Discomfort: The Ills of the Canadian Health System," *Policy Review*, Number 58 (Fall, 1991), pp. 32-37.

Krasny, Jacques, "The Wrong Health-Care Model," *National Review*, Volume XLIV (February 17, 1992), pp. 43-44, 59.

McDonald, Kenneth, *Keeping Canada Together* (Agincourt, Canada: Ramsay Business Systems, Ltd., 1990).

McDonald, Kenneth, "Letter From Canada: Ici On Parle Anglais," *Chronicles*, Volume 14 (July, 1990), pp. 44-46.

Richler, Mordecai, *Oh Canada! Oh Quebec! Requiem for a Divided Country* (New York: Knopf, 1992).

Stark, Andy, "Canadian Conundrums: Nationalism, Socialism, and Free Trade," *The American Spectator*, Volume 22 (April,1989), pp. 20-22.

Walker, Michael, "Cold Reality: How They Don't Do It In Canada," *Reason*, Volume 23 (March, 1992), pp. 35-39.

Zink, Lubor, J., "The Unpenetrated Problem of Pierre Trudeau," *National Review*, Volume XXXIV (June 25, 1982), pp. 751-756.

CANCER

Books and Articles

Altman, Roberta and Sarg, Michael J., *The Cancer Dictionary* (New York: Facts on File, 1992).

Ames, Bruce N., "Misconceptions About Pollution and Cancer," *National Review*, Volume XLII (December 3, 1990), pp. 34-35.

Ames, Bruce N., "Of Mice and Men: Finding Cancer's Causes," Interview by Virginia I. Postrel, *Reason*, Volume 23 (December, 1991), pp. 18-22.

Bracken, Jean Munn, *Children with Cancer: A Comprehensive Reference Guide for Parents* (New York: Oxford University Press, 1986).

Efron, Edith, *The Apocalyptics: Cancer and the Big Lie: How Environmental Politics Controls What We Know About Cancer* (New York: Simon & Schuster, 1985).

Fumento, Michael, "The Politics of Cancer Testing," *The American Spectator*, Volume 23 (August, 1990), pp. 18-23.

Larschan, Edward and Richard, *The Diagnosis Is Cancer: A Psychological and Legal Resource Handbook for Cancer Patients, Their Families, and Helping Professionals* (Menlo Park, CA: Bull Publishing, 1986).

Moss, Ralph W., *The Cancer Industry: Unraveling the Politics* (New York: Paragon House, 1991).

Pollack, Richard D., "The Science of Cancer," *The Public Interest*, Number 106 (Winter, 1992), pp. 122-134.

Whelan, Elizabeth M., "The Charge of the Cancer Brigade," *National Review*, Volume XXXIII (February 6, 1981), pp. 84-86.

Whelan, Elizabeth M., *Toxic Terror: The Truth About the Cancer Scare* (Ottawa, IL: Jameson Books, 1985).

Organizations

American Cancer Society 1599 Clifton Road, NE, Atlanta, GA 30329, (404)-320-3333. Publications: *Annual Report, Cancer, Cancer Facts and Figures, Cancer News*. Provides special services to cancer patients.

National Cancer Institute Cancer Information Service, National Institutes of Health Building 31, Room 10A24, Bethesda, MD 20892, (301)-496-5583.

CAPITAL PUNISHMENT

Books and Articles

Baker, William H., *On Capital Punishment* (Chicago, IL: Moody Press, 1985).

Berger, Raoul, *Death Penalties: The Supreme Court's Obstacle Course* (Cambridge, MA: Harvard University Press, 1982).

Berns, Walter, *For Capital Punishment: Crime and the Morality of the Death Penalty* (New York: Basic Books, 1979).

Brandon, Ruth and Davies, Christie, *Wrongful Imprisonment: A Study of Mistaken Convictions and Their Consequences* (London: Allen and Unwin, 1973).

Carrington, Frank, *Neither Cruel nor Unusual: The Case for Capital Punishment* (New York: Crown, 1978).

Cohen, Bernard Lande, *Law Without Order: Capital Punishment and the Liberals* (New York: Arlington House, 1970).

Davies, Christie, "Safely Executed," *National Review*, Volume XLIII (August 12, 1991), pp. 44-45.

Flanders, Stephen A., *Capital Punishment* (New York: Facts on File, 1991).

Goldberg, Steven, "So What If the Death Penalty Deters?," *National Review*, Volume XLI (June 30, 1989), pp. 42-44.

Gorecki, Jan, *Capital Punishment: Criminal Law and Social Evolution* (New York: Columbia University Press, 1983).

Mallon, Thomas, "Death Rally Days," *The American Spectator*, Volume 23 (June, 1990), pp. 16-20.

Pakaluk, Michael, "Until Death Do Us Part: Does the Death Penalty Satisfy Christian Standards of Justice and Compassion?," *Crisis*, Volume 7 (September, 1989), pp. 23-28, 56.

Spence, Karl and Conrad, John P., "Crime and Punishment," *National Review*, Volume XXXV (September 16, 1983), pp. 1140-1144, 1161.

van den Haag, Ernest, *The Death Penalty: A Debate* (New York: Plenum Books, 1983).

Organizations

National Criminal Justice Reference Service National Institute of Justice, Department of Justice, Box 6000, Rockville, MD 20850, (301)-251-5500.

CAPITALISM

Books and Articles

Berger, Peter L., *The Capitalist Revolution: Fifty Propositions About Prosperity, Equality, and Liberty* (New York: Basic Books, 1986).

Berger, Peter, et al., "The Pope, Liberty, and Capitalism: Essays on *Centesimus Annus,*" *National Review*, Volume XLIII (June 24, 1991), pp. S1 - S16.

Braudel, Fernand, *The Structures of Everyday Life: Civilization and Capitalism 15th-18th Century, Vol. I* (New York: Harper & Row, 1982).

Braudel, Fernand, *The Wheels of Commerce: Civilization and Capitalism 15th-18th Century, Vol. II* (New York: Harper & Row, 1983).

Braudel, Fernand, *The Perspective of the World: Civilization and Capitalism 15th-18th Century, Vol. III* (New York: Harper & Row, 1984).

Buchholz, Todd G., *New Ideas From Dead Economists* (New York: New American Library, 1989).

Chamberlain, John, *The Enterprising Americans: A Business History of the United States* (New York: Harper & Row, 1974).

Chamberlain, John, *The Roots of Capitalism* (Princeton, NJ: D. Van Nostrand Co., 1965).

de Soto, Hernando, *The Other Path: The Invisible Revolution in the Third World* (New York: Harper & Row, 1989).

Fortin, Ernest L., "Two Cheers for Capitalism: Free Markets Have Their Limits," *Crisis*, Volume 10 (July/August, 1992), pp. 20-25.

Friedman, Milton, *Capitalism and Freedom* (Chicago, IL: University of Chicago Press, 1962).

Gilder, George, *The Spirit of Enterprise* (New York: Simon & Schuster, 1984).

Gilder, George, *Wealth and Poverty* (New York: Basic Books, 1981).

Gray, John, "Social Injustice: What Hayek Taught Communists, He Can Now Teach Us," *Crisis*, Volume 8 (September, 1990), pp. 30-32.

Griffiths, Brian, *The Creation of Wealth: A Christian's Case for Capitalism* (Downers Grove, IL: Inter-Varsity Press, 1984).

Griffiths, Brian, *Morality and the Marketplace* (London: Hodder and Stoughton, 1982).

Hayek, Friedrich A., ed., *Capitalism and the Historians* (Chicago, IL: University of Chicago Press, 1954).

Johnson, Paul, "The Capitalist Commandments: Ten Ways for Businessmen to Promote Social Justice," *Crisis*, Volume 7 (November, 1989), pp. 10-16.

Kirzner, Israel M., *Competition and Entrepreneurship* (Chicago, IL: University of Chicago Press, 1973).

Kirzner, Israel M., *Discovery, Capitalism, and Distributive Justice* (New York: Basil Blackwell, 1989).

Kristol, Irving, "The Cultural Revolution and the Capitalist Future," *The American Enterprise*, Volume 3 (March/April, 1992), pp. 43-51.

Kristol, Irving, *Two Cheers for Capitalism* (New York: New American Library, 1978).

Lefever, Ernest W., ed., *Will Capitalism Survive?: A Challenge by Paul Johnson with Twelve Responses* (Washington, DC: Ethics and Public Policy Center, 1979).

Lepage, Henri, *Tomorrow, Capitalism: The Economics of Economic Freedom* (LaSalle, IL: Open Court, 1982).

Lindsell, Harold, *Free Enterprise: A Judeo-Christian Defense* (Wheaton, IL: Tyndale House, 1982).

Mises, Ludwig, Von, *The Anti-Capitalistic Mentality* (South Howard, IL: Libertarian Press, 1956).

Muller, Jerry Z., *Adam Smith in His Time and Ours: Designing the Decent Society* (new York: Free Press, 1992).

Muller, Jerry Z., "Capitalism: The Wave of the Future," *Commentary*, Volume 86 (December, 1988), pp. 21-26.

Neuhaus, Richard John, *Doing Well and Doing Good: The Challenge to the Christian Capitalist* (New York: Doubleday, 1992).

Novak, Michael, *The American Vision: An Essay on the Future of Democratic Capitalism* (Washington, DC: American Enterprise Institute for Public Policy Research, 1978).

Novak, Michael, "Boredom, Virtue, and Democratic Capitalism," *Commentary*, Volume 88 (September, 1989), pp. 34-37.

Novak, Michael, ed., *Capitalism and Socialism: A Theological Inquiry* (Washington, DC: American Enterprise Institute for Public Policy Research, 1979).

Novak, Michael, "Capitalism With a Heart: The Man They Called the Last Socialist Comes Out in Favor of Free Market Capitalism," *Crisis*, Volume 9 (June, 1991), pp. 21-22.

Novak, Michael, *The Catholic Ethic and the Spirit of Capitalism* (New York: The Free Press, 1993).

Novak, Michael, ed., *The Denigration of Capitalism: Six Points of View* (Washington, DC: American Enterprise Institute for Public Policy Research, 1979).

Novak, Michael, *The Spirit of Democratic Capitalism* (New York: Simon & Schuster, 1982).

Opitz, Edmund A., *Religion and Capitalism: Allies, Not Enemies* (New Rochelle, NY: Arlington House, 1970).

Porter, Michael E., *The Competitive Advantage of Nations* (New York: The Free Press, 1990).

Rand, Ayn, *Capitalism: The Unknown Ideal* (New York: Signet Books, 1946).

Rockwell, Llewellyn H., Jr., ed., *The Free-Market Reader: Essays in the Economics of Liberty* (Burlingame, CA: The Ludwig Von Mises Institute, 1988).

Ropke, Wilhelm, *A Humane Economy: The Social Framework of the Free Market* (South Bend, IN: Gateway Editions, 1960).

Rosenberg, Nathan and Birdzell, L. E., *How the West Grew Rich: The Economic Transformation of the Industrial World* (New York: Basic Books, 1986).

Rothschild, Michael, *Bionomics: The Inevitability of Capitalism* (New York: Henry Holt, 1990).

Schaeffer, Franky, ed., *Is Capitalism Christian?* (Westchester, IL: Crossway Books, 1985).

Schumpeter, Joseph A., *Capitalism, Socialism, and Democracy* (New York: Harper & Row, 1942).

Slattery, Michael, "The Catholic Origins of Capitalism: Max Weber Clarified," *Crisis*, Volume 6 (April, 1988), pp. 24-29.

Smith, Adam, *An Inquiry into the Nature and Causes of the Wealth of Nations,* Edwin Canaan, ed. (New York: Modern Library, 1937).

Tucker, Jeffrey A., "Papal Economics 101: The Catholic Ethic and the Spirit of Capitalism," *Crisis*, Volume 9 (June, 1991), pp. 16-21.

Urena, Enrique M., *Capitalism or Socialism? An Economic Critique for Christians* (Chicago, IL: Franciscan Herald Press, 1988).

van den Haag, Ernest, *Capitalism: Sources of Hostility* (New Rochelle, NY: Epoch Books, 1979).

Organizations

American Business Conference 1730 K Street, NW, Suite 1200, Washington, DC 20006, (202)-822-9300. Publications: *Winning Performance of Midsize, High Growth Companies, High Cost of Capital: Handicap of American Industry, Winning in the World Market, Overconsumption: The Challenge to the U.S. Economy.* Concerns itself with tax policy, regulatory reform, and international trade issues; works to preserve the free enterprise system.

American Enterprise Institute for Public Policy Research 1150 17th Street, NW, Washington, DC 20036, (202)-862-5800. Publications: *The American Enterprise, Regulation: A Journal on Government and Society.* Provides conservative-leaning studies of matters foreign and domestic to all interested parties.

America's Future P.O. Box 1625, Milford, PA 18337, (717)-296-2800. Publications: *America's Future, Textbook Evaluation Reports.* Seeks to educate Americans on the history, character, importance, and value of the U.S. constitutional republic and institutions and the social, economic, and political principles upon which such government and institutions are founded, emphasizing the advantages of the free enterprise system.

Cato Institute 224 Second Street, SE, Washington, DC 20003, (202)-546-0200. Publications: *Cato Journal: An Interdisciplinary Journal on Public Policy Analysis, Cato Policy Report, Regulation.* A public policy research foundation dedicated to increasing policy debate to allow consideration of more options the institute believes are consistent with traditional American principles of limited government, individual liberty, and peace.

Center for the Defense of Free Enterprise Liberty Park, 12500 N.E. 10th Place, Bellevue, WA 98005, (206)-455-5038. Publications: *Advise and Consent, Impressions, The Private Sector, Free Enterprise Press.* Defends and promotes the principles of the American free enterprise system and relates their application to contemporary American society.

Center for Libertarian Studies 875 Mahler Road, Suite 150, Burlingame, CA 94011, (415)-348-3000. Publications: *In Pursuit of Liberty Newsletter, Journal of Libertarian Studies.* Promotes scholarly analysis of social, economic, political, and philosophical problems from a libertarian perspective.

Citizens for a Sound Economy 470 L'Enfant Plaza, East, SW, Suite 7112, Washington, DC 20024, (202)-488-8200. Publications: *Annual Report, Capital Comment, CSE Report, Economic Perspective, Facts and Figures on Governmental Finance, Issues and Answers, Legal Perspective, On Alert for America's Taxpayers, Tax Features, A Citizens Guide to Deficit Reduction, Myths About Foreign Investment.* Strives to advance understanding of the market process in order to restore a sound economy.

Coalition for Freedom P.O. Box 19458, Raleigh, NC 27619, (919)-850-9035. Publication: *Newsletter.* Sponsors television programs designed to inform the public of the fundamentals of the free enterprise system.

Entrepreneurial Leadership Center Galvin Road at Harvell Drive, Bellevue College, Bellevue, NE 68005, (402)-291-8100. Publications: *The Bottom Line, Missing Dimensions in Economics.* Promotes worldwide understanding of the free enterprise system.

Foundation for Economic Education 30 South Broadway, Irvington-on-Hudson, NY 10533, (914)-591-7230. Publication: *The Freeman: Ideas on Liberty.* Encourages the study and promotion of private ownership, free exchange, open competition, and limited government; maintains library.

The Heritage Foundation 214 Massachusetts Avenue, NE, Washington, DC 20002, (202)-546-4400. Publications: *Backgrounder/Issue Bulletin, Educational Update, Heritage Members' News, Heritage Today, National Security Record, Policy Review, Publications Catalog.* Public policy research institute dedicated to the principles of free competitive enterprise, limited government, individual liberty, and a strong national defense.

Ludwig Von Mises Institute Auburn University, Auburn, AL 36849-5301,

(205)-844-2500. Publications: *Austrian Economics Newsletter, Free Market, Review of Austrian Economics.* Interested in the study of the Austrian school of economics.

Mid America Institute for Public Policy Research 5220 South Harper, #107, Chicago, IL 60615, (312)-786-9575. Publication: *Newsletter.* Non-profit, independent, scholarly organization that studies issues affecting national and international financial market institutions.

Private Enterprise Research Center 459 Blocker Building, Texas A&M University, College Station, TX 77843-4231, (409)-845-7722. Publications: *Pathfinder, Studies in Political Economy, The Foundation of Free Enterprise.* Objectives are: to increase basic understanding of economics; provide information on the dynamics of federal government growth; promote awareness of "the importance of individual freedom to the strength and vitality of our economy."

Students in Free Enterprise 1959 E. Kerr, Springfield, MO 65803, (417)-831-9505. Publications: *SIFE Lines Newsletter, Students in Free Enterprise.* College students, usually business majors, who develop educational programs that teach free enterprise principles to college peers and local citizens.

United States Business and Industrial Council 220 National Press Building, 14th and F Streets, NW, Washington, DC 20045, (202)-662-8744. Publications: *Bulletin, Declaration of Policy, Washington Business Wire.* Conservative council promoting private enterprise, national security, and a strong national economy.

CATHOLIC CHURCH

Books and Articles

Abbott, Walter M. and Gallagher, Joseph, eds., *The Documents of Vatican II* (New York: The America Press, 1966).
Berger, Peter, et al., "The Pope, Liberty, and Capitalism: Essays on *Centesimus Annus*," *National Review*, Volume XLIII (June 24, 1991), pp. S1 - S16.
Blehl, Vincent F., ed., *Essential Newman* (New York: Herder and Herder, 1963).
Bokenkotter, Thomas S., *A Concise History of the Catholic Church* (New York: Image Books, 1977).
Buckley, Reid, "Does the Pope Love America?," *The American Spectator*, Volume 21 (May, 1988), pp. 19-21.
Canavan, Francis, *Pins in the Liberal Balloon* (New York: Catholic Eye, 1990).
Carlen, Claudia, ed., *Papal Encyclicals 1740 - 1981*, 5 vols. (Ann Arbor, MI: Pierian Press, 1981).

Carlen, Claudia, ed., *Papal Pronouncements: A Guide, 1740 - 1978.* 2 vols. (Ann Arbor, MI: Pierian Press, 1990).

Craycraft, Kenneth R., Jr., "Why Marx Hated Christianity: A Reply to Leonardo Boff," *Crisis,* Volume 7 (March, 1989), pp. 32-36.

Delany, John J., *Pocket Dictionary of Saints* (New York: Image Books, 1983).

Dubay, Thomas, "No Longer Groovy: Catholic Dissent Is Going the Way of Abbie Hoffman," *Crisis,* Volume 7 (October, 1989), pp. 12-16.

Eberstadt, Mary, "The Lost Orthodoxies of Vatican II: A Case of Selected Memory," *Crisis,* Volume 9 (May, 1991), pp. 24-29.

Finn, James, ed., *Private Virtue and Public Policy: Catholic Thought and National Life* (New Brunswick, NJ: Transaction Books, 1990).

Hardon, John, *The Catholic Catechism* (New York: Doubleday, 1975).

Hardon, John, *Modern Catholic Dictionary* (New York: Doubleday, 1966).

Hitchcock, James, *Catholicism and Modernity: Confrontation or Capitulation* (New York: Seabury Press, 1979).

Hitchcock, James, "Hijacking Vatican II: Can Catholicism Survive Subversion From Within?," *Crisis,* Volume 10 (April, 1992), pp. 18-26.

Hughes, Philip, *Popular History of the Catholic Church* (New York: Macmillan, 1962).

Hughes, Philip, *Popular History of the Reformation* (New York: Image Books, 1969).

Kelly, George A., *The Battle for the American Church* (New York: Image Books, 1979).

Kelly, J. N., *The Oxford Dictionary of Popes* (New York: Oxford University Press, 1986).

Knox, Ronald, *The Belief of Catholics* (Garden City, NY: Image Books, 1958).

Lawler, Phil, et al., *Catholic Sexual Ethics: A Summary, Explanation, and Defense* (Huntington, IN: Our Sunday Visitor, 1985).

McGurn, William, "Is the Pope Capitalist?," *The American Spectator,* Volume 24 (August, 1991), pp. 12-14.

Molnar, Thomas, *Authority & Its Enemies* (New Rochelle, NY: Arlington House, 1976).

Molnar, Thomas, *The Church, Pilgrim of the Centuries* (Grand Rapids, MI: William Eerdmans, 1990).

Molnar, Thomas, *Politics and the State: The Catholic View* (Chicago, IL: Franciscan Herald Press, 1980).

Molnar, Thomas, *Twin Powers: Politics & the Sacred* (Grand Rapids, MI: William Eerdmans, 1988).

Muggeridge, Anne Roche, *The Desolate City: Revolution in the Catholic Church* (New York: Harper & Row, 1986).

Myers, Kenneth, ed., *Aspiring to Freedom: Commentaries on John Paul II's Encyclical "The Social Concerns of the Church"* (Grand Rapids, MI: William Eerdmans, 1988).

Neuhaus, Richard J., *Biblical Interpretation in Crisis: The Ratzinger Conference on Bible and Church* (Grand Rapids, MI: William Eerdmans, 1989).

Neuhaus, Richard J., *The Catholic Moment: The Paradox of the Church in the Postmodern World* (New York: Harper & Row, 1987).

Neuhaus, Richard J., *Freedom for Ministry* (San Francisco, CA: Harper Religious Books, 1984).

Novak, Michael, "Capitalism With a Heart: The Man They Called the Last Socialist Comes Out in Favor of Free Market Capitalism," *Crisis*, Volume 9 (June, 1991), pp. 21-22.

Novak, Michael, *The Catholic Ethic and the Spirit of Capitalism* (New York: The Free Press, 1993).

Novak, Michael, *Freedom With Justice: Catholic Social Thought & Liberal Institutions* (San Francisco, CA: Harper & Row, 1984).

Pegis, Jessie Corrigan, *A Practical Catholic Dictionary* (New York: All Saints Press, 1961).

Pelikan, Jaroslav, *The Riddle of Roman Catholicism: Its History, Its Beliefs, Its Future* (Nashville, TN: Abingdon Press, 1959).

Pieper, Josef, *In Search of the Sacred: Contributions to an Answer* (San Francisco, CA: Ignatius Press, 1991).

Ratzinger, Joseph Cardinal, *Introduction to Christianity* (New York: Crossroad, 1970; San Francisco, CA: Ignatius Press, 1990).

Ratzinger, Joseph Cardinal, *The Ratzinger Report: An Exclusive Interview on the State of the Church*, With Vittorio Messori (San Francisco, CA: Ignatius Press, 1985).

Reese, Thomas, *Archbishop: Inside the Power Structure of the American Catholic Church* (New York: Harper & Row, 1989).

Rutler, George William, *Beyond Modernity: Reflections of a Post-Modern Catholic* (San Francisco, CA: Ignatius Press, 1986).

Schall, James V., *The Church, the State, and Society in the Thought of John Paul II* (Chicago, IL: Franciscan Herald, 1982).

Schall, James V., *Religion, Wealth, and Poverty* (Vancouver, British Columbia: The Fraser Institute, 1991).

Sheed, F. J., *Theology For Beginners* (Ann Arbor, MI: Servant Books, 1958).

Sigmund, Paul E., *Liberation Theology at the Crossroads: Democracy or Revolution?* (New York: Oxford University Press, 1990).

Simon, William E., "The Bishops' Folly," *National Review*, Volume XXXVII (April 5, 1985), pp. 28-31.

Slattery, Michael, "The Catholic Origins of Capitalism: Max Weber Clarified," *Crisis*, Volume 6 (April, 1988), pp. 24-29.

Steichen, Donna, *Ungodly Rage: The Hidden Face of Catholic Feminism* (San Francisco, CA: Ignatius Press, 1991).

Tucker, Jeffrey A., "Papal Economics 101: The Catholic Ethic and the Spirit of Capitalism," *Crisis*, Volume 9 (June, 1991), pp. 16-21.

Weigel, George, *Catholicism and the Renewal of American Democracy* (Mahwah, NJ: Paulist Press, 1989).

Weigel, George, "The New Anti-Catholicism," *Commentary*, Volume 93 (June, 1992), pp. 25-31.

Weigel, George, "Secularism R.I.P.: Reclaiming the Catholic Intellectual Tradition," *Crisis*, Volume 7 (October, 1989), pp. 22-31.

Weigel, George, *Tranquillitas Ordinis: The Present Failure and Future Promise of American Catholic Thought on War and Peace* (New York: Oxford University Press, 1987).

Woodward, Kenneth L., *Making Saints: How the Church Determines Who Becomes a Saint, Who Doesn't and Why* (New York: Simon & Schuster, 1990).

Zagano, Phyllis, "In Whose Image? - Feminist Theology at the Crossroads," *This World*, Number 15 (Fall, 1986), pp. 78-86.

CATHOLIC EDUCATION

Books and Articles

Aragones, Jay J., "Beyond Bork and Brennan: Should Catholic Law Schools Teach Natural Law?," *Crisis*, Volume 8 (November, 1990), pp. 20-24.

Bethell, Tom, "Orthodoxy and the Liberal Arts," *National Review*, Volume XXXVIII (September 26, 1986), pp. 40-44.

Buetow, Harold A., *Of Singular Benefit: The Story of U.S. Catholic Education* (New York: Macmillan, 1970).

May, William, ed., *Vatican Authority and American Catholic Dissent: The Curran Case and Its Consequences* (New York: Crossroad, 1987).

Schubert, Frank D., "Theology Without God: A New Study Documents the Secularization of the Catholic Curriculum," *Crisis*, Volume 7 (June, 1989), pp. 22-26.

Wolfe, Gregory, "Killing the Spirit: Problems of Conformity, Anti-Intellectualism and Loss of Mission at Alternative Catholic Colleges," *Crisis*, Volume 9 (September, 1991), pp. 19-24.

Organizations

National Catholic Educational Association 1077 30th Street, NW, Suite 100, Washington, DC 20007, (202)-337-6232. Publications: *Current Issues in Catholic Higher Education, Data Bank Report, Momentum, Private Law School Digest, Parish Coordinator/Directors of Religious Education, Seminary News.* Catholic schools and religious education centers from kindergarten through graduate school.

CATHOLIC SCHOOLS
(see **Catholic Education**)

CATHOLICS

Books and Articles

Bozell, L. Brent, *Mustard Seeds: A Conservative Becomes a Catholic* (Manassas, VA: Trinity Publications, 1986).

Day, Thomas, *Why Catholics Can't Sing: The Culture of Catholicism and the Triumph of Bad Taste* (New York: Crossroad, 1990).

Maritain, Jacques, *The Peasant of Garonne* (New York: Holt Rinehart and Winston, 1968).

Maritain, Jacques, *St. Thomas Aquinas* (New York: Meridian Books, 1958).

Newman, John Henry Cardinal, *An Essay in Aid of a Grammar of Assent* (New York: Oxford University Press, 1985).

Novak, Michael, *Confessions of a Catholic* (San Francisco, CA: Harper Religious Books, 1983).

Occhiogrosso, Peter, *Once a Catholic: Prominent Catholics and Ex-Catholics Discuss the Influence of the Church on Their Lives and Work* (Boston, MA: Houghton Mifflin, 1987).

O'Neil, Dan, ed., *The New Catholics: Contemporary Converts Tell Their Stories* (New York: Crossroad, 1987).

Pakaluk, Michael, "A Grammar of Dissent: The Case Against 'Cafeteria Catholics,'" *Crisis*, Volume 6 (July/August, 1988), pp. 20-24.

Organizations

American Catholic Historical Association Mullen Library, Room 318, Catholic University of America, Washington, DC 20064, (202)-319-5079. Publication: *Catholic Historical Review*. Professional society of historians, educators, students, and others interested in the history of the Catholic church in the United States and abroad and in the promotion of historical scholarship among Catholics.

Catholic Biblical Association of America 620 Michigan Avenue, NE, Washington, DC 20064, (202)-319-5519. Publications: *Catholic Biblical Quarterly, Old Testament Abstracts*. Research scholars in the biblical field.

Catholic Book Publishers Association 333 Glen Head Road, Old Brookville, NY 11545, (516)-671-9342. Faciltitates professional information exchange and cooperation.

Catholic League for Religious and Civil Rights 1011 First Avenue, New York, NY 10022. Publication office: 6324 West North Avenue, Wauwatosa, WI 53213, (414)-476-8911. Publication: *Catholic League Newsletter*. Combats all forms of religious prejudice and discrimination and defends human rights, family rights, and the sanctity of all human life, born and unborn.

Catholic News Service 3211 Fourth Street, N.E., Washington, DC 20017, (202)-541-3250. Publication: *Catholic Trends.*

Catholic Press Association 119 North Park Avenue, Rockville Centre, NY 11570, (516)-766-3400. Publications: *Bulletin, Catholic Journalist, Catholic Press Directory.* Sponsors research and education programs; provides job placement service.

Catholic Traditionalist Movement 210 Maple Avenue, Westbury, NY 11590, (516)-333-6470. Publications: *Quote Unquote: A Public Information Service of the Catholic Traditionalist Movement, Sounds of Truth and Tradition.* Opposes liturgical misinterpretation of Vatican II; calls for an end to regimented group participation in the Mass, restricted use of English in the liturgy, and recognition that Latin is the official liturgical language of the Church; has information service and conducts opinion surveys.

Foundation for Catholic Reform P.O. Box 255, Harrison, NY 10528. Publication: *The Latin Mass: Chronicle of a Catholic Reform.* Catholic traditonalists dedicated to correcting abuses in the post-Vatican II Mass; supports reintroduction of regularly scheduled Latin and Tridentine Masses.

Knights of Columbus One Columbus Plaza, New Haven, CT 06507, (203)-772-2130. Publication: *Columbia.* Fraternal society of Catholic men.

National Committee of Catholic Laymen 150 East 35th Street, Room 840, New York, NY 10016, (212)-685-6666. Publication: *catholic eye.* Orthodox Catholics who support Pope John Paul II and who wish to present a united voice in the debate over the direction of the Church.

Paul VI Institute for the Arts 924 G Street, NW, Washington, DC 20001, (202)-347-1450. Publications: *Art and Religion, Cultural Resources for Leisure Clubs, Newsletter,.* Promotes the arts as part of the Catholic Church's evangelical mission and seeks to reestablish and promote the Church's role as sponsor of the arts.

CELEBRITIES

Books and Articles

Celebrity Services International Staff, *Celebrity Register* (Detroit, MI: Gale Research Inc., annual).
Hubbard, Linda S., *Notable Americans: What They Did From 1620 to the Present* (Detroit, MI: Gale Research, Inc., 1988).
Mooney, Louise, ed., *Newsmakers* (Detroit, MI: Gale Research, Inc., annual).

Stetler, Susan L., ed., *Almanac of Famous People,* 3 vols. (Detroit, MI: Gale Research, Inc., 1989).
Who's Who in America (Wilmette, IL: Marquis, annual).
Who's Who in the World (Wilmette, IL: Marquis, annual).

CENSORSHIP
(see **First Amendment**)

CENTRAL INTELLIGENCE AGENCY

Books and Articles

Cline, Ray, et al., *The Central Intelligence Agency: A Photographic History* (Chelsea, MI: Scarborough House, 1986).
Cline, Ray, *The CIA: The Reality vs. Myth* (Washington, DC: Acropolis, 1981).
Cline, Ray, *The CIA Under Reagan, Bush, and Casey: The Evolution of the Agency from Roosevelt to Reagan* (Washington, DC: Acropolis, 1981).
Cline, Ray, *Secrets, Spies, and Scholars: Blueprint of the Essential CIA* (Washington, DC: Acropolis, 1976).
Codevilla, Angelo, "The Arrogance of the Clerks," *National Review*, Volume XLIII (November 4, 1991), pp. 38-40.
Coleman, Peter, *The Liberal Conspiracy: The Congress for Cultural Freedom and the Struggle for the Mind of Postwar Europe* (New York: The Free Press, 1989).
Copeland, Miles, *Beyond Cloak and Dagger: Inside the CIA* (New York: Pinnacle Books, 1975).
Copeland, Miles, "CIA: The Case for Intelligence," *National Review*, Volume XXVII (July 4, 1975), pp. 712-719.
Eberstadt, Nicholas, "Where Did the CIA Go Wrong?," *National Review*, Volume XLIII (June 10, 1991), pp. 31-34.
Epstein, Edward J., *Deception: The Invisible War Between the KGB and the CIA* (New York: Simon & Schuster, 1989).
Ranelagh, John, *The Agency: The Rise and Decline of the CIA* (New York: Touchstone, 1986).
Winks, Robin W., *Cloak and Gown: Scholars in the Secret War 1939-1961* (New York: Morrow, 1987).

Organizations

Central Intelligence Agency Washington, DC 20505, (202)-482-1100.

Association of Former Intelligence Officers 6723 Whittier Avenue, McLean, VA 22101, (703)-790-0320. Encourages public support for intelligence agencies and supports increased intelligence education in colleges and universities.

CHARITIES
(see **Philanthropy**)

CHEMICAL-BIOLOGICAL WARFARE

Books and Articles

Ledeen, Michael, "The Curious Case of Chemical Warfare," *Commentary*, Volume 88 (July, 1989), pp. 37-41.

Ledeen, Michael, "Iraq's German Connection," *Commentary*, Volume 91 (April, 1991), pp. 27-30.

Seagrave, Sterling, *Yellow Rain: A Journey Through the Terror of Chemical Warfare* (New York: M. Evans & Co., 1981).

CHEMISTRY

Books and Articles

Considine, Douglas M., ed., *Van Nostrand Reinhold Encyclopedia of Chemistry* (New York: Van Nostrand Reinhold, 1984).

Daintith, John, ed., *The Facts on File Dictionary of Chemistry* (New York: Facts on File, 1988).

Ihde, Aron J., *The Development of Modern Chemistry* (New York: Dover, 1983).

Organizations

American Chemical Society 1155 16th Street, NW, Washington, DC 20036, (202)-872-4600. Publications: *Accounts of Chemical Research*, *Analytical Chemistry*. Scientific and educational society of chemists and chemical engineers.

American Institute of Chemical Engineers 345 East 47th Street, New York, NY 10017, (212)-705-7338. Publication: *AIChE Journal*. Professional society of chemical engineers. Establishes standards for chemical engineering curricula.

CHESS

Books and Articles

Alburt, Lev and Parr, Larry, "Life Itself," *National Review*, Volume XLIII (September 9, 1991), pp. 48-50.

Organizations

United States Chess Federation 186 Rt 9 W, New Windsor, NY 12553, (914)-562-8350. The governing body of chess in the United States.

CHILD CARE
(see **Day Care**)

CHILDREN

Books and Articles

Allen, Charlotte Low, "Special Delivery: Overcoming the Barriers to Adoption," *Policy Review*, Number 49 (Summer, 1989), pp. 46-53.

Besharov, Douglas J., "Protecting the Innocent," *National Review*, Volume XLII (February 19, 1990), pp. 44-46.

Besharov, Douglas J., *Recognizing Child Abuse: A Guide for the Concerned* (New York: Free Press, 1990).

Best, Joel, "Missing Children, Misleading Statistics," *The Public Interest*, Number 92 (Summer, 1988), pp. 84-92.

Billingsley, K. D., "The Scientific War on Child Abuse," *National Review*, Volume XLV (February 15, 1993), pp. 25-26.

Blits, Jan H., "What's Wrong With Children's Rights," *This World*, Number 7 (Winter, 1984), pp. 5-19.

Dobson, James and Bauer, Gary L., *Children at Risk: The Battle for the Hearts and Minds of Our Kids* (Irving, TX: Word Publishing, 1991).

Dunlap, John R., "Kiddie Litter," *The American Spectator*, Volume 22 (December, 1989), pp. 18-21.

Eberstadt, Nicholas, "America's Infant-Mortality Puzzle," *The Public Interest*, Number 105 (Fall, 1991), pp. 30-47.

Eberstadt, Nicholas, "Is Illegitimacy a Public-Health Hazard?," *National Review*, Volume XL (December 30, 1988), pp. 36-39.

Eberstadt, Nicholas, "Why Are so Many American Babies Dying?," *The American Enterprise*, Volume 2 (September/October, 1991), pp. 37-45.

Farber, Seth, "The Real Abuse," *National Review*, Volume XLV (April 12, 1993), pp. 44-50.

Frohnen, Bruce, "Mother Knows Best," *Chronicles*, Volume 13 (November, 1989), pp. 50-52.

Gilbert, Neil, "Teaching Children to Prevent Sexual Abuse," *The Public Interest*, Number 93 (Fall, 1988), pp.3-15.

Gill, Richard T., "For the Sake of the Children," *The Public Interest*, Number 108 (Summer, 1992), pp. 81-96.

Gosman, Fred, *Spoiled Rotten: Today's Children and How to Change Them* (New York: Villard Books, 1992).

Hood, John, "Children's Crusade: Armed With Business Rhetoric and Dubious 'Facts,' the Children's Defense Fund Has Become the Most Potent Lobbyist for a Renewed Welfare State," *Reason*, Volume 24 (June, 1992), pp. 32-35.

Kramer, Rita, *In Defense of the Family: Raising Children in America Today* (New York: Basic Books, 1983).

Lowry, Richard and Samuelson, Richard, "How Many Battered Children?," *National Review*, Volume XLV (April 12, 1993), p. 46.

O'Beirne, Kate Walsh, "Children's Hour," *National Review*, Volume XLIII (July 29, 1991), pp. 34-36.

Olasky, Marvin, "The War on Adoption," *National Review*, Volume XLV (June 7, 1993), pp. 38-44.

Pakaluk, Michael, "War Games: Why Little Boys Should Play With Toy Guns," *Crisis*, Volume 9 (October, 1991), pp. 16-20.

Singh, Harmeet K. D., "Stork Reality: Why America's Infants are Dying," *Policy Review*, Number 52 (Spring, 1990), pp. 56-63.

Stein, Sara Bonnett, *Girls and Boys: The Limits of Nonsexist Childrearing* (New York: Scribner's, 1983).

Wexler, Richard, *Wounded Innocents: The Real Victims of the War Against Child Abuse* (Buffalo, NY: Prometheus Books, 1990).

CHILE

Books and Articles

Rosett, Claudia, "Looking Back on Chile, 1973-1984," *National Review*, Volume XXXVI (June 1, 1984), pp. 25-28, 53.

CHINA

Books and Articles

Butterfield, Fox, *China: Alive in the Bitter Sea* (New York: Times Books, 1982).

Elegant, Robert, "Chinese Communism Turns Seventy," *National Review*, Volume XLIII (July 29, 1991), pp. 31-34.

Heng, Liang and Shapiro, Judith, *After the Nightmare* (New York: Knopf, 1986).
Leys, Simon, *Chinese Shadows* (New York: Viking Press, 1977).
Lin, Chong-Pin, "China's Enemies Within," *The American Enterprise*, Volume 1
   (January/February, 1990), pp. 41-45.
McGurn, William, *Perfidious Albion: The Abandonment of Hong Kong*
   (Washington, DC: Ethics and Public Policy Center, 1992).
Mosher, Steven W., *China Misperceived: American Illusions and Chinese Reality*
   (New York: Basic Books, 1990).
Mosher, Steven W., "The China Syndrome," *Reason*, Volume 21 (October,
   1989), pp. 22-28.
Munro, Ross H., "Who Lost Hong Kong?," *Commentary*, Volume 90 (December,
   1990), pp. 33-39.
Spence, Jonathan D., *The Gate of Heavenly Peace: The Chinese and Their
   Revolution 1895-1980* (New York: Viking, 1981).

Organizations

Free the Fathers 1120 Applewood Circle, Signal Mountain, TN 37377, (615)-
886-2134. Publication: *Free the Fathers*. Works to free imprisoned priests, nuns,
and laity in China and other communist and totalitarian states.

Independent Federation of Chinese Students and Scholars 733 15th Street, NW,
Suite 440, Washington, DC 20005, (202)-347-0017. Publications: *IFCSS
Newsletter, Press Freedom Herald*. Umbrella group representing the Chinese pro-
democracy movement; seeks to educate both Americans and those still in China
about the suppression of the pro-democracy movement.

CHRISTIANITY
(see also **Catholic Church, Religion**)

Books and Articles

Atkins, Stanley and McConnell, Theodore, eds., *Churches on the Wrong Road*
   (Chicago, IL: Regnery Gateway, 1986).
Atwood, Thomas C., "Through a Glass Darkly: Is the Christian Right
   Overconfident It Knows God's Will?," *Policy Review*, Number 54 (Fall,
   1990), pp. 44-52.
Barlow, Geoffrey, ed., *Vintage Muggeridge: Religion and Society* (Grand
   Rapids, MI: William Eerdmans, 1985).
Barrett, David, ed., *World Christian Encyclopedia: A Comparative Survey of
   Churches and Religions in the Modern World* (New York: Oxford University
   Press, 1982).

Cross, F. L., and Livingstone, Elizabeth A., *The Oxford Dictionary of the Christian Church* (NewYork: Oxford University Press, 1974).

Eliot, T. S., *Christianity and Culture. Including The Idea of a Christian Society; Notes Towards the Definition of Culture* (San Diego, CA: Harcourt Brace Jovanovich, 1960).

Hamilton, Kenneth, *Earthly Good: The Churches and the Betterment of Human Existence* (Grand Rapids, MI: William Eerdmans, 1990).

Harvey, Van A., *A Handbook of Theological Terms* (New York: Macmillan, 1964).

Hatch, Nathan. *The Democratization of American Christianity* (New Haven, CT: Yale University Press, 1989).

Johnson, Paul, *A History of Christianity* (New York: Atheneum, 1976).

Lewis, C. S., *The Case for Christianity* (New York: Macmillan, 1989).

Lewis, C. S., *Mere Christianity* (New York: Macmillan, 1969).

Lewis, C. S., *Miracles* (New York: Macmillan, 1978).

Lewis, C. S., *Screwtape Letters* (New York: Macmillan, 1982).

McManners, John, ed., *The Oxford Illustrated Encyclopedia of Christianity* (New York: Oxford University Press, 1990).

McManners, John, *The Oxford Illustrated History of Christianity* (New York: Oxford University Press, 1990).

Mead, Frank S. and Hill, Samuel S., *Handbook of Denominations in the United States* (Nashville, TN: Abingdon Press, 1990).

Mead, Walter B., "Christianity and the Modern Political Order: The Question of Functionality," *Modern Age,* Volume 32 (Spring, 1988), pp. 122-130.

Muggeridge, Malcolm, *Chronicles of Wasted Time* (Washington, DC: Regnery Gateway, 1989).

Muggeridge, Malcolm, *The End of Christendom* (Grand Rapids, MI: William Eerdmans, 1980).

Muggeridge, Malcolm, *Jesus, the Man Who Lives* (San Francisco, CA: Harper Religious Books, 1975).

Muggeridge, Malcolm, *Jesus Rediscovered* (New York: Doubleday, 1979).

Neuhaus, Richard John, *Doing Well and Doing Good: The Challenge to the Christian Capitalist* (New York: Doubleday, 1992).

Oddie, William, "The Goddess Squad," *National Review,* Volume XLIII (November 18, 1991), pp. 44-46.

Panichas, George A., et al., "Christianity in Sight of the Third Millenium: A Symposium," *Modern Age,* Volume 33 (Summer, 1990), pp. 98-212.

Pelikan, Jaroslav, *The Christian Tradition: A History of the Development of Doctrine, Vol. I: Emergence of the Catholic Tradition* (Chicago, IL: University of Chicago Press, 1971).

Pelikan, Jaroslav, *The Christian Tradition: A History of the Development of Doctrine, Vol. II: The Spirit of Eastern Christendom* (Chicago, IL: University of Chicago Press, 1974).

Pelikan, Jaroslav, *The Christian Tradition: A History of the Development of Doctrine, Vol. III: The Growth of Medieval Theology* (Chicago, IL: University of Chicago Press, 1978).

Pelikan, Jaroslav, *Jesus Through the Centuries: His Place in the History of Culture* (New York: Harper & Row, 1987).

Rahner, Karl, *A Dictionary of Theology* (New York: Crossroad, 1985).

Ratzinger, Joseph Cardinal, *Introduction to Christianity,* (San Francisco, CA: Ignatius Press, 1990).

Reid, Daniel G., et al., eds. *Dictionary of Christianity in America* (Downers Grove, IL: Inter-Varsity Press, 1990).

Schall, James V., *Christianity and Politics* (Jamaica Plains, MA: Daughters of Saint Paul, 1981).

Schall, James V., *The Distinctiveness of Christianity* (San Francisco, CA: Ignatius Press, 1983).

Schall, James V., *The Politics of Heaven and Hell: Christian Themes From Classical, Medieval, and Modern Political Philosophy* (Lanham, MD: University Press of America, 1984).

Schlossberg, Herbert, *Idols for Destruction: Christian Faith and its Confrontation with American Society* (Washington, DC: Regnery Gateway, 1983).

Tinder, Glenn, *The Political Meaning of Christianity: An Interpretation* (Baton Rouge, LA: Louisiana State University Press, 1988).

Walsh, David, *After Ideology: Recovering the Spiritual Foundations of Freedom* (New York: Harper Collins, 1991).

Organizations

Christian Voice 208 North Patrick, Alexandria, VA 22314, (703)-548-1421. Publications: *Christian Voice Scorecard, Congressional Report Card.* Major lobbying group representing traditional Christians; supports Christian agenda, including pro-life legislation; conducts seminars in Christian activism.

CHURCH/STATE

Books and Articles

Carey, George W., and Schall, James V., eds., *Essays on Christianity and Political Philosophy* (Lanham, MD: The Intercollegiate Studies Institute and University Press of America, 1984).

Dreisbach, Daniel, *Real Threat and Mere Shadow: Religious Liberty and the First Amendment* (Westchester, IL: Crossway Books, 1987).

Molnar, Thomas S., *Twin Powers: Politics and the Sacred* (Grand Rapids, MI: William Eerdmans, 1988).

Schall, James V., *The Politics of Heaven and Hell: Christian Themes From Classical, Medieval, and Modern Political Philosophy* (Lanham, MD: University Press of America, 1984).
Schall, James V., *Reason, Revelation, and the Foundations of Political Philosophy* (Baton Rouge, LA: Louisiana State University Press, 1987).

Organizations

Plymouth Rock Foundation Fisk Mill, P.O. Box 577, Marlborough, NH 03455 (603)-876-4685. Publications: *The Correspondent, FAC-Sheet, Letter From Plymouth Rock, The Pilgrims' Progress, Correspondent, Fundamentals for American Christians.* Purposes are: "to advance God's Biblical principles of self and civil government as the only real basis for a society of free people; to help restore the foundation of the American Christian Republic; to be a vital part of the total ministry commissioned by our Lord and Savior."

CIGARETTES
(see **Tobacco**)

CITIES
(see **Urban Affairs**)

CITIZENSHIP
(see also **American Government, Immigration**)

Organizations

Patriotic Education/Inc. 435 N. Lee Street, Alexandria, VA 22314, (703)-548-3350. Publications: *The Making of George Washington, The Key to the Constitution of the United States.* Promotes and develops constructive citizenship through education.

CIVIL RIGHTS

Books and Articles

Berger, Raoul, *Government by Judiciary: The Transformation of the Fourteenth Amendment* (Cambridge, MA: Harvard University Press, 1977).
Bolick, Clint, "Betting on Bush," *National Review*, Volume XLII (August 6, 1990), pp. 33-35.

Bolick, Clint, *Changing Course: Civil Rights at the Crossroads* (New Brunswick, NJ: Transaction Books, 1988).

Bolick, Clint, *Unfinished Business: A Civil Rights Strategy for America's Third Century* (San Francisco, CA: Pacific Research Institute for Public Policy, 1990).

Capaldi, Nicholas, *Out of Order: Affirmative Action and the Crisis of Doctrinaire Liberalism* (Buffalo, NY: Prometheus Books, 1985).

Detlefsen, Robert, *Civil Rights Under Reagan* (San Francisco, CA: Institute for Contemporary Studies Press, 1991).

Eastland, Terry, "George Bush's Quota Bill: The Dismaying Impact of *Griggs*," *Policy Review*, Number 57 (Summer, 1991), pp. 45-49.

Eastland, Terry, "Toward a Real Restoration of Civil Rights," *Commentary*, Volume 88 (November, 1989), 25-29.

Epstein, Richard A., *Forbidden Grounds: The Case Against Employment Discrimination Laws* (Cambridge, MA: Harvard University Press, 1992).

Glendon, Mary Ann, *Rights Talk: The Impoverishment of Political Discourse* (New York: The Free Press, 1991).

Graglia, Lino, *Disaster by Decree: The Supreme Court Decisions on Race and the Schools* (Ithaca, NY: Cornell University Press, 1976).

Graham, Hugh Davis, *The Civil Rights Era: Origins and Development of National Policy* (New York: Oxford University Press, 1990).

Morgan, Richard E., *Disabling America: The "Right Industry" in Our Time* (New York: Basic Books, 1986).

Roth, Byron M., "Social Psychology's Racism," *The Public Interest*, Number 98 (Winter, 1990), pp. 26-36.

Sowell, Thomas, *Civil Rights: Rhetoric or Reality?* (New York: William Morrow, 1984).

Thernstrom, Abigail M., *Whose Votes Count? Affirmative Action and Minority Voting Rights* (Cambridge, MA: Harvard University Press, 1987).

Organizations

Institute for Justice 1001 Pennsylvania Avenue, NW, #200-S, Washington, DC 20004, (202)-457-4240.

Landmark Legal Foundation 1006 Grand Avenue, 8th Floor, Kansas City, MO 64106, (816)-474-6600. Publications: *In Brief, Executive Memorandum*.

Washington Legal Foundation 1705 N Street, NW, Washington, DC 20036, (202)-857-0240. Publications: *Legal Backgrounders, WLF Working Papers Studies*. Public interest law firm "dedicated to supporting the precepts of individual liberties and the free enterprise system in the administrative agencies and the courts."

CIVIL WAR
(see **U.S. Civil War**)

COLD WAR
(see also **U.S. Foreign Policy**)

Books and Articles

Allen, Richard V., et al., "The Cold War's Magnificent Seven," *Policy Review*, Number 59 (Winter, 1992), pp. 44-54.

Burnham, James, *Containment or Liberation: An Inquiry into the Aims of United States Foreign Policy* (New York: John Day, 1952).

Crozier, Brian, et al., *This War Called Peace* (New York: Universe Books, 1985).

Harries, Owen, "The Cold War and the Intellectuals: 'In Mockery of the Promise and Fitness of Things,'" *Commentary*, Volume 92 (October, 1991), pp. 13-20.

Lee, William and Star, Richard F., *Soviet Military Policy Since World War II* (Stanford, CA: Hoover Institution Press, 1986).

Puddington, Arch, "The Anti-Cold War Brigade," *Commentary*, Volume 90 (August, 1990), pp. 30-38.

Puddington, Arch, "Why Aren't These People Smiling?," *National Review*, Volume XLIII (November, 4, 1991), pp. 44-46, 60.

Thomas, Hugh, *Armed Truce: The Beginnings of the Cold War 1945 - 46* (New York: Atheneum, 1987).

COLLEGES
(see **Universities**)

COMMONWEALTH OF INDEPENDENT STATES

Books and Articles

Aron, Leon, "After Communism," *National Review*, Volume XLIII (September 23, 1991), pp. 28-32.

Beichman, Arnold, *The Long Pretense: Soviet Treaty Diplomacy from Lenin to Gorbachev* (New Brunswick, NJ: Transaction Books, 1991).

Bernstam, Mikhail, "The Collapse of the Soviet Welfare State," *National Review*, Volume XXXIX (November 6, 1987), pp. 40-41.

Carrere d'Encausse, Helene, *Big Brother: The Soviet Union and Soviet Europe* (New York: Holmes and Meier, 1987).

Carrere d'Encausse, Helene, *Confiscated Power* (New York: Harper & Row, 1982).

Carrere d'Encausse, Helene, *Decline of an Empire: The Soviet Socialist Republics in Revolt* (New York: Newsweek Books, 1979).

Conquest, Robert, "The Beginning of the End," *National Review*, Volume XLIII (September 9, 1991), pp. 19-20.

Conquest, Robert, "History, Humanity, and Truth," *National Review*, Volume XLV (June 7, 1993), pp. 28-35.

Conquest, Robert, *Kolyma: The Arctic Death Camps* (New York: Viking Press, 1978).

Conquest, Robert, ed., *The Last Empire: Nationality and the Soviet Future* (Stanford, CA: Hoover Institution Press, 1986).

Conquest, Robert, *The Nation Killers: The Soviet Deportation of Nationalities* (New York: Macmillan, 1970).

Conquest, Robert, "Reflections on the Revolution," *National Review*, Volume XLIII (September 23, 1991), pp. 24-26.

Diuk, Nadia and Karatnycky, Adrian, *The Hidden Nations: The People Challenge the Soviet Union* (New York: William Morrow and Co., 1990).

Eberstadt, Nicholas and Tombes, Jonathan, "The Soviet Economy: How Big?," *The American Enterprise*, Volume 1 (July/August, 1990), pp. 76-80.

Fairbanks, Charles, "Getting It Wrong," *National Review*, Volume XLIII (September 23, 1991), pp. 26-28.

Heller, Mikhail, *Cogs in the Soviet Wheel: The Formation of Soviet Man* (New York: Knopf, 1988).

Heller, Mikhail and Nekrich, Aleksandr M., *Utopia in Power: The History of the Soviet Union From 1917 to the Present* (New York: Summit Books, 1986).

Horowitz, David, "Still Taking the Fifth," *Commentary*, Volume 88 (July, 1989), pp. 53-55.

Hosking, Geoffrey, *The Awakening of the Soviet Union* (Cambridge, MA: Harvard University Press, 1990).

Karatnycky, Adrian, "The Empire Strikes Out," *The American Spectator*, Volume 24 (February, 1991), pp. 20-25.

Labedz, Leopold, *The Use and Abuse of Sovietology*. Melvin J. Lasky, ed., (New Brunswick, NJ: Transaction Books, 1989).

Laqueur, Walter, *The Long Road to Freedom: Russia and Glasnost* (New York: Scribner's, 1989).

Laqueur, Walter, *Soviet Realities: Culture and Politics From Stalin to Gorbachev* (New Brunswick, NJ: Transaction Books, 1990).

Levine, Alan J., *The Soviet Union, the Communist Movement, and the World: Prelude to the Cold War 1917-1941* (New York: Praeger, 1990).

Luttwak, Edward, *The Grand Strategy of the Soviet Union*, With Appendix by Herbert Block and W. Seth Carus. (New York: St. Martin's Press, 1983).

Lyons, Eugene, *Workers Paradise Lost* (New York: Funk and Wagnalls, 1967).

Malia, Martin E., *The Soviet Tragedy: A History of Socialism in Russia* (New York: The Free Press, 1993).

Malia, Martin E., "Yeltsin and Us," *Commentary*, Volume 93 (April, 1992), pp. 21-28.

Menges, Constantine C., "That Old Summit Magic," *National Review*, Volume XL (June 24, 1988), pp. 37-40.

Methvin, Eugene H., "Yeltsin Spoils the Party," *National Review*, Volume XLII (March 19, 1990), pp. 29-33.

Muller, Jerry Z., "Communism, Anti-Semitism, and the Jews," *Commentary*, Volume 86 (August, 1988), pp. 28-39.

Oberg, James E., *Uncovering Soviet Disasters: Exploring the Limits of Glasnost* (New York: Random House, 1988).

Odom, William E., "Smashing an Icon: The Soviet Military Today," *The National Interest*, Number 21 (Fall, 1990), pp. 62-74.

Pipes, Richard, "Russia's Chance," *Commentary*, Volume 93 (March, 1992), pp. 28-33.

Pipes, Richard, *Survival is not Enough: Soviet Realities and America's Future* (New York: Simon and Schuster, 1984).

Revel, Jean-Francois, "Hastening the Death of Communism," *Commentary*, Volume 88 (October, 1989), pp. 19-23.

Revel, Jean-Francois, "Is Communism Reversible?," *Commentary*, Volume 87 (January, 1989), pp. 17-24.

Rubinfien, Elizabeth and Sneider, Daniel, "Yeltsin's Unfinished Revolution," *National Review*, Volume XLIV (December 14, 1992), pp. 21-24.

Schapiro, Leonard, *The Communist Party of the Soviet Union* (New York: Random House, 1971).

Schapiro, Leonard, *Russian Studies* (New York: Viking, 1986).

Scherr, James, "Yeltsin Rolls the Dice," *National Review*, Volume XLV (April 12, 1993), pp. 36-40.

Seaton, Albert and Seaton, Jan, *The Soviet Army: 1918 to the Present* (New York: New American Library, 1986).

Shelton, Judy, *The Coming Soviet Crash: Gorbachev's Desperate Pursuit of Credit in Western Financial Markets* (New York: The Free Press, 1989).

Simis, Konstantin M., *USSR - The Corrupt Society: The Secret World of Soviet Capitalism* (New York: Simon & Schuster, 1982).

Ulam, Adam, *Dangerous Relations: The Soviet Union in World Politics, 1970-1982* (New York: Oxford University Press, 1983).

Ulam, Adam, *Expansion and Coexistence: The History of Soviet Foreign Policy 1917-73* (New York: Praeger, 1974).

Ulam, Adam, *The Rivals: America and Russia Since World War II* (New York: Viking Press, 1971).

Voslenskii, Michael, *Nomenklatura: The Soviet Ruling Class* (New York: Doubleday, 1984).

Willis, David K., *Klass: How Russians Really Live* (New York: St. Martin's Press, 1985).

COMMUNICATIONS

Books and Articles

Ellig, Jerome, "Consumers on Hold: The Future Could Be Today If the Baby Bells Were Allowed to Grow Up," *Reason*, Volume 21 (July, 1989), pp. 34-37.

Hazlett, Thomas W., "The Fairness Doctrine and the First Amendment," *The Public Interest*, Number 96 (Summer, 1989), pp. 103-116.

Shew, William, "The Economics of Communication: Auctioning the Airwaves," *The American Enterprise*, Volume 2 (September/October, 1991), pp. 21-23.

Organizations

Competitive Telecommunications Association 1140 Connecticut Avenue, NW, Suite 220, Washington, DC 20036, (202)-296-6650. Publication: *COMPTEL Bulletin*. Serves as a voice for the competitve long distance telephone industry on both the legislative and regulatory levels.

COMMUNISM
(see also **Socialism**)

Books and Articles

Besancon, Alain, *The Rise of the Gulag: The Intellectual Origins of Leninism* (New York: Continuum Publishing Corp., 1981).

Bethell, Tom, "Will Success Spoil Anti-Communists?," *National Review*, Volume XLII (March 5, 1990), pp. 38-40.

Brown, Anthony Cave and MacDonald, Charles B., *On a Field of Red: The Communist International and the Coming of World War II* (New York: Putnam, 1981).

Brzezinski, Zbigniew, *The Grand Failure: The Birth and Death of Communism in the Twentieth Century* (New York: Scribners, 1989).

Burnham, James, *The Coming Defeat of Communism* (New York: John Day, 1949).

Burnham, James, *The Web of Subversion: Underground Networks in the U.S. Government* (New York: John Day, 1954).

Chambers, Whittaker, *Witness* (Washington, DC: Regnery Gateway, 1952).

Daniels, Anthony, *The Wilder Shores of Marx: Journeys in a Vanishing World* (New York: Crown, 1991).

Eberstadt, Nicholas, *The Poverty of Communism* (New Brunswick, NJ: Transaction Books, 1988).

Farah, Joseph, "The Real Blacklist," *National Review*, Volume XLI (October 27, 1989), pp. 42-43.

Gray, John, "The End of History - or of Liberalism?," *National Review*, Volume XLI (October 27, 1989), pp. 33-35.

Grenier, Richard, "The New Treason of the Clerks," *National Review*, Volume XLII (July 23, 1990), pp. 42-45.

Haraszti, Miklos, *The Velvet Prison: Artists Under State Socialism* (New York: Basic Books, 1987).

Harries, Owen, "The Cold War and the Intellectuals: In Mockery of the Promise and Fitness of Things," *Commentary*, Volume 92 (October, 1991), pp. 13-20.

Heller, Mikhail, *Cogs in the Soviet Wheel: The Formation of Soviet Man* (New York: Knopf, 1986).

Hessen, Robert, ed., *Breaking with Communism: The Intellectual Odyssey of Bertram D. Wolfe* (Stanford, CA: Hoover Institution Press, 1990).

Karetnikova, Inga and Golomstock, Igor, "Totalitarian Culture: The Encounter in Paris," *National Review*, Volume XXXVIII (May 9, 1986), pp. 42-45.

Klehr, Harvey, *The Heyday of American Communism: The Depression Decade* (New York: Basic Books, 1984).

Leites, Nathan, *A Study of Bolshevism* (Glencoe, IL: The Free Press, 1953).

Leonhard, Wolfgang, *Child of the Revolution* (Chicago, IL: Henry Regnery, 1958).

Lewy, Guenter, *The Cause That Failed: Communism in American Political Life* (New York: Oxford University Press, 1990).

Lyons, Eugene, *The Red Decade: The Stalinist Penetration of America* (New Rochelle, NY: Arlington House, 1970).

Meyer, Frank S., *The Moulding of Communists: The Training of the Communist Cadre* (New York: Harvest/Harcourt Brace Jovanovich, 1961).

Minogue, Kenneth, *Alien Powers: The Pure Theory of Ideology* (New York: St. Martin's, 1985).

Puddington, Arch, "Why Johnny's Not an Anti-Communist," *National Review*, Volume XLII (February 5, 1990), pp. 44-46.

Puddington, Arch, "The Wounds of Glasnost," *National Review*, Volume XLI (November 24, 1989), pp. 26-28.

Rajic, Negovan, "On Liberty and the Grand Idea," *Chronicles*, Volume 12 (December, 1988), pp. 14-17.

Revel, Jean-Francois, *How Democracies Perish* (New York: Doubleday, 1983).

Revel, Jean-Francois, *The Totalitarian Temptation* (Garden City, NY: Doubleday, 1977).

Schapiro, Leonard, *The Russian Revolutions of 1917: The Origins of Modern Communism* (New York: Basic Books, 1984).

Smith, Tony, *Thinking Like a Communist: State and Legitimacy in the Soviet Union, China, and Cuba* (New York: Norton, 1987).

Sowell, Thomas, *Marxism: Philosophy and Economics* (New York: Quartet Books, 1985).

Ulam, Adam B., *The Communists: The Story of Power and Lost Illusions: 1948-1991* (New York: Scribner's, 1992).

Weigel, George, "Death of a Heresy," *National Review*, Volume XLIV (January 20, 1992), pp. 42-46.

Weigel, George, *The Final Revolution: The Resistance Church and the Collapse of Communism* (New York: Oxford, 1992).

Wolfe, Bertram D., *Strange Communists I Have Known* (Lanham, MD: Madison Books, 1982).

Zinsmeister, Karl, "All the Hungry People," *Reason*, Volume 20 (June, 1988), pp. 22-30.

COMMUNITARIANISM

Books and Articles

Anderson, Digby, ed., *The Loss of Virtue: Moral Confusion and Social Disorder in Britain and America* (new York: National Review Books, 1993).

Bellah, Robert N., et al., *The Good Society* (New York: Knopf, 1991).

Bellah, Robert N., et al., *Habits of the Heart: Individualism and Commitment in American Life* (New York: Harper & Row, 1985).

Deutsch, Morton, *Distributive Justice: A Social-Psychological Perspective* (New Haven, CT: Yale University Press, 1985).

Etzioni, Amatai, *The Spirit of Community: Rights, Responsibilities, and the Communitarian Agenda* (New York: Crown, 1993).

Glass, James M., *Delusion: Internal Dimensions of Political Life* (Chicago, IL: University of Chicago Press, 1985).

Glendon, Mary Ann, *Rights Talk: The Impoverishment of Political Discourse* (New York: The Free Press, 1991).

Montgomery, Marion, *Liberal Arts and Community: The Feeding of the Larger Body* (Baton Rouge, LA: Louisiana State University Press, 1990).

Nisbet, Robert, *The Quest for Community: A Study in the Ethics of Order and Freedom* (San Francisco, CA: Institute for Contemporary Studies Press, 1990).

Novak, Michael, *Free Persons and the Common Good* (Lanham, MD: Madison Books, 1989).

COMPETITIVENESS
(see **Economic Planning, Economics, International Trade**)

COMPUTERS

Books and Articles

Costikyan, Greg, "Closing the Net: Will Over Zealous Investigations of
    Computer Crime Render Freedom of the Press Technologically Obsolete?,"
    Reason, Volume 22 (January, 1991), pp. 22-27.
Kurzweil, Raymond, *The Age of Intelligent Machines* (Cambridge, MA: The
    MIT Press, 1990).

Organizations

Software Publishers Association 1730 M Street, NW, Suite 700, Washington, DC
20036-4510, (202)-452-1600. Publications: *SPA Membership Directory, SPA
News.* Purpose is to examine and research topics raised by the growth in
software manufacturing, especially the unauthorized duplication and distribution of
microcomputer software.

Town Hall 214 Massachusetts Avenue, NE, Washington, DC 20002, (800)-441-
4142; via modem: (301)-262-8610. Interactive 24-hour conservative meeting place
accessed via desktop computers. Joint project of *National Review* and the Heritage
Foundation.

CONDOMS
(see **Contraceptives**)

CONGRESS
(see also **Federal Government**)

Books and Articles

Barnes, Fred, "Congressional Despots, Then and Now," *The Public Interest*,
    Number 100 (Summer, 1990), pp. 45-50.
Barnes, Fred, "So You Want to Reform Congress?," *The American Spectator*,
    Volume 22 (September, 1989), pp. 14-16.
Brock, David, "Mr. Symms Goes to Jamba: A Kind Word for Congress in
    Foreign Policy," *Policy Review*, Number 59 (Winter, 1992), pp. 32-39.
Brock, David, "The Prince Metternichs of Congress," *The American Spectator*,
    Volume 23 (February, 1990), pp. 22-27.
Crovitz, L. Gordon, "The Least Responsive Branch," *Commentary*, Volume 87
    (March, 1989), pp. 38-41.
Felton, Eric, *The Ruling Class: Inside the Imperial Congress* (Washington, DC:
    Regnery Gateway, 1993).

Fredenburg, Michael, "Cleaning House," *National Review*, Volume XLIV (October 19, 1992), pp. 44-48.

Jackley, John L., *Hill Rat: Blowing the Lid Off Congress* (Washington, DC: Regnery Gateway, 1992).

Jones, Gordon S. and Marini, John A., *The Imperial Congress: Crisis in the Separation of Powers* (Washington, DC: The Heritage Foundation, 1988).

Ladd, Carll Everett, "Public Opinion and the 'Congress Problem,'" *The Public Interest*, Number 100 (Summer, 1990), pp. 57-67.

McDowell, Gary L., "Congress and the Courts," *The Public Interest*, Number 100 (Summer, 1990), pp. 89-101.

McFadden, Edward, "There's No Accounting for Congress: Especially If the GAO Is Cooking the Numbers," *The American Spectator*, Volume 25 (July, 1992), pp. 24-28.

Payne, James L., "The Congressional Brainwashing Machine," *The Public Interest*, Number 100 (Summer, 1990), pp. 3-14.

Payne, James L., *The Culture of Spending: Why Congress Lives Beyond Our Means* (San Francisco, CA: Institute for Contemporary Studies, 1991).

Polsby, Nelson W., "Congress-Bashing for Beginners," *The Public Interest*, Number 100 (Summer, 1990), pp. 15-23.

Rabkin, Jeremy, "Micromanaging the Administrative Agencies," *The Public Interest*, Number 100 (Summer, 1990), pp. 116-130.

Rodman, Peter W., "The Imperial Congress," *The National Interest*, Number 1 (Fall, 1985), pp. 26-35.

Will, George F., *Restoration: Congress, Term Limits, and the Recovery of Deliberative Democracy* (New York: Free Press, 1992).

Organizations

American Conservative Union 38 Ivy Street, SE, Washington, DC 20003, (202)-546-6555. Publication: *Capitol Review.* Lobbies to further the general cause of conservatism; maintains information service on conservative publications; issues congressional ratings.

Capitol Research Center 727 15th Street, NW, 8th Floor, Washington, DC 20005 (202)-737-5677. Publications: *Organizational Trends, Alternatives in Philanthropy, Philanthropy, Culture and Society.* Provides grantmakers with information on which public policy, special interest and traditional charitable organizations promote the principles of free enterprise, individual initiative and responsibility, and limited government.

Center for Judicial Studies Box 113, Hampden-Sydney College, Hampden, VA 23943, (804)-223-2207. Publications: *Benchmark, Constitutional Commentaries.* Goal is to reform the U.S. constitutional and judicial systems.

The Conservative Caucus Research, Analysis and Education Foundation
450 Maple Street, East, Suite 309, Vienna, VA 22180, (703)-281-6782.
Publications: *Senate Issues Yearbook, Senate Report*. Disseminates information
about federal government actions and expenditures, focusing on Congress;
monitors federal monies given to political activists; issues congressional ratings.

Conservative Leadership Political Action Committee 717 Second Street, NE,
Washington, DC 20002, (202)-546-5106. Assists in the campaigns of conservative
congressional candidates; trains and places campaign staffers.

Free Congress Research and Education Foundation 717 Second Street, NE,
Washington, DC 20002, (202)-546-3000. Publications: *Empowerment, Spotlight
on Congress, Political Report*. Analyzes U.S. House and Senate races and studies
political trends considered to have national significance. "Networks" conservative
organizations active in social, economic and foreign causes.

Fund for a Conservative Majority 1200 G Street, NW, Suite 800, Washington,
DC 20005, (202)-546-3993. Publication: *FCM Report*. Seeks a conservative
majority in Congress; trains young campaign workers and offers financial aid to
candidates.

United States Capitol Historical Society 200 Maryland Avenue, NE,
Washington, DC 20002, (202)-543-8919. Publications: *The Capital Dome,
Congress and the Presidency, Congressional Journal*. Encourages understanding
of the founding, growth, and significance of the Capitol as a tangible symbol of
representative government; conducts research into the history of the Congress and
the Capitol.

CONSERVATISM
(see also **State/Regional Conservatism**)

Books and Articles

Abrams, Elliot, "Breaking Ranks," *National Review*, Volume XLV (January 18,
     1992), pp. 40-41.
Allison, Wick, et al., "Conservative Movement R.I.P.?," *Chronicles*, Volume 15
     (May, 1991), pp. 18-22.
Allison, Wick, et al., "National Review Special Supplement: Rebuilding
     America: A Citizens' Guide," *National Review*, Volume XLII (May 28,
     1990), pp. 1S-15S.
Andrews, John K., et al., "The Vision Thing: Conservatives Take Aim at the
     '90s," *Policy Review*, Number 52 (Spring, 1990), pp. 4-37.

Ashford, Nigel and Davies, Stephen, eds., *Dictionary of Conservative and Libertarian Thought* (New York: Routledge, 1991).

Atwood, Thomas C., "Through a Glass Darkly: Is the Christian Right Overconfident It Knows God's Will?," *Policy Review*, Number 54 (Fall, 1990), pp. 44-52.

Bakshian, Aram, Jr., "New Paradigm or Old Paradox?," *National Review*, Volume XLIII (June 24, 1991), pp. 36-37.

Barnes, Fred, "Why Can't Conservatives Govern?," *The American Spectator*, Volume 21 (May, 1988), pp. 14-15.

Bethel, Tom, et al., "The Conservative Summit," *National Review*, Volume XLV (March 29, 1993), pp. 33-48.

Bradford, M. E., "Collaborators With the Left: The Monstrosity of Big-Government Conservatism," *Policy Review*, Number 57 (Summer, 1991), pp. 78-81.

Bradford, M. E., *The Reactionary Imperative: Essays Literary and Political* (LaSalle, IL: Sherwood Sudgen, 1990).

Bradford, M. E., *Remembering Who We Are: Observations of a Southern Conservative* (Athens, GA: University of Georgia Press, 1985).

Bradford, M. E., "Rhetoric and Respectability," *Modern Age,* Volume 32 (Summer, 1989), pp. 238-243.

Brookhiser, Richard, *The Way of the WASP: How It Made America, and How It Can Save It, So to Speak* (New York: The Free Press, 1991).

Buchanan, Patrick J., *Right From the Beginning* (Boston, MA: Little, Brown, 1988).

Buckley, William F., Jr., ed., *American Conservative Thought in the Twentieth Century* (Indianapolis, IN and New York: Bobbs-Merrill, 1970).

Buckley, William F., Jr., "Agenda for the Nineties," *National Review*, Volume XLII (February 19, 1990), pp. 34-40.

Buckley, William F., Jr., *Execution Eve and Other Contemporary Ballads* (New York: G.P. Putnam's Sons, 1975).

Buckley, William F., Jr., *The Governor Listeth: A Book of Inspired Political Revelations* (New York: G. P. Putnam's Sons, 1970).

Buckley, William F., Jr., *A Hymnal: The Controversial Arts* (New York: G.P. Putnam's Sons, 1978).

Buckley, William F., Jr., and Kesler, Charles R., eds., *Keeping the Tablets: Modern American Conservative Thought* (New York: Perennial Library/Harper and Row, 1988).

Buckley, William F., Jr., *Overdrive: A Personal Documentary* (Boston, MA: Little, Brown, 1984).

Buckley, William F., Jr., *Quotations from Chairman Bill*, Compiled by David Franke. (New Rochelle, NY: Arlington House, 1970).

Buckley, William F., Jr., *Right Reason*, Richard Brookhiser, ed. (Garden City, NY: Doubleday, 1985).

Bunzel, John H., ed., *Political Passages: Journeys of Change Through Two Decades, 1968 - 1988* (New York: Free Press, 1988).

Carey, George W., ed., *Freedom and Virtue: The Conservative/Libertarian Debate* (Lanham, MD: University Press of America, 1984).

Chambers, Whittaker, *Odyssey of a Friend: Letters to William F. Buckley, Jr. 1954 - 1961* (Washington, DC: Regnery Gateway, 1987).

Cranston, Maurice, "American vs. British Conservatism: An Even Match?," *The American Spectator*, Volume 23 (April, 1990), pp. 20-22.

Cranston, Maurice, "Freedom and Nationhood," *National Review*, Volume XLV (January 18, 1993), pp. 44-46, 61.

Crozier, Brian, "Political Thought of James Burnham," *National Review*, Volume XXXV (April 15, 1983), pp. 434-438.

Devine, Donald, "A Free Market in Government," *National Review*, Volume XLI (October 27, 1989), pp. 40-41.

East, John, *The American Conservative Movement: The Philosophical Founders* (Washington, DC: Regnery Gateway, 1986).

Eastland, Terry, "Rush Limbaugh: Talking Back," *The American Spectator*, Volume 25 (September, 1992), pp. 22-27.

Eatwell, Roger and O'Sullivan, Noel, *The Nature of the Right: American and European Politics and Political Thought Since 1789* (Boston, MA: Twayne Publishers, 1991).

Filler, Louis, *Dictionary of American Conservatism* (New York: Philosophical Library, 1987).

Finn, Chester E., Jr., "Giving Shape to Cultural Conservatism," *The American Spectator*, Volume 19 (November, 1986), pp. 14-16.

Fleming, Thomas, "Be Angry at the Sun," *Chronicles*, Volume 14 (May, 1990), pp. 12-15.

Fleming, Thomas, "The Closing of the Conservative Mind," *Chronicles*, Volume 13 (September, 1989), pp. 10-13.

Fleming, Thomas, "The New Fusion," *Chronicles*, Volume 15 (May, 1991), pp. 10-12.

Fleming, Thomas, *The Politics of Human Nature* (New Brunswick, NJ: Transaction Books, 1988).

Francis, Samuel, "Beautiful Losers: The Failure of American Conservatism," *Chronicles*, Volume 15 (May, 1991), pp. 14-17.

Francis, Samuel, "Imperial Conservatives," *National Review*, Volume XLI (August 4, 1989), pp. 37-38.

Francis, Samuel and van den Haag, Ernest, "Paleolithics," *National Review*, Volume XLI (April 7, 1989), pp. 43-46.

Francis, Samuel, *Power and History: The Political Thought of James Burnham* (Lanham, MD: University Press of America, 1984).

Francis, Samuel, "Prophet Sustained: James Burnham and the Managerial Revolution," *Chronicles*, Volume 16 (January, 1992), pp. 14-18.

Frohnen, Bruce, *Virtue and the Promise of Conservatism: The Legacy of Burke and Tocqueville* (Lawrence, KS: University of Kansas Press, 1993).

Fussell, Paul, *Thank God for the Atom Bomb, and Other Essays* (New York: Summit Books, 1988).

Gottfried, Paul and Fleming, Thomas, *The Conservative Movement* (Boston, MA: Twayne Publishers, 1988).

Gottfried, Paul Edward, *The Search for Historical Meaning: Hegel and the Postwar American Right* (DeKalb, IL: Northern Illinois University Press, 1986).

Gray, John, "The Virtues of Toleration," *National Review*, Volume XLIV (October 5, 1992), pp. 28-36.

Himmelfarb, Dan, "Conservative Splits," *Commentary*, Volume 85 (May, 1988), pp. 54-58.

Himmelfarb, Milton, "American Jews: Diehard Conservatives," *Commentary*, Volume 87 (April, 1989), pp. 44-49.

Hoeveler, J. David, Jr., *Watch on the Right: Conservative Intellectuals in the Reagan Era* (Madison, WI: University of Wisconsin Press, 1991).

Hook, Sidney, et al., "James Burnham: 1905 - 1987," *National Review*, Volume XXXIX (September 11, 1987), pp. 31-54.

Hook, Sidney, *Out of Step: An Unquiet Life in the Twentieth Century* (New York: Harper & Row, 1987).

Horowitz, David, "Back to Our Roots," *National Review*, Volume XLIII (May 13, 1991), pp. 42-44.

Jaffa, Harry V., *American Conservatism and the American Founding* (Durham, NC: Carolina Academic Press, 1984).

Johnston, Joseph F., "Conservative Flirtation: Conservative Populism - A Dead End," *National Review*, Volume XXXVI (October 19, 1984), pp. 38-42.

Kersten, Katherine, "What Do Women Want? A Conservative Feminist Manifesto," *Policy Review*, Number 56 (Spring, 1991), pp. 4-15.

Kirk, Russell, *The Conservative Mind: From Burke to Eliot,* 7th ed. (Chicago, IL: Regnery Gateway, 1986).

Kirk, Russell, *Enemies of the Permanent Things: Observations of Abnormality in Literature and Politics* (La Salle, IL: Sherwood Sugden, 1984).

Kirk, Russell, *The Wise Men Know What Wicked Things Are Written on the Sky* (Washington, DC: Regnery Gateway, 1987).

Kramer, Hilton, ed., *The New Criterion Reader: The First Five Years* (New York: Free Press, 1988).

Lasky, Melvin J., *Utopia and Revolution* (Chicago, IL: University of Chicago Press, 1976).

McGurn, William, "Pat Buchanan and the Intellectuals," *National Review*, Volume XLIV (February 17, 1992), pp. 41-43.

Meyer, Frank, *The Conservative Mainstream* (New Rochelle, NY: Arlington House, 1969).

Moritz, Amy, "Family Feud: Is the Conservative Movement Falling Apart?," *Policy Review*, Number 57 (Summer, 1991), pp. 50-54.

Nagle, Robert, *American Conservatism: An Illustrated History* (New York: Philosophical Library, 1989).

Nash, George H., *The Conservative Intellectual Movement in America Since 1945* (New York: Basic Books, 1976).

Nash, George H., "Pilgrims' Progress: America's Tradition of Conservative Reform," *Policy Review*, Number 58 (Fall, 1991), pp. 50-56.

Neusner, Jacob, "Letter From a State of Mind: The Religion of Neoconservatism," *Chronicles*, Volume 12 (June, 1988), pp. 44-45.

Nisbet, Robert, *The Present Age: Progress and Anarchy in Modern America* (New York: Harper & Row, 1988).

Novak, Michael, "Father of Neoconservatives," *National Review*, Volume XLIV (May 11, 1992), pp. 39-42.

Nuechterlein, James, "William F. Buckley, Jr. and American Conservatism," *Commentary*, Volume 85 (June, 1988), pp. 31-41.

Ortega y Gasset, Jose, *The Revolt of the Masses* (New York: W.W. Norton, 1964).

O'Sullivan, John, "Is the Heroic Áge of Conservatism Over?," *National Review*, Volume XLIII (January 28, 1991), pp. 32-37.

Panichas, George, ed., *Modern Age: The First Twenty Five Years: A Selection* (Indianapolis, IN: Liberty Press, 1988).

Podhoretz, Norman, "Buchanan and the Conservative Crackup," *Commentary*, Volume 93 (May, 1992), pp. 30-34.

Podhoretz, Norman, "Enter the Peace Party," *Commentary*, Volume 91 (January, 1991), pp. 17-21.

Regnery, Henry, "Richard Weaver: A Southern Agrarian at the University of Chicago," *Modern Age*, Volume 32 (Spring, 1988), pp. 102-112.

Richardson, Heather S., "The Politics of Virtue: A Strategy for Transforming the Culture," *Policy Review*, Number 58 (Fall, 1991), pp. 18-23.

Rusher, William A., *The Making of the New Majority Party* (Ottawa, IL: Green Hill Publishers, 1975).

Rusher, William A., *The Rise of the Right* (New York: Morrow, 1984).

Ryn, Claes, *Will, Imagination, and Reason* (Washington, DC: Regnery Gateway, 1986).

Scruton, Roger, ed., *Conservative Texts: An Anthology* (New York: St. Martin's, 1990).

Scruton, Roger, *Untimely Tracts* (New York: St. Martin's, 1987).

Sobran, Joseph, "*Pensées*: Notes For the Reactionary of Tomorrow," *National Review*, Volume XXXVII (December 31, 1985), pp. 23-58.

Sowell, Thomas, *Compassion Versus Guilt and Other Essays* (New York: William Morrow, 1987).

Sowell, Thomas, *A Conflict of Visions: Ideological Origins of Political Struggles* (New York: William Morrow, 1987).

Stelzer, Irwin, et al., "The Shape of Things to Come," *National Review*, Volume XLIII (July 8, 1991), pp. 26-30.

Strauss, Leo, *The Rebirth of Classical Political Rationalism: An Introduction to the Thought of Leo Strauss*, Thomas Pangle, ed., (Chicago, IL: University of Chicago Press, 1989).

Sumner, William Graham, *The Conquest of the United States by Spain and Other Essays*, Murray Polnar, ed. (Chicago, IL: Regnery Gateway, 1965).

Sunic, Tomislav, *Against Democracy and Equality: The European New Right* (New York: Peter Lang, 1990).

Tanenhaus, Sam, "What the Anti-Communists Knew," *Commentary*, Volume 90 (July, 1990), pp. 32-36.

Teachout, Terry, ed., *Beyond the Boom: New Voices on American Life, Culture, and Politics* (New York: Poseidon Press, 1990).

Tyrrell, R. Emmett, Jr., *The Conservative Crack-Up* (New York: Simon & Schuster, 1992).

Tyrrell, R. Emmett, Jr., *Orthodoxy: The American Spectator Anniversary Anthology* (New York: Harper and Row, 1987).

van den Haag, Ernest, "The War Between Paleos and Neos," *National Review*, Volume XLI (February 24, 1989), pp. 21-23.

Viguerie, Richard, "Conservative Flirtation: A Populist, and Proud of It," *National Review*, Volume XXXVI (October 19, 1984), pp. 42-44.

Waugh, Auberon, *Brideshead Benighted* (Boston, MA: Little, Brown, 1986).

Weaver, Richard M., *Ideas Have Consequences* (Chicago, IL: University of Chicago Press, 1984).

Will, George F., "Recovering America," *National Review*, Volume XLV (April 12, 1993), pp. 30-33.

Wolfe, Gregory, *Right Minds: A Sourcebook of American Conservative Thought* (Washington, DC: Regnery Gateway, 1987).

Organizations

American Enterprise Institute for Public Policy Research 1150 17th Street, NW, Washington, DC 20036, (202)-862-5800. Publications: *The American Enterprise, Regulation: A Journal on Government and Society.* Provides conservative-leaning studies of matters foreign and domestic to all interested parties.

John M. Ashbrook Center for Public Affairs Ashland University, Ashland, OH 44805, (419)-289-5411. Publications: *The Ashbrook Principle, Res Publica.* Undergraduate program dedicated to study, research and discussion of the principles and practice of American constitutional government and politics. Directed to the scholarly defense of individual liberty, limited constitutional government and civic morality.

Citizens for America 919 Prince Street, Alexandria, VA 22314, (703)-683-6833. Publications: *Call For Action, Conservative Report.* National civic league for those who believe in policies fostering economic growth and a strong national defense.

The Claremont Institute for the Study of Statesmanship and Political Philosophy 250 West 1st Street, #330, Claremont, CA 91711, (909)-621-5831.

Publication: *Principles.* Non-partisan foundation dedicated to recovering America's first principles and the institutions that proceed from them.

Coalitions for America 717 Second Street, NE, Washington, DC 20002, (202)-546-3003. Seeks to develop a common conservative strategy on political, regulatory, and legislative issues; tries to coordinate conservative business and single-issue groups to counter liberal initiatives at all levels of government.

Concerned Women for America 370 L'Enfant Promenade, SW, Suite 800, Washington, DC 20024, (202)-488-7000. Publication: *The Family Voice.* Seeks to preserve traditional family values and protect the rights of the family.

The Conservative Caucus 450 Maple Avenue, East, Suite 309, Vienna, VA 22180 (703)-938-9626. Publication: *Members Report.* Seeks to build a grassroots lobbying coalition in every congressional district; wants conservatives to be able to set the public agenda and determine the limits to the public policy debate.

Conservative Victory Committee 113 South West.Street, 2nd Floor, Alexandria, VA, 22314, (703)-684-6603. Publications: *Annual Report, Newsletter.* Individuals promoting a strong American conservative political movement; supports strong defense and an anti-communist foreign policy; aids conservative congressional candidates; calls for deployment of SDI.

Eagle Forum Box 618, Alton, IL 62002, (618)-462-5415. Publication: *The Phyllis Schlafly Report.* Lobbies in support of a variety of conservative legislative initiatives, with emphasis on morality, the family, and education; strongly pro-defense; opposes the Equal Rights Amendment.

Education and Research Institute 800 Maryland Avenue, NE, Washington, DC 20002, (202)-546-1710. Publication: *Newsletter.* Promotes awareness of America's traditional values and the free enterprise system; publishes studies on public policy issues; trains young conservative journalists for employment in the field; maintains job bank.

Ethics and Public Policy Center 1015 15th Street, NW, #900, Washington, DC 20005, (202)-682-1200. Publication: *Ethics and Public Policy - Newsletter.* Attempts to clarify the relationship "between the specific and the general, and between political necessity and moral principle; focuses on the role of organized religion in the public policy arena.

Empower America 1776 Eye Street, NW, Suite 890, Washington, DC 20006, (202)-452-8200. Conservative advocacy group aimed at developing individual "empowerment" policies as solutions to various problems afflicting America.

Family Research Council 700 13th Street, NW, Suite 500, Washington, DC 20005, (202)-393-2100. Publications: *Family Policy, Washington Watch.* Provides expertise and information to government agencies, members of Congress, policymakers, the media, and the public.

Free the Eagle 666 Pennsylvania Avenue, SE, Suite 300, Washington, DC 20003, (202)-543-6090. Publications: *International Economic Report, State of the Nation.* Citizens' lobbying group which supports legislation in Congress reducing government waste; supports democratic resistance movements in totalitarian countries; conducts legislative research and classes on lobbying techniques.

The Heritage Foundation 214 Massachusetts Avenue, NE, Washington, DC 20002, (202)-546-4400. Publications: *Backgrounder/Issue Bulletin, Educational Update, Heritage Members' News, Heritage Today, National Security Record, Policy Review, Publications Catalog.* Public policy research institute dedicated to the principles of free competitive enterprise, limited government, individual liberty, and a strong national defense.

The Hoover Institution Stanford University, Stanford, CA 94305-6010, (415)-723-1687. A public policy research center devoted to advanced study on domestic public policy and international affairs. Has one of the world's largest archives and most complete libraries devoted to the economic, social and political changes of the twentieth century.

The Hudson Institute Herman Kahn Center, P.O. Box 26-919, Indianapolis, IN 46226, (317)-545-1000. Publications: *Hudson Institute Briefing, Hudson Institute Opinion, Hudson Institute Report.* Studies public policy issues in areas of national security, international and domestic economics, employment and education, energy and technology, and future studies. Conducts briefings; maintains library.

Institute for Contemporary Studies 243 Kearny Street, San Francisco, CA 94108, (415)-981-5353. Publication: *The Letter.* Public policy think tank; studies issues that meet the following criteria: have an effect on the free market system, are of topical concern, and appear likely to have a long-term influence.

Institute on Religion and Democracy 1331 H Street, NW, Suite 900, Washington, DC 20005, (202)-393-3200. Publications: *Briefing Paper, Religion and Democracy, The Religion and Economics Report.* Churches, ministers, and laity concerned about the increasing leftward tilt of various denominations; critical of religious support for Marxist-Leninist insurgencies; maintains information service.

Intercollegiate Studies Institute 14 South Bryn Mawr Avenue, Bryn Mawr, PA 19010, (215)-525-7501. Publications: *Modern Age, The Intercollegiate Review: A*

Journal of Scholarship and Opinion, Continuity: A Journal of History, The Political Science Reviewer. Seeks to develop "the conservative philosophy of individual liberty, limited government, free-market economics, the right of private property, and the spiritual and moral underpinnings of this philosophy."

Leadership Institute 8001 Braddock Road, Suite 502, Springfield, VA 22151, (703)-321-8580. Publications: *Building Leadership, Leadership Training Service Directory.* Seeks to prepare conservatives for employment in Congress and other public policy organizations.

National Center for Policy Analysis First Interstate Plaza, 12655 North Central Expressway, #720, Dallas, TX 75243, (214)-386-6272. Non-profit, non-partisan public policy research institute established to uncover and promote private sector alternatives to government regulation and control, solving problems by relying on the strengths of innovative individuals and on the competitive, entrepreneurial private sector.

National Center for Public Policy Research 1776 K Street, NW, Washington, DC 20006, (202)-429-7360. Publications: *A Letter from Central America, Catholic Study Council - Bulletin.* Educates the public about public policy issues by distributing brochures, article reprints and other materials; maintains library.

National Conservative Foundation 618 South Alfred Street, Alexandria, VA 22314, (703)-548-0900. Publication: *Newswatch.* Conservative education and research organization; promotes media fairness; provides voters with information on issues; operates school for political managers on how to run an effective campaign.

National Forum Foundation 511 C Street, NE, Washington, DC 20002, (202)-543-3515. Publications: *Forum News, Policy Forum.* Legislative and executive branch personnel, business and religious leaders who are dedicated to a strong defense, welfare reform, and preservation of the family; maintains library; conducts research.

National Institute for Public Policy 3031 Javier Road, Suite 300, Fairfax, VA 22031, (703)-698-0563. Examines public policy and its relation to international and security issues with an emphasis on military affairs; analyzes the domestic economy and provides accurate trend projections.

Pacific Research Institute for Public Policy 177 Post Street, Suite 500, San Francisco, CA 94108, (415)-989-0833. Informs the public about issues that affect the free enterprise system and the rights of individuals. Areas of special interest include education, school choice, health care, and moral philosophy.

Rockford Institute Center on Religion and Society 934 North Main, Rockford, IL 61103, (815)-964-5811. Publications: *Religion and Society Report, Encounter Series.* Interreligious research center; aims to examine in a scholarly manner the relation of religion, culture, and societal change.

CONSPIRACY THEORIES

Books and Articles

Brock, David, "Christic Mystics and Their Drug-Running Theories," *The American Spectator*, Volume 21 (May, 1988), pp. 22-26.

Cohen, Jacob, "Yes, Oswald Alone Killed Kennedy," *Commentary*, Volume 93 (June, 1992), pp. 32-40.

Collier, Peter, "Ollie über Alles," *The American Spectator*, Volume 25 (April, 1992), pp. 28-31.

CONSTITUTION

Books and Articles

Arkes, Hadley, *Beyond the Constitution* (Princeton, NJ: Princeton University Press, 1990).

Arkes, Hadley, "Who's the Laissez-Fairest of Them All? The Tradition of Natural Rights in American Law," *Policy Review*, Number 60 (Spring, 1992), pp. 78-85.

Ball, William Bentley, "The Tempting of Robert Bork: What's a Constitution Without Natural Law?," *Crisis*, Volume 8 (June, 1990), pp. 28-32.

Bloom, Allan, ed., *Confronting the Constitution* (Washington, DC: American Enterprise Institute for Public Policy Research, 1990).

Carey, George W., *The Federalist: Design for a Constitutional Republic* (Champaign, IL: University of Illinois Press, 1989).

Epstein, David F., *The Political Theory of "The Federalist"* (Chicago, IL: University of Chicago Press, 1984).

Francis, Samuel, "Who's In Charge Here: If Presidents Have a Free Hand in Foreign Policy, Who Needs a Constitution?," *Chronicles*, Volume 12 (March, 1988), pp. 12-15.

Goldwin, Robert and Schambra, William, ed., *How Capitalistic Is the Constitution?* (Washington, DC: American Enterprise Institute for Public Policy Research, 1982).

Graglia, Lino, "Of Rights and Choices," *National Review*, Volume XLIV (February 17, 1992), pp. 39-41.

Graglia, Lino, "Saving the Constitution: A Theory of Power," *National Review*, Volume XXXIX (July 17, 1987), pp. 33-36.

Jaffa, Harry V., "The Closing of the Conservative Mind," *National Review*, Volume XLII (July 9, 1990), pp. 40-43.

Kesler, Charles, *Saving the Revolution: The Federalist Papers and the American Founding* (New York: The Free Press, 1987).

Kirk, Russell, *The Conservative Constitution* (Washington, DC: Regnery Gateway, 1990).

Lerner, Ralph, "Believers and the Founders' Constitution," *This World*, Number 26 (Summer, 1989), pp. 80-91.

McDonald, Forrest, *Novus Ordo Seclorum: The Intellectual Origins of the Constitution* (Lawrence, KS: University Press of Kansas, 1985).

Noonan, John T., Jr., "Calling for a Constitutional Convention," *National Review*, Volume XXXVII (July 26, 1985), pp. 25-28.

Ryn, Claes G., "Political Philosophy and the Unwritten Constitution," *Modern Age*, Volume 34 (Summer, 1992), pp. 303-309.

Siegan, Bernard H., *Economic Liberties and the Constitution* (Chicago, IL: University of Chicago Press, 1981).

Storing, Herbert and Day, Murray S., eds., *The Complete Anti-Federalist* (Chicago, IL: University of Chicago Press, 1981).

van den Haag, Ernest, "Not Above the Law," *National Review*, Volume XLIII (October 7, 1991), pp. 35-36.

Walker, Graham, *Moral Foundations of Constitutional Thought: Current Problems, Augustinian Prospects* (Princeton, NJ: Princeton University Press, 1990).

Organizations

Center for Individual Rights 1300 19th Street, NW, Suite 260, Washington, DC 20036, (202)-833-8400. Public interest law firm which litigates academic freedom and constitutional and regulatory issues. Seeks to limit the growth and size of government.

Center for Judicial Studies Box 113, Hampden-Sydney College, Hampden, VA 23943, (804)-223-2207. Publications: *Benchmark, Constitutional Commentaries*. Seeks to reform the U.S. constitutional and judicial systems.

Committee to Restore the Constitution P.O. Box 986, Fort Collins, CO 80522 (303)-484-2575. Publication: *CRC Bulletin*. Seeks to educate the public about the nature of America's constitutional crisis; calls for the abolition of the Federal Reserve; opposes federal encroachment at the expense of property owners; trains local leaders and maintains information service.

The Federalist Society for Law & Public Policy Studies 1700 K Street, NW,

#901, Washington, DC 20006, (202)-822-8138. Publications: *The Federalist Paper, Harvard Journal of Law and Public Policy*. Seeks to bring about a reordering of priorities within the U.S. legal system that will emphasize individual liberty, traditional values, and the rule of law; considers the interpretation of the constitution to be the province of the judiciary, not the legislatures.

National Center for Constitutional Studies P.O. Box 841, West Jordan, UT 84084, (800)-565-1787. Publications: *Behind the Scenes in Washington, The Constitution: Special Reports*. Researches, develops, and produces programs which stress the benefits of a strict constructionalist approach to the Constitution; strongly in favor of states' rights; maintains research files, biographical archives, and a library.

Pacific Legal Foundation 2700 Gateway Oaks Drive, #200, Sacramento, CA 95833, (916)-641-8888. Publications: *At Issue, In Perspective, Achieving a Balanced Environmental Policy*. Litigates nationally on behalf of personal freedoms, free enterprise, private property rights, and a balanced approach to environmental consideration; encourages limits on governmental power.

CONSUMER ISSUES

Books and Articles

Clarke, Betsy, "The War Toys Meltdown," *Chronicles*, Volume 12 (July, 1988), pp. 45-47.
Curtin, Richard T., "The Index of Consumer Sentiment at Forty," *The American Enterprise*, Volume 3 (May/June, 1992), pp. 18-24.
England, Robert Stowe, "Congress, Nader, and the Ambulance Chasers," *The American Spectator*, Volume 23 (September, 1990), pp. 18-23.
Rubin, Paul H., "The Economics of Regulating Deception," *The Cato Journal*, Volume 10 (Winter, 1991), pp. 667-690.
Sapolsky, Harvey M., et al., *Consuming Fears: The Politics of Product Risks* (New York: Basic Books, 1986).
Viscusi, W. Kip., *Reforming Products Liability* (Cambridge, MA: Harvard University Press, 1991).

Organizations

Consumer Alert 1555 Wilson Boulevard, Suite 300, Arlington, VA 22209, (703)-875-8644. Publications: *Comments, Testimony*. Opposes excessive regulation, supports free enterprise; seeks to prevent public interest groups from using student fees to further their own agendas; conducts lectures; maintains library.

CONTRACEPTION

Books and Articles

Bethell, Tom, "Imperialism and the Pill," *National Review*, Volume XXXVIII (March 14, 1986), pp. 38-40.
Neuhaus, Richard John, "The Wrong Way to Go," *National Review*, Volume XLV (February 1, 1993), p. 53.

Organizations

International Federation for Family Life Promotion 2009 North 14th Street, Arlington, VA 22201, (703)-516-0388. Publication: *IFFLP Bulletin*. Supports natural family planning; offers educational programs; maintains library.

Couple to Couple League P.O. Box 111184, Cincinnati, OH 45211, (513)-661-7612. Publication: *CCL Family Foundations*. Supports natural birth control; promotes premarital chastity through speakers and literature.

COPYRIGHTS

Organizations

American Intellectual Property Law Association 2001 Jefferson Davis Highway, Suite 203, Arlington, VA 22202, (703)-415-0780. Publications: *AIPLA Bulletin, AIPLA Quarterly*. Aids in the operation and improvement of U.S. patent, trademark, and copyright systems, including the laws by which they are governed and rules and regulations under which federal agencies administer those laws.

Patent and Trademark Service 2001 Jefferson Davis Highway, Suite 1209, Arlington, VA 22205, (800)-336-7575. Provides aid and information with regard to all facets of obtaining a patent or trademark.

CORPORATIONS

Books and Articles

Bhide, Amar, "In Praise of Corporate Raiders: Junking Three Fallacies About Hostile Takeovers," *Policy Review*, Number 47 (Winter, 1989), pp. 21-23.
Blasi, Joseph, *Employee Ownership: Revolution or Ripoff?* (Cambridge, MA: Ballinger, 1988).

Easterbrook, Frank H., *The Economic Structure of Corporate Law* (Cambridge, MA: Harvard University Press, 1991).

Giuffra, Robert J., "Sentencing Corporations," *The American Enterprise,* Volume 1 (May/June 1990), pp. 85-87.

Gray, Arthur, Jr. and Laffer, Arthur B., "Debt and Taxes," *National Review,* Volume XLI (September 1, 1989), pp. 38-39.

Horowitz, Irving Louis and Curtis, Mary E., "The 'Bottom Line' as American Myth and Metaphor," *Chronicles,* Volume 15 (April, 1991), pp. 26-30.

Jacobs, Michael T., *Short-Term America* (Cambridge, MA: Harvard Business School Press, 1991).

Kapstein, Ethan B., "We Are Us: The Myth of the Multinational," *The National Interest,* Number 26 (Winter, 1991/92), pp. 55-62.

Lipset, Seymour Martin and Schneider, William, *The Confidence Gap: Business, Labor, and Government in the Public Mind* (New York: The Free Press, 1983).

Mackay, Robert J., and Mix, Phoebe A., "Uncertain Future: The Tax Treatment of Hedging," *The American Enterprise,* Volume 3 (May/June, 1992), pp. 67-71.

Makin, John H., "The New Superpowers," *The American Enterprise,* Volume 1 (September/October, 1990), pp. 17-18.

Poole, William T., "How Big Business Bankrolls the Left," *National Review,* Volume XLI (March 10, 1989), pp. 34-37.

Stein, Benjamin J., "Takeovers and Acquistions: Who's Responsible?," *The American Spectator,* Volume 21 (September, 1988), pp. 16-19.

Stelzer, Irwin M., "The Truth About Takeovers," *The American Spectator,* Volume 20 (June, 1987), pp. 14-15.

Vogel, David, *Fluctuating Fortunes: The Political Power of Business in America* (New York: Basic Books, 1989).

Weaver, Paul H., *The Suicidal Corporation: How Big Business Fails America* (New York: Simon & Schuster, 1988).

Weidenbaum, Murray L. and Chilton, Kenneth, eds., *Public Policy Toward Corporate Takeovers* (New Brunswick, NJ: Transaction Books, 1988).

COURTS

Books and Articles

Bork, Robert H., "The Full Court Press: The Drive for Control of the Courts," *The American Enterprise,* Volume 1 (January/February, 1990), pp. 58-61.

Caplan, Gerald, "Battered Wives, Battered Justice," *National Review,* Volume XLIII (February 25, 1991), pp. 39-43.

Christainsen, Gregory B., "Law as a Discovery Procedure," *The Cato Journal,* Volume 9 (Winter, 1990), pp. 497-530.

England, Robert Stowe, "Congress, Nader, and the Ambulance Chasers," *The American Spectator*, Volume 23 (September, 1990), pp. 18-23.

Huber, Peter W., *Galileo's Revenge: Junk Science in the Courtroom* (New York: Basic Books, 1991).

Huber, Peter W., *Liability: The Legal Revolution and Its Consequences* (New York: Basic Books, 1988).

Methvin, Eugene H., "Texas on Trial," *National Review*, Volume XLII (December 31, 1990), pp. 32-35.

Olson, Walter K., *The Litigation Explosion: What Happened When America Unleashed the Lawsuit* (New York: E.P. Dutton, 1991).

Posner, Richard A., *The Federal Courts: Crisis and Reform* (Cambridge, MA: Harvard University Press, 1985).

Schuck, Peter H., "The New Ideology of Tort Law," *The Public Interest*, Number 92 (Summer, 1988), pp. 93-109.

Szasz, Thomas, "Whose Competence?," *National Review*, Volume XLI (September 15, 1989), pp. 38, 60.

Tucker, William, "Private Prosecutions," *The American Spectator*, Volume 19 (May, 1986), pp. 16-18.

Viscusi, W. Kip., *Reforming Products Liability* (Cambridge, MA: Harvard University Press, 1991).

Organizations

American Arbitration Association 140 W. 51st Street, New York, NY 10020, (212)-484-4000. Publications: *Arbitration Journal, Arbitration and the Law, Arbitration in the Schools.* Dedicated to the resolution of disputes of all kinds through the use of arbitration, mediation, democratic elections, and other voluntary methods.

American Tort Reform 1212 New York Avenue, NW, Suite 515, Washington, DC 20005, (202)-682-1163. Publications: *Leaders' Update, Legislative Watch, The Reformer, Tort Reform Report.* Seeks to remedy the current liability insurance "crisis" by developing, promoting, and coordinating the U.S. tort law system.

CRIME
(see also **Organized Crime**)

Books and Articles

Anderson, Lorrin, "Crime, Race, and the Fourth Estate," *National Review*, Volume XLII (October 15, 1990), pp. 52-56.

DiIulio, John J., Jr., "The Underclass: The Impact of Inner-City Crime," *The Public Interest*, Number 96 (Summer,1989), pp. 28-46.

Gilbert, Neil, "The Phantom Epidemic of Sexual Assault," *The Public Interest*, Number 103 (Spring, 1991), pp. 54-65.

Katz, Jack, *Seductions of Crime: Moral and Sensual Attractions in Doing Evil* (New York: Basic Books, 1988).

Novak, Michael, "Crime and Character," *This World*, Number 14 (Spring/Summer, 1986), pp. 26-54.

Reiss, Albert, Jr. and Tonry, Michael, eds., *Communities and Crime* (Chicago, IL: University of Chicago Press, 1987).

Samenow, Stanton E., *Inside the Criminal Mind* (New York: Times Books, 1984).

Shackley, Theodore G.,et al., *You're the Target: Coping With Terror and Crime* (Fairhaven, NJ: New World Publishing, 1989).

Skogan, Wesley, *Disorder and Decline: Crime and the Spiral of Decay in American Neighborhoods* (New York: The Free Press, 1990).

Wilson, Colin, *The Mammoth Book of True Crime 1* (New York: Carroll and Graf, 1988).

Wilson, Colin, *The Mammoth Book of True Crime 2* (New York: Carroll and Graf, 1990).

Wilson, James Q., ed., *Crime and Public Policy* (San Francisco, CA: Institute for Contemporary Studies Press, 1983).

The World's Most Infamous Crimes and Criminals (New York: Gallery Books, 1987).

Organizations

Americans for Effective Law Enforcement 5519 North Cumberland Avenue, #1008, Chicago, IL 60656, (312)-763-2800. Publications: *Jail and Prison Law Bulletin, Law Enforcement Legal Liability Reporter, Security Legal Update*. Seeks to promote more effective administration of criminal law by aiding the courts, police, and prosecutors; assists police agencies accused of misconduct; compiles statistics and maintains a library.

CRIME/PUNISHMENT
(see also **Capital Punishment**)

Books and Articles

Brubaker, Stanley C., "In Praise of Punishment," *The Public Interest*, Number 97 (Fall 1989), pp. 44-55.

Calabresi, Steven G., "Designer Sentences and the Criminal Justice System," *The American Enterprise*, Volume 1 (January/February, 1990), pp. 18-21.

Colson, Charles, "Crime and Restitution: The Alternative to Lock-Them-Up Liberalism," *Policy Review*, Number 43 (Winter, 1988), pp. 14-18.

Giuffra, Robert J., "Sentencing Corporations," *The American Enterprise,*
    Volume 1 (May/June, 1990), pp. 85-87.
van den Haag, Ernest, "Worse Than a Crime," *National Review*, Volume XLIV
    (January 20, 1992), pp. 48-51.

CRIMINAL LAW

Books and Articles

Crovitz, L. Gordon, "How Law Destroys Order," *National Review*, Volume
    XLIII (February 11, 1991), pp. 28-33.
Crovitz, L. Gordon, "R.I.C.O. and the Man: When an Ambitious Prosecutor
    Meets a Bad Law, No One Is Safe," *Reason*, Volume 21 (March, 1990), pp.
    26-30.
Maeder, Thomas, *Crime and Madness: The Origins and the Evolution of the
    Insanity Defense* (New York: Harper & Row, 1985).
Morris, Norval, *Madness and the Criminal Law* (Chicago, IL: University of
    Chicago Press, 1984).
Nagel, Robert F., "The Myth of the General Right to Bail," *The Public Interest*,
    Number 98 (Winter, 1990), pp. 84-97.
Nelson, Caleb, "The Paradox of the Exclusionary Rule," *The Public Interest*,
    Number 96 (Summer, 1989), pp. 117-130.
Scully, Leon, "Civil Wrongs," *National Review*, Volume XLIV (May 25, 1992),
    pp. 22-28.
Szasz, Thomas, "Whose Competence?," *National Review*, Volume XLI
    (September 15, 1989), pp. 38, 60.
Tucker, William, "Private Prosecutions," *The American Spectator*, Volume 19
    (May, 1986), pp. 16-18.
Winslade, William S. and Ross, Judith Wilson, *The Insanity Plea* (New York:
    Scribner's, 1983).

Organizations

American Prosecutors Research Institute 1033 N. Fairfax Street, Suite 200,
Alexandria, VA 22314, (703)-549-4253. Publications: *Mainline, Prosecutor's
Perspective.* Acts as clearinghouse, providing information and referrals to
members and interested individuals in regard to all areas of criminal justice.

National Association of Crime Victim Compensation Boards P.O. Box 16003,
Alexandria, VA 22302, (703)-370-2996. Publication: *Newsletter.* Seeks to
formulate crime victim compensation programs; encourages legislation at all levels
of government regarding such programs.

CUBA

Books and Articles

Arostegui, Martin, "Castro's Scapegoat," *National Review*, Volume XLIV (December 28, 1992), pp. 33-35.

Carbonell, Nestor, *And the Russians Stayed: The Soviet-ization of Cuba* (New York: William Morrow, 1989).

Cruz, Arturo J., Jr., "Anatomy of an Execution," *Commentary*, Volume 88 (November, 1989), pp. 54-56.

Falcoff, Mark, "Castro Bombs in Madrid," *National Review*, Volume XLIV (October 5, 1992), pp. 49-52.

Falcoff, Mark, "The Last Communist," *Commentary*, Volume 91 (June, 1991), pp. 27-33.

Falcoff, Mark, "Why Latins Still Love Fidel," *The American Enterprise*, Volume 1 (November/December, 1990), pp. 42-49.

Geyer, Georgie Anne, *Guerrilla Prince: The Untold Story of Fidel Castro* (Boston, MA: Little, Brown, 1991).

Grenier, Richard, "The Albania of the Caribbean," *National Review*, Volume XLI (May 5, 1989), pp. 41-43.

Horowitz, Irving, ed., *Cuban Communism* (New Brunswick, NJ: Transaction Publishers, 1991).

Kerrigan, Anthony, "Literacy, Yes, Books, No: A Personal Report From Cuba," *This World*, Number 26 (Summer, 1989), pp. 125-131.

Llovio-Menendez, Jose Louis, *Insider: My Hidden Life as a Revolutionary in Cuba* (New York: Bantam, 1988).

Montaner, Carlos Alberto, *Cuba, Castro, and the Caribbean: The Cuban Revolution and the Crisis in Western Conscience* (New Brunswick, NJ: Transaction Books, 1985).

Ratliff, William, et al., *The Selling of Fidel Castro: The Media and the Cuban Revolution* (New Brunswick, NJ: Transaction Books, 1987).

Rojas Bruce, Matias, "Cuba's Open Boats," *The American Spectator*, Volume 24 (September, 1991), pp. 12-13.

Symmes, Patrick, "Fidel's World," *The American Spectator*, Volume 25 (July, 1992), pp. 18-23.

Valladares, Armando, *Against All Hope: The Prison Memoirs of Armando Valladares* (New York: Knopf, 1986).

Organizations

Cuban American Foundation 7300 Northwest 35th Terrace, Miami, FL 33122, (305)-477-1202. Publication: *Cuban Monitor*. Lobbies for freedom and democracy in Cuba; offers educational and research programs.

Cuban American National Foundation 1000 Thomas Jefferson Street, Suite 507, Washington, DC 20007, (202)-265-2822. Publication: *The Issue Is Cuba.* Gathers and disseminates information on Cuba and its exiles; conducts research and maintains library.

CULTS

Books and Articles

Barker, Eileen, *The Making of a Moonie: Choice or Brainwashing?* (Cambridge, MA: Basil Blackwell, 1984).
Evanier, David, "A Jonestown Reader," *National Review*, Volume XXXIV (April 16, 1982), pp. 428-436.

Organizations

Cult Awareness Network 2421 West Pratt Boulevard, Suite 1173, Chicago, IL 60645, (312)-267-7777. Publication: *Cult Awareness Network - News.* Offers information and counseling on destructive cults; opposes underhanded recruiting methods; functions as national referral network for parents and offers support groups for former cult members; compiles statistics and maintains library.

Spiritual Counterfeits Project P.O. Box 4308, Berkeley, CA 94704, (510)-540-0300. Publications: *Journal, Newsletter.* Exposes cults as they emerge; critiques cults from a Christian perspective; offers referral service and maintains library.

DAY CARE
(see also **Children**, **Family**)

Books and Articles

Christensen, Bryce J., *Day Care: Child Psychology and Adult Economics* (Rockford, IL: The Rockford Institute, 1989).
Gallagher, Maggie, "Do Congressmen Have Mothers?," *National Review*, Volume XLI (October 27, 1989), pp. 38-39, 59.
Gilder, George, "An Open Letter to Orrin Hatch," *National Review*, Volume XL (May 13, 1988), pp. 32-34.
Gill, Richard T., "Day Care or Parental Care," *The Public Interest*, Number 105 (Fall, 1991), pp. 3-16.
Gress-Wright, Jessica, "ABC and Me," *Commentary*, Volume 89 (January, 1990), pp. 29-35.

Gress-Wright, Jessica, "Liberals, Conservatives, and the Family," *Commentary*, Volume 3 (April, 1992), pp. 43-46.

Haskins, Ron and Brown, Hank, "The Day Care Reform Juggernaut," *National Review*, Volume XLI (March 10, 1989), pp. 40-41.

Marshner, Connaught, "Socialized Motherhood: As Easy as ABC," *National Review*, Volume XL (May 13, 1988), pp. 28-31.

Zinsmeister, Karl, "Brave New World: How Day Care Harms Children," *Policy Review*, Number 44 (Spring, 1988), pp. 40-48.

DEATH

Books and Articles

Aries, Phillipe, *The Hour of Our Death* (New York: Oxford University Press, 1991).

Sullum, Jacob, "Cold Comfort: Cryonicists Seek Better Living Through Liquid Nitrogen," *Reason*, 22 (April, 1991), pp. 22-29.

DEATH PENALTY
(see **Capital Punishment**)

DEFICIT
(see **Federal Budget**)

DEMOCRACY
(see also **Federalism**)

Books and Articles

Abrams, Elliott, "Can Democracy Drive Foreign Policy?," *National Review*, Volume XLIV (May 11, 1992), pp. 25-28.

Bryan, Frank, "Going It Alone: The Case for Vermont's Secession," *Chronicles*, Volume 15 (April, 1991), pp. 45-48.

Bryan, Frank and McClaughry, John, *The Vermont Papers: Recreating Democracy on a Human Scale* (Post Mills, VT: Chelsea Green Publishing, 1989).

Fleming, Thomas, "Freedom of Opinion and Democracy," *Chronicles*, Volume 12 (June, 1988), pp. 8-10.

Fleming, Thomas, "Peace on Earth Among Men of Good Will," *Chronicles*, Volume 14 (February, 1990), pp. 12-14.

Gordon, David, "Democracy and the Missing Argument," *This World*, Number 27 (Winter, 1992), pp. 8-13.

Kagan, Donald, *Pericles of Athens and the Birth of Democracy* (New York: The Free Press, 1990).

Kauffman, Bill, "The Last Jeffersonian," *Chronicles*, Volume 14 (December, 1990), pp. 46-47.

Kirkwood, R. Cort, "Missionaries for Democracy," *Chronicles*, Volume 14 (March, 1990), pp. 22-25.

Kuehnelt-Leddihn, Erik von, "Utopias and Ideologies," *Chronicles*, Volume 12 (December, 1988), pp. 21-23.

Murray, Charles, "Thomas Jefferson Goes East," *National Review*, Volume XLIV (March 30, 1992), pp. 21-29.

Ornstein, Norman and Coursen, Kimberly, "As the World Turns Democratic, Federalism Finds Favor," *The American Enterprise*, Volume 3 (January/February, 1992), pp. 20-24.

Pangle, Thomas L., *The Enobling of Democracy: The Challenge of the Post Modern Age* (Baltimore, MD: Johns Hopkins University Press, 1992).

Revel, Jean-Francois, *How Democracies Perish* (New York: Doubleday, 1983).

Ryn, Claes, "The Democracy Boosters," *National Review*, Volume XLI (March 24, 1989), pp. 30-32, 52.

Ryn, Claes G., *The New Jacobinism: Can Democracy Survive?* (Washington, DC: National Humanities Institute, 1991).

Sunic, Tomislav, "A Global Village or the Rights of the Peoples?," *Chronicles*, Volume 15 (January, 1991), pp. 22-24.

Usher, Dan, *The Economic Prerequisite to Democracy* (New York: Columbia University Press, 1981).

Wilson, Clyde, "The Future of American Nationalism," *Chronicles*, Volume 14 (November, 1990), pp. 16-21.

DEMOCRATIC PARTY

Books and Articles

Brown, Peter, *Minority Party: Why the Democrats Face Defeat in 1992 and Beyond* (Washington, DC: Regnery Gateway, 1991).

Mead, Lawrence M., "The Democrats' Dilemma," *Commentary*, Volume 93 (January, 1992), pp. 43-47.

Novak, Michael, "The Long-Time Democrat Blues," *National Review*, Volume XLIV (July 20, 1992), pp. 24-27.

Rothenberg, Stuart, "The No Growth Party?," *The American Enterprise*, Volume 2 (November/December, 1991), pp. 16-21.

Stelzer, Irwin M., "Bad Advice for the Democrats," *Commentary*, Volume 92 (July, 1991), pp. 19-23.

Organizations

Conservative Democratic Forum 1211 Longworth House Office Building, Washington, DC 20515, (202)-225-6605. Caucus of Conservative Democrats in the U.S. House of Reprsentatives.

Democratic Leadership Council 316 Pennsylvania Avenue, SE, Suite 500, Washington, DC 20003, (202)-546-0007. Publication: *The New Democrat.* Coalition of moderate Democratic politicians and policymakers trying to bring the party back towards the political center. Has regional chapters.

DESEGREGATION

Books and Articles

Anderson, Lorrin, "The Siege of Yonkers," *National Review*, Volume XLIII (May 13, 1991), pp. 28-33.
Crovitz, L. Gordon, "Judge, Jury, and Executioner," *National Review*, Volume XL (October 14, 1988), pp. 30-33.
Erler, Edward J., *"Brown v. Board of Education* at 30," *National Review*, Volume XXXVI (September 7, 1984), pp. 26-31, 53.
Walters, Raymond, *The Burden of* Brown: *Thirty Years of School Desegregation* (Knoxville, TN: University of Tennessee Press, 1984).

DÉTENTE
(see **Cold War**, **U.S. Foreign Policy**)

DISABLED

Books and Articles

Rockwell, Llewellyn H., Jr., "Wheelchairs at Third Base," *National Review*, Volume XLV (June 7, 1993), pp. 47-50.
Weaver, Carolyn L., "The ADA: Another Mandated Benefits Program," *The American Enterprise*, Volume 1 (May/June, 1990), pp. 81-84.
Weaver, Carolyn L., "Reassessing Federal Disability Insurance," *The Public Interest*, Number 106 (Winter, 1992), pp. 108-121.

DISARMAMENT
(see **Arms Control**)

DISEASE
(see **Medicine**)

DISTRICT ATTORNEYS

Organizations

National District Attorneys Association 1033 N. Fairfax Street, Suite 200, Alexandria, VA 22314, (703)-549-9222. Publications: *Case Commentaries and Briefs, Directory of Prosecuting Attorneys, NDAA Bulletin, The Prosecutor.* Seeks to serve prosecuting attorneys and to improve and facilitate the administration of justice in the U.S.

DIVORCE
(see also **Family**)

Books and Articles

Neely, Richard, *The Divorce Decision: The Legal and Human Consequences of Ending a Marriage* (New York: McGraw-Hill, 1984).
Phillips, Roderick, *Putting Asunder: A History of Divorce in Western Society* (New York: Cambridge University Press, 1988).
Smith, Janet E., "The Health of Nations: What America Can Learn from Other Countries About Abortion and Divorce," *Crisis*, Volume 8 (April, 1990), pp. 20-24.

DOCTORS

Books and Articles

Brodsky, Archie, "Home Delivery: Midwifery Works. So Should Midwives," *Reason*, Volume 23 (March, 1992), pp. 28-34.

DOMESTIC VIOLENCE
(see **Children**, **Family**, **Homosexuals**, **Women**)

DRAMA
(see **Authors**, **Literature**, **Theater**)

DRUGS
(see **Pharmaceuticals**)

EASTERN EUROPE

Books and Articles

Applebaum, Anne, "Who Owns Central Europe?," *The American Spectator*,
Volume 24 (February, 1991), pp. 14-16.

Aslund, Anders, "Four Key Reforms: The Eastern European Experiment,
Phase II," *The American Enterprise*, Volume 2 (July/August, 1991), pp. 49-
55.

Bauer, Peter, "Western Subsidies and Eastern Reform," *The Cato Journal*,
Volume 11 (Winter, 1992), pp. 343-353.

Brozyna, Piotr and Lilla, Mark, "Dismantling Socialism in One Country," *The
American Spectator*, Volume 23 (February, 1990), pp. 28-30.

Brozyna, Piotr and Lilla, Mark, "Dismantling Socialism in One Country (II),"
The American Spectator, Volume 23 (April, 1990), pp. 23-25.

Codevilla, Angelo, "Is Olof Palme the Wave of the Future?," *Commentary*,
Volume 89 (March, 1990), pp. 26-32.

d'Encausee, Helene Carrere, *Big Brother: The Soviet Union and Soviet Europe*
(New York: Holmes and Meier, 1987).

Eberstadt, Nicholas, "How Not to Aid Eastern Europe," *Commentary*, Volume
92 (November, 1991), pp. 24-30.

Friedman, Milton, "Four Steps to Freedom," *National Review*, Volume XLII
(May 14, 1990), pp. 33-36.

Michnik, Adam, *Letters From Prison and Other Essays* (Berkeley, CA:
University of California Press, 1985).

Molnar, Thomas, "Don't Go West Young Man: A Report From the Hungarian
Front," *Crisis*, Volume 10 (June, 1992), pp. 39-42.

Molnar, Thomas, "Letter From Eastern Europe: A Difficult Road," *Chronicles*,
Volume 15 (January, 1991), pp. 43-45.

Pejovich, Steve, "Liberty, Property Rights and Innovation in Eastern Europe,"
The Cato Journal, Volume 9 (Spring/Summer, 1989), pp. 57-71.

Puddington, Arch, "Voices in the Wilderness: The Western Heroes of Eastern
Europe," *Policy Review*, Number 53 (Summer, 1990), pp. 34-39.

Sikorski, Radek, "Poland's Erhard?," *National Review*, Volume XLIV
(November 2, 1992), pp. 23-24.

Stelzer, Irwin M., "A Marshall Plan for Eastern Europe?," *Commentary*, Volume
89 (January, 1990), pp. 17-22.

Tismaneanu, Vladimir, *The Crisis of Marxist Ideology in Eastern Europe* (New
York: Routledge, Chapman and Hall, 1988).

Troy, Tevi, "Praguelodytes," *National Review*, Volume XLIV (October 19, 1992), pp. 62-64.

Organizations

The Kreible Institute 214 Massachusetts Ave., NE, Washington, DC 20002, (202)-547-4042. Publication: *Kreible Monitor*. Resource center whose principal mission is to assist Eastern Europe and the former Soviet Republics in progressing to democratic and capitalistic societies through education and training. Provides financial support to programs that articulate and advocate these principles.

ECONOMIC PLANNING

Books and Articles

Barfield, Claude E., "Bush-League Industrial Policy: Scrambled Signals," *The American Enterprise*, Volume 1 (March/April, 1990), pp. 95-96.

Beltz, Cynthia A., "How to Lose the Race: Industrial Policy and the Lessons of HDTV," *The American Enterprise*, Volume 2 (May/June, 1991), pp. 22-27.

Harrigan, Anthony and Hawkins, William R., *American Economic Preeminence: Goals for the 1990s* (Washington, DC: U.S. Industrial Council Educational Foundation, 1989).

Lindsey, Brink, "Dram Scam: How the United States Built an Industrial Policy on Sand," *Reason*, Volume 23 (February, 1992), pp. 40-48.

McKenzie, Richard B., *Competing Visions: The Political Conflict Over America's Economic Future* (Washington, DC: The Cato Institute, 1985).

Porter, Michael E., *The Competitive Advantage of Nations* (New York: The Free Press, 1990).

Schlosstein, Steven, *Trade War: Greed, Power, and Industrial Policy on Opposite Sides of the Pacific* (New York: Congdon and Weed, 1984).

Stein, Herbert, "Recycling Industrial Policy," *The American Enterprise*, Volume 3 (July/August), pp. 5-7.

Stelzer, Irwin M., "Corporatism Ousts Reaganomics," *The American Spectator*, Volume 22 (May, 1989), pp. 31-34.

ECONOMIC THEORIES

Books and Articles

Baird, Charles W., "James Buchanan and the Austrians: The Common Ground," *The Cato Journal*, Volume 9 (Spring/Summer, 1989), pp. 201-230.

Bandow, Doug, "Meet Uncle Sam, Pickpocket: Exposing the Private Vices of the Public Sector," *Crisis*, Volume 7 (September, 1989), pp. 29-33.

Buchanan, James M., *Explorations into Constitutional Economics* (College Station, TX: Texas A&M University Press, 1989).

Buchholz, Todd G., *New Ideas from Dead Economists* (New York: New American Library, 1989).

Burnham, James, *The Managerial Revolution: What Is Happening in the World* (New York: John Day, 1968).

Fossedal, Gregory, "The Lehrman-Mueller Hypothesis: A New Theory of Deficits, Stagflation, and Monetary Disorder," *Policy Review*, Number 59 (Winter, 1992), pp. 71-81.

Francis, Samuel, "Prophet Sustained: James Burnham and the Managerial Revolution," *Chronicles*, Volume 16 (January, 1992), pp. 14-18.

Gilder, George, *Microcosm: The Quantum Revolution in Economics and Technology* (New York: Simon & Schuster, 1990).

Goldman, David, "Growth Economics vs. Macroeconomics," *The Public Interest*, Number 105 (Fall, 1991), pp. 78-92.

Hazlitt, Henry, *Man vs. the Welfare State* (Lanham, MD: University Press of America, 1983).

Kirzner, Israel, *Discovery, Capitalism and Distributive Justice* (New York: Basil Blackwell, 1989)

Kirzner, Israel, "The Use of Labels in Doctrinal History: Comment on Baird," *The Cato Journal*, Volume 9 (Spring/Summer, 1989), pp. 231-235.

Lasch, Christopher, "The New Class Controversy," *Chronicles*, Volume 14 (June, 1990), pp. 21-25.

Lynn, Richard, "What Makes People Rich?," *National Review*, Volume XLIII (September 9, 1991), pp. 30-33.

McCloskey, Donald N., *If You're So Smart: The Narrative of Economic Expertise* (Chicago, IL: University of Chicago Press, 1990).

North, Douglass C., "Private Property and the American Way," *National Review*, Volume XXXV (July 8, 1983), pp. 805-812.

Reynolds, Alan, "Who's on Next?," *National Review*, Volume XLIII (August 26, 1991), pp. 31-34.

Roberts, Paul Craig, "'Supply-Side' Economics - Theory and Results," *The Public Interest*, Number 93, (Fall, 1988), pp. 16-36.

Roberts, Paul Craig, *The Supply-Side Revolution: An Insider's Account of Policymaking in Washington* (Cambridge, MA: Harvard University Press, 1984).

Rockwell, Llewellyn H., Jr., "Morning After in America: The Austrian View of the Recession," *Policy Review*, Number 60 (Spring, 1992), pp. 73-77.

Rothbard, Murray N., *What Has Government Done to Our Money?* (Auburn, AL: Ludwig von Mises Institute, 1990).

Sowell, Thomas, *Marxism: Philosophy and Economics* (New York: Quartet Books, 1985).

Stein, Herbert, "The Master of the 'No School' School of Economics," *The American Enterprise*, Volume 3 (May/June, 1992), pp. 5-8.

Stelzer, Irwin M., "Bad Advice for the Democrats," *Commentary*, Volume 92 (July, 1991), pp. 19-23.

Stigler, George, *Memoirs of an Unregulated Economist* (New York: Basic Books, 1988).

Ulmer, Melville J., "Mainstream Marxism Rebutted," *The American Spectator*, Volume 21 (February, 1988), pp. 26-27.

ECONOMICS

Books and Articles

Bernstein, Peter L., "Savings-and-Investment and Other Myths," *The Public Interest*, Number 107 (Spring, 1992), pp. 87-94.

Brookes, Warren T., "America Dragged Down," *National Review*, Volume XLII (October 15, 1990), pp. 34-43.

Friedman, Milton, et al., "What Is the 'Right' Amount of Savings?," *National Review*, XLI (June 16, 1989), pp. 25-32.

Goldstein, Henry N., "Should We Fret About Our Low Net National Savings Rate?," *The Cato Journal,* Volume 9 (Winter, 1990), pp. 647-662.

Hulten, Charles R., "Is the U.S. Economy in Decline? That Depends on How You Look at It," *The American Enterprise*, Volume 1 (May/June, 1990), pp. 62-69.

Lindsey, Lawrence B., *The Growth Experiment: How the New Tax Policy is Transforming the U.S. Economy* (New York: Basic Books, 1990).

Lipset, Seymour Martin, "The Work Ethic - Then and Now," *The Public Interest*, Number 98 (Winter, 1990), pp. 61-69.

McKenzie, Richard B., "American Competitiveness - Do We Really Need to Worry?," *The Public Interest*, Number 90 (Winter, 1988), pp. 65-80.

Rothbard, Murray N., "Repudiating the National Debt," *Chronicles*, Volume 16 (June, 1992), pp. 49-52.

Shaw, Peter, "The Competitiveness Illusion," *National Review*, Volume XLV (January 18, 1993), pp. 41-44.

Stein, Herbert, "A Guide to the American Economy," *The American Enterprise*, Volume 2 (November/December, 1991), pp. 6-9.

Stein, Herbert, "The Next Trillion Dollars," *The American Enterprise*, Volume 2 (September/October, 1991), pp. 6-8.

Stein, Herbert, "Problems and Non-Problems in the American Economy," *The Public Interest*, Number 97 (Fall, 1989), pp. 56-70.

Stein, Herbert, "Reflections on Recessions," *The American Enterprise*, Volume 2 (July/August, 1991), pp. 6-9.

Stein, Herbert. "The U.S. Economy: A Visitor's Guide," *The American Enterprise*, Volume 1 (July/August, 1990), pp. 6-12.

Tolchin, Martin and Tolchin, Susan, *Buying Into America: How Foreign Money Is Changing the Face of Our Nation* (New York: Times Books, 1988).

Weidenbaum, Murray, *Rendezvous with Reality: The American Economy After Reagan* (New York: Basic Books, 1988).

Organizations

Atlas Economic Research Foundation 4210 Roberts Road, Fairfax, VA 22032, (703)-352-0525. Publications: *Bulletin, Newsletter*. Seeks to improve public understanding of economic issues and their wider social ramifications.

Citizens for a Sound Economy 470 L'Enfant Plaza, E., SW, Suite 7112, Washington, DC 20024, (202)-488-8200. Publications: *Annual Report, Capital Comment, CSE Report, Economic Perspective, Facts and Figures on Governmental Finance, Issues and Answers, Legal Perspective, On Alert for America's Taxpayers, Tax Features, A Citizens Guide to Deficit Reduction, Myths About Foreign Investment*. Strives to advance understanding of the market process in order to restore a sound economy.

The Conference Board 845 Third Avenue, New York, NY 10022, (212)-759-0900. Publications: *Across the Board, Business Executives' Expectations, Cumulative Index, Statistical Bulletin, Consumer Confidence Survey, Manufacturing Investment Outlook, Regional Economies and Markets, Survey of Financial Indicators*. Fact-finding institution that conducts research and publishes studies on business economics and management experience.

Manhattan Institute for Policy Research 52 Vanderbilt Avenue, New York, NY 10017, (212)-599-7000. Publication: *City Journal*. Assist scholars, government officials, and the public in obtaining a better understanding of economic processes and the effect of government programs on the economic situation.

ECOLOGY
(see **Environment**)

EDUCATION, HIGHER

Books and Articles

Anderson, Martin, *Impostors in the Temple: The Decline of the American University* (New York: Simon & Schuster, 1992).

Barzun, Jacques, *The Culture We Deserve* (Middletown, CT: Wesleyan University Press, 1989).

Barzun, Jacques, *The House of Intellect* (New York: Harper and Brothers, 1959).

Bethell, Tom, "Totem and Taboo at Stanford," *National Review*, Volume XXXIX (October 9, 1987), pp. 42-50.

Biechman, Arnold, "Stopping the Long March Through the University," *Chronicles*, Volume 12 (January, 1988), pp. 15-19.

Blits, Jan H., "Liberal Education and the Modern University," *This World*, Number 11 (Spring/Summer, 1985), pp. 63-74.

Bloom, Allan, *The Closing of the American Mind* (New York: Simon & Schuster, 1987).

Bradford, M. E., et al., "The State of the Humanities: A Symposium," *Modern Age*, Volume 34 (Winter, 1992), pp. 98-167.

Bryden, David P., "It Ain't What They Teach, It's the Way That Teach It," *The Public Interest*, Number 103 (Spring, 1991), pp. 38-53.

Cantor, Paul, "The Fixed Canon: The Maginot Line of the College Curriculum," *The American Enterprise*, Volume 2 (September/October, 1991), pp. 14-20.

Damerell, Reginald G., *Education's Smoking Gun: How Teachers Colleges Have Destroyed Education in America* (New York: Freundlich Books, 1985).

Dannhauser, Werner J., "Allan Bloom and the Critics," *The American Spectator*, Volume 21 (October, 1988), pp. 17-21.

D'Souza, Dinesh, *Illiberal Education: The Politics of Race and Sex on Campus* (New York: The Free Press, 1991).

Epstein, Joseph, "The Sad Story of the Boy Wonder," *Commentary*, Volume 89 (March, 1990), pp. 44-51.

Finn, Chester E., Jr., "The Campus: 'An Island of Repression in a Sea of Freedom,'" *Commentary*, Volume 88 (September, 1989), pp. 17-23.

Fleming, Thomas, "Revolution and Tradition in the Humanities Curriculum," *Chronicles*, Volume 14 (September, 1990), pp. 13-16.

Fuller, Timothy, *The Voice of Liberal Learning: Michael Oakeshott on Education* (New Haven, CT: Yale University Press, 1989).

Gottfried, Paul, "Academics, Therapists, and the German Connection," *Chronicles*, Volume 14 (September, 1990), pp. 21-23.

Gustin, Kimberly J., "Women's Studies, A Major Error: Our Campus Scout Reports from the Front," *Crisis*, Volume 9 (January, 1991), pp. 31-33.

Hirsch, E. D., Jr., "Another Part of the Forest," *Chronicles*, Volume 14 (September, 1990), pp. 18-20.

Henry, Carl F. H., "The Crisis of Modern Learning," *This World*, Number 7 (Winter, 1984), pp. 95-105.

Hook, Sidney, "Civilization and Its Malcontents," *National Review*, Volume XLI (October 13, 1989), pp. 30-33.

Howard, John A., "Taking the King's Shilling: Federal Aid to Higher Education," *Chronicles*, Volume 13 (September, 1989), pp. 20-22.

Kimball, Roger, *Tenured Radicals: How Politics Has Corrupted Our Higher Education* (New York: Harper & Row, 1990).

Lehman, David, *Signs of the Times: Deconstruction and the Fall of Paul de Man* (New York: Poseidon Press, 1991).

Miner, Brad and Sykes, Charles, *The National Review College Guide: America's Top Liberal Arts Colleges* (New York: Simon & Schuster, 1993).

Molnar, Thomas, "The Teaching of Humanities and Other Trivia," *Chronicles*, Volume 14 (September, 1990), pp. 24-25.

Montgomery, Marion, "Academic Afterword: On the Occasion of My Retirement from the Academy," *Chronicles*, Volume 12 (January, 1988), pp. 19-23.

Montgomery, Marion, *Liberal Arts and Community: The Feeding of the Larger Body* (Baton Rouge, LA: Louisiana State University Press, 1990).

Neusner, Jacob, "Can Humanity Forget What It Knows?," *Chronicles*, Volume 15 (September, 1991), pp. 19-22.

Neusner, Jacob, "Why Are Universities Different from All Other Centers of Learning?," *Chronicles*, Volume 13 (September, 1989), pp. 45-46.

Oakeshott, Michael, *The Voice of Liberal Learning: Michael Oakeshott on Higher Education,* Timothy Fuller, ed. (New Haven, CT: Yale University Press, 1990).

Panichas, George A., et al., "A Symposium on Allan Bloom's *The Closing of the American Mind,*" *Modern Age*, Volume 32 (Winter, 1988), pp. 4-60.

Pelikan, Jaroslav, *The Idea of the University: A Re-Examination* (New Haven, CT: Yale University Press, 1992).

Platt, Michael, "Thomas Aquinas and America: How One College Might Strengthen the Souls of Youth and Reinvigorate the Republic," *Crisis*, Volume 9 (July, August, 1991), pp. 21-25, 42.

Schall, James V., *Another Sort of Learning* (San Francisco, CA: Ignatius Press, 1988).

Schwartz, Joel, "Antihumanism in the Humanities," *The Public Interest*, Number 99 (Spring, 1990), pp. 29-44.

Shaw, Peter, *The War Against the Intellect: Episodes in the Decline of Discourse* (Iowa City, IA: University of Iowa Press, 1989).

Sowell, Thomas, *Inside American Education: The Decline, the Deception, the Dogmas* (New York: The Free Press, 1992).

Sowell, Thomas, "On Higher Learning in America: Some Comments," *The Public Interest*, Number 99 (Spring, 1990), pp. 68-78.

Sterling, Arlene, "Class Conflict," *National Review*, Volume XLV (June 21, 1993), pp. 78-79.

Stockdale, James Bond, "Learning Goodness: Why Western Civ Is the Best Refuge in Adversity," *Chronicles*, Volume 12 (July, 1988), pp. 9-12.

Sykes, Charles, *The Hollow Men: Politics and Corruption in Higher Education* (Washington, DC: Regnery Gateway, 1990).

Sykes, Charles, *Profscam: Professors and the Demise of Higher Education* (Washington, DC: Regnery Gateway, 1988).

Waters, Brent, "Moral Issues and the University," *This World*, Number 11
(Spring/Summer, 1985), pp. 75-82.

Organizations

Accuracy in Academia 1275 K Street, NW, Suite 1150, Washington, DC 20005,
(202)-789-4076. Publications: *The Campus Report, Academic License: The War
on Academic Freedom*. Seeks accurate use of facts and historical information on
college and university campuses.

Intercollegiate Studies Institute 14 S. Bryn Mawr Avenue, Bryn Mawr, PA
19010, (215)-525-7501. Publications: *Continuity: A Journal of History, The
Intercollegiate Review: A Journal of Scholarship and Opinion, Modern Age, The
Political Science Reviewer*. Seeks to develop among college students and
professors an understanding of "the conservative philosophy of individual liberty,
limited government, free-market economics, the right of private property, and the
spiritual and moral underpinnings of this philosophy."

National Association of Scholars 575 Ewing Street, Princeton, NJ 08540, (609)-
683-7878. Publications: *Academic Questions, Update*. Provides a forum for the
discussion of curricular issues and trends in higher education. Seeks to restore
scholarship and higher education to their high academic standards.

National Humanities Institute 214 Massachusetts Avenue, NE, Suite 470,
Washington, DC 20002, (202)-544-3158. Publication: *Humanitas*. Seeks to
educate students about the practical and aesthetic value of humanities study.

University Professors for Academic Order c/o COMCOA, Inc., 101 S.W.
Western Blvd., P.O. Box Q, Corvallis, OR 97339, (503)-752-6512. Publication:
Universitas. Upholds the university's function to "impart knowledge, wisdom, and
culture rather than serve as a center for political activity and social activism."

Young America's Foundation 110 Elden Street, Suite A, Herndon, VA 22070,
(703)-318-9608. Publications: *Libertas, Campus Leader, Continuity*. Service
organization for politically conservative high school and college students;
committed to bringing balance to college campuses.

EDUCATION, LOWER

Books and Articles

Adelson, Joseph, "The Nuclear Bubble," *Commentary*, Volume 90 (November,
1990), pp. 39-44.

Adler, Mortimer, *The Paideia Proposal: An Educational Manifesto* (New York: Macmillan, 1982).

Baer, Richard A., Jr., "Public Education as 'Brutal Censorship,'" *This World*, Number 22 (Summer, 1988), pp. 110-115.

Ball, G. Carl, et al., "In Search of Educational Excellence: Business Leaders Discuss School Choice and Accountability," *Policy Review*, Number 54 (Fall, 1990), pp. 54-59.

Bennett, William J., *Our Children and Our Country: Improving America's Schools and Affirming the Common Culture* (New York: Simon & Schuster, 1988).

Besharov, Douglas J., "A New Start for Head Start," *The American Enterprise*, Volume 3 (March/April, 1992), pp. 52-57.

Borden, Enid and O'Beirne, Kate Walsh, "False Start? The Fleeting Gains at Head Start," *Policy Review*, Number 47 (Winter, 1989), pp. 48-51.

Brock, David, "Selling Globaloney in the Schools," *The American Spectator*, Volume 21 (December, 1988), pp. 22-26.

Castelli, Jim, "Morality Without Theology: How to Teach Values in Public Schools," *Crisis*, Volume 8 (September, 1990), pp. 37-39.

Coleman, James S. and Hoffer, Thomas, *Public and Private High Schools: The Impact of Communities* (New York: Basic Books, 1987).

Crouse, James and Trusheim, Dale, "The Case Against the SAT," *The Public Interest*, Number 93 (Fall, 1988), pp. 97-110.

Doyle, Denis P., "Bright Lights, Big Questions: The Edison Project and Our Schools," *The American Enterprise*, Volume 3 (July/August, 1992), pp. 24-26.

Doyle, Denis P., et al., "Education Ideas and Strategies for the 1990s: How the States Can Do a World of Good," *The American Enterprise*, Volume 2 (March/April, 1991), pp. 25-33.

Finn, Chester E., Jr., et al., eds., *Against Mediocrity: The Humanities in America's High Schools* (New York: Holmes and Meier, 1984).

Finn, Chester E., Jr., "Biased Against Everyone," *The American Spectator*, Volume 25 (June, 1992), p. 37.

Finn, Chester E., Jr., "Dropouts and Grownups," *The Public Interest*, Number 96 (Summer, 1989), pp. 131-134.

Finn, Chester E., Jr., "Narcissus Goes to School," *Commentary*, Volume 89 (June, 1990), pp. 40-45.

Finn, Chester E., Jr., "A Nation Still at Risk," *Commentary*, Volume 87 (May, 1989), pp. 17-23.

Finn, Chester E., Jr., "The Science of Bad Science," *The American Spectator*, Volume 22 (August, 1989), pp. 34-35.

Finn, Chester E., Jr., "The Social Studies Debacle," *The American Spectator*, Volume 21 (May, 1988), pp. 35-36.

Finn, Chester E., Jr., "Taking Charge," *National Review*, Volume XLIV (July 6, 1992), pp. 42-44.

Finn, Chester E., Jr., "Unwillingly to School," *National Review*, Volume XLIV (March 2, 1992), pp. 45-46, 61.

Finn, Chester E., Jr., "Up From Mediocrity: What Next in School Reform?," *Policy Review*, Number 61 (Summer, 1992), pp. 80-83.

Finn, Chester E., Jr., *We Must Take Charge: Our Schools and the Future* (New York: The Free Press, 1991).

Fuller, Timothy, *The Voice of Liberal Learning: Michael Oakeshott on Education* (New Haven, CT: Yale University Press, 1989).

Glazer, Nathan, "The Real World of Urban Education," *The Public Interest*, Number 106 (Winter, 1992), pp. 57-75.

Herrnstein, R. J., and Murray, Charles, "What's Really Behind the SAT-Score Decline?," *The Public Interest*, Number 106 (Winter, 1992), pp. 32-56.

Holt, Thomas Harvey, "Growing Up Green: Are Schools Turning Our Kids Into Eco-Activists?," *Reason*, Volume 23 (October, 1991), pp. 37-41.

Jaki, Stanley L., "The Only Chaos," *This World*, Number 22 (Summer, 1988), pp. 98-109.

Kosters, Marvin H., "Be Cool, Stay in School," *The American Enterprise*, Volume 1 (March/April, 1990), pp. 60-67.

Kramer, Rita, "Are Girls Shortchanged at School?," *Commentary*, Volume 93 (June, 1992), pp. 48-49.

Lawler, Philip F., "Lessons from Chelsea: Silber Crusades to Save Public Schools," *Crisis*, Volume 10 (January, 1992), pp. 21-24.

Lederer, Richard, "56 B.C. and All That," *National Review*, Volume XLV (March 1, 1993), pp. 51-52.

Lerman, Robert I. and Pouncy, Hillard, "The Compelling Case for Youth Apprenticeships," *The Public Interest*, Number 101 (Fall, 1990), pp. 62-77.

Lerner, Barbara, "How Shakespeare Can Save Our Kids," *National Review*, Volume XLIV (January 20, 1992), pp. 30-37.

London, Herbert I., *Armageddon in the Classroom: An Examination of Nuclear Education* (Lanham, MD: University Press of America, 1987).

London, Herbert I., *Why Are They Lying to Our Children?* (New York: Stein and Day, 1984).

Lynn, Richard, "Why Johnny Can't Read - But Yoshio Can," *National Review*, Volume XL (October 28, 1988), pp. 40-43.

Mitchell, Richard, *The Gift of Fire* (New York: Fireside/Simon and Schuster, 1986).

Mitchell, Richard, *The Graves of Academe* (New York: Fireside/Simon and Schuster, 1987).

Mitchell, Richard, *The Leaning Tower of Babel* (Boston, MA: Little, Brown, 1984).

Morris, Geoffrey, "Whittling at the Wall," *National Review*, Volume XXLIV (September 14, 1992), pp. 50-51.

Nelson, Caleb, "Bring Back the Old Math," *The American Spectator*, Volume 22 (November, 1989), pp. 36-37.

Pauly, Edward, *The Classroom Crucible: What Really Works, What Doesn't, and Why* (New York: Basic Books, 1991).

Porter, Rosalie Pedalino, *Forked Tongue: The Politics of Bilingual Education* (New York: Basic Books, 1990).

Puddington, Arch, "Why Johnny's Not an Anti-Communist," *National Review*, Volume XLII (February 5, 1990), pp. 44-46.

Ravitch, Diane, *The Schools We Deserve: Reflections on the Educational Crises of Our Time* (New York: Basic Books, 1987).

Ravitch, Diane, *The Troubled Crusade: American Education 1945 - 1980* (New York: Basic Books, 1983).

Schall, James V., *Another Sort of Learning* (San Francisco, CA: Ignatius Press, 1988).

Shaw, Peter, "The Competitiveness Illusion," *National Review*, Volume XLV (January 18, 1993), pp. 41-44.

Sowell, Thomas, *Inside American Education: The Decline, the Deception, the Dogmas* (New York: The Free Press, 1992).

Stevenson, Harold W. and Stigler, James W., *The Learning Gap: Why Our Schools Are Failing and What We Can Learn from Japanese and Chinese Education* (New York: Summit Books, 1992).

Toby, Jackson and Armor, David, "Carrots or Sticks for High School Dropouts?," *The Public Interest*, Number 106 (Winter, 1992), pp. 76-91.

Uzzell, Lawrence A., "Want to Reform Public Education? First De-Fund the Department of Ed," *Chronicles*, Volume 14 (June, 1990), pp. 26-28.

van den Haag, Ernest, "Why Do American Kids Learn So Little?," *National Review*, Volume XLIV (August 3, 1992), pp. 34-36.

Vigilante, Richard, "Winning in New York," *National Review*, Volume XLV (January 18, 1993), pp. 18-20.

Whitehead, John W., *The Freedom of Religious Expression in the Public High Schools* (Westchester, IL: Crossway Books, 1983).

Wood, Regna Lee, "That's Right - They're Wrong: Nothing Can Be Done with Our Schools Until the Basic Problem Is Solved - And No One Even Sees What It Is," *National Review*, Volume XLIX (September 14, 1992), pp. 49-52.

Wooster, Martin Morse, "Control Freaks: How Progressives and Efficiency Experts Abolished School-Based Management," *Reason*, Volume 24 (May, 1992), pp. 33-35.

Wooster, Martin Morse, "First Principals: The Leadership Vacuum in American Schools," *Policy Review*, Number 57 (Summer, 1991), pp. 55-61.

Organizations

Council for Basic Education 725 15th Street, NW, Washington, DC 20005, (202)-347-4171. Publications: *Basic Education, Basic Education: Issues, Answers, and Facts.* Promotes the teaching and learning of the liberal arts.

National Center for Education Statistics U.S. Department of Education/OERI, 555 New Jersey Avenue, NW, Room 400, Washington, DC 20208, (202)-219-1828. Publications: *The Condition of Education, Digest of Education Statistics, Education Directory - Colleges and Universities, Projections of Education Statistics*. Agency of the U.S. Department of Education. Collects and disseminates statistics and other data related to education in the U.S.

ELDERLY
(see **Old Age**)

ELECTION REFORM
(see **American History**)

ELECTIONS

Organizations

Elections Research Center 5508 Greystone Street, Chevy Chase, MD 20815, (301)-654-3541 or (301)-654-5541. Publications: *America Votes, America at the Polls*. Purpose is to collect data and statistics on state and national election returns.

Federal Election Commission Library, 990 E Street, NW, Washington, DC 20463, (202)-219-3440.

Federal Election Commission Public Records Office, 1325 K Street, NW, Washington, DC 20463, (202)-219-4140.

ELECTORAL REFORM

Books and Articles

Jeffe, Douglas and Jeffe, Sherry Bebitch, "Absence Counts: Voting by Mail," *The American Enterprise*, Volume 1 (November/December, 1990), pp. 19-21.
Kesler, Charles R., "Bad Housekeeping: The Case Against Congressional Term Limitations," *Policy Review*, Number 53 (Summer, 1990), pp. 20-25.
Payne, James L., "Limiting Government By Limiting Congressional Terms," *The Public Interest*, Number 103 (Spring, 1991), pp. 106-117.
Reynolds, Alan, "Time for Term Limits," *National Review*, Volume XLIV (April 13, 1992), pp. 43-44.

Will, George, *Restoration: Congress, Term Limits and the Recovery of Deliberative Democracy* (New York: The Free Press, 1992).

ELECTORATE

Books and Articles

Black, Earl and Black, Merle, *The Vital South: How Presidents Are Elected* (Cambridge, MA: Harvard University Press, 1992).

Reddy, Patrick, "Democrats and Demographics," *The American Enterprise*, Volume 2 (March/April, 1991), pp. 65-67.

Rothenberg, Stuart, "The Politics of Independents," *The American Enterprise*, Volume 1 (November/December, 1990), pp. 13-15.

Scammon, Richard, "Mega-Trends, Mega-Counties," *The American Enterprise*, Volume 1 (March/April, 1990), pp. 16-17.

Schneider, William and Reddy, Patrick, "Altered States: The Demographic Changes and Partisan Shifts of Four Decades," *The American Enterprise*, Volume 1 (July/August 1990), pp. 45-55.

Teixeira, Ruy A., *The Disappearing American Voter* (Washington, DC: The Brookings Institution, 1992).

Teixeira, Ruy A., *Why Americans Don't Vote: Turnout Decline in the United States, 1960 - 1984* (Westport, CT: Greenwood Press, 1987).

EMPLOYMENT

Books and Articles

Blits, Jan H. and Gottfredson, Linda S., "Employment Testing and Job Performance," *The Public Interest*, Number 98 (Winter, 1990), pp. 18-25.

Burtless, Gary, *A Future of Lousy Jobs: The Changing Structure of U.S. Wages* (Washington, DC: The Brookings Institution, 1990).

Frieden, Bernard J., "The Downtown Job Puzzle," *The Public Interest*, Number 97 (Fall, 1989), pp. 71-86.

Kosters, Marvin H., "A White-Collar Recession?," *The American Enterprise*, Volume 3 (March/April, 1992), pp. 20-23.

Mead, Lawrence, "The Hidden Jobs Debate," *The Public Interest*, Number 92 (Spring, 1988), pp. 40-58.

McKenzie, Richard B., *The American Job Machine* (New York: Universe Books, 1988).

Vedder, Richard and Gallaway, Lowell, "How to Increase Unemployment," *National Review*, Volume XLIV (November 16, 1992), pp. 44-47.

ENDANGERED SPECIES

Books and Articles

Gordon, Robert E., Jr., and Dunlop, George S., "Creature Comfort: The Revitalization of American Wildlife," *Policy Review*, Number 53 (Summer, 1990), pp. 60-64.

Miniter, Richard, "Saving the Species," *National Review*, Volume XLIV (July 6, 1992), pp. 32-35.

Oliver, Charles, "All Creatures Great and Small: Species Preservation Out of Control," *Reason*, Volume 23 (April, 1992), pp. 22-27.

Rice, James Owen, "Where Many an Owl Is Spotted," *National Review*, Volume XLIV (March 2, 1992), pp. 41-43.

Weaver, Stephen M., "The Elephant's Best Friend," *National Review*, Volume XLIII (August 12, 1991), pp. 42-43.

ENERGY

Books and Articles

Bohi, Douglas R., "Thinking Through Energy Security Issues," *The American Enterprise*, Volume 2 (September/October, 1991), pp. 32-35.

Crandall, Robert W. and Graham, John D., "New Fuel-Economy Standards?," *The American Enterprise*, Volume 2 (March/April, 1991), pp. 68-69.

Miniter, Richard, "The Oil Shortage That Wasn't," *National Review*, Volume XLIII (April 15, 1991), pp. 36-38.

Singer, S. Fred, "NOPEC - The Future of Oil," *The National Interest*, Number 7 (Spring, 1987), pp. 61-67.

Stelzer, Irwin, "National Energy Planning Redux," *The Public Interest*, Number 101 (Fall, 1990), pp. 43-54.

Organizations

American Petroleum Institute 1220 L Street, NW, Washington, DC 20005, (202)-682-8000. Publication: *Director*. Seeks to maintain cooperation between government and industry on all matters of national concern; fosters foreign and domestic trade in American petroleum products; promotes the interests of the petroleum industry; encourages the study of the arts and sciences connected with the petroleum industry.

Gas Research Institute 8600 W. Bryn Mawr Avenue, Chicago, IL 60631-3562, (312)-399-8100. Publications: *Baseline Projection of U.S. Natural Gas Supply and Demand, Gas Research Insights, Annual Report.* Plans and manages research related to supply of natural and synthetic gas, efficient gas-fueled appliances and equipment, distribution, safety and environmental impacts, and basic research.

ENERGY ALTERNATIVES

Books and Articles

Fumento, Michael, "Some Dare Call Them Robber Barons," *National Review*, Volume XXXIX (March 13, 1987), pp. 32-38.
Fumento, Michael, "What Kind of Fuel Am I?," *The American Spectator*, Volume 23 (November, 1990), pp. 25-31.

Organizations

Alternative Sources of Energy 107 S. Central Avenue, Milaca, MN 56353, (612)-983-6892. Publication: *Directory of the Independent Power Industry*. Seeks to publicize the applications of alternative technologies for power production.

ENVIRONMENT

Books and Articles

Adler, Jonathan H., "Little Green Lies: The Environmental Miseducation of America's Children," *Policy Review*, Number 61 (Summer, 1992), pp. 18-26.
Anderson, William, "Acid Test: Edward Krug Flunks Political Science," *Reason*, Volume 23 (January, 1992), pp. 20-26.
Bailey, Ronald, "Captain Planet for Veep," *National Review*, Volume XLIV (September 14, 1992), pp. 40-46.
Bailey, Ronald, *Ecoscam: The False Prophets of Ecological Apocalypse* (New York: St. Martins, 1993).
Bailey, Ronald, "The Hole Story: The Science Behind the Scare," *Reason*, Volume 24 (June, 1992), pp. 24-31.
Bailey, Ronald, "Raining in Their Hearts," *National Review*, Volume XLII (December 3, 1990), pp. 32-36.
Balling, Robert C., Jr., *The Heated Debate: Greenhouse Predictions Versus Climate Reality* (San Francisco, CA: Pacific Research Institute, 1992).
Bethell, Tom, "The New Environmentalism: Too Many People, Too Few Trees," *Crisis*, Volume 8 (June, 1990), pp. 22-26.
Bolch, Ben and Lyons, Harold, "A Multibillion-Dollar Radon Scare," *The Public Interest*, Number 99 (Spring, 1990), pp. 61-67.
Bovard, James, "A Hazardous Waste: What Else Can You Call Environmental Regulations the Prevent Recycling, Discourage Cleanups, And Stifle

Improvements in Waste Management?," *Reason*, Volume 21 (November, 1989), pp. 32-35.

Bray, Anna J., "The Ice Age Cometh: Remembering the Scare of Global Cooling," *Policy Review*, Number 58 (Fall, 1991), pp. 82-84.

Brookes, Warren T., "America Dragged Down," *National Review*, Volume XLII (October 15, 1990), pp. 34-43.

Brooks, David, "Environmentalists: High, Low, and Dangerous," *National Review*, Volume XLII (April 1, 1990), pp. 28-31.

Chase, Alston, *Playing God in Yellowstone: The Destruction of America's First National Park* (New York: Atlantic Monthly Press, 1986).

Dunn, James R., "America the Beautiful," *National Review*, Volume XLIV (July 6, 1992), pp. 34-35.

Fleming, Thomas, "Short Views on Earth Day," *Chronicles*, Volume 14 (August, 1990), pp. 12-15.

Fumento, Michael, "The Asbestos Rip-Off," *The American Spectator*, Volume 22 (October, 1989), pp. 21-26.

Fumento, Michael, *Science Under Siege: Balancing Technology and the Environment* (New York: Morrow, 1993).

Greve, Michael S. and Smith, Fred L., Jr., eds., *Environmental Politics: Public Costs, Private Rewards* (New York: Praeger Publishers, 1992).

Greve, Michael S., "Bounty Hunting and Environmentalism," *The Public Interest*, Number 97 (Fall, 1989), pp. 15-29.

Greve, Michael S., "The EPA Rediscovers the Environment," *The American Enterprise*, Volume 2 (November/December, 1991), pp. 52-61.

Hahn, Robert W., "Reshaping Environmental Policy: The Test Case of Hazardous Waste," *The American Enterprise*, Volume 2 (May/June, 1991), pp. 73-80.

Henderson, Rick, "Dirty Driving: Donald Stedman and the EPA's Sins of Emission," *Policy Review*, Number 60 (Spring, 1992), pp. 56-60.

Henderson, Rick, "Insufficient Data," *Reason*, Volume 24 (June, 1992), pp. 55-57.

Henderson, Rick, "Going Mobile: On-Road Emissions Tests Promise a Cheap and Effective Way to Clean Up Auto Pollution," *Reason*, Volume 22 (August/September, 1990), pp. 32-36.

Henderson, Rick, "The Swamp Thing: Under New Federal Policy, Wetlands Need Not Be Picturesque, Ecologically Valuable, or Even Wet," *Reason*, Volume 22 (April, 1991), pp. 30-35.

Hill, Peter J., "The Christian and Creation," *Chronicles*, Volume 12 (February, 1988), pp. 19-25.

Holt, Thomas Harvey, "Growing Up Green: Are Schools Turning Our Kids Into Eco-Activists?," *Reason*, 23 (October, 1991), pp. 37-41.

Horowitz, David, "Making the Green One Red," *National Review*, Volume XLII (March 19, 1990), pp. 39-40.

Idso, Sherwood B., *Carbon Dioxide and Global Change: Earth in Transition* (Tempe, AZ: Institute for Biospheric Research Press, 1989).

Jordan, William R., III, "The Reentry of Nature: Ecological Restoration," *Chronicles*, Volume 14 (August, 1990), pp. 19-22.

Krug, Edward C., "Fish Story: The Great Acid Rain Flimflam," *Policy Review*, Number 52 (Spring, 1990), pp. 44-48.

Krutch, Joseph Wood, *The Desert Year* (Tucson, AZ: University of Arizona Press, 1985).

Krutch, Joseph Wood, *The Forgotten Peninsula: A Naturalist in Baja, California* (Tucson, AZ: University of Arizona Press, 1986).

Krutch, Joseph Wood, *Grand Canyon: Today and All Its Yesterdays* (Tucson, AZ: University of Arizona Press, 1989).

Lyon, Thomas J., *This Incomparable Lande: A Book of American Nature Writing* (Boston, MA: Houghton Mifflin, 1989).

McPhee, John, *The Control of Nature* (New York: Farrar, Straus Giroux, 1989).

Miniter, Richard, "Muddy Waters: The Quagmire of Wetlands Regulation," *Policy Review*, Number 56 (Spring, 1991), pp. 70-77.

Mueller, William, "Prometheus in Overalls," *Chronicles*, Volume 12 (December, 1988), pp. 53-55.

Nelson, Robert H., "Unoriginal Sin: The Judeo-Christian Roots of Ecotheology," *Policy Review*, Number 53 (Summer, 1990), pp. 52-59.

Ray, Dixy Lee, with Guzzo, Lou, *Trashing the Planet: How Science Can Help Us Deal With Acid Rain, Depletion of the Ozone, and Nuclear Waste (Among Other Things)* (Washington, DC: Regnery Gateway, 1990).

Ray, Dixy Lee, "The Great Acid Rain Debate," *The American Spectator*, Volume 20 (January, 1987), pp. 21-25.

Samuel, Peter, "Fog from Foggy Bottom," *National Review*, Volume XLIV (May 25, 1992), pp. 36, 53.

Samuel, Peter, "Green Grows the Downturn, O!," *National Review*, Volume XLIII (December 2, 1991), pp. 38-40.

Samuel, Peter, "Honor Among Environmentalists," *National Review*, Volume XLV (March 29, 1993), pp. 56-58.

Schwartz, Joel, "The Rights of Nature and the Death of God," *The Public Interest*, Number 97 (Fall, 1989), pp. 3-14.

Seitz, Russell, "Spirits of the Air," *National Review*, Volume XLII (April 1, 1990), 46-47.

Seitz, Russell, "A War Against Fire: The Uses of 'Global Warming,'" *The National Interest*, Number 20 (Summer, 1990), pp. 54-62.

Shaw, Jane S. and Stroup, Richard L., "Getting Warmer?," *National Review*, Volume XLI (July 14, 1989), pp. 26-28.

Shaw, Peter, "Apocalypse Again," *Commentary*, Volume 87 (April, 1989), pp. 50-52.

Singer, S. Fred, "My Adventures in the Ozone Layer," *National Review*, Volume XLI (June 30, 1989), pp. 34-38.

Smith, Fred L., Jr., "Carnival of Dunces," *National Review*, Volume XLIV (July 6, 1992), pp. 30-32.

Smith, Fred L., Jr., "A Free-Market Environmental Program," *The Cato Journal*, Volume 11 (Winter, 1992), pp. 457-475.

Smith, Fred L., Jr., and Kushner, Kathy H., "Good Fences Make Good Neighbors," *National Review*, Volume XLII (April 1, 1990), pp. 31-33, 59.

Stewart, Richard B. and Wiener, Jonathan B., "A Comprehensive Approach to Climate Change: Using the Market to Protect the Environment," *The American Enterprise*, Volume 1 (November/December, 1990), pp. 75-80.

Stroup, Richard L., and Shaw, Jane S., "The Free Market and the Environment," *The Public Interest*, Number 97 (Fall, 1989), pp. 30-43.

Tucker, William, *Progress and Privilege: America in the Age of Environmentalism* (New York: Doubleday, 1982).

Turner, Frederick, "Natural Technology," *Chronicles*, Volume 14 (August, 1990), pp. 27-31.

Whelan, Elizabeth, *Toxic Terror* (Ottawa, IL: Jameson, 1985).

Wilson, Edward O., "The New Environmentalism," *Chronicles*, Volume 14 (August, 1990), pp. 16-18.

Yandle, Bruce, "Taxation, Political Action, and Superfund," *The Cato Journal*, Volume 8 (Winter, 1989), pp. 751-764.

Organizations

Foundation for Research on Economics and the Environment 4900 25th Avenue, NE, Suite 201, Seattle, WA 98105, (206)-548-1776; or, during the summer months: 502 South 19th Street, #35, Bozeman, MT 59715, (406)-585-1776.

National Asbestos Council 1777 N.E. Expressway, Suite 150, Atlanta, GA 30329, (404)-633-2622. Publications: *Council Currents, Membership Directory, NAC Journal.* Goal is to collect and disseminate information to building owners, interested professionals, and the public concerning asbestos in buildings. Serves as a clearinghouse of information on safe asbestos control.

National Wilderness Institute 25766 Georgetown Station, Washington, DC 20007, (703)-836-7404. Publication: *NWI Resource.* Dedicated to using sound, objective science for the wise management of natural resources. Recognizes the direct, positive relationship between progress and environmental quality and champions private sector stewardship; supports policies which protect or extend private property rights and reduce the regulatory burden of government.

Pacific Legal Foundation, 2700 Gateway Oaks Drive, Suite 200, Sacramento, CA 95833, (916)-641-8888. Publications: *At Issue, In Perspective, Achieving a Balanced Environmental Policy.* Litigates nationally on behalf of personal freedoms, free enterprise, private property rights, and a balanced approach to environmental consideration; encourages the concept of limited government.

World Resources Institute 1709 New York Avenue, NW, Suite 700, Washington, DC 20006, (202)-638-6300. Publications: *Center for International Development and Environment-Annual Report, World Resources Report*. Seeks to achieve balance between the long-term conservation of natural resources, the environment, and human needs.

EQUAL RIGHTS AMENDMENT
(see **Constitution, Women**)

ESPIONAGE
(see **Intelligence**)

ETHICS

Books and Articles

Castelli, Jim, "Morality Without Theology: How to Teach Values in Public Schools," *Crisis*, Volume 8 (September, 1990), pp. 37-39.

Eisele, Thomas D., "Must Virtue Be Taught?," *Modern Age*, Volume 33 (Fall, 1990), pp. 235-248.

Fleming, Thomas, "Science, Wisdom, and Judgment," *Chronicles*, Volume 14 (April, 1990), pp. 12-14.

Garment, Suzanne, *Scandal: The Crisis of Mistrust in American Politics* (New York: Times Books, 1991).

Molnar, Thomas, "Technology and the Ethical Imperative," *Chronicles*, Volume 12 (February, 1988), pp. 14-15.

Vogel, David, "Business Ethics Past and Present," *The Public Interest*, Number 102 (Winter, 1991), pp. 49-64.

Organizations

Council on Governmental Ethics Laws c/o Council of State Governments, P.O. Box 11910, Iron Works Pike, Lexington, KY 40578-1910, (606)-231-1909. Publications: *Campaign Finance, Ethics, and Lobby Law Blue Book, COGEL Guardian*. Compiles and disseminates information regarding state elections, campaign finance, ethics, and lobbying registration and regulations.

Society of Christian Ethics School of Theology, Boston University, 475 Commonwealth Avenue, Boston, MA 02215, (617)-353-7322. Publication: *The Annual of the Society of Christian Ethics*. Promotes scholarly work in the field of

Christian ethics, in relation to other traditions of ethics, and to social, economic, political, and cultural problems.

ETHNIC GROUPS
(see **Minorities**)

ETIQUETTE
(see **Manners**)

EUROPE
(see **Eastern Europe**, **European Community**, **Western Europe**)

EUROPEAN COMMUNITY

Books and Articles

Brzezinski, Zbigniew, "Beyond Chaos: A Policy for the West," *The National Interest*, Number 19 (Spring, 1990), pp. 3-12.

Congdon, Tim, "Is Europe on the Road to Serfdom?," *National Review*, Volume XLII (September 17, 1990), pp. 40-43.

Codevilla, Angelo, "The Coming Euromess," *National Review*, Volume XLIV (June 8, 1992), pp. 44-46.

Fratianni, Michele, "The European Monetary System: How Well Has It Worked?," With Comment by Alan Walters. *The Cato Journal*, Volume 8 (Fall, 1988), pp. 477-506.

Hartley, Anthony, "After 1992: Multiple Choice," *The National Interest*, Number 15 (Spring, 1989), pp. 29-32.

Hartley, Anthony, "The Once and Future Europe," *The National Interest*, Number 26 (Winter, 1991/92), pp. 44-53.

Kaplan, Roger, "Watch on the Rhine," *National Review*, Volume XLIV (October 19, 1992), pp. 24-26.

Lagon, Mark P., "The Future of the CSCE," *The American Enterprise*, Volume 3 (July/August, 1992), pp. 16-22.

Malcolm, Noel, "Heads in the Sand," *National Review*, Volume XLIV (July 20, 1992), pp. 34-36.

Malcolm, Noel, "Other People's Money," *National Review*, Volume XLV (January 18, 1993), pp. 20-22.

Molnar, Thomas, "Europe Is Not What It Seems," *Chronicles*, Volume 15 (April, 1991), pp. 18-20.

Sacco, Giuseppe, "Saving Europe from Itself," *Commentary*, Volume 92 (September, 1991), pp. 36-39,

Sked, Alan, "Myths of European Unity," *The National Interest*, Number 22 (Winter 1990/91), pp. 67-73.

Szamuely, George, "The Politics of 1992," *Commentary*, Volume 88 (October, 1989), pp. 42-45.

EUTHANASIA

Books and Articles

Gomez, Carlos, M.D., *Regulating Death: Euthanasia and the Case of the Netherlands* (New York: The Free Press, 1991).

Kass, Leon R., "Death with Dignity and the Sanctity of Life," *Commentary*, Volume 89 (March, 1990), pp. 33-43.

Kass, Leon R., "Neither for Love nor Money: Why Doctors Must Not Kill," *The Public Interest*, Number 94 (Winter, 1989), pp. 25-46.

Spitzer, Robert, "A Reason to Die: Euthanasia Comes to Washington State," *Crisis*, Volume 9 (October, 1991), pp. 21-25, 45.

EVOLUTION

Books and Articles

Denton, Michael, *Evolution: A Theory in Crisis* (Bethesda, MD: Adler and Adler, 1985).

Johnson, Phillip, *Darwin on Trial* (Washington, DC: Regnery Gateway, 1991).

Johnston, George Sim, "The Genesis Controversy: Darwin's Theory of Evolution Is Losing Support in the Scientific Community," *Crisis*, Volume 7 (May, 1989), pp. 12-18.

Kass, Leon R., "Evolution and the Bible: Genesis I Revisited," *Commentary*, Volume 86 (November, 1988), pp. 29-39.

Rentz, Mark D., "Darwin for Sissies, or What Ever Happened to Survival of the Fittest?," *Chronicles*, Volume 12 (December, 1988), pp. 55-56.

FAMILY

Books and Articles

Bauer, Gary L., "Leaving Families Out," *National Review*, Volume XLV (March 29, 1993), pp. 58-60.

Berger, Brigitte and Berger, Peter L., *The War over the Family: Capturing the Middle Ground* (New York: Doubleday, 1983).

Blankenhorn, David., et al., eds., *Rebuilding the Nest: A New Commitment to the American Family* (Milwaukee, WI: Family Service America, 1990).

Carlson, Allan, "'Be Fruitful and Multiply': Religious Pronatalism in a Depopulating America," *This World*, Number 21 (Spring, 1988), pp. 18-30.

Carlson, Allan, "The Fertility Gap: The Need for a Pro-Family Agenda," *This World*, Number 26 (Summer, 1989), pp. 34-45.

Carlson, Allan, "A Pro-Family Income Tax," *The Public Interest*, Number 94 (Winter, 1989), pp. 69-76.

Carlson, Allan, *The Swedish Experiment in Family Politics: The Myrdals and the Interwar Population Crisis* (New Brunswick, NJ: Transaction Books, 1990).

Christensen, Bryce J., "The Costly Retreat from Marriage," *The Public Interest*, Number 91 (Spring, 1988), pp. 59-66.

Christensen, Bryce J., *The Family Wage: Work, Gender, and Children in the Modern Economy* (Rockford, IL: The Rockford Institute, 1989).

Christensen, Bryce J., "In Sickness and in Health: The Medical Costs of Family Meltdown," *Policy Review*, Number 60 (Spring, 1992), pp. 70-72.

Christensen, Bryce J., *Utopia Against the Family: The Problems and Politics of the American Family* (San Francisco, CA: Ignatius Press, 1990).

Davidson, Nicholas, "Life Without Father: America's Greatest Social Catastrophe," *Policy Review*, Number 51 (Winter, 1990), pp. 40-44.

Eberstadt, Nicholas, "Is Illegitimacy a Public-Health Hazard?," *National Review*, Volume XL (December 30, 1988), pp. 36-39.

Fleming, Thomas, "The Facts of Life," *Chronicles*, Volume 14 (October, 1990), pp. 12-15.

Gallagher, Maggie, *Enemies of Eros* (Chicago, IL: Bonus Books, 1990).

Gill, Richard T., "For the Sake of the Children," *The Public Interest*, Number 108 (Summer, 1992), pp. 81-96.

Glendon, Mary Ann, *The Transformation of Family Law: State, Law, and Family in the United States and Western Europe* (Chicago, IL: University of Chicago Press, 1989).

Hafen, Bruce C., "Custom, Law, and the American Family," *This World*, Number 18 (Summer, 1987), pp. 28-42.

Kamerman, Sheila B. and Kahn, Alfred J., "What Europe Does for Single Parent Families," *The Public Interest*, Number 93 (Fall, 1988), pp. 70-86.

Levine, Edward M., "Homosexuality and the Family," *Chronicles*, Volume 12 (July, 1988), pp. 21-22.

Marshner, Connaught C., "What Social Conservatives Really Want," *National Review*, Volume XL (September 2, 1988), pp. 38-40.

Mattox, William R., Jr., "The Parent Trap: So Many Bills, So Little Time," *Policy Review*, Number 55 (Winter, 1991), pp. 6-13.

Mount, Ferdinand, *The Subversive Family: An Alternative History of Love and Marriage* (New York: The Free Press, 1982).

Popenoe, David, *Disturbing the Nest: Family Change and Decline in Modern Societies* (Hawthorne, NY: Aldine de Gruyter, 1988).

Tucker, William, "Why We Have Families," *The American Spectator*, Volume 18 (December, 1985), pp. 14-18.

Zinsmeister, Karl, "Is Poverty the Problem? Why We Need More Intact Families and Fewer Transfer Programs," *Crisis*, Volume 7 (July/August, 1989), pp. 28-32.

Organizations

American Family Association P.O. Drawer and Federal Box 2440, Tupelo, MS 38803, (601)-844-5036. Publication: *AFA Journal*. Fosters "the biblical ethic of decency in American society with a primary emphasis on television."

Christian Family Renewal Box 73, Clovis, CA 93613, (209)-297-7818. Publication: *Jesus And Mary Are Calling You*. Promotes Christian solutions to problems in business, politics, and education counseling.

Family Research Council 700 13th Street, NW, Suite 500, Washington, DC 20005, (202)-393-2100. Publications: *Family Policy, Washington Watch*. Provides expertise and information to government agencies, members of Congress, policymakers, the media, and the public.

Focus on the Family 8655 Explorer Drive, Colorado Springs, CO 80920, (719)-531-3400. Publications: *Family Newsletter, Focus on the Family Magazine*. Non-profit communications, resource and counseling organization dedicated to the preservation of the home, a Judeo-Christian ethic, and the traditional family.

Free Congress Research and Education Foundation 717 Second Street, NE, Washington, DC 20002, (202)-546-3004. Publications: *Family Protection Report, Journal of Family and Culture*. Focuses on public policy as it affects the traditional family; seeks to present alternatives to abortion and euthanasia; conducts seminars.

Pro-Family Forum P.O. Box 8907, Fort Worth, TX 76124, (817)-531-3605. Publication: *The Family Educator*. Christian-oriented group concerned with strengthening family structures and educating others on family issues.

FAMILY PLANNING
(see **Abortion, Contraceptives**)

FAR EAST
(see **Asia**)

FEDERAL BUDGET

Books and Articles

Archer, Bill, "Who's the Fairest of Them All? The Truth About the 80s," *Policy Review*, Number 57 (Summer, 1991), pp. 67-73.

Attarian, John, "No Time for Gimmicks," *National Review*, Volume XLV (May 10, 1993), pp.27-33.

Bartley, Robert, et al., "The Great Deficit Debate," *National Review*, Volume XLI (January 27, 1989), pp. 46-51.

Brookes, Warren T., "Dead Wrong Again," *National Review*, Volume XLIII (October 7, 1991), pp. 29-35.

Cogan, John F. and Muris, Timothy J., "The Great Budget Shell Game: Now You See Them, Now You Don't - Budget Cuts in the Reagan and Bush Administrations," *The American Enterprise*, Volume 1 (November/December, 1990), pp. 35-41.

Cox, Christopher, "Capitol Offenders: A Budget Reform to Stop Congress from Breaking the Law," *Policy Review*, Number 54 (Fall, 1990), pp. 38-42.

Daxson, Thomas E., "Shrinking Mortgage: Ronald Reagan Was a Friend to Future Taxpayers," *Policy Review*, Number 47 (Winter 1989), pp. 68-69.

Dewald, William G. and Ulan, Michael, "The Twin-Deficit Illusion," *The Cato Journal*, Volume 9 (Winter, 1990), pp. 689-707.

Eastland, Terry, "Bush's Fatal Attraction: Anatomy of the Budget Fiasco," *Policy Review*, Number 60 (Spring, 1992), pp. 20-24.

Grace, J. Peter, *Burning Money: The Waste of Your Tax Dollars* (New York: Macmillan, 1984).

Haskins, Ron and Brown, Hank, "A Billion Here, a Billion There: Social Spending Under Ronald Reagan," *Policy Review*, Number 49 (Summer, 1989), pp. 22-28.

Hatch, Orrin G., et al., "The $25-Billion Question: How Five Senators Would Cut Domestic Spending," *Policy Review*, Number 61 (Summer, 1992), pp. 70-73.

Hodge, Scott A., "Pork Chop: Budget Questions for Your Congressman," *Policy Review*, Number 58 (Fall, 1991), pp. 58-59.

Lindsey, Lawrence B., "The Surplus of 1999," *National Review*, XLII (April 30, 1990), pp. 34-36.

Martino, Antonio, "Budget Deficits and Constitutional Constraints," *The Cato Journal*, Volume 8 (Winter, 1989), pp. 695-711.

Meadows, Edward, "Peter Grace Knows 2,478 Ways to Cut the Deficit," *National Review*, Volume XXXVI (March 9, 1984), pp. 26-36.

Meigs, A. James, "Dollars and Deficits: Substituting False for Real Problems," *The Cato Journal*, Volume 8 (Fall, 1988), pp. 533-553.

Mitchell, Daniel J., "Bush's Rasputin," *National Review*, Volume XLIV (December 28, 1992), pp. 29-31.

Mitchell, Daniel J., "The Grim Truth About Gramm-Rudman: The Deficit Law Is Working," *Policy Review*, Number 52 (Spring, 1990), pp. 76-79.

Moe, Ronald and Fisher, Louis, "Line-Item Imaginings," *The American Spectator*, Volume 21 (August, 1988), pp. 38-39.

Moore, Stephen, "Balancing Act," *National Review*, Volume XLIV (June 8, 1992), pp. 42-44.

Moore, Stephen, "All Pain, No Gain," *National Review*, Volume XLIII (September 9, 1991), pp. 33-35.

Moore, Stephen, "Reaganomics in Reverse," *National Review*, Volume XLIII (February 25, 1991), pp. 43-44.

Niskanen, William A., "The Uneasy Relation Between the Budget and Trade Deficits," With Comments by Gary Stern and John Williamson, *The Cato Journal*, Volume 8 (Fall, 1988), pp. 507-532.

Pitney, John J., Jr., "Budget Balancing Act: Would a Constitutional Convention Undo Everything ... or Accomplish Nothing?," *Reason*, Volume 20 (January, 1989), pp. 28-31.

Reynolds, Alan, "Public Works Won't Work," *National Review*, Volume XLV (March 15, 1993), pp. 50-51.

Rothbard, Murray N., "Repudiating the National Debt," *Chronicles*, Volume 16 (June, 1992), pp. 49-52.

Stein, Herbert, "The Next Trillion Dollars," *The American Enterprise*, Volume 2 (September/October, 1991), pp. 6-8.

White, Joseph and Wildavsky, Aaron, "How to Fix the Deficit - Really!," *The Public Interest*, Number 94 (Winter, 1989), pp. 3-24.

Wildavsky, Aaron, *The New Politics of the Budgetary Process* (New York: Harper Collins College, 1991).

Organizations

Citizens Against Government Waste 1301 Connecticut Avenue, NW, Suite 400, Washington, DC 20036, (202)-467-5300. Publications: *War on Waste Digest, Burning Money: The Waste of Your Tax Dollars*. Bipartisan organization that seeks to educate the public, individuals in public administration, and Congress on eliminating waste, mismanagement, and inefficiency in government spending.

FEDERAL BUREAU OF INVESTIGATION

Books and Articles

Kurins, Andris and O'Brien, Joseph F., *Boss of Bosses: The Fall of the Godfather: The FBI and Paul Castellano* (New York: Simon and Schuster, 1991).

Lamphere, Robert J. and Schachtman, Tom, *The FBI-KGB War: A Special Agent's Story* (New York: Random House, 1986).

Pistone, Joseph D. and Woodley, Richard, *Donnie Brasco: My Undercover Life in the Mafia* (New York: New American Library, 1987).

Welch, Neil J., and Marston, David W., *Inside Hoover's FBI: The Top Field Chief Reports* (New York: Doubleday, 1984).

FEDERAL BUREAUCRACY

Books and Articles

Lynch, Edward J., "Politics, Nonpartisanship, and the Public Service," *The Public Interest*, Number 98 (Winter, 1990), pp. 118-132.

Mills, Edwin, *The Burden of Government* (Stanford, CA: Hoover Institution Press, 1986).

Rector, Robert and Sanera, Michael, eds., *Steering the Elephant: How Washington Works* (New York: Universe Books, 1987).

Roche, George, *America by the Throat: The Stranglehold of Federal Bureaucracy* (Greenwich, CT: Devin-Adair, 1983).

FEDERAL DEFICIT
(see **Federal Budget**)

FEDERAL RESERVE
(see also **Banking/Banks, International Economy**)

Books and Articles

Coyne, Andrew, "Elect the Fed: The Vote Standard," *National Review*, Volume XLIII (June 10, 1991), pp. 23-29.

Friedman, Milton, *Money Mischief* (New York: Harcourt Brace Jovanovich, 1992).

FEDERALISM
(see also **American Government**)

Books and Articles

Aranson, Peter H., "Federalism: The Reasons of Rules," *The Cato Journal*, Volume 10 (Spring/Summer, 1990), pp. 17-38.

Berger, Raoul, *Federalism: The Founders' Design* (Norman, OK: University of Oklahoma Press, 1987).

Bryan, Frank, "Going It Alone: The Case for Vermont's Secession," *Chronicles,* Volume 15 (April, 1991), pp. 45-48.

Carey, George W., *The Federalist: Design for a Constitutional Republic* (Champaign, IL: University of Illinois Press, 1989).

Devine, Donald, "A Federalist Agenda: Some Advice for the Republicans," *Chronicles,* Volume 14 (May, 1990), pp. 21-24.

Moore, Stephen, "Reform Afoot," *National Review,* Volume XLIV (May 11, 1992), pp. 36-39.

Ornstein, Norman and Coursen, Kimberly, "As the World Turns Democratic, Federalism Finds Favor," *The American Enterprise*, Volume 3 (January/February, 1992), pp. 20-24.

Wildavsky, Aaron, "A Double Security: Federalism as Competition," *The Cato Journal,* Volume 10 (Spring/Summer, 1990), pp. 39-58.

FETAL TISSUE RESEARCH

Books and Articles

Fumento, Michael, "Fetal Attraction," *The American Spectator*, Volume 25 (July, 1992), pp. 30-36.

Ryskind, Rebecca, "Fatal Tissue: The Horror and the Lure," *The Human Life Review,* Volume 18 (Summer, 1992), pp. 27-34.

FIBER OPTICS
(see **Communications, Technology**)

FICTION
(see **Authors, Literature**)

FILM
(see **Movies**)

FIRST AMENDMENT

Books and Articles

Baer, Richard A., Jr., "Public Education as 'Brutal Censorship,'" *This World,*

Number 22 (Summer, 1988), pp. 110-115.

Berns, Walter, "Flag-Burning and Other Modes of Expression," *Commentary*, Volume 88 (October, 1989), pp. 37-41.

Costikyan, Greg, "Closing the Net: Will Overzealous Investigations of Computer Crime Render Freedom of the Press Obsolete?," *Reason*, Volume 22 (January, 1991), pp. 22-27.

Hazlett, Thomas W., "The Fairness Doctrine and the First Amendment," *The Public Interest*, Number 96 (Summer, 1989), pp. 103-116.

Himmelfarb, Gertrude, "The Right to Misquote," *Commentary*, Volume 91 (April, 1991), pp. 31-34.

Organizations

Libel Defense Resource Center 404 Park Avenue, South, 16th Floor, New York, NY 10016, (212)-889-2306. Publications: *Annual LDRC 50-State Survey of Current Developments in Media Libel and Invasion of Privacy Law*, *Bulletin*. Provides support for defendants in libel and privacy cases.

Rutherford Institute P.O. Box 7482, Charlottesville, VA 22906-7482, (804)-978-3888. Publications: *Rutherford Institute Action Newsletter*, *Rutherford Journal*. Provides legal services without charge to individuals whose First Amendment freedoms have been threatened by state action.

FLAGS

Organizations

Flag Research Center P.O. Box 580, Winchester, MA 01890, (617)-729-9410. Publications: *The Flag Bulletin*, *News from the Vexillarium*. Professional and amateur vexillologists seeking to coordinate flag research activities and promote vexillology as a historical discipline and hobby and to increase knowledge of and appreciation for flags of all kinds.

National Flag Foundation Flag Plaza, Pittsburgh, PA 15219-3630, (412)-261-1776. Publication: *Flag Plaza Standard*. Formed to further charitable, literary, educational, and patriotic purposes through research, scholarship, production, distribution, and promulgation of patriotic works of art and literature relating to the historic flags of the U.S. and their heritage.

FOOD STAMPS
(see **Hunger, Welfare**)

FOREIGN AID

Books and Articles

Bandow, Doug, "Foreign-Aid Addiction," *National Review*, Volume XLIV
(June 8, 1992), pp. 46, 61.
Bandow, Doug, "Foreign Aid Prescriptions," *The American Spectator*, Volume
19 (September, 1986), pp. 21-23.
Bauer, P. T., *Economic Analysis & Policy in Underdeveloped Countries*
(Westport, CT: Greenwood, 1982).
Bauer, P. T., *Equality, the Third World, and Economic Delusion* (Cambridge,
MA: Harvard University Press, 1981).
Bauer, P. T. *Reality and Rhetoric: Studies in the Economics of Development*
(Cambridge, MA: Harvard University Press, 1984).
Bauer, Peter, "Western Subsidies and Eastern Reform," Comment by Doug
Bandow, *The Cato Journal*, Volume 11 (Winter, 1992), pp. 343-353.
Eberstadt, Nicholas, "How Not to Aid Eastern Europe," *Commentary*, Volume
92 (November, 1991), pp. 24-30.
Hancock, Graham, *The Lords of Poverty: The Power, Prestige, and Corruption of
the International Aid Business* (New York: The Atlantic Monthly Press,
1989).
Krauss, Melvyn, *Development Without Aid: Growth, Poverty, and Government*
(New York: McGraw-Hill, 1983).
Lamm, Richard D., "The New Wealth of Nations," *Chronicles*, Volume 15
(October, 1991), pp. 25-27.
McKitterick, Nathaniel M., "The World Bank and the McNamara Legacy," *The
National Interest*, Number 4 (Summer, 1986), pp. 45-52.

FOREIGN INVESTMENT

Books and Articles

Dewald, William G. and Ulan, Michael, "Appreciating America's Foreign
Investments," *The American Enterprise*, Volume 1 (September/October,
1990), pp. 73-75.
Kelman, Steven, "The 'Japanization' of America?," *The Public Interest*, Number
98 (Winter, 1990), pp. 70-83.
Reynolds, Alan, "Put Money in Thy Purse: The Case for Foreign Investment,"
Chronicles, Volume 14 (January, 1990), pp. 22-24.
Stelzer, Irwin M., "Independence Day Blues," *The American Spectator*, Volume
22 (September, 1989), pp. 28-29.
Stelzer, Irwin M., "The Selling of America," *The American Spectator*, Volume
21 (June, 1988), pp. 35-36.

FOREIGN LANGUAGES
(see **Bilingual Education**)

FOREIGN POLICY
(see **U.S. Foreign Policy**)

FOSTER CARE
(see **Children**)

FOUNDATIONS

Books and Articles

Muravchik, Joshua, "MacArthur's Millions," *The American Spectator*, Volume 25 (January, 1992), pp. 34-41.

Nielson, Waldemar A., *The Golden Donors* (New York: Truman Talley Books/E.P. Dutton, 1985).

FRANCE

Books and Articles

Grenier, Richard, "The New Treason of the Clerks," *National Review*, Volume XLII (July 23, 1990), pp. 42-45.

Peyrefitte, Alain, *The Trouble with France* (New York: Knopf, 1981).

Schama, Simon, *Citizens: A Chronicle of the French Revolution* (New York: Knopf, 1989).

Sutton, Michael, *Nationalism, Positivism, and Catholicism: The Politics of Charles Maurras and French Catholics* (New York: Cambridge University Press, 1982).

FREEDOM OF INFORMATION

Books and Articles

Guida, Richard A., "The Costs of Free Information," *The Public Interest*, Number 97 (Fall, 1989), pp. 87-95.

Ledeen, Michael A., "Secrets," *The National Interest,* Number 10 (Winter 1987/8), pp. 48-55.

GENEALOGY

Organizations

Genealogical Institute P.O. Box 22045, Salt Lake City, UT 84122, (801)-257-6174. Publications: *Research News, Immigration Digest, Teaching Genealogy.* Publisher and distributor of genealogical how-to-do-it materials. Conducts training activities and client research.

GENETICS

Books and Articles

Bishop, Jerry E. and Waldholz, Michael, *Genome* (New York: Simon & Schuster, 1990).
Gallagher, Maggie, "Womb to Let," *National Review,* Volume XXXIV (April 24, 1987), pp. 27-30.
Gladwell, Malcolm, "Risk, Regulation, and Biotechnology," *The American Spectator,* Volume 22 (January, 1989), pp. 21-24.
Mueller, William, "Prometheus in Overalls," *Chronicles,* Volume 12 (December, 1988), pp. 53-55.
Neuhaus, Richard John, "The Return of Eugenics," *Commentary,* Volume 85 (April, 1988), pp. 15-26.

Organizations

Genetics Society of America 9650 Rockville Pike, Bethesda, MD 20814-3998, (301)-571-1825. Publications: *Genetics, Membership Directory, Supplement to Genetics, Career Opportunities in Genetics.* Individuals and organizations interested in any field of genetics.

GENOCIDE

Books and Articles

Browning, Christopher, *Ordinary Men: Reserve Police Battalion 101 and the Final Solution in Poland* (New York: Harper-Collins, 1992).

Dawidowicz, Lucy, *The Holocaust and the Historians* (Cambridge, MA: Harvard University Press, 1981).

Dawidowicz, Lucy, "How They Teach the Holocaust," *Commentary*, Volume 90 (December, 1990), pp. 25-32.

Dawidowicz, Lucy, "Perversions of the Holocaust," *Commentary*, Volume 88 (October, 1989), pp. 56-60.

Dawidowicz, Lucy, *From That Place and Time: A Memoir 1938 - 1947* (New York: Norton, 1989).

Kogon, Eugen, *The Theory and Practice of Hell* (New York: Farrar, Straus and Cudahy, 1950).

Levi, Primo, *Survival in Auschwitz* (New York: MacMillan, 1987).

Lukas, Richard C., *The Forgotten Holocaust: The Poles Under German Occupation 1939 - 1944* (Lexington, KY: University Press of Kentucky, 1986).

Maier, Charles S., *The Unmasterable Past: History, Holocaust, and German National Identity* (Cambridge, MA: Harvard University Press, 1988).

Mayer, Arno J., *Why Did the Heavens Not Darken? The "Final Solution" in History* (New York: Pantheon Books, 1988).

Muller, Jerry Z., "German Historians at War," *Commentary*, Volume 87 (May, 1989), pp. 33-41.

Rutherford, Ward, *Genocide: The Jews in Europe 1939-45* (New York: Ballantine Books, 1973).

Steiner, Jean-Francoise, *Treblinka* (New York: NAL-Dutton, 1968).

Watson, George, "Buchenwald's Second Life," *Chronicles,* Volume 13 (July, 1989), pp. 16-18.

GEOGRAPHY

Organizations

Association of American Geographers 1710 16th Street, NW, Washington, DC 20009, (202)-234-1450. Publications: *AAG Newsletter, Directory, Geography Department Guide, History of Geography Newsletter, Professional Geographer.* Seeks to further professional investigations in geography and to encourage the application of geographic research in education, government, and business.

GERMANY

Books and Articles

Bailey, George, *Germans: Biography of An Obsession* (New York: The Free Press, 1991).

Fest, Joachim, "The Silence of the Clerks," *National Review,* Volume XLII
　　(April 16, 1990), pp. 33-35.
Gedmin, Jeffrey, "Germany's Growing Pains," *The American Enterprise,*
　　Volume 3 (March/April, 1992), pp. 58-66.
Joffe, Josef, "One-and-a-Half Cheers for German Unification," *Commentary,*
　　Volume 89 (June, 1990), pp. 26-33.
Szamuely, George, "Germany Neither East Nor West," *The American Spectator,*
　　Volume 24 (March, 1991), pp. 16-19.

GOLD/GOLD STANDARD

Books and Articles

Friedman, Milton, et al., "As Good as Gold," *National Review,* Volume XLII
　　(June 11, 1990), pp. 28-35.
Friedman, Milton, *Money Mischief* (San Diego, CA: Harcourt Brace Jovanovich,
　　1992).
Lehrman, Lewis and Paul, Ron, *The Case for Gold: A Minority Report of the U.S.
　　Gold Commission* (Washington, DC: The Cato Institute, 1982).
Lehrman, Lewis, "An Exorbitant Privilege," *National Review,* Volume XXVIII
　　(November 21, 1986), pp. 40-46.
McKinnon, Ronald I., "An International Gold Standard without Gold,"
　　Comments by Rudiger Dornbusch and Robert E. Keleher, *The Cato
　　Journal,* Volume 8 (Fall, 1988), pp. 351-392.

GOVERNMENT AGENCIES
(see **Federal Bureaucracy**, **Municipal Government**)

GOVERNMENT AND THE ARTS

Books and Articles

Banfield, Edward C., *The Democratic Muse: Visual Arts and the Public Interest*
　　(New York: Basic Books, 1984).
Barlow, Janet Scott, "Letter from Cincinnati: Stranger in Paradise," *Chronicles,*
　　Volume 14 (October, 1990), pp. 46-49.
Berns, Walter, "Saving the N.E.A," *National Review,* Volume XLII (November
　　19, 1990), pp. 34-36.
Fleming, Thomas, "The Art of Revolution," *Chronicles,* Volume 14 (June,
　　1990), pp. 14-17.

Garrett, George, "Art Is Always Political When the Government Starts Giving Grants," *Chronicles,* Volume 14 (June, 1990), pp. 18-20.

Grampp, William D., *Pricing the Priceless: Art, Artists & Economics* (New York: Basic Books, 1989).

Grenier, Richard, "The Ecstasies of John Frohnmayer," *National Review,* Volume XLIV (August 3, 1992), pp. 36-37.

Hyde, Henry, "The Culture War," *National Review,* Volume XLII (April 30, 1990), pp. 25-27.

Lipman, Samuel, "Backward and Downward with the Arts," *Commentary,* Volume 89 (May, 1990), pp. 23-26.

Lipman, Samuel, "Can We Save Culture?," *National Review,* Volume XLIII (August 26, 1991), pp. 36-38.

Lipman, Samuel, "The New American Arts Order," *National Review,* Volume XLIII (February 11, 1991), pp. 39-40.

Molnar, Thomas, "Notes on Art Patronage," *Chronicles,* Volume 14 (March, 1990), pp. 53-54.

Neusner, Jacob, "The End of the N.E.A.," *National Review,* Volume XLIII (May 13, 1991), pp. 39-41.

Ryerson, Andre, "Abolish the NEA: Government Is Incapable of Detecting Artistic Genius," *Policy Review,* Number 54 (Fall, 1990), pp. 32-37.

GOVERNORS

Organizations

National Governors' Association Hall of States, 444 N. Capital Street, Suite 267, Washington, DC 20001, (202)-624-5300. Publications: *Capital Ideas, Current Developments in Employment and Training, Directory of Governors of the American States, Commonwealths, and Territories, Federal Funds Information for States Newsletter, Fiscal Survey of the States, Governors' Staff Directory, Governors' Weekly Bulletin, Labor Notes, Legisline, Policy Positions, Regsline.* Serves as vehicle through which governors influence the development and implementation of national policy and apply creative leadership to state problems.

GRAMMAR

Books and Articles

Barzun, Jacques and Graff, Henry F., *The Modern Researcher,* 5th ed. (Boston, MA: Houghton Mifflin, 1992).

Bridges, Linda and Rickenbacker, William F., *The Art of Persuasion: A National Review Rhetoric for Writers* (New York: National Review Books, 1992).

Kilpatrick, James J., *The Writer's Art* (Kansas City, MO: Andrews and McMeel, 1985).

Mitchell, Richard, *Less Than Words Can Say* (Boston, MA: Little, Brown, 1979).

Simon, John, *Paradigms Lost: Reflections on Literacy and Its Decline* (New York: Clarkson N. Potter, 1980).

Organizations

Society for the Preservation of English Language P.O. Box 118, Waleska, GA 30183. Publications: *Spell/Binder, SPELL Error-Avoidance Handbook*. Promotes the proper use of Standard English in schools and the mass media; encourages newspapers to improve their use of the language; strives to eliminate grammatical errors in print and on television and radio.

GUN CONTROL

Books and Articles

Austerman, Wayne R., "Those Deadly, Depressing, Syncopated Semi-automatic Assault Rifle Blues: An Exercise in Calculated Hysteria," *Chronicles,* Volume 13 (November, 1989), pp. 21-25.

Kates, Don B., Jr., and Harris, Patricia Terrell, "How to Make Their Day," *National Review,* Volume XLIII (October 21, 1991), pp. 30-32.

Kopel, David B., *The Samurai, the Mountie, and the Cowboy: Should America Adopt the Gun Controls of Other Democracies?* (Buffalo, NY: Prometheus Books, 1992).

Sullum, Jacob, "Gun-Shy Judges," *Reason,* Volume 23 (May, 1991), pp. 47-49.

Wright, James D. and Rossi, Peter H., *Armed and Considered Dangerous: A Survey of Felons and Their Firearms* (Hawthorne, NY: Aldine de Gruyter, 1986).

Wright, James D., "Guns and Sputter," *Reason,* Volume 21 (July, 1989), pp. 46-47.

Wright, James D., "In the Heat of the Moment," *Reason,* Volume 22 (August/September, 1990), pp. 44-45.

Wright, James D., "Second Thoughts About Gun Control," *The Public Interest*, Number 91 (Spring, 1988), pp. 23-39.

Wright, James D., et al., *Under the Gun: Weapons, Crime, and Violence in America* (Hawthorne, NY: Aldine de Gruyter, 1983).

Organizations

Citizens Committee for the Right to Keep and Bear Arms Liberty Park, 12500 N.E. Tenth Place, Bellevue, WA 98005, (206)-454-4911. Publications: *Point*

Blank, Our Vanishing Freedom, The Gun Owners Political Action Manual, The Rights of Gun Owners. Citizens interested in defending the Second Amendment.

National Association of Federally Licensed Firearms Dealers 2455 East Sunrise Boulevard, Suite 916, Ft. Lauderdale, FL 33304, (305)-561-3505. Publications: *AFI Shot Show Magazine, American Firearms Industry.* Provides firearm retailers with low-cost liability insurance, current information on new products for the industry, and retail business guidance.

National Rifle Association of America 1600 Rhode Island Avenue, NW, Washington, DC 20036, (202)-828-6000. Publications: *American Hunter, American Rifleman, Insights, Tournament News: The American Marksman, NRAction.* Promotes rifle, pistol, and shotgun shooting, hunting, gun collecting, home firearm safety, and wildlife conservation.

Second Amendment Foundation James Madison Building, 12500 N.E. Tenth Place, Bellevue, WA 98005, (206)-454-7012. Publications: *Gun Week, Monograph, Reporter.* Dedicated to promoting a better understanding of "our constitutional right to privately own and possess firearms."

HANDICAPPED
(see **Disabled**)

HEALTH CARE

Books and Articles

Arnett, Grace-Marie, "The Clinton Plan and Others," *National Review,* Volume XLV (May 24, 1993), pp. 30-34.

Baker, Charles D., "Do You Sincerely Want to Be Healthy?," *National Review,* Volume XLIII (June 24, 1991), pp. 32-36.

Baumol ,William J., "Containing Medical Costs: Why Price Controls Won't Work," *The Public Interest,* Number 93 (Fall, 1988), pp. 37-53.

Butler, Stuart, "Freeing Health Care," *National Review,* Volume XLI (December 22, 1989), pp. 34-36.

Christensen, Bryce J., "In Sickness and in Health: The Medical Costs of Family Meltdown," *Policy Review,* Number 60 (Spring, 1992), pp. 70-72.

Danzon, Patricia M., "Other Models and Hidden Costs," *The American Enterprise,* Volume 3 (January/February, 1992), pp. 71-75.

Docksai, Ronald F., "Putting the Patient First: A Kinder, Gentler Health System," *Policy Review,* Number 47 (Winter, 1989), pp. 74-80.

Eberstadt, Nicholas, "America's Infant Mortality Puzzle," *The Public Interest*, Number 105 (Fall, 1991), pp. 30-47.

Eberstadt, Nicholas, "Why Are so Many American Babies Dying?," *The American Enterprise*, Volume 2 (September/October, 1991), 37-45.

England, Robert S., "The Catastrophic Health Care Blunder," *The American Spectator*, Volume 21 (November, 1988), pp. 25-30.

Goodman, John C., "An Expensive Way to Die," *National Review*, Volume XLII (April 16, 1990), pp. 30-32.

Haislmaier, Edmund F., "Northern Discomfort: The Ills of the Canadian Health System," *Policy Review*, Number 58 (Fall, 1991), pp. 32-37.

Krasny, Jacques, "The Wrong Health-Care Model," *National Review*, Volume XLIV (February 17, 1992), pp. 43-44, 59.

Macrae, Norman, "The Good Health Guide," *National Review*, Volume XLIII (December 16, 1991), pp. 28-33.

Makin, John, "Runaway Health Care Costs," *The American Enterprise*, Volume 1 (January/February, 1990), pp. 52-57.

Meyer, Jack A., "Helping the Uninsured," *The American Enterprise*, Volume 1 (January/February, 1990), pp. 71-73.

Moore, William J. and Newman, Robert J., "Drug Restrictions and Medicaid Costs," *The American Enterprise*, Volume 1 (September/ October, 1990), pp. 76-78.

Morrisey, Michael A., "Mandates: What Most Proposals Would Do," *The American Enterprise*, Volume 3 (January/February, 1992), pp. 63-66.

Pauly, Mark, et al., "How We Can Get Responsible National Health Insurance: What Constitutes a Good Plan. What Present Proposals Lack," *The American Enterprise*, Volume 3 (July/August, 1992), pp. 61-69.

Pauly, Mark V., "Why Is American Health Care So Hard to Reform?," *The American Enterprise*, Volume 3 (January/February, 1992), pp. 60-63.

Prout, Curtis and Ross, Robert, *Care and Punishment: The Dilemma of Prison Medicine* (Pittsburgh, PA: University of Pittsburgh Press, 1988).

Samuel, Peter, "Health-Reform Politics," *National Review*, Volume XLV (May 24, 1993), pp. 34-37.

Santerre, Rexford E., et al., "Government Intervention in Health Care Markets and Health Care Outcomes: Some International Evidence," *The Cato Journal*, Volume 11 (Spring/Summer, 1991), pp. 1-12.

Schambra, William A., "Health Care Blues: And an Ancient Remedy," *Crisis*, Volume 10 (March, 1992), pp. 23-28.

Schwartz, Harry, "The Right Medicine," *National Review*, Volume XLI (March 10, 1989), pp. 26-29.

Seidman, Laurence S., "Reconsidering National Health Insurance," *The Public Interest*, Number 101 (Fall, 1990), pp. 78-88.

Steuerle, C. Eugene, "The Search for a Better Approach," *The American Enterprise*, Volume 3 (January/February, 1992), pp. 67-70.

Sullum, Jacob, "Market Medicine: We Don't Have It. But We Could," *Reason*, Volume 23 (March, 1992), pp. 23-27.

Walker, Michael, "Cold Reality: How They Don't Do It in Canada," *Reason*, Volume 23 (March, 1992), pp. 35-39.
Warshawsky, Mark J., "Retiree Health Benefits: Promises Uncertain?," *The American Enterprise*, Volume 2 (July/August, 1991), pp. 57-63.

HEALTH INSURANCE
(see **Health Care**)

HIGHWAYS

Books and Articles

Hulten, Charles R., "Getting on the Right Road: Highway Policy in the 1990s," *The American Enterprise*, Volume 2 (May/June, 1991), pp. 39-43.
Samuel, Peter, "Private Extension," *Reason*, Volume 21 (January, 1990), pp. 46-47.

HISPANICS

Books and Articles

Chavez, Linda, "Hispanics vs. Their Leaders," *Commentary*, Volume 92 (October, 1991), pp. 47-49.
Chavez, Linda, *Out of the Barrio: Toward a New Politics of Hispanic Assimilation* (New York: Basic Books, 1991).
Estrada, Richard, "From El Paso to Plymouth: Hispanic Contributions to American Culture," *Chronicles*, Volume 16 (April, 1992), pp. 18-20.
Gann, Lewis H. and Duignan, Peter J., *The Hispanics in the United States: A History* (Stanford, CA: Hoover Institution Press, 1986).
Nelson, B. A., *The Coming Triumph of Mexican Irredentism* (Monterey, VA: American Immigration Control Foundation, 1984).
Porter, Rosalie Pedalino, "Language Choice for Latino Students," *The Public Interest*, Number 105 (Fall, 1991), pp. 48-60.
Skerry, Peter, "Hispanic Dropouts: A Social Problem, a Political Cause?," *The American Enterprise*, Volume 1 (July/August, 1990), pp. 20-21.
Skerry, Peter, *Mexican Americans: The Reshaping of the American Dream* (New York: The Free Press, 1992).
Skerry, Peter, "On Edge: Blacks and Mexicans in Los Angeles," *The American Spectator*, Volume 21 (May, 1988), pp. 16-18.
Vargas Llosa, Mario, "The Miami Model," *Commentary*, Volume 93 (February, 1992), pp. 21-27.

HISTORIOGRAPHY

Books and Articles

Barzun, Jacques, *Clio and the Doctors: History, Psycho-History, and Quanto-History* (Chicago, IL: University of Chicago Press, 1974).

Cantor, Norman F., *Inventing the Middle Ages: The Lives, Works, and Ideas of the Great Medievalists of the Twentieth Century* (New York: William Morrow, 1991).

Clive, John, *Not by Fact Alone: Essays on the Writing and Reading of History* (Boston, MA: Houghton Mifflin, 1989).

Conquest, Robert, "History, Humanity, and Truth," *National Review*, Volume XLV (June 7, 1993), pp. 28-35.

Dawidowicz, Lucy, "How They Teach the Holocaust," *Commentary*, Volume 90 (December, 1990), pp. 25-32.

Gottfried, Paul, "What Ails the Historical Profession?," *Chronicles*, Volume 12 (December, 1988), pp. 17-20.

Himmelfarb, Gertrude, *The New History and the Old* (Cambridge, MA: Harvard University Press, 1987).

Himmelfarb, Gertrude, "Of Heroes, Villans, and Valets," *Commentary*, Volume 91 (June, 1991), pp. 20-26.

Horgan, Paul, *A Certain Climate: Essays on History, Arts, and Letters* (Middletown, CT: Wesleyan University, Press, 1988).

Johnston, J. F., Jr., "Decadence Revisited," *Modern Age*, Volume 33 (Spring, 1990), pp. 23-32.

Kagan, Donald, "The First Revisionist Historian," *Commentary*, Volume 85 (May, 1988), pp. 43-49.

Momigliano, Arnaldo, *The Classical Foundations of Modern Historiography* (Berkeley, CA: University of California Press, 1990).

Muller, Jerry Z., "German Historians at War," *Commentary*, Volume 87 (May, 1989), pp. 33-41.

Ortega y Gasset, Jose, *Man and Crisis* (New York: W. W. Norton, 1958).

Plumb, J. H., *The Collected Essays of J. H. Plumb, Vol. I: The Making of an Historian* (Athens, GA: University of Georgia Press, 1989).

Schram, Glenn N., "Western Civilization in the Light of the Philosophy of History," *Modern Age*, Volume 33 (Fall, 1990), pp. 249-258.

HISTORY

Books and Articles

Bloom, Allan, et al., "Responses to Fukuyama," *The National Interest*, Number 16 (Summer, 1989), pp. 19-35.

Burckhardt, Jacob, *On History and Historians* (New York: Harper Torchbooks, 1965).

Falcoff, Mark, "Was 1492 a Mistake? Did Columbus Go Too Far?," *The American Enterprise*, Volume 3 (January/February, 1992), pp. 38-47.

Feur, Lewis, S., *Imperialism and the Anti-Imperialist Mind* (Buffalo, NY: Prometheus Books, 1986).

Fraser, George MacDonald, *The Hollywood History of the World: From "One Million Years B.C." to "Apocalypse Now"* (Holt, MI: Beech Tree Press, 1988).

Fukuyama, Francis, "The End of History?," *The National Interest*, Number 16 (Summer, 1989), pp. 3-18.

Fukuyama, Francis, "A Reply to My Critics," *The National Interest*, Number 18 (Winter, 1989/90), pp. 21-28.

Fuller, Timothy, et al., "More Responses to Fukuyama," *The National Interest*, Number 17 (Fall, 1989), pp. 93-100.

Fussell, Paul, *Thank God for the Atom Bomb and Other Essays* (New York: Summit Books, 1988).

Gottfried, Paul, "*Quis Judicabit:* Have We Reached the End of History, Or Just the End of Historical Knowledge?," *Chronicles*, Volume 14 (February, 1990), pp. 16-18.

Howard, Michael, *The Lessons of History* (New Haven, CT: Yale University Press, 1991).

Huntington, Samuel P., "No Exit: The Errors of Endism," *The National Interest*, Number 17 (Fall, 1989), pp. 3-11.

Johnson, Paul, *Intellectuals* (New York: Harper & Row, 1988).

Laqueur, Walter, *Europe In Our Time: A History, 1945 - 1992* (New York: Viking Press, 1992).

Lukacs, John, *Confessions of an Original Sinner* (New York: Ticknor and Fields, 1990).

Nisbet, Robert, *History of the Idea of Progress* (New York: Basic Books, 1980).

Oakeshott, Michael, *On History and Other Essays* (New York: Barnes and Noble, 1983).

Plumb, J. H., *Men and Centuries* (Boston, MA: Houghton Mifflin, 1963).

Taylor, A. J. P., *From Napoleon to Lenin: Historical Essays* (New York: Harper Torchbooks, 1966).

Taylor, A. J. P., *Politicians, Socialism, and Historians* (New York: Stein and Day, 1981).

Thomas, Hugh, *A History of the World* (New York: Harper & Row, 1979).

Wedgwood, C . V., *The Spoils of Time: A World History from the Dawn of Civilization Through the Early Renaissance* (New York: Doubleday, 1985).

Wilford, John Noble, *The Mapmakers: The Story of the Great Pioneers in Cartography From Antiquity to the Space Age* (New York: Knopf, 1981).

HISTORY, ANCIENT

Books and Articles

Andrewes, Antony, *The Greek Tyrants* (New York: Harper Torchbooks, 1963).

Brunt, P. A., *Social Conflicts in the Roman Republic* (New York: W. W. Norton, 1971).

Cowell, F. R., *Life in Ancient Rome* (Toronto: General Publishing Co., Ltd., 1988).

Eckstein, Arthur M., *Senate and General: Individual Decision Making and Roman Foreign Relations 264 - 194 B.C.* (Berkeley, CA: University of California Press, 1987).

Ferrill, Arther, *The Fall of the Roman Empire: The Military Explanation* (New York: Thames and Hudson, 1986).

Grant, Michael, *The Founders of the Western World: A History of Greece and Rome* (New York: Scribner's, 1991).

Grant, Michael, *From Alexander to Cleopatra: The Hellenistic World* (New York: Simon and Schuster, 1982).

Hamilton, Edith, *The Greek Way* (New York: W. W. Norton, 1983).

Hamilton, Edith, *The Roman Way* (New York: W.W. Norton, 1984).

Kagan, Donald, *The Archidamian War* (Ithaca, NY: Cornell University Press, 1990).

Kagan, Donald, *The Fall of the Athenian Empire* (Ithaca, NY: Cornell University Press, 1987).

Kagan, Donald, "The First Revisionist Historian," *Commentary*, Volume 85 (May, 1988), pp. 43-49.

Kagan, Donald, *The Outbreak of the Peloponnesian War* (Ithaca, NY: Cornell University Press, 1969).

Kagan, Donald, *The Peace of Nicias and the Sicilian Expedition* (Ithaca, NY: Cornell University Press, 1981).

Kagan, Donald, *Pericles of Athens and the Birth of Democracy* (New York: The Free Press, 1990).

Oliphant, Margaret, *The Atlas of the Ancient World: Charting the Great Civilizations of the Past* (New York: Simon and Schuster, 1992).

Tarnas, Richard, *The Passion of the Western Mind: Understanding the Ideas that Have Shaped Our World View* (New York: Crown, 1991).

Wilken, Robert, *The Christians as the Romans Saw Them* (New Haven, CT: Yale University Press, 1984).

HISTORY, DARK AGES

Books and Articles

Asser, et al., *Alfred the Great: Asser's Life of King Alfred and Other Contemporary Sources* (New York: Penguin Books, 1983).

Blair, Peter Hunter, *An Introduction to Roman Britain and Early England 55 B.C. to A.D. 871* (New York: Norton, 1966).

Dixon, Philip, *Barbarian Europe* (Oxford, England: Elsevier-Phaidon, 1976).

Duckett, Eleanor Shipley, *Alfred the Great: The King and His England* (Chicago, IL: University of Chicago Press, 1958).

Fichtenau, Heinrich, *The Carolingian Empire*, Peter Munz, trans. (Toronto: University of Toronto Press, 1968).

Ganshof, Francois Louis, *Frankish Institutions Under Charlemagne* (New York: Norton, 1970).

Hodges, Richard, *Dark Age Economics: The Origins of Towns and Trade A.D. 600 - 1000* (New York: St. Martin's Press, 1982).

Morris, John, *The Age of Arthur: A History of the British Isles from 350 - 650* (New York: Scribner's, 1973).

Munz, Peter, *Life In the Age of Charlemagne* (New York: Capricorn Books, 1971).

Riche, Pierre, *Daily Life in the World of Charlemagne* (Philadelphia, PA: University of Pennsylvania Press, 1978).

Wallace-Hadrill, J. M., *The Barbarian West: The Early Middle Ages A.D. 400 - 1000* (New York: Harper Torchbooks, 1962).

HISTORY, MEDIEVAL

Books and Articles

Barber, Richard, *The Knight and Chivalry* (New York: Harper Colophon Books, 1974).

Barraclough, Geoffrey, trans., *Medieval Germany, 950 to 1250: Essays by German Historians*, 2 Vols. (New York: AMS Press, 1938).

Barraclough, Geoffrey, *The Origins of Modern Germany* (New York: W. W. Norton, 1984).

Bloch, Marc, *Land and Work in Medieval Europe* (New York: Harper Torchbooks, 1969).

Brewer, Derek, *Chaucer in His Time* (London: Thomas Nelson and Sons, 1963).

Brooke, Rosalind and Brooke, Christopher, *Popular Religion in the Middle Ages* (New York: Thames and Hudson, 1984).

Cantor, Norman F., *Inventing the Middle Ages: The Lives, Works, and Ideas of the Great Medievalists of the Twentieth Century* (New York: William Morrow, 1991).

Cantor, Norman, *Medieval History: The Life and Death of a Civilization*, 2nd ed. (New York: Macmillan, 1969).

Chambers, James, *The Devil's Horsemen: The Mongol Invasion of Europe* (New York: Atheneum, 1979).

Contamine, Philippe, *War in the Middle Ages* (New York: Basil Blackwell, 1984).

Curtius, Ernst Robert, *European Literature and the Latin Middle Ages* (Princeton, NJ: Princeton University Press, 1990).

Daly, L. J., *The Medieval University 1200 - 1400* (New York: Sheed and Ward, 1962).

Dawson, Christopher, *Medieval Religion and Other Essays* (London: Sheed and Ward, 1934).

Duby, Georges, *A History of Private Life Vol. II: Revelations of the Medieval World* (Cambridge, England: The Belknap Press of Harvard University Press, 1988).

Duby, Georges, *William Marshal: The Flower of Chivalry* (New York: Pantheon Books, 1985).

Fletcher, Richard, *The Quest for El Cid* (New York: Knopf, 1989).

Furhrmann, Horst, *Germany in the High Middle Ages,* Timothy Reuter, trans. (New York: Cambridge University Press, 1986).

Ganshof, F. L., *Feudalism,* Philip Grierson, trans. (New York: Harper Torchbooks, 1961).

Gillingham, John, *The Life and Times of Richard I* (London: Weidenfeld and Nicolson, 1973).

Gillingham, John, *The Wars of the Roses: Peace and Conflict in Fifteenth Century England* (Baton Rouge, LA: Louisiana State University Press, 1981).

Gilson, Etienne, *Reason and Revelation in the Middle Ages* (New York: Scribner's, 1938).

Gimpel, Jean, *The Medieval Machine: The Industrial Revolution of the Middle Ages* (New York: Penguin Books, 1976).

Gottfried, Robert S., *The Black Death: Natural and Human Disaster in Medieval Europe* (New York: The Free Press, 1983).

Haskins, Charles Homer, *Norman Institutions* (Cambridge, MA: Harvard University Press, 1918).

Haskins, Charles Homer, *The Rise of Universities* (Ithaca, NY: Cornell University Press, 1957).

Heer, Friedrick, *The Medieval World: Europe Eleven Hundred to Thirteen Fifty* (New York: George Weidenfeld and Nicolson, 1961).

Hogue, Arthur R., *Origins of the Common Law* (Indianapolis, IN: Liberty Press, 1986).

Holmes, George, ed., *The Oxford Illustrated History of Medieval Europe* (New York: Oxford University Press, 1988).

Howard, Donald R., *Chaucer: His Life, His Works, His World* (New York: Dutton, 1987).

Howarth, David, *1066: The Year of the Conquest* (New York: Viking, 1978).

Huizinga, Johan, *The Waning of the Middle Ages: A Study of Forms of Life, Thought, and Art in France and the Netherlands in the XIVth and XVth Centuries* (New York: St. Martin's Press, 1969).

Kantorowicz, Ernst H., *Frederick the Second, 1194 - 1250,* E. O. Lorimer, trans. (New York: F. Ungar, 1967).

Keen, Maurice, *Chivalry* (New Haven, CT: Yale University Press, 1984).

Keen, Maurice, *A History of Medieval Europe* (New York: Praeger, 1967).

Kieckhefer, Richard, *Repression of Heresy in Medieval Germany* (Liverpool, England: Liverpool University Press, 1978).

Knowles, David, *The Evolution of Medieval Thought,* D. E. Luscombe and C. N. L. Brooke, eds. (New York: Longman, 1988).

Koch, H. W., *Medieval Warfare* (New York: Crescent Books, 1983).

Lewis, C. S., *The Discarded Image: An Introduction to Medieval and Renaissance Literature* (Cambridge, England: Cambridge University Press, 1968).

McCall, Andrew, *The Medieval Underworld* (London: Hamish Hamilton, 1979).

Matthews, William, *The Ill-Framed Knight: A Skeptical Inquiry into the Identity of Sir Thomas Malory* (Berkeley, CA: University of California Press, 1966).

Newark, Timothy, *Medieval Warfare* (London: Bloomsbury Books, 1988).

Platt, Colin, *The Atlas of Medieval Man* (New York: St. Martin's Press, 1979).

Pollack, Frederick and Maitland, William Frederick, *The History of English Law Before the Time of Edward I,* 2 Vols. (London: Cambridge University Press, 1968).

Power, Eileen, *Medieval People* (New York: Barnes and Noble, 1963).

Prestwich, Michael, *The Three Edwards: War and State in England, 1272 - 1377* (London: Weidenfeld and Nicolson, 1980).

Rorig, Fritz, *The Medieval Town* (Berkeley, CA: University of California Press, 1967).

Ross, Charles, *The War of the Roses* (New York: Thames and Hudson, 1977).

Runciman, Steven, *A History of the Crusades,* 3 Vols. (New York: Cambridge University Press, 1980).

Russell, Jeffrey Burton, *Witchcraft in the Middle Ages* (Ithaca, NY: Cornell University Press, 1972).

Seward, Desmond, *The Hundred Years War: The English in France, 1337 - 1453* (New York: Atheneum, 1978).

Smail, R. C., *The Crusaders in Syria and the Holy Land* (London: Thames and Hudson, 1973).

Southern, R. W., *The Making of the Middle Ages* (New Haven, CT: Yale University Press, 1953).

Southern, R. W., *Western Society and the Church in the Middle Ages* (New York: Penguin, 1970).

Strayer, Joseph R., *On the Medieval Origins of the Modern State* (Princeton, NJ: Princeton University Press, 1972).

Strayer, Joseph R., *Western Europe in the Middle Ages* (Prospect Heights, IL: Waveland Press, 1991).

Trevor-Roper, Hugh, *The Rise of Christian Europe* (New York: Harcourt Brace and World, 1965).

Vinogradoff, Paul, *Roman Law in Medieval Europe,* 3rd ed. (Oxford, England: Oxford University Press, 1961).

Warren, W. L., *Henry II* (Berkeley, CA: University of California Press, 1973).

White, Lynn, Jr., *Medieval Technology and Social Change* (New York: Oxford University Press, 1962).

Woods, William, *England in the Age of Chaucer* (Briarcliff Manor, NY: Stein and Day, 1976).

HISTORY, 16TH CENTURY

Books and Articles

Elton, G. R., *Reformation Europe 1517 - 1559* (New York: Harper Torchbooks, 1963).

Graham, Winston, *The Spanish Armadas* (Garden City, NY: Doubleday, 1972).

Huizinga, Johan, *Erasmus and the Age of Reformation* (New York: Harper Torchbooks, 1957).

Johnson, Paul, *Elizabeth I* (London: Weidenfeld and Nicolson, 1974).

Mattingly, Garrett, *The Armada* (Boston, MA: American Heritage Library, 1959).

Plumb, J. H., *The Italian Renaissance* (New York: Harper Torchbooks, 1965).

Sugden, John, *Sir Francis Drake* (New York: Simon and Schuster, 1990).

HISTORY, 17TH CENTURY

Books and Articles

Carr, John Laurence, *Life in France Under Louis XIV* (New York: Capricorn/G.P. Putnam's Sons, 1970).

Schama, Simon, *The Embarassment of Riches: An Interpretation of Dutch Culture in the Golden Age* (New York: Knopf, 1987).

Trevelyan, G. M., *The English Revolution, 1688 - 1689* (London: Oxford University Press, 1938).

Wedgwood, C. V., *The Thirty Years War* (New York: Doubleday/Anchor, 1961).

Wedgwood, C. V., *A Coffin for King Charles: The Trial and Execution of Charles I* (New York: Time-Life Books, 1966).

HISTORY, 18th CENTURY

Books and Articles

Acton, John Emerich Edward Dalberg, *Lectures on the French Revolution* (New York: Noonday Press, 1969).

Cooper, Duff, *Talleyrand* (London, England: Jonathan Cape, 1932).

Cranston, Maurice, "Should We Celebrate the French Revolution?," *The American Spectator*, Volume 22 (June, 1989), pp. 15-17.

Fleming, Thomas, "The Legacy of 1789," *Chronicles*, Volume 13 (June, 1989), pp. 10-12.

Gress, David, "Demystifying the French Revolution," *Commentary*, Volume 88 (July, 1989), pp. 42-49.

Hancock, Ralph C., "Robespierre and the Rights of Man: The Terror of 1793 Sprang from the Theories of 1789," *Policy Review*, Number 49 (Summer, 1989), pp. 38-44.

Jarrett, Derek, *England in the Age of Hogarth* (New Haven, CT: Yale University Press, 1976).

Molnar, Thomas, "The French Revolution: Two Centuries After," *This World*, Number 26 (Summer, 1989), pp. 116-124.

Molnar, Thomas, "New Thoughts on the French Revolution," *Chronicles*, Volume 13 (June, 1989), pp. 48-50.

O'Brien, Conor Cruise, "A Vindication of Edmund Burke," *National Review*, Volume XLII (December 17, 1990), pp. 28-35.

Plumb, J. H., *England in the Eighteenth Century, 1714 - 1815* (New York: Penguin Books, 1963).

Prebble, John, *Culloden* (New York: Penguin Books, 1967).

Schama, Simon, *Citizens: A Chronicle of the French Revolution* (New York: Knopf, 1989).

Schama, Simon, *Patriots and Liberators: Revolution in the Netherlands 1780 - 1813* (New York: Knopf, 1977).

Stanlis, Peter J., "A True Vindication of Edmund Burke," *Chronicles*, Volume 15 (May, 1991), pp. 51-54.

Tonsor, Stephen, ed., *Reflections on the French Revolution: A Hillsdale Symposium* (Washington, DC: Regnery Gateway, 1990).

Watson, George, "The Cost of Revolution: England and 1789," *Chronicles*, Volume 13 (June, 1989), pp. 14-18.

HISTORY, 19TH CENTURY

Books and Articles

Ackroyd, Peter, *Dickens* (New York: Harper Collins, 1990).

De Segur, Phillippe Paul, *Napoleon's Russian Campaign* (New York: Time Incorporated, 1958).

Erickson, Carolly, *Our Tempestuous Day: A History of Regency England* (New York: William Morrow, 1986).

Farwell, Byron, *Queen Victoria's Little Wars* (New York: Harper and Row, 1973).

Himmelfarb, Gertrude, *Marriage and Morals Among the Victorians* (New York: Knopf, 1986).

Himmelfarb, Gertrude, *Poverty and Compassion: The Moral Imagination of the Late Victorians* (New York: Knopf, 1991).

Mayhew, Henry, *Mayhew's London,* Peter Quennell, ed. (London: Bracken Books, 1984).

HOME SCHOOLING

Books and Articles

Pride, Mary, *The Big Book of Home Learning: The Complete Guide to Everything Educational for You and Your Children* (Westchester, IL: Crossway Books, 1987).

Pride, Mary, *The New Big Book of Home Learning: The Basic Guide to Everything Educational for You and Your Children* (Westchester, IL: Crossway Books, 1988).

Pride, Mary, *The Next Book of Home Learning: Everything Enriching for You and Your Children* (Westchester, IL: Crossway Books, 1987).

Seuffert, Virginia, "Home Remedy: A Mom's Prescription for Ailing Schools," *Policy Review*, Number 52 (Spring, 1990), pp. 70-75.

Organizations

Home School Legal Defense Association P.O. Box 159, Paeonian Springs, VA 22129, (703)-882-3838. Publications: *The Home School Court Report, Home School Chart of the 50 States.* Provides legal assistance to families whose attempts to educate their children at home are challenged by state government or the local school board.

National Association for Legal Support of Alternative Schools P.O. Box 2823, Santa Fe, NM 87501, (505)-471-6928. Publication: *National Association for the Legal Support of Alternative Schools - Tidbits.* National information and legal service center designed to research, coordinate, and support legal actions involving nonpublic educational alternatives.

Seton Home Study School 1350 Progress Drive, Front Royal, VA 22630, (703)-636-9990. Publication: *The Seton Home Study Newsletter.* Catholic home schooling organization.

HOMELESSNESS

Books and Articles

Bethell, Tom, "Mitch Snyder's Sendoff," *The America Spectator*, Volume 23 (September, 1990), pp. 9-11.

Ellickson, Robert C., "The Homelessness Muddle," *The Public Interest*, Number 99 (Spring, 1990), pp. 45-60.

Horowitz, Carl F., "Mitch Snyder's Phony Numbers: The Fiction of Three Million Homeless," *Policy Review*, Number 49 (Summer, 1989), pp. 66-69.

Isaac, Rael Jean and Armat, Virginia C., *Madness in the Streets: How Psychiatry and the Law Abandoned the Mentally Ill* (New York: The Free Press, 1990).

McMurry, Dan, "Down and Out in America: A Sociologist Lives Among the Homeless and Returns with a Surprising Tale," *Crisis*, Volume 7 (February, 1989), pp. 27-31.

McMurry, Dan, "The Myth of the Homeless Family," *Chronicles*, Volume 14 (October, 1990), pp. 52-54.

Main, Thomas J., "What We Know About the Homeless," *Commentary*, Volume 85 (May, 1988), pp. 26-31.

Rossi, Peter H., *Down and Out in America: The Origins of Homelessness* (Chicago, IL: University of Chicago Press, 1989).

Schiff, Laurence, "Would They Be Better Off in a Home?," *National Review*, Volume XLII (March 5, 1990), pp. 33-35.

Torrey, E. Fuller, *Nowhere to Go: The Tragic Odyssey of the Homeless Mentally Ill* (New York: Harper & Row, 1988).

Torrey, E. Fuller, "Who Goes Homeless?," *National Review*, Volume XLIII (August 26, 1991), pp. 34-36.

Tucker, William, *The Excluded Americans: Homelessness and Housing Policies* (Washington, DC: Regnery Gateway, 1989).

Tucker, William, "Homeless People, Peopleless Homes," *The American Spectator*, Volume 20 (February, 1987), pp. 18-21.

Tucker, William, "How Housing Regulations Cause Homelessness," *The Public Interest*, Number 102 (Winter, 1991), pp. 78-88.

Tucker, William, "Visits with the Homeless," *The American Spectator*, Volume 18 (May, 1985), pp. 10-13.

Tucker, William, "Where Do the Homeless Come From?," *National Review*, Volume XXXIX (September 25, 1987), pp. 32-43.

van den Haag, Ernest, "Who Goes Homeless?," *National Review*, Volume XLV (March 1, 1993), pp. 49-50.

White, Richard W., *Rude Awakenings: What the Homeless Crisis Tells Us* (San Francisco, CA: Institute for Contemporary Studies, 1992).

Organizations

Manhattan Institute for Policy Research 52 Vanderbilt Avenue, New York, NY 10017, (212)-599-7000. Publication: *City Journal*. Purpose is to assist scholars, government officials, and the public in obtaining a better understanding of economic processes and the effect of government programs on the economic situation.

HOMOSEXUALS
(see also **Acquired Immune Deficiency Syndrome**)

Books and Articles

Bacevich, A. J., "Gays and Military Culture," *National Review*, Volume XLV (April 26, 1993), pp. 26-31.

Fumento, Michael, "How Many Gays?," *National Review*, Volume XLV (April 26, 1993), pp. 28-29.

Goldberg, Steven, "What Is Normal?," *National Review*, Volume XLIV (February 3, 1992), pp. 36-39.

Grenier, Richard, "The Homosexual Millenium: Is It Here? Is It Approaching?," *National Review*, Volume XLV (June 7, 1993), pp. 52-56.

Guay, Paul Edward, "Setting Freud Straight: Homosexuality as Repressed Friendship," *Crisis*, Volume 8 (May, 1990), pp. 27-31.

Klingeman, Henry, "Anonymous Sex," *National Review*, Volume XXXIX (June 19, 1987), pp. 42-43.

Levine, Edward M., "Homosexuality and the Family," *Chronicles*, Volume 12 (July, 1988), pp. 21-22.

Magnuson, Roger J., *Are Gay Rights Right?* (Minneapolis, MN: Straitgate Press, 1985).

Pattullo, E. L., "Why Not Gays in the Military?," *National Review*, Volume XLV (March 1, 1993), p. 38-41.

Rueda, Enrique, *The Homosexual Network: Private Lives and Public Policy* (Greenwich, CT: Devin-Adair, 1982).

Short, Thomas, "Gay Rights or Closet Virtues?," *National Review*, Volume XLII (September 17, 1990), pp. 43-44.

Teachout, Terry, "Gay Rights and Straight Realities," *National Review*, Volume XXXV (November 11, 1983), pp. 1408-1412, 1433.

Thompson, John B., "The Link Line: The Art of Indoctrination," *Chronicles*, Volume 15 (December, 1991), pp. 43-46.

Van den Aardweg, Gerard, *Homosexuality and Hope: A Psychologist Talks About Treatment and Change* (Ann Arbor, MI: Servant Publications, 1985).

van den Haag, Ernest, "Sodom and Begorrah," *National Review*, Volume XLIII (April 29, 1991), pp. 35-38.

"Woolman, John," "Letter From a Friend: A Conservative Speaks Out for Gay Rights," *National Review*, Volume XXXVIII (September 12, 1986), pp. 28-31, 58-59.

Organizations

Aesthetic Realism Foundation 141 Greene Street, New York, NY 10012, (212)-777-4490. Publications: *The Right of Aesthetic Realism to Be Known, The Aesthetic Realism of Eli Siegel and the Change from Homosexuality.* Purpose is to teach Aesthetic Realism, the philosophy founded in 1941 by poet and critic Eli Siegel. Aesthetic Realism is defined as "the art of liking the world and oneself at the same time by seeing the world and oneself as aesthetic opposites." Conducts class on changing one's sexual affiliation from homosexuality to heterosexuality.

HONG KONG
(see **China**)

HOUSE OF REPRESENTATIVES, U.S.
(see **Congress**)

HOUSING

Books and Articles

Fuerst, J. S. and Petty, Roy, "High-Rise Housing for Low-Income Families,"
    The Public Interest, Number 103 (Spring, 1991), pp. 118-130.
Husock, Howard, "Mocking the Middle Class: The Perverse Effects of Housing
    Subsidies," *Policy Review,* Number 56 (Spring, 1991), pp. 65-69.
Husock, Howard, "Rediscovering the Three-Decker House," *The Public
    Interest,* Number 98 (Winter, 1990), pp. 49-60.
McWilliams, Rita, "Revolution in the Projects," *Reason,* Volume 20 (July,
    1988), pp. 24-30.
Messenger, Paul H., "Public Housing Perversity: A View From the Trenches,"
    The Public Interest, Number 108 (Summer, 1992), pp. 132-143.
Tucker, William, "The Economics of Public Housing," *The American Spectator,*
    Volume 22 (November, 1989), pp. 26-29.
Tucker, William, *The Excluded Americans: Homelessness and Housing Policies*
    (Washington, DC: Regnery Gateway, 1990).
Tucker, William, "It's a Rotten Life: Rent Control and the Loss of Civility,"
    Reason, Volume 20 (February, 1989), pp. 22-26.
Tucker, William, "Pity the New York Landlord," *The American Spectator,*
    Volume 22 (February, 1989), pp. 19-22.
Weber, Peter, "Scenes from the Squatting Life," *National Review,* Volume
    XXXIX (February 27, 1987), pp. 28-32.

Welfeld, Irving, "Our Nonexistent Housing Crisis," *The Public Interest*, Number 101 (Fall, 1990), pp. 55-61.

Welfeld, Irving, "Poor Tenants, Poor Landlords, Poor Policy," *The Public Interest*, Number 92 (Summer, 1988), pp. 110-121.

Organizations

Manhattan Institute for Policy Research 52 Vanderbilt Avenue, New York, NY 10017, (212)-599-7000. Publication: *City Journal*. Purpose is to assist scholars, government officials, and the public in obtaining a better understanding of economic processes and the effect of government programs on the economic situation.

HUMAN RIGHTS

Books and Articles

Barrett, William, et al., "Human Rights and American Foreign Policy: A Symposium," *Commentary*, Volume 72 (November, 1981), pp. 25-63.

Fleming, Thomas, "The Dangerous Myth of Human Rights," *Chronicles*, Volume 12 (December, 1988), pp. 6-8.

Kristol, Irving, "'Human Rights': The Hidden Agenda," *The National Interest*, Number 6 (Winter, 1986/87), pp. 3-11.

Muravchik, Joshua, *The Uncertain Crusade: Jimmy Carter and the Dilemmas of Human Rights Policy* (Lanham, MD: Hamilton Press, 1986).

Orwin, Clifford and Pangle, Thomas L., "Restoring the Human Rights Tradition," *This World*, Number 3 (Fall, 1982), pp. 21-41.

Veatch, Henry B., *Human Rights: Fact or Fancy?* (Baton Rouge, LA: Louisiana State University Press, 1985).

Organizations

Freedom House 120 Wall Street, 26th Floor, New York, NY 10005, (212)-514-8040. Publications: *Freedom at Issue, Freedom Monitor, Freedom in the World: Political Rights and Civil Liberties, Prospective on Freedom*. To strengthen free institutions at home and abroad.

International Freedom Foundation 200 G Street, NE, Suite 300, Washington, DC 20002, (202)-546-5788. Publications: *European Freedom Review, Freedom Research, Southern African Freedom Review*. Promotes individual freedom, open societies, and free enterprise; critiques "people's democracies"; conducts research on and publishes studies of groups that support leftist regimes and movements.

National Endowment for Democracy 1101 15th Street, NW, Suite 700, Washington, DC 20005, (202)-293-9072. Publication: *Annual Report*. Promotes development of democracy and human rights world-wide; supports non-governmental participation in democratic training programs and institution building.

HUMOR

Books and Articles

Barry, Dave and O'Rourke, P. J., "Literary Logrolling," *The American Spectator*, Volume 22 (September, 1989), pp. 22-23.

Davies, Christie, *Ethnic Humor Around the World: A Comparative Analysis* (Bloomington, IN: Indiana University Press, 1990).

King, Florence, *With Charity Toward None: A Fond Look at Misanthropy* (New York: St. Martin's Press, 1992).

O'Rourke, P. J., *Give War a Chance: Eyewitness Accounts of Mankind's Struggle Against Tyranny, Injustice, and Alcohol-Free Beer* (New York: Atlantic Monthly Press, 1992).

O'Rourke, P. J., *Holidays in Hell* (New York: Atlantic Monthly Press, 1988).

O'Rourke, P. J., *Modern Manners: An Etiquette Book for Rude People* (New York: Atlantic Monthly Press, 1989).

O'Rourke, P. J., *Republican Party Reptile* (New York: Atlantic Monthly Press, 1987).

O'Rourke, P. J., "The '60s Kids and the Crash," *The American Spectator*, Volume 21 (February, 1988), pp. 16-17.

Shalit, Gene, ed., *Laughing Matters: A Celebration of American Humor* (New York: Doubleday, 1987).

HUNGER

Books and Articles

Rector, Robert, "Food Fight: How Hungry Are America's Children?," *Policy Review*, Number 58 (Fall, 1991), pp. 38-43.

Zinsmeister, Karl, "All the Hungry People," *Reason*, Volume 20 (June, 1988), pp. 22-30

HYDRO-ELECTRIC POWER
(see **Energy**, **Utilities**)

ILLEGAL ALIENS
(see **Immigration**)

IMMIGRATION

Books and Articles

Aron, Leon, "The Russians Are Coming: Millions of Soviet Refugees Will Be Fleeing to the West," *Policy Review*, Number 58 (Fall, 1991), pp. 44-49.

Auster, Lawrence, "The Forbidden Topic," *National Review*, Volume XLIV (April 27, 1992), pp. 42-44.

Auster, Lawrence, *The Path to National Suicide: An Essay on Immigration and Multiculturalism* (Monterey, VA: American Immigration Control Foundation, 1990).

Bethell, Tom, "A New Statute of Liberty," *National Review*, Volume XXXIX (December 18, 1987), pp. 38-43.

Borjas, George J., *Friends or Strangers: The Impact of Immigrants on the U.S. Economy* (New York: Basic Books, 1990).

Bouvier, Leon F., *Peaceful Invasions: Immigration and Changing America* (Washington, DC: Center for Immigration Studies, 1992).

Bradford, M. E., *Sentiment or Survival: The Crisis in the Immigration Policy of the United States* (Monterey, VA: American Immigration Control Foundation).

Brimelow, Peter, "Time to Rethink Immigration?," *National Review*, Volume XLIV (June 22, 1992), pp. 30-46.

Citrin, Jack, "Language, Politics and American Identity," *The Public Interest*, Number 99 (Spring, 1990), pp. 96-109.

Elmer, Evelyn E. and Elmer, Glaister A., *Ethnic Conflicts Abroad: Clues to America's Future?* (Monterey, VA: American Immigration Control Foundation, 1988).

Fleming, Thomas, "A Not So Wonderful Life," *Chronicles*, Volume 14 (July, 1990), pp. 11-13.

Hardin, Garrett, "Conspicuous Benevolence and the Population Bomb," *Chronicles*, Volume 15 (October, 1991), pp. 18-22.

Harwood, Edwin, *In Liberty's Shadow: Illegal Aliens and Immigration Law Enforcement* (Stanford, CA: Hoover Institution Press, 1986).

Huddle, Donald L., et al., *Illegal Immigration: Job Displacement and Social Costs* (Monterey, VA: American Immigration Control Foundation, 1985).

Kirkwood, R. Cort, "Your Papers, Please," *Chronicles*, Volume 14 (November, 1990), pp. 45-46.

Krikorian, Mark, "Taking Leave of Our Census," *Chronicles*, Volume 14 (February, 1990), pp. 44-45.

Lamm, Richard D. and Imhoff, Gary, *The Immigration Time Bomb: The Fragmenting and Destruction of America by Immigration* (New York: Dutton, 1986).

Lutton, Wayne, *The Myth of Open Borders: The American Tradition of Immigration Control* (Monterey, VA: American Immigration Control Foundation, 1988).

Marcus, Philip, "No-Fault Citizenship," *Chronicles*, Volume 14 (July, 1990), p. 48.

Martin, Philip L., *Illegal Immigration and the Colonization of the American Labor Market* (Washington, DC: Center for Immigration Studies, 1986).

Mehlman, Ira H., "Mixing Oil and Water: The Common Problems of Assimilating Immigrants in Israel and the United States," *Chronicles*, Volume 14 (March, 1990), pp. 18-21.

Mehlman, Ira H., "The New Jet Set," *National Review*, Volume XLV (March 15, 1993), pp. 40-46.

Nelson, B. A., *The Coming Triumph of Mexican Irredentism* (Monterey, VA: American Immigration Control Foundation, 1984).

Neusner, Jacob H., et al., "The Pros and Cons of Immigration: A Debate," *Chronicles*, Volume 14 (July, 1990), pp. 14-19.

Schuck, Peter and Smith, Rogers M., *Citizenship Without Consent: Illegal Aliens in the American Polity* (New Haven, CT: Yale University Press, 1985).

Simon, Julian L., et al., "Why Control the Borders?," *National Review*, Volume XLV (February 1, 1993), pp. 27-34.

Skerry, Peter, "Borders and Quotas: Immigration and the Affirmative-Action State," *The Public Interest*, Number 96 (Summer, 1989), pp. 86-102.

Sowell, Thomas, *Ethnic America: A History* (New York: Basic Books, 1981).

Ten Steps to Securing America's Borders (Washington, DC: Federation for American Immigration Reform, 1989).

Wagner, Geoffrey, "The Intransigent Uninvited," *Chronicles*, Volume 14 (July, 1990), pp. 24-26.

Wilson, Clyde, "The Future of American Nationalism," *Chronicles*, Volume 14 (November, 1990), pp. 16-21.

Winnick, Louis, "America's 'Model Minority,'" *Commentary*, Volume 90 (August, 1990), pp. 22-29.

Organizations

American Immigration Control Foundation Box 525, Monterey, VA 24465, (703)-468-2022. Publications: *Border Watch, Immigration Time Bomb.*
Objective is to educate Americans and their leaders about the need for immigration control and problems the AICF believes are caused by illegal immigration.

Americans for Immigration Control 717 Second Street, NE, Suite 307,

Washington, DC 20002, (202)-543-3719. Lobbies for: an increase in the budget of the U.S. Immigration and Naturalization Service in an effort to increase the effectiveness of border patrols; no amnesty for illegal immigrants in the U.S.; sanctions against employers who knowingly hire illegal immigrants.

Emerald Isle Immigration Center 6705 Roosevelt Avenue, Woodside, NY 11377, (718)-478-5502. Seeks to: secure amnesty for illegal immigrants in the U.S.; obtain a quota of nonpreference visas from the U.S. government for immigrants from Ireland and other European countries.

Federation for American Immigration Reform 1666 Connecticut Avenue, NW, Washington, DC 20009. Seeks end to illegal immigration and cap on legal immigration; urges political leaders to develop comprehensive U.S. immigration policy consistent with national goals.

INDEPENDENT COUNSEL
(see **Special Prosecutor**)

INDUSTRIAL POLICY
(see **Economic Planning**)

INSURANCE
(see also **Auto Insurance**)

Books and Articles

Armentano, D. T., "Antitrust and Insurance: Should the McCarran Act Be Repealed?," *The Cato Journal*, Volume 8 (Winter, 1989), pp. 729-749.
England, Robert Stowe, "Congress, Nader, and the Ambulance Chasers," *The American Spectator*, Volume 23 (September, 1990), pp. 18-23.
Litan, Robert and Winston, Clifford, eds., *Liability: Perspectives and Policy* (Washington, DC: Brookings Institution, 1988).

Organizations

American Insurance Association 1130 Connecticut Avenue, NW, Suite 1000, Washington, DC 20036, (202)-828-7100. Represents companies providing property and liability insurance and suretyship.

American Tort Reform Association 1212 New York Avenue, NW, Suite 515,

Washington, DC 20005, (202)-682-1163. Publications: *Leaders' Update, Legislative Watch, The Reformer, Tort Reform Report.* Seeks to remedy the current liability insurance "crisis" by developing, promoting, and coordinating the U.S. tort law system.

Insurance Information Institute 110 William Street, New York, NY 10038, (212)-669-9200. Publications: *Data Base News, Data Base Reports, Educators' Letter, Executive Letter, Insurance Facts, Insurance Pulse, Insurance Review, Insurance Update.* Represents interests of property and liability insurance companies and provides information to trade associations, businesses, other groups, and the public.

INTELLIGENCE

Books and Articles

Barron, John, *KGB: The Secret Work of Soviet Secret Agents* (New York: Reader's Digest Press, 1974).

Barros, James, *No Sense of Evil: The Espionage Case of E. Herbert Norman* (Toronto: Deneau Publishers, 1986).

Bethell, Nicholas, *Betrayed* (New York: Times Books, 1984).

Bittman, Ladislav, *The Deception Game* (New York: Ballantine Books, 1981).

Bittman, Ladislav, *The KGB and Soviet Disinformation: An Insider's View* (McLean, VA: Pergamon-Brassey's, 1985).

Blitzer, Wolf, *Territory of Lies: The Elusive Story of Jonathon J. Pollard - The American Who Spied on His Country for Israel and How He Was Betrayed* (New York: Harper & Row, 1989).

Breindel, Eric M., "Do Spies Matter?," *Commentary*, Volume 85 (March, 1988), pp. 53-58.

Codevilla, Angelo and Godson, Roy, *Informed Statecraft: Intelligence for a New Century* (New York: The Free Press, 1992).

Cohen, Jacob, "Innocent After All?," *National Review*, Volume XLV (January 18, 1993), pp. 26-33.

Corson, William R. and Crowley, Robert T., *The New KGB: Engine of Soviet Power* (New York: Quill Books, 1986).

Daily, Brian D., and Parker, Patrick J., eds., *Soviet Strategic Deception* (Lexington, MA: Lexington Books/Hoover Institution Press, 1987).

Dziak, John J., *Chekisty: A History of the KGB* (Lexington, MA: Lexington Books, 1988).

Epstein, Edward Jay, *Deception: The Invisible War Between the KGB and the CIA* (New York: Simon & Schuster, 1989).

Gehlen, Reinhard, *The Service: The Memoirs of General Reinhard Gehlen* (New York: Popular Library, 1972).

Godson, Roy S. and Shultz, Richard H., Jr., *Dezinformatsia: Active Measures in Soviet Strategy* (Elmsford, NY: Pergamon Press, 1984).

Golitsyn, Anatoliy, *New Lies for Old: The Communist Strategy of Deception and Disinformation* (New York: Dodd, Mead, 1984).

Haselkorn, Avigdor, "Why Spy?," *The American Spectator*, Volume 25 (July, 1992), pp. 38-41.

Knightley, Phillip, *The Master Spy: The Story of Kim Philby* (New York: Knopf, 1989).

Koch, Stephen, *Double Lives: Espionage and the War of Ideas* (New York: The Free Press, 1992).

Krasnov, Vladislav, *Soviet Defectors: The KGB Wanted List* (Stanford, CA: Hoover Institution Press, 1985).

Lamphere, Robert J. and Schachtman, Tom, *The FBI-KGB War: A Special Agent's Story* (New York: Random House, 1986).

Ledeen, Michael A., "Secrets," *The National Interest*, Number 10 (Winter, 1987/88), pp. 48-55.

Miller, Stephen, "The Disinformation Virus: How U.S. Scientists Invented AIDS and Other Russian Folktales," *Policy Review*, Number 46 (Fall, 1988), pp. 75-79.

O'Toole, G. J. A., *The Encyclopedia of American Intelligence and Espionage: From the Revolutionary War to the Present* (New York: Facts on File, 1988).

Perlmutter, Amos, "Soviet Historiography, Western Journalism," *National Review*, Volume XLV (January 18, 1993), pp. 30-31.

Radosh, Ronald and Milton, Joyce, *The Rosenberg File: A Search for the Truth* (Fort Worth, TX: Holt, Rinehart, 1983).

Romerstein, Herbert and Levchenko, Stanislav, *The KGB Against the Main Enemy: How the Soviet Intelligence Service Operates Against the United States* (Lexington, MA: Lexington Books, 1989).

Shultz, Richard H. and Godson, Roy, *Dezinformatsia: Active Measures in Soviet Strategy* (Washington, DC: Pergamon Brassey's, 1984).

Tanenhaus, Sam, "Witness for the Truth," *National Review*, Volume XLV (February 15, 1993), pp. 42-46.

Weinstein, Allen, *Perjury: The Hiss - Chambers Case* (New York: Knopf, 1978).

West, Nigel, *Molehunt: Search for Soviet Spies in MI-5* (New York: William Morrow, 1989).

Organizations

The Jamestown Foundation 1528 18th Street, NW, Washington, DC 20002, (202)-483-8888. Conducts research on defection; houses library containing biographies and volumes on the Soviet Union, the KGB, and intelligence activities; compiles statistics.

National Intelligence Study Center 1800 K Street, NW, Suite 1102, Washington, DC 20006, (202)-466-6029. Publications: *The Foreign Intelligence Literary Scene, Notes, The Scholar's Guide to Intelligence Literature: Bibliography of the Russell J. Bowen Collection, Teaching Intelligence in the Mid-1980s.* Seeks to put intelligence in its proper perspective and to enlighten the public on the subject of intelligence in order to "raise the level of sophistication in thinking about the intellectual and government process called intelligence on which our national security depends so much."

INTELLIGENCE QUOTIENT

Books and Articles

Herrnstein, R. J., "Still an American Dilemma," *The Public Interest*, Number 98 (Winter, 1990), pp. 3-17.

Jensen, Arthur R., "IQ and Science: The Mysterious Burt Affair," *The Public Interest*, Number 105 (Fall, 1991), pp. 93-106.

Jensen, Arthur, *Straight Talk About Mental Tests* (New York: The Free Press, 1981).

Seligman, Daniel, "Is America Smart Enough?," *National Review*, Volume XLIII (April 15, 1991), pp. 24-31.

Snyderman, Mark and Rothman, Stanley, *The IQ Controversy, the Media, and Public Policy* (New Brunswick, NJ: Transaction Books, 1989).

INTERNAL REVENUE SERVICE
(see **Taxation**)

INTERNATIONAL ECONOMY

Books and Articles

Bartley, Robert L. and Luttwak, Edward N., "Is America on the Way Down?," *Commentary*, Volume 93 (March, 1992), pp. 15-27.

Berger, Peter L., et al., "Is America on the Way Down? (Round II)," *Commentary*, Volume 93 (May, 1992), pp. 19-29.

Bovard, James, "Inside the World Bank: What They're Doing with Your Money Is a Crime," *Reason*, Volume 20 (April, 1989), pp. 27-31.

Cooper, Richard N., "Toward an International Commodity Standard?," Comments by Lawrence H. White and Paul Craig Roberts, *The Cato Journal*, Volume 8 (Fall, 1988), pp. 315-349.

Culp, Christopher L., "The Coordination of Economies," *The National Interest*, Number 13 (Fall, 1988), pp. 36-42.

Entin, Stephen J., "See How They Run," *National Review*, Volume XLIV (May 25, 1992), pp. 29-31.

Finn, James, ed., *Global Economics and Religion* (New Brunswick, NJ: Transaction Books, 1983).

Fleming, Thomas, "Surviving in the New World Order," *Chronicles*, Volume 15 (April, 1991), pp. 12-16.

Friedman, Milton, et al., "As Good as Gold," *National Review*, Volume XLII (June 11, 1990), pp. 28-35.

Friedman, Milton, *Money Mischief* (New York: Harcourt Brace Jovanovich, 1992).

Hale, David D., "Global Super Market: The Real Peace Dividend Is Three Billion New Customers," *Policy Review*, Number 60 (Spring, 1992), pp. 4-8.

Harrigan, Anthony, "The Corporate Citizen: National vs. Transnational Economic Strategies," *Chronicles*, Volume 14 (January, 1990), pp. 25-28.

Hazlitt, Henry, *From Bretton Woods to World Inflation: A Study of Causes and Consequences* (Washington, DC: Regnery Gateway, 1984).

Johnson, Manuel H., "Current Perspectives on Monetary Policy," *The Cato Journal*, Volume 8 (Fall, 1988), pp. 253-260.

Kapstein, Ethan B., "Losing Control: National Security and the Global Economy," *The National Interest*, Number 18 (Winter, 1989/90), pp. 85-90.

Lamm, Richard D., "The New Wealth of Nations," *Chronicles*, Volume 15 (October, 1991), pp. 25-27.

Luttwak, Edward N., "From Geopolitics to Geo-Economics: Logic of Conflict, Grammar of Commerce," *The National Interest*, Number 20 (Summer, 1990), pp. 17-23.

McKenzie, Richard B. and Lee, Dwight R., *Quicksilver Capital: How the Rapid Movement of Wealth Has Changed the World* (New York: Free Press, 1991).

Meltzer, Allan H., et al., "Is Monetarism Dead?," *National Review*, Volume XLIII (November 4, 1991), pp. 30-36.

Nau, Henry R., *The Myth of America's Decline: Leading the World Economy into the 1990s* (New York: Oxford University Press, 1990).

Porter, Michael E., *The Competitive Advantage of Nations* (New York: The Free Press, 1990).

INTERNATIONAL RELATIONS

Books and Articles

Bork, Robert H., "The Limits of 'International Law,'" *The National Interest*, Number 18 (Winter, 1989/90), pp. 3-10.

Hawkins, William R., "How to Give Away Your Future: Law of the Sea," *National Review*, Volume XXXIV (April 16, 1982), pp. 410-414.

Luttwak, Edward N., "The Shape of Things to Come," *Commentary*, Volume 89 (June, 1990), pp. 17-25.

Nixon, Richard, *Seize the Moment: America's Challenge in a One-Superpower World* (New York: Simon & Schuster, 1992).

Sofaer, Abraham D., "International Law and the Use of Force," *The National Interest*, Number 13 (Fall, 1988), pp. 53-64.

Sunic, Tomislav, "The Decline and Splendor of Nationalism," *Chronicles*, Volume 16 (January, 1992), pp. 22-25.

Organizations

Center for Strategic and International Studies 1800 K Street, NW, Suite 400, Washington, DC 20006, (202)-887-0200. Publications: *The Washington Quarterly, Washington Papers, Panel Reports.* A public policy research institute that provides policymakers with a strategic perspective on issues relating to international economics, politics, security and business. Committed to serving the common interests of the United States and other countries around the world that support representative government and the rule of law.

INTERNATIONAL TRADE

Books and Articles

Barfield, Claude, "The Americas and World Trade," *The American Enterprise*, Volume 3 (July/August, 1992), pp. 10-14.

Bhagwati, Jagdish, *The World Trading System at Risk* (Princeton, NJ: Princeton University Press, 1991).

Bovard, James, *The Fair Trade Fraud* (New York: St. Martin's Press, 1991).

Bovard, James, "The Agricultural Swamp," *National Review*, Volume XLI (February 10, 1989), pp. 46-48.

Bovard, James, "Mismanaged Trade," *National Review*, Volume XLIII (August 12, 1991), pp. 40-42.

Dam, Kenneth W., "U.S. Policy Options in International Trade: Why the GATT Negotiations Must Succeed," *The American Enterprise*, Volume 1 (July/August, 1990), pp. 31-37.

Dewald, William G. and Ulan, Michael, "The Twin-Deficit Illusion," *The Cato Journal*, Volume 9 (Winter, 1990), pp. 689-707.

Gilder, George, "The Planetary Utility: America's Most Creative Enterprises Depend on Imports," *Policy Review*, Number 44 (Spring, 1988), pp. 50-53.

Gordon, Bernard K., "Who Really Buys American?," *The National Interest*, Number 22 (Winter, 1990/91), pp. 48-55.

Grennes, Thomas, "The Multifiber Arrangement and the Management of International Textile Trade," *The Cato Journal*, Volume 9 (Spring/Summer, 1989), pp. 107-131.

Harrigan, Anthony, et al., *Putting America First: A Conservative Trade Alternative* (Washington, DC: United States Industrial Council Educational Foundation, 1987).

Hawkins, William, "Free Trade Is No Free Lunch," *National Review*, Volume XXXIX (August 28, 1987), pp. 38-39.

Hawkins, William, "Neomercantilism: Is There a Case for Tariffs?," With Comments by J. K. Galbraith and Milton Friedman, *National Review*, Volume XXXVI (April 6, 1984), pp. 25-45.

Kirkwood, R. Cort, "Inside the Red Trade Lobby," *National Review*, Volume XL (April 29, 1988), pp. 35-40.

Kirkwood, R. Cort., "Trading with Gorbachev: The Case for Export Controls," *Chronicles*, Volume 14 (May, 1990), pp. 55-58.

Lindsey, Brink, "Trade Secret: The Global Import Boom No One Talks About," *Policy Review*, Number 51 (Winter, 1990), pp. 56-61.

McCracken, Paul W., "Will the Third Great Wave Continue?," *The American Enterprise*, Volume 2 (March/April, 1991), pp. 52-57.

Meltzer, Allan H., "Making Progress: Frameworks that Produce Results," *The American Enterprise*, Volume 3 (January/February, 1992), pp. 48-57.

Meigs, A. James, "Dollars and Deficits: Substituting False for Real Problems," *The Cato Journal*, Volume 8 (Fall, 1988), pp. 533-553.

Meltzer, Allan H. and Prestowitz, C.yde V., "Trade Policy: What Next?," *The American Enterprise*, Volume 1 (May/June, 1990), pp. 88-91.

Mooney, James C., "We're Not Import Gorgers," *Reason*, Volume 20 (June, 1988), pp. 40-41.

Nau, Henry R., "Trade and Deterrence," *The National Interest*, Number 7 (Spring, 1987), pp. 48-60.

Niskanen, William A., "The Uneasy Relation Between the Budget and Trade Deficits," With Comments by Gary H. Stern and John Williamson, *The Cato Journal*, Volume 8 (Fall, 1988), pp. 507-532.

Stelzer, Irwin M., "How to Save Free Trade - And Still Trade With Japan," *Commentary*, Volume 90 (July, 1990), pp. 15-21.

Stelzer, Irwin M., "Losing on Both Fronts," *The American Spectator*, Volume 22 (June, 1989), pp. 37-38.

Stelzer, Irwin M., "The New Protectionism," *National Review*, Volume XLIV (March 16, 1992), pp. 30-34.

Taylor, Joan Kennedy, *Free Trade: The Necessary Foundation for World Peace* (Irvington-on-Hudson, NY: Foundation for Economic Education, 1986).

Organizations

American Association of Exporters and Importers 11 W. 42nd Street, New York, NY 10036, (212)-944-2230. Publications: *AAEI Membership Directory,*

Alertfax, Bulletin, International Trade Alert, Newsletter. Seeks fair and equitable conditions for world trade.

International Trade Council 3114 Circle Hill Road, Alexandria, VA 22305, (703)-548-1234. Publications: *Membership Directory, Research Report, World Agricultural Review, World Agricultural Directory, World Opportunity/Risk Review, World Trade Directory, World Trade Review, Worldbusiness Directory, Worldbusiness Review, Worldbusiness Weekly.* Promotes free trade and elimination of trade barriers and facilitates logistics, research, and marketing for members.

National Foreign Trade Council 1270 Sixth Avenue, Suite 206, New York, NY 10020, (212)-399-7128. Publications: *Bulletin, Noticias: Latin America Report.* Works to promote and protect American foreign trade and investment.

INVENTIONS
(see **Patents, Technology**)

IRELAND

Books and Articles

Holland, Jack, *The American Connection: U.S. Guns, Money and Influence in Northern Ireland* (New York: Viking, 1987).
O'Brien, Conor Cruise, "The Patriot Game," *National Review*, Volume XLV (April 26, 1993), pp. 37-38.
O'Malley, Padraig, *Biting at the Grave: The Irish Hunger Strikes and the Politics of Despair* (Boston, MA: Beacon Press, 1990).
O'Malley, Padraig, *The Uncivil Wars: Ireland Today* (Boston, MA: Houghton, Mifflin, 1983).

ISLAM

Books and Articles

Decter, Midge, "The Rushdiad," *Commentary*, Volume 87 (June, 1989), pp. 18-23.
Doughty, Charles M., *Travels In Arabia Deserta*, . 2 vols. (New York: Dover Publications, 1980).
Guillaume, Alfred, *Islam* (New York: Penguin Books, 1954).

Hartley, Anthony, "Europe's Muslims," *The National Interest*, Number 22 (Winter, 1990/91), pp. 57-66.

Naipaul, V. S., *Among the Believers: An Islamic Journey* (New York: Knopf, 1981).

Norton, Augustus Richard, *Amal and the Shi'a: Struggle for the Soul of Lebanon* (Austin, TX: University of Texas Press, 1987).

Pipes, Daniel, "The Ayatollah, the Novelist, and the West," *Commentary*, Volume 87 (June, 1989), pp. 9-17.

Pipes, Daniel, *In the Path of God: Islam and Political Power* (New York: Basic Books, 1983).

Pipes, Daniel, "The Muslims Are Coming! The Muslims Are Coming!" *National Review*, Volume XLII (November 19, 1990), pp. 28-31.

Rodman, Peter W., "Islam and Democracy," *National Review*, Volume XLIV (May 11, 1992), pp. 28-29.

Simpson, John, *Inside Iran: Life Under Khomeini's Regime* (New York: St. Martin's Press, 1988).

Taheri, Amir, *Holy Terror: Inside the World of Islamic Terrorism* (Bethesda, MD: Adler and Adler, 1987).

ISRAEL

Books and Articles

Abel, Lionel, et al., "American Jews and Israel: A Symposium," *Commentary*, Volume 85 (February, 1988), pp. 21-75.

Adams, James, *The Unnatural Alliance: Israel and South Africa* (New York: Quartet Books, 1984).

Avishai, Bernard, *The Tragedy of Zionism: Revolution and Democracy in the Land of Israel* (New York: Farrar, Straus and Giroux, 1985).

Bainerman, Joel, "Shock Treatment," *National Review*, Volume XLIV (April 13, 1992), pp. 41-43.

Bard, Mitchell, "Israel: Some Surprising Polls," *Commentary*, Volume 88 (August, 1989), pp. 45-47.

Feder, Don, "Israel," *Chronicles*, Volume 13 (June, 1989), pp. 22-23.

Harkabi, Yehoshafat, *Israel's Fateful Hour* (New York: Harper & Row, 1988).

Mehlman, Ira H., "Mixing Oil and Water: The Common Problems of Assimilating Immigrants in Israel and the United States," *Chronicles*, Volume 14 (March, 1990), pp. 18-21.

Norder, Edward, "Right Behind You, Scarlett!," *The American Spectator*, Volume 24 (August, 1991), pp. 14-16.

Perlmutter, Amos, "Now Go It Alone: Israel and the West Bank," *The National Interest*, Number 13 (Fall, 1988), pp. 122-125.

Peters, Joan, *From Time Immemorial: The Origins of the Arab-Jewish Conflict Over Palestine* (New York: Harper & Row, 1984).

Pipes, Daniel and Garfinkle, Adam, "Is Jordan Palestine?," *Commentary*, Volume 86 (October, 1988), pp. 35-42.

Podhoretz, Norman, "America and Israel: An Ominous Change," *Commentary*, Volume 93 (January, 1992), pp. 21-25.

Podhoretz, Norman, "Israel: A Lamentation from the Future," *Commentary*, Volume 87 (March, 1989), pp. 15-21.

Raab, Earl, "No Jewish Split on Israel," *Commentary*, Volume 89 (June, 1990), pp. 46-48.

Reynolds, Alan, "Draining Israel's Red Sea," *National Review*, Volume XXXIII (August 1, 1986), pp. 29-30, 44-45.

Schiff, Ze`ev, "U.S. and Israel: Friendship Under Strain," *The National Interest*, Number 10 (Winter, 1987/88), pp. 3-12.

Spiegel, Steven L., et al., "America and Israel - How Bad Is It?," *The National Interest*, Number 22 (Winter, 1990/91), pp. 11-22.

Stein, Herbert, "Israel's Economy: Observations of an Adviser," *The American Enterprise*, Volume 1 (May/June, 1990), pp. 12-18.

JAPAN

Books and Articles

Brock, David, "The Theory and Practice of Japan-Bashing," *The National Interest*, Number 17 (Fall, 1989), pp. 29-40.

Calder, Kent E., "Japan Today: The New Deal Analogy," *The American Enterprise*, Volume 2 (March/April, 1991), pp. 35-39.

Choate, Pat, *Agents of Influence* (New York: Knopf, 1990).

Courdy, Jean-Claude, *The Japanese: Everyday Life in the Empire of the Rising Sun* (New York: Harper & Row, 1984).

Cropsey, Seth, "Uncle Samurai: America's Military Alliance with Japan," *Policy Review*, Number 58 (Fall, 1991), pp. 24-31.

Feiler, Bruce S., *Learning to Bow: An American Teacher in a Japanese School* (Boston, MA: Ticknor & Fields, 1991).

Grundfest, Joseph A., "Financial Scandals in the United States and Japan," *The American Enterprise*, Volume 3 (May/June, 1992), pp. 34-45.

Hale, David D., "Must We Become Japanese?," *National Review*, Volume XLI (October 27, 1989), pp. 30-32, 59.

Hale, David D., "You Pat My Back, I'll Pat Yours," *National Review*, Volume XLII (April 16, 1990), pp. 35-37.

Hane, Mikiso, *Peasants, Rebels, and Outcasts: The Underside of Modern Japan* (New York: Pantheon Books, 1982).

Hollerman, Leon, "The Headquarters Nation," *The National Interest*, Number 25 (Fall, 1991), pp. 18-25.

Kaplan, David E. and Dubro, Alec, *Yakuza: The Explosive Account of Japan's Criminal Underworld* (New York: Collier/Macmillan, 1986).

Lynn, Richard, "Why Johnny Can't Read - But Yoshio Can," *National Review*, Volume XL (October 28, 1988), pp. 40-43.

Lynn, Richard, "What Makes People Rich?," *National Review*, Volume XLIII (September 9, 1991), pp. 30-33.

Pyle, Kenneth B., "How Japan Sees Itself: At Home, in Asia, and Around the World," *The American Enterprise*, Volume 2 (November/ December, 1991), pp. 29-37.

Rauch, Jonathan, "The Trouble with Japan," *The American Enterprise*, Volume 1 (March/April, 1990), pp. 78-82.

Rauch, Jonathan, "Why Is Japanese Baseball So Dull? And Why Should Americans Care?," *Reason*, Volume 24 (August/September, 1992), pp. 24-31.

Seligman, Daniel, "Is America Smart Enough?," *National Review*, Volume XLIII (April 15, 1991), pp. 24-31.

Stelzer, Irwin M., "How to Save Free Trade - and Still Trade with Japan," *Commentary*, Volume 90 (July, 1990), pp. 15-21.

van Wolferen, Karel, *The Enigma of Japanese Power* (New York: Knopf, 1989).

van Wolferen, Karel, "No Brakes, No Compass," *The National Interest*, Number 25 (Fall, 1991), pp. 26-35.

Woronoff, Jon, *Japan's Commercial Empire* (Armonk, NY: M. E. Sharpe, 1985).

Zinsmeister, Karl, "Raising Hiroko: The Child-Centered Culture of Japan," *The American Enterprise*, Volume 1 (March/April, 1990), pp. 52-59.

Zinsmeister, Karl, "Shadows on the Rising Sun," *The American Enterprise*, Volume 1 (May/June, 1990), pp. 52-61.

JERUSALEM
(see **Israel, Middle East**)

JOBS
(see **Employment**)

JOURNALISM
(see also **Media Bias**)

Books and Articles

Bethell, Tom, *The Electric Windmill: An Inadvertent Autobiography* (Washington, DC: Regnery Gateway, 1988).

Catto, Henry, "Anthony Agonistes," *National Review*, Volume XLI (September 1, 1989), pp. 34-37, 52.

Connolly, Cyril, ed., *The Golden Horizon* (New York: University Books, 1955).

Cooke, Alistair, *America Observed: From the 1940s to the 1980s* (New York: Knopf, 1988).

Cooke, Alistair, *The Americans: Fifty Talks on Our Life and Times* (New York: Knopf, 1979).

McConnell, Scott, "Headless Tabloid in Bottomless Pit," *National Review*, Volume XLV (April 12, 1993), pp. 51-52.

Sobran, Joseph, et al., "The Decline of American Journalism," *National Review*, Volume XLV (June 21, 1993), pp. 25-64.

Teachout, Terry, ed., *Ghosts on the Roof: Selected Journalism of Whittaker Chambers 1931-1959* (Washington, DC: Regnery Gateway, 1989).

Wolfe, Tom, *The Electric Kool-Aid Acid Test* (New York: Bantam, 1983).

Wolfe, Tom, *The Kandy-Kolored Tangerine-Flake Streamline Baby* (New York: Farrar, Straus and Giroux, 1987).

Wolfe, Tom, *The Pumphouse Gang* (New York: Farrar, Straus and Giroux, 1968).

Wolfe, Tom, *The Purple Decades: A Reader* (New York: Farrar, Straus and Giroux, 1982).

Wolfe, Tom, *Radical Chic and Mau-Mauing the Flak Catchers* (New York: Farrar, Straus and Giroux, 1970).

Worthington, Peter, *Looking for Trouble: A Journalist's Life and then Some* (Toronto: Key Porter Books, 1984).

Organizations

Education and Research Institute 800 Maryland Avenue, NE, Washington, DC 20002, (202)-544-1333. Publication: *Newsletter*. Operates National Journalism Center to train conservative college students in the trade; offers placement service.

Leadership Institute 8001 Braddock Road, Suite 502, Springfield, VA 22151, (703)-321-8580. Publications: *Building Leadership, Leadership Training Service Directory*. Seeks to prepare conservatives for employment in Congress and other public policy organizations.

JUDAISM

Books and Articles

Abramson, Glenda, *The Blackwell Companion to Jewish Culture: From the Eighteenth Century to the Present* (New York: Basil Blackwell, 1989).

Brookhiser, Richard, "Great Expectations," *National Review*, Volume XLIV (November 30, 1992), pp. 56-57.

Feder, Don, "Abortion, Judaism, and Jews," *National Review*, Volume XLIII (July 8, 1991), pp. 37, 50-53.

Feder, Don, "Into the House of Bondage," *National Review*, Volume XLII (March 5, 1990), pp. 41-43.

Feder, Don, "The Kosher Majority," *National Review*, Volume XXXIX (April 10, 1987), pp. 40-58, 64.

Friedman, Murray, *Utopian Dilemma: American Judaism and Public Policy* (Washington, DC: Ethics and Public Policy Center, 1985).

Himmelfarb, Milton, "American Jews: Diehard Conservatives," *Commentary*, Volume 87 (April, 1989), pp. 44-49.

Johnson, Paul, *A History of the Jews* (New York: Harper & Row, 1987).

Kedourie, Elie, "Who Is a Jew," *Commentary*, Volume 85 (June, 1988), pp. 25-30.

Kristol, Irving, "The Future of American Jewry," *Commentary*, Volume 92 (August, 1991), pp. 21-26.

Kristol, Irving, "Liberalism and American Jews," *Commentary*, Volume 86 (October, 1988), pp. 19-23.

Muller, Jerry Z., "Communism, Anti-Semitism, and the Jews," *Commentary*, Volume 86 (August, 1988), pp. 28-39.

Neusner, Jacob, *The Ecology of Religion: From Writing to Religion in the Study of Judaism* (Nashville, TN: Abingdon Press, 1989).

Neusner, Jacob, *The Enchantments of Judaism: Rites of Transformation from Birth Through Death* (New York: Basic Books, 1987).

Neusner, Jacob, *Judaism: The Evidence of the Mishnah* (Chicago, IL: University of Chicago Press, 1981).

Neusner, Jacob, "Letter from a State of Mind: The Religion of Neoconservatism," *Chronicles*, Volume 12 (June, 1988), pp. 44-45.

Norden, Edward, "Behind 'Who Is a Jew': A Letter From Jerusalem," *Commentary*, Volume 87 (April, 1989), pp. 21-33.

Rubinstein, W. D., *The Left, the Right, and the Jews* (New York: Universe Books, 1982).

Silberman, Charles E., *A Certain People: American Jews and Their Lives Today* (New York: Summit Books, 1985).

Tamari, Meir, *"With All Your Possessions": Jewish Ethics and Economic Life* (New York: The Free Press, 1987).

Wisse, Ruth R., *If I Am Not for Myself...: The Liberal Betrayal of the Jew* (New York: The Free Press, 1992).

Woocher, Jonathan S., *Sacred Survival: The Civil Religion of American Jews* (Bloomington, IN: Indiana University Press, 1986).

Organizations

American Jewish Committee c/o Institute of Human Relations, 165 E. 56th Street, New York, NY 10022, (212)-751-4000. Publications: *AJC Journal,*

Commentary, American Jewish Year Book: A Record of Events and Trends in American and Worldwide Jewish Life, Present Tense. Conducts program of education, research, and human relations; combats bigotry; seeks to protect religious and civil rights.

JUDGES
(see also **Courts, Supreme Court**)

Books and Articles

Bork, Robert H., "The Full Court Press: The Drive for Control of the Courts," *The American Enterprise*, Volume 1 (January/ February, 1990), pp. 58-61.

Graglia, Lino A., "Was the Constitution a Good Idea?," *National Review*, Volume XXXVI (July 13, 1984), pp. 34-39.

Knight, Robert H., "Bye Bye Birdie," *National Review*, Volume XXXVIII (September 12, 1986), pp. 42-44, 59.

McDowell, Gary L., "Congress and the Courts," *The Public Interest*, Number 100 (Summer, 1990), pp. 89-101.

McGuigan, Patrick B. and Weyrich, Dawn M., *Ninth Justice: The Fight for Bork* (Washington, DC: Free Congress Research and Education Foundation, 1990).

Sowell, Thomas, "Rose Bird on Trial," *The American Spectator*, Volume 19 (September, 1986), pp. 23-26.

Toledano, Ben C., "Judge Not," *National Review*, Volume XLII (August 20, 1990), pp. 33-37.

Troy, Daniel E., "A Difference of Opinion: Reagan/Bush Judges vs. Their Predecessors," *Policy Review*, Number 61 (Summer, 1992), pp. 27-33.

Organizations

The Federalist Society for Law and Public Policy Studies 1700 K Street, NW, #901, Washington, DC 20006, (202)-822-8138. Publications: *The Federalist Paper, Harvard Journal of Law and Public Policy.* Seeks to bring about a reordering of priorities within the U.S. legal system that will emphasize individual liberty, traditional values, and the rule of law; considers the interpretation of the constitution to be the province of the judiciary, not the legislature.

JURISPRUDENCE

Books and Articles

Arkes, Hadley, *Beyond the Constitution* (Princeton, NJ: Princeton University Press, 1990).

Bork, Robert H., "Beside the Law," *National Review*, Volume XLIV (October 19, 1992), pp. 38-44.

Bork, Robert H., "The Case Against Political Judging," *National Review*, Volume XLI (December 8, 1989), pp. 23-28.

Bork, Robert H., "An End to Political Judging?," *National Review*, Volume XLII (December 31, 1990), pp. 30-32.

Bork, Robert H., "The Struggle over the Role of the Court," *National Review*, Volume XXXIV (September 17, 1982), pp. 1137-1139.

Bork, Robert H., *The Tempting of America: The Political Seduction of the Law* (New York: The Free Press, 1990).

Brubaker, Stanley, "Rewriting the Constitution: The Mainstream According to Laurence Tribe," *Commentary*, Volume 86 (December, 1988), pp. 36-42.

Eastland, Terry, "Deconstructing David Souter," *National Review*, Volume XLII (December 3, 1990), pp. 37-39.

Ely, John Hart, *Democracy and Distrust: A Theory of Judicial Review* (Cambridge, MA: Harvard University Press, 1980).

Graglia, Lino A., "Was the Constitution a Good Idea?," *National Review*, Volume XXXVI (July 13, 1984), pp. 34-39.

Higgins, Thomas J., *Judicial Review Unmasked* (Hanover, MA: Christopher Publishing House, 1981).

Jaffa, Harry V., "The Closing of the Conservative Mind," *National Review*, Volume XLII (July 9, 1990), pp. 40-43.

McDowell, Gary L., *Equity and the Constitution: The Supreme Court, Equitable Relief & Public Policy* (Chicago, IL: University of Chicago Press, 1983).

Markman, Stephen J. and Regnery, Alfred S., "The Mind of Justice Brennan: A 25 Year Tribute," *National Review*, Volume XXXVI (May 18, 1984), pp. 30-38.

Posner, Richard A., *The Problems of Jurisprudence* (Cambridge, MA: Harvard University Press, 1990).

Scalia, Antonin and Epstein, Richard, *Two Views on Judicial Activism* (Washington, DC: Cato Institute, 1985).

van den Haag, Ernest, "Not Above the Law," *National Review*, Volume XLIII (October 7, 1991), pp. 35-36.

Wildavsky, Aaron, "Robert Bork and the Crime of Inequality," *The Public Interest*, Number 98 (Winter, 1990), pp. 98-117.

Organizations

Center for Judicial Studies Box 113, Hampden-Sydney College, Hampden-Sydney, VA 29343, (804)-223-2207. Publications: *Benchmark, Constitutional Commentaries*. Goal is to reform U.S. constitutional and judicial systems.

JURY SYSTEM
(see **Courts**)

JUST WAR

Books and Articles

Finn, James, "Pacifism, Just War, and the Bishops' Muddle," *This World*, Number 7 (Winter, 1984), pp. 31-42.

Johnson, James Turner and Weigel, George, *Just War and the Gulf War* (Lanham, MD: Ethics and Public Policy Center/University Press of America, 1991).

Johnson, James Turner, *Just War Tradition and the Restraint of War: A Moral and Historical Inquiry* (Princeton, NJ: Princeton University Press, 1981).

Johnson, James Turner, *The Quest for Peace* (Princeton, NJ: Princeton University Press, 1987).

Martino, Joseph P., *A Fighting Chance: The Moral Use of Nuclear Weapons* (San Francisco, CA: Ignatius Press, 1988).

Owens, Mackubin T., "Vietnam and the Just-War Tradition," *This World*, Number 7 (Winter, 1984), pp. 43-65.

Weigel, George, *Tranquillitas Ordinis: The Present Failure and Future Promise of American Catholic Thought on War and Peace* (New York: Oxford University Press, 1987).

JUVENILE CRIME
(see **Crime, Criminal Law, Organized Crime**)

LABOR UNIONS
(see also **Right to Work**)

Books and Articles

Baird, Charles W., "Labor Law Reform: Lessons From History," *The Cato Journal*, Volume 10 (Spring/Summer, 1990), pp. 175-209.

Bernstein, David, "Exclusionary Rule: Something's Not Kosher About Davis-Bacon," *Reason*, Volume 23 (August/September, 1991), pp. 32-35.

Dickman, Howard, *Industrial Democracy in America: Ideological Origins of National Labor Relations Policy* (LaSalle, IL: Open Court, 1987).

Kilberg, William J., "How We Pay People: Changing Compensation: More to Our Benefits?," *The American Enterprise*, Volume 1 (September/October, 1990), pp. 25-33.

Lipset, Seymour Martin and Schneider, William, *The Confidence Gap: Business, Labor, and Government in the Public Mind* (New York: The Free Press, 1983).

McMenamin, Michael, "Cleaning Up the Teamsters," *Reason*, Volume 21
    (May, 1989), pp. 26-31.
McMenamin, Michael, "Game Wardens for Dinosaurs," *Reason*, Volume 24
    (July, 1992), pp. 42-43.
Methvin, Eugene H., "The Liberation of the Teamsters," *National Review*,
    Volume XLIV (March 30, 1992), p. 35.
Puddington, Arch, "Business, Labor, and the Anti-Communist Struggle,"
    National Review, Volume XXXVI (January 27, 1984), pp. 29-37.
Reynolds, Morgan O., *Power and Privelege: Labor Unions in America* (New
    York: Universe, 1984).

Organizations

Americans Against Union Control of Government 1761 Business Center Drive,
Suite 230, Reston, VA 22090, (703)-438-3966. Publications: *Forewarned,
Political Insider.* Individual citizens united: to reverse the trend toward
compulsory public sector bargaining in America; for research, education, and
legislation relating to public sector unionism; to alert the public to the need for
action on specific legislative proposals.

Public Service Research Council 1761 Business Center Drive, Suite 230, Reston,
VA 22090, (703)-438-3966. Publications: *Bulletin, Government Union Critique.*
Conducts research in the area of public sector employer/employee relations,
including issues such as strikes, growth of unionism, and political spending.

LANGUAGE
(see also **Bilingual Education**)

Books and Articles

Barzun, Jacques, *A Word or Two Before You Go* (Middletown, CT: Wesleyan
    University Press, 1986).
Bradford, M. E., "Rhetoric and Respectability," *Modern Age*, Volume 32
    (Summer, 1989), pp. 238-243.
Brooks, Cleanth, *The Language of the American South* (Athens, GA:
    University of Georgia Press, 1985).
Citrin, Jack, "Language Politics and American Identity," *The Public Interest*,
    Number 99, (Spring, 1990), pp. 96-109.
Davies, Christie, "Letter from England: The Collapse of British English,"
    Chronicles, Volume 15 (September, 1991), pp. 49-50.
DeMaria, Robert, *Johnson's Dictionary and the Language of Learning* (Chapel
    Hill, NC: University of North Carolina Press, 1986).

Enright, D. J., ed., *Fair of Speech: The Uses of Euphemism* (New York: Oxford University Press, 1985).

Erlich, Eugene, *Amo, Amas, Amat, and More: How to Use Latin to Your Own Advantage and to the Astonishment of Others* (New York: Harper & Row, 1985).

Little, Joyce A., "Words, Words Everywhere . . . And Not a Thought to Think," *Crisis*, Volume 10 (January, 1992), pp. 25-31.

Moskovit, Leonard, "A Report on the Warfare Used Against Language Critics," *Chronicles*, Volume 12 (January, 1988), pp. 23-27.

Porter, Rosalie Pedalino, "Language Choice for Latino Students," *The Public Interest*, Number 105 (Fall, 1991), pp. 48-60.

Simon, John, *Paridigms Lost: Reflections on Literacy and Its Decline* (New York: Clarkson N. Potter, 1980).

Tulloch, Sara, ed., *The Oxford Dictionary of New Words: A Popular Guide to Words in the News* (New York: Oxford University Press, 1992).

Organizations

American Classical League Miami University, Oxford, OH 45056, (513)-529-4116. Publications: *Classical Outlook, Newsletter*. Promotes the teaching of Latin and other classical languages.

Junior Classical League Miami University, Oxford, OH 45056, (513)-529-4116. Publication: *Torch*. U.S. High school students studying Latin.

National Committee for Latin and Greek c/o Robert LaBouve, 5804 Back Court Drive, Austin, TX 78731, (512)-463-9556. Publication: *Prospects*. Purpose is to initiate and coordinate efforts to promote the study of Latin and Greek on behalf of all cooperating classical organizations by developing a variety of appropriate projects and activities.

Pompeiiana, Inc. 6026 Indianola Avenue, Indianapolis, IN 46220, (317)-255-0589. Publication: *Newsletter*. Promotes Latin and classical Greek studies at the secondary school level.

LATIN AMERICA

Books and Articles

Ashby, Timothy, *The Bear in the Backyard: Moscow's Caribbean Strategy* (Lexington, MA: Lexington Books, 1987).

Asman, David, "Wealth of Naciones: People Power Comes to Latin America," *Policy Review*, Number 60 (Spring, 1992), pp. 38-45.

Barfield, Claude, "The Americas and World Trade," *The American Enterprise*, Volume 3 (July/August, 1992), pp. 10-14.

Bethell, Tom, "De Soto in Peru," *The American Spectator*, Volume 25 (August, 1992), pp. 15-16.

De Soto, Hernando, *The Other Path: The Invisible Revolution in the Third World* (New York: Harper & Row, 1989).

Evans-Pritchard, Ambrose, "Argentina Drifts Toward Disaster," *The American Spectator*, Volume 22 (September, 1989), pp. 19-21, 41.

Falcoff, Mark, "Making Central America Safe for Communism," *Commentary*, Volume 85 (June, 1988), pp. 17-24.

Falcoff, Mark, *Modern Chile 1970 - 1989: A Critical History* (New Brunswick, NJ: Transaction Books, 1989).

Falcoff, Mark, "The Only Hope for Latin America," *Commentary*, Volume 87 (April, 1989), pp. 34-38.

Goodman, Timothy, "Latin America's Reformation: The Waning of Catholicism? The Coming of Capitalism?," *The American Enterprise*, Volume 2 (July/August, 1991), pp. 41-47.

Jaeckle, Franklin A. and Whelan, James R., *The Soviet Assault on America's Southern Flank* (Washington, DC: Regnery Gateway, 1988).

Kagan, Robert, "Losing in Latin America," *Commentary*, Volume 86 (November, 1988), pp. 45-51.

Kagan, Robert, "There to Stay: The U.S. and Latin America," *The National Interest*, Number 19 (Spring, 1990), pp. 59-67.

Martin, David, "Speaking in Latin Tongues," *National Review*, Volume XLI (September 29, 1989), pp. 30-35.

Martin, David, *Tongues of Fire: The Explosion of Protestantism in Latin America* (Cambridge, MA: Basil Blackwell, 1990).

Rosenau, William and Flanagan, Linda Head, "Blood of the Condor: The Genocidal Talons of Peru's Shining Path," *Policy Review*, Number 59 (Winter, 1992), pp. 82-85.

Rosenau, William, "Poor Peru," *The American Spectator*, Volume 23 (December, 1990), pp. 16-18.

Stoll, David, *Is Latin America Turning Protestant? The Politics of Evangelical Growth* (Berkeley, CA: University of California Press, 1990).

Symmes, Patrick W., "Out to Lunch with Sendero," *The American Spectator*, Volume 24 (December, 1991), pp. 26-28.

Vargas Llosa, Mario, "The Miami Model," *Commentary*, Volume 93 (February, 1992), pp. 21-27.

Wagner, Geoffrey, *Red Calypso: The Grenadian Revolution and Its Aftermath* (Washington, DC: Regnery Gateway, 1988).

Whelan, James R. and Bozell, Patricia B., *Catastrophe in the Caribbean: The Failure of America's Human Rights Policy in Central America* (Ottawa, IL: Green Hill Publishers, 1984).

Organizations

American Studies Center 499 South Capitol Street, Suite 417, Washington, DC 20003, (202)-488-7188.

Council for Inter-American Security 1700 K Street, NW, Suite 650, Washington, DC 20006, (202)-296-3711. Publication: *West Watch: A Report on the Americas and the World*. Seeks to broaden cross-cultural cooperation and understanding among non-Marxist, academic, corporate, and political leaders throughout the Western Hemisphere; promotes U.S. policies conducive to the freedom and security of the Americas.

LAW
(see also **Crime/Punishment, Criminal Law**)

Books and Articles

Hogue, Arthur R., *Origins of the Common Law* (Indianapolis, IN: Liberty Fund, 1986).
Posner, Richard, *Law and Literature: A Misunderstood Relation* (Cambridge, MA: Harvard University Press, 1988).
Schuck, Peter H., "The New Ideology of Tort Law," *The Public Interest*, Number 92 (Summer, 1988), pp. 93-109.

Organizations

Atlantic Legal Foundation 205 East 42nd Street, 9th Floor, New York, NY, 10017, (212)-573-1960.

The Federalist Society for Law and Public Policy Studies 1700 K Street, NW, #901, Washington, DC 20006, (202)-822-8138. Publications: *The Federalist Paper, Harvard Journal of Law and Public Policy*. Seeks to bring about a reordering of priorities within the U.S. legal system that will emphasize individual liberty, traditional values, and the rule of law; considers the interpretation of the constitution to be the province of the judiciary, not the legislature.

Free Enterprise Legal Defense Fund c/o Centre for Defense of Free Enterprise, Liberty Park, 12500 N.E. Tenth Place, Bellevue, WA 98005, (206)-455-5038. Purpose is to engage in legal action to defend the right of individuals and businesses to operate unhindered in the free market.

Institute for Justice 1001 Pennsylvania Avenue, NW, #200-S, Washington, DC 20004, (202)-457-4240.

Landmark Legal Foundation 1006 Grand Avenue, 8th Floor, Kansas City, MO 64106, (816)-474-6600.

Mountain States Legal Foundation 1660 Lincoln Street, #2300, Denver, CO 80264, (303)-861-0244.

National Legal Center for the Public Interest 1000 16th Street, NW, #301, Washington, DC 20036, (202)-296-1683. Publications: *Judicial/Legislative Watch Report, White Papers, Monographs.* Cooperates with regional foundations that litigate on behalf of free enterprise, individual liberties, and limited government regulation.

New England Legal Foundation 150 Lincoln Street, Boston, MA 02111, (617)-695-3660. Publication: *The Docket.* Seeks to challenge intrusions by governments and to offset the influence of special interest groups when either attempts to overreach its jurisdiction and interfere with the private lives of New England businesses and individuals.

Northwest Legal Foundation 557 Roy Street, #100, Seattle, WA 98109, (206)-283-0503. Non-partisan public interest law firm dedicated to promoting proper and responsible exercise of government authority and safeguarding individual rights and freedoms guaranteed by the federal and state constitutions. Provides legal representation on issues involving governmental actions or laws which have a significant public impact.

Pacific Legal Foundation 2700 Gateway Oaks Drive, #200, Sacramento, CA 95833, (916)-641-8888. Publications: *At Issue, In Perspective, Achieving a Balanced Environmental Policy.* Litigates nationally on behalf of personal freedoms, free enterprise, private property rights, and a balanced approach to environmental considerations.

LAW OF THE SEA
(see also **International Relations**)

Books and Articles

Hawkins, William R., "How to Give Away Your Future: Law of the Sea," *National Review*, Volume XXXIV (April 16, 1982), pp. 410-414.
Horner, Charles, "Two More If by Sea," *The American Spectator*, Volume 23 (August, 1990), pp. 15-17.

Organizations

Council on Ocean Law 1709 New York Avenue, NW, 7th Floor, Washington, DC 20006, (202)-347-3766. Publication: *Ocean Policy News*. Addresses and promotes American interests in the growing number of uses for ocean space; seeks to increase public awareness of the need for ocean law and international order to govern these uses.

LAWYERS

Books and Articles

England, Robert Stowe, "Can the A.B.A. Declare Independence?," *National Review*, Volume XLIII (July 8, 1991), pp. 36-37.

Isaac, Rael Jean, "Legal Services and the Farmer," *The American Spectator*, Volume 19 (November, 1986), pp. 22-27.

Kilpatrick, James J., "Anatomy of a Smear: The Legal Services Corporation," *National Review*, Volume XXXV (March 4, 1983), pp. 253-254.

Methvin, Eugene H., "Texas on Trial," *National Review*, Volume XLII (December 31, 1990), pp. 32-35.

Organizations

American Tort Reform Association 1212 New York Avenue, NW, Suite 515, Washington, DC 20005, (202)-682-1163. Publications: *Leaders' Update, Legislative Watch, The Reformer, Tort Reform Report*. Seeks to remedy the current liability insurance "crisis" by developing, promoting, and coordinating the U.S. tort law system.

National Legal Center for the Public Interest 1000 16th Street, NW, Suite 301, Washington, DC 20036, (202)-296-1683. Publications: *Judicial/Legislative Watch Report, National Legal Center for the Public Interest - Monographs, National Legal Center for the Public Interest - News, National Legal Center for the Public Interest - White Papers, Public Interest Law Review*. Serves as a national resource center and clearinghouse for public interest law.

United States Justice Foundation 2091 E. Valley Parkway, Suite 1-D, Escondido, CA 92027, (619)-741-8086. Publication: *Newsletter*. Politically conservative attorneys striving to preserve the civil, property, and human rights of U.S. citizens.

Washington Legal Foundation 1705 N Street, NW, Washington, DC 20036, (202)-857-0240. Publications: *Legal Backgrounders, WLF Working Papers Studies*. Public interest law firm "dedicated to supporting the precepts of individual liberties and the free enterprise system in the administrative agencies and the courts."

LEFTISM/LEFTISTS

Books and Articles

Beichman, Arnold, *Nine Lies About America* (New York: The Library Press, 1972).

Beichman, Arnold, "Stopping the Long March Through the University," *Chronicles*, Volume 12 (January, 1988), pp. 15-19.

Boorstin, Daniel J., *The Decline of Radicalism: Reflections on America Today* (New York: Random House, 1969).

Brock, David, "Christic Mystics and Their Drug-Running Theories," *The American Spectator*, Volume 21 (May, 1988), pp. 22-26.

Brock, David, "The Evil Empire of Irvine, California," *The American Spectator*, Volume 23 (May, 1990), pp. 22-27.

Brock, David, "The Rainbow Lobby Storms Congress," *The American Spectator*, Volume 23 (November, 1990), pp. 21-24.

Brooks, David, "Good Vibrations: The New Peace Offensive," *National Review*, Volume XXXIX (November 6, 1987), pp. 36-39.

Bunzel, John, *Political Passages: Journeys of Change Through Two Decades, 1968-1988* (New York: The Free Press, 1988).

Collier, Peter and Horowitz, David, *Deconstructing the Left: From Vietnam to the Persian Gulf* (Lanham, MD: Second Thoughts Books, 1991).

Collier, Peter and Horowitz, David, *Destructive Generation: Second Thoughts About the Sixties* (New York: Summit Books, 1989).

Collier, Peter and Horowitz, David, "McCarthyism: The Last Refuge of the Left," *Commentary*, Volume 85 (January, 1988), pp. 36-41.

Collier, Peter and Horowitz, David, "Slouching Towards Berkeley: Socialism in One City," *The Public Interest*, Number 94, (Winter, 1989), pp. 47-68.

Fleming, Thomas, "Diplomats, Dupes, and Traitors," *Chronicles*, Volume 12 (October, 1988), pp. 8-10.

Fleming, Thomas, "Second Thoughts," *Chronicles*, Volume 13 (July, 1989), pp. 8-10.

Fleming, Thomas, "A Time to Reap," *Chronicles*, Volume 12 (February, 1988), pp. 6-8.

Grenier, Richard, "The New Treason of the Clerks," *National Review*, Volume XLII (July 23, 1990), pp. 42-45.

Hollander, Paul, "An End to the Political Pilgrimage?," *Chronicles*, Volume 13 (June, 1989), pp. 28-32.

Hollander, Paul, *Anti-Americanism: Critiques at Home and Abroad, 1965 - 1990* (New York: Oxford University Press, 1992).

Hollander, Paul, *Political Pilgrims: Travels of Western Intellectuals to the Soviet Union, China, and Cuba 1928 - 1978* (New York: Oxford University Press, 1981).

Hollander, Paul, *The Survival of the Adversary Culture: Social Criticism and Political Escapism in American Society* (New Brunswick, NJ: Transaction Books, 1988).

Hook, Sidney, *Out of Step: An Unquiet Life in the Twentieth Century* (New York: Harper & Row, 1987).

Horowitz, David, "Coalition Against the U.S," *National Review*, Volume XLIII (February 25, 1991), pp. 36-38.

Horowitz, David, "Socialism: Guilty as Charged," *Commentary*, Volume 90 (December, 1990), pp. 17-24.

Isaac, Rael Jean and Isaac, Erich, *The Coercive Utopians: Social Deception by America's Power Players* (Washington, DC: Regnery Gateway, 1983).

Johns, Michael, "The Admiral Who Jumped Ship: Inside the Center for Defense Information," *Policy Review*, Number 44 (Spring, 1988), pp. 58-64.

Klehr, Harvey, *Far Left of Center: The American Radical Left Today* (New Brunswick, NJ: Transaction Books, 1988).

Koch, Stephen, *Double Lives: Espionage and the War of Ideas* (New York: The Free Press, 1992).

Kristol, Irving, "The Cultural Revolution and the Capitalist Future," *The American Enterprise*, Volume 3 (March/April, 1992), pp. 43-51.

Kuehnelt-Leddihn, Erik von, *Leftism Revisited: From de Sade and Marx to Hitler and Pol Pot* (Washington, DC: Regnery Gateway, 1990).

Lewy, Guenter, *Peace and Revolution: The Moral Crisis of American Pacifism* (Grand Rapids, MI: William B. Eerdmans, 1988).

Mallon, Thomas, "Charles Reich's Con Job," *The American Spectator*, Volume 23 (October, 1990), pp. 38-40.

Morrison, Micah, "Invasion of the Watermelons," *The American Spectator*, Volume 23 (July, 1990), p. 48.

Muravchik, Joshua, "'Glasnost', the KGB, and the 'Nation,'" *Commentary*, Volume 85 (June, 1988), pp. 47-49.

Podhoretz, Norman, "Enter the Peace Party," *Commentary*, Volume 91 (January, 1991), pp. 17-21.

Poole, William T., "How Big Business Bankrolls the Left," *National Review*, Volume XLI (March 10, 1989), pp. 34-37.

Powell, Scott Steven, *Covert Cadre: Inside the Institute for Policy Studies* (Ottawa, IL: Green Hill Publishers, 1987).

Powell, Scott Steven, "Little Policy Shop Of Horrors: Jesse Jackson's Brain Trust," *Policy Review*, Number 45 (Summer, 1988), pp. 64-68.

Puddington, Arch, "Those Were the Days: The SDS Revisited," *The American Spectator*, Volume 22 (March, 1989), pp. 18-20.

Scruton, Roger, *Thinkers on the Left* (Essex, England: Longman, 1985).

Ulmer, Melville J., "Mainstream Marxism Rebutted," *The American Spectator*, Volume 21 (February, 1988), pp. 26-27.

LIBERALISM

Books and Articles

Barash, David, *The L Word: An Unapologetic, Thoroughly Biased, Long-Overdue Explication and Celebration of Liberalism* (New York: William Morrow, 1992).

Berns, Walter, "The New Pacifism and World Government," *National Review*, Volume XXXV (May 27, 1983), pp. 613-620.

Bethell, Tom, "Will Success Spoil Anti-Communists?," *National Review*, Volume XLII (March 5, 1990), pp. 38-40.

Bruckner, Pascal, *The Tears of the White Man: Compassion as Contempt* (New York: Free Press, 1986).

Buckley, William F., Jr., *Up From Liberalism* (New York: Stein & Day, 1984).

Burnham, James, *Suicide of the West: An Essay on the Meaning and Destiny of Liberalism* (Chicago, IL: Regnery Books, 1985).

Canavan, Francis, *Pins in the Liberal Balloon* (New York: Catholic Eye, 1990).

Catto, Henry, "Anthony Agonistes," *National Review*, Volume XLI (September 1, 1989), pp. 34-37, 52.

Chodorov, Frank, *The Rise and Fall of Society* (New York: Devin-Adair, 1959).

Coleman, Peter, *The Liberal Conspiracy: The Congress for Cultural Freedom and the Struggle for the Mind of Postwar Europe* (New York: The Free Press, 1989).

Decter, Midge, "How the Rioters Won," *Commentary*, Volume 94 (July, 1992), pp. 17-22.

Decter, Midge, "The Professor and the L-Word," *Commentary*, Volume 87 (February, 1989), pp. 39-48.

D'Souza, Dinesh, "Whatever Happened to Neoliberalism?," *National Review*, XLI (June 2, 1989), pp. 34-36.

Donohue, William A., *The New Freedom: Individualism and Collectivism in the Social Lives of Americans* (New Brunswick, NJ: Transaction Books, 1991).

Ferguson, Andrew, "America's New Man," *The American Spectator*, Volume 25 (January, 1992), pp. 26-33.

Fleming, Thomas, "Flies Trapped in Honey," *Chronicles*, Volume 16 (January, 1992), pp. 10-13.

Gray, John, "The End of History - Or of Liberalism?," *National Review*, Volume XLI (October 27, 1989), pp. 33-35.

Gray, John, *Liberalisms: Essays in Political Philosophy* (New York: Routledge, Chapman and Hall, 1989).

Grenier, Richard, "The New Treason of the Clerks," *National Review*, Volume XLII (July 23, 1990), pp. 42-45.

Hamerow, Theodore S., "Exotic Revolutionism and the Western Intelligentsia," *Modern Age*, Volume 34 (Spring, 1992), pp. 203-213.

Harries, Owen, "The Cold War and the Intellectuals: In Mockery of the Promise and Fitness of Things," *Commentary*, Volume 92 (October, 1991), pp. 13-20.

Hazlitt, Henry, *Man vs. the Welfare State* (Lanham, MD: University Press of America, 1983).

Hitchcock, James, *What Is Secular Humanism?* (Ann Arbor, MI: Servant Books, 1982).

Johnson, Paul, "Idols of Destruction: Is There a Substitute for God?," *Crisis*, Volume 9 (June, 1991), pp. 24-30.

King, Florence, "The Goading of America," *Chronicles*, Volume 15 (May, 1991), pp. 23-27.

Kristol, Irving, "Liberalism and American Jews," *Commentary*, Volume 86 (October, 1988), pp. 19-23.

Kuehnelt-Leddihn, Erik von, "The Iron Rod of American 'Liberalism,'" *Chronicles*, Volume 12 (November, 1988), pp. 15-17.

Lasch, Christopher, *The True and Only Heaven: Progress and Its Critics* (New York: Norton, 1991).

Lipkis, Jeff, "The Brainchild of Earnest Gentlemen: How Liberalism Went Left," *Reason*, Volume 22 (April, 1991), pp. 36-40.

Martin, David, "What Makes People Good?," *National Review*, Volume XLIII (September 9, 1991), pp. 25-29.

Mayer, William G., "The Shifting Sands of Public Opinion: Is Liberalism Back?," *The Public Interest*, Number 107 (Spring, 1992), pp. 3-17.

Minogue, Kenneth, *Alien Powers: The Pure Theory of Ideology* (New York: St. Martin's, 1985).

Murray, Charles, "The Coming of Custodial Democracy," *Commentary*, Volume 86 (September, 1988), pp. 19-24.

Murray, Charles, "The Legacy of the 60s," *Commentary*, Volume 94 (July, 1992), pp. 23-30.

Pangle, Thomas, "The Liberal Paradox: Might Religion Have an Answer?," *Crisis*, Volume 10 (May, 1992), pp. 18-25.

Puddington, Arch, "Why Aren't These People Smiling?," *National Review*, Volume XLIII (November 4, 1991), pp. 44-46, 60.

Sandel, Michael, *Liberalism and the Limits of Justice* (Cambridge, MA: Cambridge University Press, 1982).

Shils, Edward, "Liberalism: Collectivist and Conservative," *Chronicles*, Volume 13 (July, 1989), pp. 12-14.

Sobran, Joseph, "A Nation of Loners," *National Review*, Volume XLI (September 1, 1989), pp. 28-29.

Sobran, Joseph, "The Party of Compassion," *National Review*, Volume XXXIII (June 26, 1981), pp. 716-722.

Spinello, Richard A., "Fatal Attraction: The Problem of Cultural Relativism," *Crisis*, Volume 8 (September, 1990), pp. 20-24.

Tyrrell, R. Emmett, *The Liberal Crack-Up* (New York: Simon & Schuster, 1984).

Tyrrell, R. Emmett, *Public Nuisances* (New York: Basic Books, 1979).
Weaver, Richard, *Ideas Have Consequences* (Chicago, IL: University of Chicago Press, 1984).
Wisse, Ruth R., *If I Am Not for Myself … : The Liberal Betrayal of the Jews* (New York: The Free Press, 1992).

LIBERTARIANISM

Books and Articles

Carey, George W., ed., *Freedom and Virtue: The Conservative/Libertarian Debate* (Lanham, MD: University Press of America, 1984).
Dennis, Richard, "Libertarian Is an L-Word, Too," *Reason*, Volume 20 (March, 1989), pp. 28-30.
Garris, Eric, "Libertarians Belong in the GOP," *Reason*, Volume 20 (March, 1989), pp. 27-28.
Rockwell, Llewellyn H., Jr. and Tucker, Jeffrey A., "Ayn Rand Is Dead," *National Review*, Volume XLII (May 28, 1990), pp. 35-36.
Rockwell, Llewellyn H., ed., *The Free-Market Reader: Essays in the Economics of Liberty* (Auburn, AL: The Ludwig von Mises Institute, 1991).

Organizations

Cato Institute 224 Second Street, SE, Washington, DC 20003, (202)-546-0200. Publications: *Cato Journal: An Interdisciplinary Journal on Public Policy Analysis, Cato Policy Report, Regulation.* A public policy research foundation dedicated to increasing policy debate to allow consideration of more options the institute believes are consistent with traditional American principles of limited government, individual liberty, and peace.

LibertyTree Network 134 98th Avenue, Oakland, CA 94603, (510)-568-6047. Publications: *LibertyTree, Review and Catalog for Your Life, Liberty, and Prosperity.* Persons and organizations promoting the history and practice of individual liberty, with emphasis on limited government intervention.

Reason Foundation 3415 South Sepulveda Boulevard, Suite 400, Los Angeles, CA 90034, (310)-391-2245. Publications: *Reason, Privatization Watch.* Provides a better understanding of the intellectual basis of a free society and develops new ideas in public policy.

LIQUOR
(see **Alcohol**)

LITERACY

Books and Articles

Bishop, Meredith, "Why Johnny's Dad Can't Read: The Elusive Goal of Universal Adult Literacy," *Policy Review*, Number 55 (Winter, 1991), pp. 19-25.

Organizations

Barbara Bush Foundation for Family Literacy 1002 Wisconsin Avenue, NW, Washington, DC 20007, (202)-338-2006. Publications: *First Teachers: A Family Literacy Handbook for Parents, Policy Makers, Literacy Providers.* To establish literacy as a family value and break the intergenerational cycle of illiteracy in American families.

Christian Literacy Associates 541 Perry Highway, Pittsburgh, PA 15229, (412)-364-3777. Publications: *Profiles and Practices, TLC Gossip, Christian Literacy Outreach, The Light Is Coming.* Christian professionals and para-professionals who prepare literacy materials for children and adults for use through churches; volunteers also train tutors and plan literacy campaigns.

LITERATURE
(see also **Authors, Poetry, Theater**)

Books and Articles

Aldridge, John W., *Talents and Technicians: Literary Chic and the New Assembly-Line Fiction* (New York: Scribner's, 1992).

Alter, Robert, *The Pleasures of Reading in an Ideological Age* (New York: Simon & Schuster, 1989).

Bawler, Bruce, *Diminishing Fictions: Essays on the Modern American Novel and Its Critics* (St. Paul, MN: Graywolf Press, 1988).

Bowman, James, "Ghost Writer," *National Review*, Volume XLIV (August 3, 1992), pp. 42-45.

Bradford, M. E., *Against the Barbarians and Other Reflections on Familiar Themes* (Columbia, MO: University of Missouri Press, 1992).

Bradford, M. E., *Generation of the Faithful Heart: On the Literature of the South* (LaSalle, IL: Sherwood Sugden, 1983).

Bradford, M. E., *The Reactionary Imperative: Essays Literary and Political* (LaSalle, IL: Sherwood Sugden, 1990).

Bradford, M. E., "A View from the Top of the Ridge: On the Literature of the American West," *Chronicles*, Volume 13 (February, 1989), pp. 43-47.

Crews, Frederick, *The Critics Bear It Away: Fiction and the Academy* (New York: Random House, 1992).

Cronin, Richard, "Politicizing Literature," *Modern Age*, Volume 32 (Fall, 1989), pp. 311-317.

Dalton, Katherine, "Books and Book Reviewing, or Why All Press Is Good Press," *Chronicles*, Volume 13 (January, 1989), pp. 20-22.

Davenport, Guy, *The Geography of the Imagination: Forty Essays* (San Francisco, CA: North Point Press, 1981).

Decter, Midge, "The Rushdiad," *Commentary*, Volume 87 (June, 1989), pp. 18-23.

D'Souza, Dinesh, "Multiculturalism 101: Great Books of the Non-Western World," *Policy Review*, Number 56 (Spring, 1991), pp. 22-30.

Dunlap, John R., "Kiddie Litter," *The American Spectator*, Volume 22 (December, 1989), pp. 19-21.

Epstein, Joseph, "Educated by Novels," *Commentary*, Volume 88 (August, 1989), pp. 33-39.

Epstein, Joseph, *A Line Out for a Walk: Familiar Essays* (New York: Norton, 1991).

Epstein, Joseph, *Partial Payments: Essays on Writers and Their Lives* (New York: Norton, 1989).

Epstein, Joseph, *Plausible Prejudices: Essays on American Writing* (New York: Norton, 1985).

Epstein, Joseph, "Who Killed Poetry?," *Commentary*, Volume 86 (August, 1988), pp. 13-20.

Fleming, Thomas, "Kazin and Caligula?," *Chronicles*, Volume 13 (January, 1989), pp. 8-10.

Fleming, Thomas, "Place of Asylum," *Chronicles*, Volume 12 (January, 1988), pp. 6-7.

Fleming, Thomas, "Science Fictions," *Chronicles*, Volume 15 (August, 1991), pp. 12-14.

Fussell, Paul, *Thank God for the Atom Bomb, and Other Essays* (New York: Summit Books, 1988).

Garrett, George, "Inch by Inch," *Chronicles*, Volume 14 (April, 1990), pp. 18-20.

Garrett, George, "Publishing Is...," *Chronicles*, Volume 13 (January, 1989), pp. 12-15.

Griffin, Bryan F., *Panic Among the Philistines* (Washington, DC: Regnery Gateway, 1983).

Groth, Janet, *Edmund Wilson: A Critic for Our Time* (Athens, OH: Ohio University Press, 1989).

Hart, Jeffrey, *Acts of Recovery: Essays on Politics and Culture* (Hanover, NH: University Press of New England, 1989).

Heard, Alex, "Brat Pack II," *The American Spectator*, Volume 22 (October, 1989), pp. 27-29.

Horgan, Paul, *A Certain Climate: Essays on History, Arts, and Letters* (Middletown, CT: Wesleyan University Press, 1988).

Iannone, Carol, "Feminism vs. Literature," *Commentary*, Volume 86 (July, 1988), pp. 49-53.

Iannone, Carol, "From 'Lolita' to 'Piss Christ,'" *Commentary*, Volume 89 (January, 1990), pp. 52-54.

Iannone, Carol, "PC and the Ellis Affair," *Commentary*, Volume 92 (July, 1991), pp. 52-54.

Iannone, Carol, "A Turning of the Critical Tide?," *Commentary*, Volume 88 (November, 1989), pp. 57-59.

James, Henry, *Essays, American and English Writers* (New York: The Library of America, 1984).

James, Henry, *European Writers and The Prefaces* (New York: The Library of America, 1984).

Johnson, Paul, *Intellectuals* (New York: Harper & Row, 1988).

Kaminsky, Alice R., *The Victim's Song* (Buffalo, NY: Prometheus Books, 1985).

Kernan, Alvin, *The Death of Literature* (New Haven, CT: Yale University Press, 1990).

Kenner, Hugh, *A Colder Eye: The Modern Irish Writers* (New York: Knopf, 1983).

Kenner, Hugh, *Gnomon: Essays in Contemporary Literature* (Durham, NC: Duke University Library, 1970).

Kenner, Hugh, *A Homemade World: The American Modernist Writers* (Baltimore, MD: Johns Hopkins University Press, 1988).

Kenner, Hugh, *Mazes: Essays* (San Francisco, CA: North Point Press, 1989).

Kenner, Hugh, *The Mechanic Muse* (New York: Oxford University Press, 1988).

Kenner, Hugh, *A Sinking Island: The Modern English Writers* (New York: Knopf, 1988).

Kopff, E. Christian, "Publishers and Sinners," *Chronicles*, Volume 13 (January, 1989), pp. 16-18.

Leavis, Q. D., "Solzhenitsyn, the Creative Artist, and the Totalitarian State," *Modern Age*, Volume 32 (Fall, 1989), pp. 294-310.

Lejeune, Anthony, "The Rise and Fall of the Western," *National Review*, Volume XLI (December 31, 1989), pp. 23-26.

Lind, Michael, "The Two Cultures (continued)," *Commentary*, Volume 92 (August, 1991), pp. 31-35.

McDonnell, Thomas P., "Emily and the Feminists," *Chronicles*, Volume 12 (July, 1988), pp. 12-14.

McNamee, Gregory, "Plundered Province: The American West as Literary Region," *Chronicles*, Volume 15 (November, 1991), pp. 46-48.

Molnar, Thomas, "Beyond Good and Evil: Contemporary Fiction's Strange New Vision of Morality," *Crisis*, Volume 7 (July/August, 1989), pp. 40-44.

Panichas, George A., "Growing Wings to Overcome Gravity," *Modern Age*, Volume 34 (Spring, 1992), pp. 194-202.

Percy, Walker, "Physician as Novelist, or Why the Best Training for a Novelist in These Last Years of the 20th Century Is an Internship at Bellevue or Cook

County Hospital, and How This Training Best Prepares Him for Diagnosing T. S. Eliot's 'Waste Land,'" *Chronicles*, Volume 13 (May, 1989), pp. 10-12.

Percy, Walker, *Signposts in a Strange Land,* Patrick Samway, ed. (New York: Farrar, Straus and Giroux, 1991).

Pipes, Daniel, "The Ayatollah, the Novelist, and the West," *Commentary*, Volume 87 (June, 1989), pp. 9-17.

Podhoretz, Norman, *The Bloody Crossroads: Where Literature and Politics Meet* (New York: Simon & Schuster, 1986).

Posner, Richard, *Law and Literature: A Misunderstood Relation* (Cambridge, MA: Harvard University Press, 1988).

Queenan, Joe, "Character Assassins," *The American Spectator*, Volume 21 (December, 1988), pp. 14-16.

Ryn, Claes, *Will, Imagination, and Reason* (Washington, DC: Regnery Gateway, 1986).

Sampson, Robert, "Adventure Fiction: The Machinery of the Dark," *Chronicles*, Volume 15 (August, 1991), pp. 16-19.

Schwartz, Stephen A., "Paz in Our Time," *The American Spectator*, Volume 23 (December, 1990), pp. 32-33.

Selic, Momcilo, "Writers' Union," *Chronicles*, Volume 13 (January, 1989), pp. 23-25.

Simon, John, *The Sheep From the Goats: Selected Literary Essays of John Simon* (New York: Weidenfield and Nicolson, 1989).

Spiller, Robert E., et al., eds., *Literary History of the United States,* 3rd ed. (New York: Macmillan, 1963).

Tanner, Stephen L., "Religion and Critical Theory," *Chronicles*, Volume 14 (July, 1990), pp. 51-53.

Tate, J. O., "Don't Get Your Knickers in a Twist," *National Review*, Volume XXXVII (November 15, 1985), pp. 48-54.

Trilling, Lionel, *Beyond Culture: Essays on Literature and Learning* (New York: Harvest/Harcourt Brace Jovanovich, 1978).

Tuttleton, James W., "City Literature: States of Mind," *Modern Age*, Volume 33 (Fall, 1990), pp. 269-279.

Vargas Llosa, Mario, "Literature and Freedom," *Chronicles*, Volume 16 (April, 1992), pp. 14-17.

Vargas Llosa, Mario, "Transforming a Lie into Truth: A Metaphor of the Novelist's Task," *National Review*, Volume XLII (October 15, 1990), pp. 68-70.

Wheeler, Richard S., "Notes from a Writer of Trash," *Chronicles*, Volume 15 (November, 1991), pp. 48-50.

Wheeler, Richard S., "Writing Offbeat Westerns," *Chronicles*, Volume 15 (August, 1991), pp. 20-23.

Williamson, Chilton, Jr., "Big Little House in American Literature," *Chronicles*, 15 (November, 1991), pp. 20-25.

Williamson, Chilton, Jr., "The Cow in the Trail," *Chronicles*, Volume 13 (November, 1989), pp. 12-14.

Williamson, Chilton, Jr., "Western Is as Western Does," *Chronicles*, Volume 15 (November, 1991), pp. 12-13.
Winchell, Mark Royden, *Neoconservative Criticism: Norman Podhoretz, Kenneth S. Lynn, and Joseph Epstein* (Boston, MA: Twayne Publishers, 1991).

LOBBYISTS

Books and Articles

Abramson, Alan J. and Penner, Rudolph G., "Special Interests, Public Opinion, and Public Policy," *The American Enterprise*, Volume 1 (September/October, 1990), pp. 79-80.
Brock, David, "The Rainbow Lobby Storms Congress," *The American Spectator*, Volume 23 (November, 1990), pp. 21-24.
Choate, Pat, *Agents of Influence* (New York: Knopf, 1990).
Hood, John, "Children's Crusade: Armed with Business Rhetoric and Dubious 'Facts', The Children's Defense Fund Has Become the Most Potent Lobbyist for a Renewed Welfare State," *Reason*, Volume 24 (June, 1992), pp. 32-35.
Navarro, Peter, *The Policy Game: How Special Interests and Ideologues Are Stealing America* (New York: John Wiley and Sons, 1984).
Ornstein, Norman J. and Schmitt, Mark, "The New World of Interest Politics," *The American Enterprise*, Volume 1 (January/February, 1990), pp. 47-51.

LOCAL GOVERNMENT
(see **Municipal Government**)

LOVE

Books and Articles

Polhemus, Robert M., *Erotic Faith: Being in Love From Jane Austin to D.H. Lawrence* (Chicago, IL: University of Chicago Press, 1990).
Scruton, Roger, *Sexual Desire: A Moral Philosophy of the Erotic* (New York: The Free Press, 1986).

MAFIA
(see **Organized Crime**)

MANNERS

Books and Articles

Kasson, John F., *Rudeness and Civility: Manners in Nineteenth Century Urban America* (New York: Hill and Wang, 1990).

Lukacs, John, "American Manners," *Chronicles*, Volume 12 (November, 1988), pp. 9-14.

Martin, Judith, *Common Courtesy: In Which Miss Manners Solves the Problem that Baffled Mr. Jefferson* (New York: Atheneum, 1985).

O'Rourke, P. J., *Modern Manners: An Etiquette Book for Rude People* (New York: Atlantic Monthly Press, 1989).

MARIJUANA

Books and Articles

Anderson, Patrick, *High in America: The True Story Behind NORML and the Politics of Marijuana* (New York: Viking, 1981).

Kleiman, Mark, *Marijuana: Costs of Abuse, Costs of Control* (Westport, CT: Greenwood Press, 1989).

Mano, D. Keith, "Marijuana," *National Review*, Volume XLII (May 14, 1990), pp. 58-59.

Miner, Brad, "How Sweet Is Mary Jane?," *National Review*, Volume XLI (June 25, 1990), p. 44.

Vigilante, Richard and Cowan, Richard, "Is Decriminalization Advisable?," *National Review*, Volume XXV (April 29, 1983), pp. 485-495.

Organizations

National Organization for the Reform of Marijuana Laws (NORML) 1636 R Street, NW, 3rd Floor, Washington, DC 20009, (202)-483-5500. Publications: *Common Sense for America, Drug Law Report, A Legal Reporting Service for Attorneys, Marijuana Penalty Pamphlet, The Leaflet, Legal Challenges to the Marijuana Laws.* Seeks an end to all criminal penalties for personal possession, use, and cultivation of marijuana.

MARINE CORPS
(see **Military (U.S.)**)

MARITIME ISSUES

Books and Articles

Guralnick, Morris, "Reviving the Merchant Marine," *Chronicles*, Volume 13
    (May, 1989), pp. 53-54.
Myles, Douglas, *The Great Waves* (New York: McGraw Hill, 1985).
Wisgerhof, Paul R., "Look, No Ships!," *The National Interest*, Number 10
    (Winter, 1987/88), pp. 105-108.

Organizations

American Association of Port Authorities 1010 Duke Street, Alexandria, VA
22314, (703)-684-5700. Publications: *Committee Reports, Newsletter, Seaports
of the Western Hemisphere, Graphics Manual, Mitigation Handbook, Finance
Survey, Salary Survey.*

American Institute of Merchant Shipping 1000 16th Street, NW, Suite 511,
Washington, DC 20036, (202)-775-4399. Publications: *American Institute of
Merchant Shipping - Newsline, Maritime Highlights.* Serves as a spokesman for
the U.S. Merchant Marine industry, with respect to maritime issues and
establishment of a strong, well-balanced American flag fleet adequate to meet the
national needs for both commerce and defense.

Federation of American Controlled Shipping 50 Broadway, 34th Floor, New
York, NY 10004, (212)-344-1483. Formed to counterbalance U.S. maritime union
efforts to discredit the economic and strategic value of American-controlled
Liberian, Bahamian, and Panamanian shipping, and to establish worldwide
shipping policies and practices as they affect FACS ships, other shipping
organizations, labor matters, ship operations, maritime safety, and pollution
prevention.

MATHEMATICS

Books and Articles

Finn, Chester E., Jr., "Math Angles & Saxon," *National Review*, Volume XL
    (November 25, 1988), pp. 30-31.
Guillen, Michael, *Bridges to Infinity: The Human Side of Mathematics* (Los
    Angeles, CA: Jeremy Tarcher, 1984).
Nelson, Caleb, "Bring Back the Old Math," *The American Spectator*, Volume
    22 (November, 1989), pp. 36-37.
Paulos, John Allen, *Innumeracy: Mathematical Illiteracy and Its Consequences*
    (New York: Hill and Wang, 1988).

Saxon, John, "Algebra Made ... Understandable," *National Review*, Volume XXXIII (May 29, 1981), pp. 611-613.

Saxon, John, "The Breakthrough in Algebra," *National Review*, Volume XXXIII (October 16, 1981), pp. 1204-1206.

Saxon, John, "Save Our Mathematics," *National Review*, Volume XXXV (August 19, 1983), pp. 1016-1033.

MEDIA BIAS

Books and Articles

Anderson, Lorrin, "Guilt and Gasoline," *National Review*, Volume XLIV (June 8, 1992), pp. 35-37.

Anderson, Lorrin, "Here Now, the News ...," *National Review*, Volume XLIV (November 16, 1992), pp. 47-52, 69.

Anderson, Lorrin, "Race, Lies, and Videotape," *National Review*, Volume XLII (January 22, 1990), pp. 40-42.

Anderson, Lorrin, "The Way It Was: The Ethics of Docudrama," *Chronicles*, Volume 15 (September, 1991), pp. 53-56.

Bethell, Tom, "Major Media Stylebook," *National Review*, Volume XLIV (November 16, 1992), pp. 48-49.

Bethell, Tom, "Now They Tell Us," *National Review*, Volume XLIV (November 30, 1992), pp. 24-27.

Bethell, Tom, "Will Success Spoil Anti-Communists?," *National Review*, Volume XLII (March 5, 1990), pp. 38-40.

Bowman, James, "Ghost Writer," *National Review*, Volume XLIV (August 3, 1992), pp. 42-45.

Bozell, L. Brent III and Baker, Brent, eds., *And That's the Way It Isn't: A Reference Guide to Media Bias* (Alexandria, VA: Media Research Center, 1990).

Bozell, L. Brent III and Baker, Brent, "Henry Luce, Call Your Medium," *National Review*, Volume XLI (September 15, 1989), p. 37.

Braley, Russell, *Bad News: The Foreign Policy of The New York Times* (Chicago, IL: Regnery Gateway, 1984).

Brookhiser, Richard, "Public Opinion and the Jogger," *Commentary*, Volume 88 (July, 1989), pp. 50-52.

Catto, Henry, "Anthony Agonistes," *National Review*, Volume XLI (September 1, 1989), pp. 34-37, 52.

Clurman, Richard M., *Beyond Malice: The Media's Years of Reckoning* (New Brunswick, NJ: Transaction Books, 1988).

Cowden-Guido, Richard, "The Post-*Webster* Press," *National Review*, Volume XLII (November 19, 1990), pp. 36-39.

Dinsmore, Herman H., *All the News That Fits: A Critical Analysis of the News and Editorial Content of the New York Times* (New Rochelle, NY: Arlington House, 1969).

Drummond, William J., "About Face: From Alliance to Alienation - Blacks and the News Media," *The American Enterprise*, Volume 1 (July/August, 1990), pp. 23-29.

Garment, Suzanne, *Scandal: The Crisis of Mistrust in American Politics* (New York: Times Books, 1991).

Goldstein, Tom, *The News at Any Cost: How Journalists Compromise Their Ethics to Shape the News* (New York: Simon & Schuster, 1985).

Hannaford, Peter, *Talking Back to the Media* (New York: Facts on File, 1986).

Iyengar, Shanto and Kinder, Donald R., *News that Matters: Television and American Opinion* (Chicago, IL: University of Chicago Press, 1987).

Krosnick, Jon A., "The Uses and Abuses of Public Opinion Polls: The Case of Louis Harris and Associates," *Chronicles*, Volume 14 (February, 1990), pp. 47-49.

Ledeen, Michael, "The New McCarthyism," *The American Spectator*, Volume 21 (October, 1988), pp. 34-36.

Levin, Andrea, "CNN vs. Israel," *Commentary*, Volume 92 (July, 1991), pp. 48-51.

Lichter, S. Robert and Noyes, Richard E., "In the Media Spotlight: Bush at Midpoint," *The American Enterprise*, Volume 2 (January/February, 1991), pp. 49-53.

Lichter, S. Robert , et al., *The Media Elite: America's New Powerbrokers* (Bethesda, MD: Adler and Adler, 1986).

Lichter, S. Robert., et al., *Watching America: What Television Tells Us About Our Lives* (Englewood, NJ: Prentice Hall, 1991).

Moore, Gary, "Reporting Nicaragua," *The National Interest*, Number 4 (Summer, 1986), pp. 79-87.

Muravchik, Joshua, *News Coverage of the Sandinista Revolution* (Washington, DC: American Enterprise Institute for Public Policy Research, 1988).

Neuhaus, Richard John, "Those Turbulent Bishops," *National Review*, Volume XLI (December 31, 1989), pp. 32-33.

Oliver, Charles, "Beyond Big Bird: PBS Is a Relic in an Age of TV Choice," *Reason*, Volume 23 (June, 1991), pp. 32-37.

Perlmutter, Amos, "Soviet Historiography, Western Journalism," *National Review*, Volume XLV (January 18, 1992), pp. 30-31.

Rusher, William A., *The Coming Battle for the Media: Curbing the Power of the Media Elite* (New York: William Morrow, 1988).

Smith, Ted J. III, *Moscow Meets Main Street* (Washington, DC: The Media Institute, 1988).

Smith, Ted J. III, "The Watchdog's Bite," *The American Enterprise*, Volume 1 (January/February, 1990), pp. 63-70.

Sobran, Joseph, et al., "The Decline of American Journalism," *National Review*, Volume XLV (June 21, 1993), pp. 25-64.

Stein, Benjamin J., "The Real Amerika: The Story that ABC Bought but Didn't Sell," *The American Spectator*, Volume 20 (May, 1987), pp. 16-18.

Taylor, S. J., *Stalin's Apologist: Walter Duranty, The New York Times' Man in Moscow* (New York: Oxford University Press, 1990).

Thompson, Loren B., "The Press and the Pentagon: Old Battles, New Skirmishes," *The American Enterprise*, Volume 3 (January/ February, 1992), pp. 14-18.

Wattenberg, Ben J., *The Good News Is the Bad News Is Wrong* (New York: Simon & Schuster, 1984).

Organizations

Accuracy In Media 1275 K Street, NW, Suite 1150, Washington, DC 20005, (202)-371-6710. Publications: *AIM Report, Index of AIM Reports*. Nonpartisan, news media watchdog organization.

Center for Media and Public Affairs 2101 L Street, NW, #405, Washington, DC 20037, (202)-223-2942. Publication: *Media Monitor*. Analyzes how media treat social and political issues; conducts surveys to determine media impact on public opinion.

Media Research Center 113 South West Street, Suite 200, Alexandria, VA 22314, (703)-683-9733. Publications: *MediaWatch, TV, etc.* News media watchdog organization; also tracks political activism of Hollywood community.

National Conservative Foundation 618 South Alfred Street, Alexandria, VA 22314-4002, (703)-684-1800. Publication: *Newswatch*. Promotes media fairness by exposing liberal domination thereof.

MEDICAID/MEDICARE
(see **Health Care**)

MEDICINE
(see **Doctors, Health Care, Pharmaceuticals**)

MENTAL HEALTH
(see **Psychiatry**)

MEXICO

Books and Articles

Pastor, Robert A. and Castaneda, Jorge G., *Limits to Friendship: The United States and Mexico* (New York: Knopf, 1988).

MIDDLE EAST

Books and Articles

Ajami, Fouad, *The Arab Predicament: Arab Political Thought and Practice Since 1967* (New York: Cambridge University Press, 1981).

Cohen, Eliot A., "How to Fight Iraq," *Commentary*, Volume 90 (November, 1990), pp. 21-27.

Doughty, Charles M., *Travels in Arabia Deserta*, 2 vols. (New York: Dover Publications, 1980).

Fisk, Robert, *Pity the Nation: Lebanon's Abduction* (New York: Atheneum, 1990).

Hourani, Albert, *A History of the Arab Peoples* (Cambridge, MA: The Belknap Press of Harvard University Press, 1991).

Horne, Alistair, *A Savage War of Peace: Algeria 1954 - 1962* (London: MacMillan, 1977).

Kedourie, Elie, *Politics in the Middle East* (New York: Oxford University Press, 1992).

Kelly, J. B., et al., "Can America Bring Peace?," *National Review*, Volume XLIII (August 26, 1991), pp. 26-30.

Lewis, Bernard, *Race and Slavery in the Middle East - An Historical Enquiry* (New York: Oxford University Press, 1990).

Norton, Augustus Richard, *Amal and the Shi'a: Struggle for the Soul of Lebanon* (Austin, TX: University of Texas Press, 1987).

O'Sullivan, John, "Arabian Days," *National Review*, Volume XLII (April 1, 1990), pp. 39-41.

O'Sullivan, John, "More Arabian Days," *National Review*, Volume XLII (April 16, 1990), pp. 38-42.

Pipes, Daniel and Garfinkle, Adam, "Is Jordan Palestine?," *Commentary*, Volume 86 (October, 1988), pp. 35-42.

Pipes, Daniel, "The Tarbabies of American Politics," *National Review*, Volume XLIV (November 16, 1992), pp. 40-44.

Pryce-Jones, David, *The Closed Circle: An Interpretation of the Arabs* (New York: Harper & Row, 1989).

Rabin, Yitzhak, et al., "Can America Bring Peace?," *National Review*, Volume XLIII (October 7, 1991), pp. 24-28.

Rubin, Barry, *Paved with Good Intentions: The American Experience in Iran* (New York: Penguin, 1981).

Simpson, John, *Inside Iran: Life Under Khomeini's Regime* (New York: St. Martin's Press, 1988).

Singer, S. Fred, "NOPEC - The Future of Oil," *The National Interest*, Number 7 (Spring, 1987), pp. 61-67.

Tamir, Abraham, et al., "Can Israel Make Peace?," *National Review*, Volume XLII (June 25, 1990), pp. 28-35.

Wohlstettter, Albert, "High Time," *National Review*, Volume XLV (February 15, 1993), pp. 30-33.

MILITARY (U.S.)

Books and Articles

Adelman, Kenneth L. and Augustine, Norman R., *The Defense Revolution: Intelligent Downsizing of America's Military* (San Francisco, CA: Institute for Contemporary Studies Press, 1992).

Bacevich, A. J., "Gays and Military Culture," *National Review*, Volume XLV (April 26, 1993), pp. 26-31.

Campbell, Kurt M., "All Rise for Chairman Powell," *The National Interest*, Number 23 (Spring, 1991), pp. 51-60.

Codevilla, Angelo M., et al., "After the Cold War: A Symposium on New Defense Priorities," *Policy Review*, Number 53 (Summer, 1990), pp. 6-16.

Currey, Cecil B. ("Cincinnatus"), *Self-Destruction: The Disintegration and Decay of the United States Army During the Vietnam Era* (New York: Norton, 1981).

Donnelly, Elaine, "What Did You Do in the Gulf, Mommy?," *National Review*, Volume XLIII (November 18, 1991), pp. 41-44.

Dupuy, Trevor N., "How the War Was Won," *National Review*, Volume XLIII (April 1, 1991), pp. 29-31.

Goldich, Robert L., "The Strategic Importance of Mass," *The National Interest*, Number 6 (Winter 1986/87), pp. 66-74.

Hawkins, William R., "Strategy and 'Freedom of Navigation,'" *The National Interest*, Number 12 (Summer, 1988), pp. 48-56.

Howarth, Stephen, *To Shining Sea: A History of the United States Navy 1775 - 1991* (New York: Random House, 1991).

Huntington, Samuel P., "Playing to Win," *The National Interest*, Number 3 (Spring, 1986), pp. 8-16.

Horowitz, David, "The Feminist Assault on the Military," *National Review*, Volume XLIV (October 15, 1992), pp. 46-49.

Ikle, Fred Charles, "The Ghost in the Pentagon: Rethinking America's Defense," *The National Interest*, Number 19 (Spring, 1990), pp. 13-20.

Kosminsky, Jay, "Arsenal of Democracy: Defense Strategies for a Revolutionary Decade," *Policy Review*, Number 58 (Fall, 1991), pp. 66-71.

Lehman, John, "Half-Speed Ahead: Budget Strategy for a Strong Navy," *Policy Review*, Number 53 (Summer, 1990), pp. 17-19.

Luttwak, Edward N., *The Pentagon and the Art of War: The Question of Military Reform* (New York: Simon & Schuster, 1985).

Mitchell, Brian, *Weak Link: The Feminization of the American Military* (Washington, DC: Regnery Gateway, 1989).

Mitchell, Brian, "Women in Arms: What Happened in Panama," *Chronicles*, Volume 14 (May, 1990), pp. 54-55.

Moskin, J. Robert, *The U.S. Marine Corps Story* (New York: McGraw-Hill, 1988).

Murray, Williamson, "Grading the War Colleges," *The National Interest*, Number 6 (Winter, 1986/87), pp. 12-19.

Norden, Edward, "Right Behind You, Scarlett!" *The American Spectator*, Volume 24 (August, 1991), pp. 14-16.

Pattullo, E. L., "Why Not Gays in the Military?," *National Review*, Volume XLV (March 1, 1993), p. 38-41.

Weltman, John J., "The Short, Unhappy Life of the Maritime Strategy," *The National Interest*, Number 15 (Spring, 1989), pp. 79-86.

Wilson, George C., *Mud Soldiers: Life Inside the New American Army* (New York: Charles Scribner's Sons, 1989).

Worden, Simon P. and Jackson, Bruce P., "Space, Power, and Strategy," *The National Interest*, Number 13 (Fall, 1988), pp. 43-52.

Zakheim, Dov S., "Top Guns: Rating the Weapons Systems in the Gulf War," *Policy Review*, Number 57 (Summer, 1991), pp. 14-21.

Organizations

Air Force Association 1501 Lee Highway, Arlington, VA 22209-1198, (703)-247-5800. Publication: *Air Force Magazine*. U.S. citizens, both civilian and military, united to address the responsibilities imposed by the impact of aerospace technology on modern society; support armed strength adequate to maintain the security and peace of the United States and the Free World.

American Defense Preparedness Association 2101 Wilson Blvd., Suite 400, Arlington, VA 22201-3061, (703)-522-1820. Publications: *Annual Report, National Defense, National Notes, Washington Corporate Directory*. Concerned citizens and military and government personnel interested in industrial preparedness for the national defense of the United States.

Society for Military History Virginia Military Institute, Journal Office, Lexington, VA 24450, (703)-464-7468. Publication: *Journal of Military History*. Persons interested in the writing and study of military history and the preservation of manuscripts, publications, relics, and other materials related to military history.

Association of the United States Army 2425 Wilson Blvd., Arlington, VA 22201, (703)-841-4300. Publications: *Army, AUSA News, Defense Reports*. Seeks to advance the security of the United States and consolidate the efforts of all who support the United States Army as an indispensable instrument of national security.

Marine Corps Association 715 Broadway, Quantico, VA 22134, (703)-640-6161. Publications: *Leatherneck Magazine, Marine Corps Gazette*. Comprised of active duty, reserve, retired, Fleet Reserve, honorably discharged Marines, and members of other services who have served with Marine Corps units.

Marine Corps Historical Foundation Marine Corps Historical Center, Building 58, Washington Navy Yard, Washington, DC 20374, (202)-433-3914. Publications: *Membership Directory, Newsletter*. Interested in the preservation of Marine Corps history. Promotes the Marine Corps' historical role and encourages the study of its history and traditions.

Naval Historical Foundation Building 57, Washington Navy Yard, Washington, DC 20374, (202)-433-2005. Publications: *History Monograph Series, Pull Together, Naval Historical Foundation Manuscript Collection Catalog*. Members of the Navy, Marine Corps, and Coast Guard, and civilians interested in U.S. naval history.

United States Naval Institute 118 Maryland Avenue, Annapolis, MD 21402-5035, (301)-268-6110. Publications: *Flag and General Officers of the U.S. Navy, Marine Corps, and Coast Guard, Naval History, Naval Review, Proceedings*. Interested in advancing professional, literary, and scientific knowledge in the naval and maritime services and in the advancement of the knowledge of seapower.

MILITARY SPENDING
(see also **Arms Sales**)

Books and Articles

Carpenter, Ted Galen, et al., "Fighting Trim: How to Cut the Defense Budget by $100 Billion," *Policy Review*, Number 60 (Spring, 1992), pp. 50-55.

Higgs, Robert, ed., *Arms, Politics, and the Economy: Historical and Contemporary Perspectives* (New York: Holmes & Meier, 1990).

Lehman, John, "Half-Speed Ahead: Budget Strategy for a Strong Navy," *Policy Review*, Number 53 (Summer, 1990), pp. 17-19.

Owens, Mackubin Thomas, "Micromanaging the Defense Budget," *The Public Interest*, Number 100 (Summer, 1990), pp. 131-146.

Payne, James L., "Wrong Numbers: Lies and Distortions About Defense Spending," *The National Interest*, Number 14 (Winter, 1988/89), pp. 60-71.
Stein, Herbert, "Remembrance of Peace Dividends Past," *The American Enterprise*, Volume 1 (March/April, 1990), pp. 18-25.
Snyder, Jed C., "Must the U.S. Disengage?," *National Review*, Volume XLIV (November 16, 1992), pp. 29-33.
Weidenbaum, Murray, "Why Defense Spending Doesn't Matter," *The National Interest*, Number 16 (Summer, 1989), pp. 91-96.

MINORITIES

Books and Articles

Friedman, Fred, "Ladders of Opportunity: Why Some Groups Succeed Faster," *Crisis*, Volume 10 (February, 1992), pp. 22-28.
Sowell, Thomas, ed., *American Ethnic Groups* (Washington, DC: The Urban Institute Press, 1978).
Sowell, Thomas, *Ethnic America: A History* (New York: Basic Books, 1983).
Winnick, Louis, *New People in Old Neighborhoods: The Role of New Immigrants in Rejuvenating New York's Communities* (New York: Russell Sage Foundation, 1990).

MODERNISM

Books and Articles

Cantor, Norman F., *Twentieth Century Culture: Modernism to Deconstruction* (New York: Peter Lang, 1988).
Eksteins, Modris, *The Rites of Spring: The Great War and the Birth of the Modern Age* (Boston, MA: Houghton Mifflin, 1989).
Gablik, Suzi, *Has Modernism Failed?* (New York: Thames and Hudson, 1984).
Johnson, Paul, *The Birth of the Modern: World Society 1815 - 1830* (New York: Harper Collins, 1991).
Kirk, Russell, et al., "Essays on the Crisis of Modernity," *Modern Age*, Volume 31 (Summer/ Fall, 1987), pp. 195-377.
McKnight, Stephen A., *Sacralizing the Secular: The Renaissance Origins of Modernity* (Baton Rouge, LA: Louisiana State University Press, 1989).
Malloch, Theodore R., "Ideology: The Relativistic Skepticism of Modernity," *Modern Age*, Volume 32 (Summer, 1989), pp. 224-230.
Molnar, Thomas, "Modernity," *This World*, Number 23 (Fall, 1988), pp. 40-49.
Rutler, George William, *Beyond Modernity: Reflections of a Post-Modern Catholic* (San Francisco, CA: Ignatius Press, 1987).

MOVIES

Books and Articles

Brooks, David, "More Kafka Than Capra," *National Review*, Volume XL (September 30, 1988), pp. 28-31.

Chetwynd, Lionel, "Reclaiming Hollywood," *National Review*, Volume XLV (April 26, 1993), pp. 41-44.

Collier, Peter, "Ollie uber Alles," *The American Spectator*, Volume 25 (April, 1992), pp. 28-31.

Farah, Joseph, "The Real Blacklist," *National Review*, Volume XLI (October 27, 1989), pp. 42-43.

Fraser, George MacDonald, *The Hollywood History of the World: From* One Million Years B.C. *to* Apocalypse Now (Holt, MI: Beech Tree Press, 1988).

Grenier, Richard, *Capturing the Culture: Film, Art, and Politics* (Washington, DC: Ethics and Public Policy Center, 1991).

Grenier, Richard, "Killer Bimbos," *Commentary*, Volume 92 (September, 1991), pp. 50-52.

Grenier, Richard, "Spike Lee Fever," *Commentary*, Volume 92 (August, 1991), pp. 50-53.

Heston, Charlton, "And the West Is History," *National Review*, Volume XLIV (December 28, 1992), pp. 38-40.

Kopff, E. Christian, "Arms and the Man: Clint Eastwood as Hero and Filmmaker," *Chronicles*, Volume 13 (August, 1989), pp. 21-23.

Lejeune, Anthony, "The Rise and Fall of the Western," *National Review*, Volume XLI (December 31, 1989), pp. 23-26.

Lejeune, Anthony, "The Way We Were," *National Review*, Volume XLIII (April 15, 1991), pp. 43-45.

Medved, Michael, "The Politics of Hollywood: What Sort of Moral Universe Do Film Producers Inhabit?," *Crisis*, Volume 9 (April, 1991), pp. 30-36.

Simon, John, *Private Screenings: Views of the Cinema of the Sixties* (New York: Macmillan, 1967).

Simon, John, *Reverse Angle: A Decade of American Films* (New York: Clarkson N. Potter, 1982).

Simon, John, *Something to Declare: Twelve Years of Films from Abroad* (New York: Clarkson N. Potter, 1983).

Sobran, Joseph, "Weird America," *National Review*, Volume XLII (October 1, 1990), pp. 38-40, 50.

Sterling, Arlene, "Class Conflict," *National Review*, Volume XLV (June 21, 1993), pp. 78-79.

Szamuely, George, "Hollywood Goes to Vietnam," *Commentary*, Volume 85 (January, 1988), pp. 48-53.

Wakeman, John, ed., *World Film Directors,* 2 vols. (New York: H. W. Wilson Co., 1987).

Organizations

Academy of Motion Picture Arts and Sciences 333 La Cienega Boulevard, Beverly Hills, CA 90211, (310)-247-3000. Publications: *Academy Players Directory, Annual Index of Motion Picture Credits*. Motion picture producers, actors, and technicians. Presents Oscar Awards. Operates National Film Information Service.

MULTICULTURALISM

Books and Articles

Alexander, Edward, "Race Fever," *Commentary*, Volume 90 (November, 1990), pp. 45-48.

Cantor, Paul, "The Fixed Canon: The Maginot Line of the College Curriculum," *The American Enterprise*, Volume 2 (September/ October, 1991), pp. 14-20.

Decter, Midge, "E Pluribus Nihil: Multiculturalism and Black Children," *Commentary*, Volume 92 (September, 1991), pp. 25-29.

D'Souza, Dinesh, "Multiculturalism 101: Great Books of the Non-Western World," *Policy Review*, Number 56 (Spring, 1991), pp. 22-30.

Falcoff, Mark, "Was 1492 a Mistake? Did Columbus Go Too Far?," *The American Enterprise*, Volume 3 (January/February, 1992), pp. 38-47.

Finn, Chester E., Jr., "Narcissus Goes to School," *Commentary*, Volume 89 (June, 1990), pp. 40-45.

Gourevitch, Philip, "The Jeffries Affair," *Commentary*, Volume 93 (March, 1992), pp. 34-38.

Ryan, Richard, "1492 and All That," *Commentary*, Volume 93 (May, 1992), pp. 41-46.

Ryerson, Andre, "Dead Asian Male: Confucius and Multiculturalism," *Policy Review*, Number 61 (Summer, 1992), pp. 74-79.

Short, Thomas, "A 'New Racism' on Campus," *Commentary*, Volume 86 (August, 1988), pp. 46-50.

Sowell, Thomas, "Cultural Diversity: A World View," *The American Enterprise*, Volume 2 (May/June, 1991), pp. 44-55.

Teachout, Terry, "Dead Center: The Myth of the Middle," *National Review*, Volume XLIV (November 2, 1992), pp. 53-55.

Washburn, Wilcomb E., "Columbus: On and Off the Reservation," *National Review*, Volume XLIV (October 5, 1992), pp. 55-58.

MULTINATIONAL CORPORATIONS
(see **Corporations, International Economy, International Trade**)

MUNICIPAL GOVERNMENT

Books and Articles

Buckley, William F., Jr., *The Unmaking of a Mayor* (New York: Viking Press, 1966).

Devine, Donald, "A Free Market in Government," *National Review*, Volume XLI (October 27, 1989), pp. 40-41.

Mysak, Joe, "The Beauty of Municipal Bonds," *The American Spectator*, Volume 22 (June, 1989), pp. 18-20.

Newfield, Jack and Barrett, Wayne, *City for Sale: Ed Koch and the Betrayal of New York* (New York: Harper & Row, 1988).

MUSIC

Books and Articles

Bayles, Martha, *Hole In Our Soul: The Loss of Beauty and Meaning in American Popular Music* (New York: The Free Press, 1993).

Bethell, Tom, "They Had a Right to Sing the Blues," *National Review*, Volume XLIII (July 8, 1991), pp. 31-33.

Bowman, James, "Plain Brown Rappers," *National Review*, Volume XLIV (July 20, 1992), pp. 36-38, 53.

Brendel, Alfred, *Music Sounded Out: Essays, Lectures, Interviews, Afterthoughts* (New York: Farrar, Straus and Giroux, 1991).

Brendel, Alfred, *Musical Thoughts and Afterthoughts* (New York: Farrar, Straus and Giroux, 1990).

Burgess, Anthony, *This Man and Music* (New York: McGraw-Hill, 1982).

Davidson, Roger and Davidson, Nicholas, "Between Tyranny and Chaos: An Appraisal of 20th-Century Music," *Chronicles*, Volume 14 (February, 1990), pp. 45-47.

Denisoff, R. Serge, *Tarnished Gold: The Record Industry Revisited* (New Brunswick, NJ: Transaction Books, 1987).

Ewen, David, *American Songwriters: An H. W. Wilson Biographical Dictionary* (New York: H. W. Wilson Co., 1987).

Ewen, David, ed., *Composers Since 1900: A Biographical and Critical Guide* (New York: H. W. Wilson Co., 1969).

Ewen, David, ed., *Composers Since 1900: First Supplement* (New York: H. W. Wilson Co., 1981).

Ewen, David, ed., *Great Composers 1300 - 1900* (New York: H. W. Wilson Co., 1986).

Ewen, David, ed., *Musicians Since 1900: Performers in Concert and Opera* (New York: H. W. Wilson Co., 1978).

Fleming, Thomas, "Rock and Roll Never Forgets," *Chronicles*, Volume 13 (August, 1989), pp. 10-13.

Hamilton, David, *The Listener's Guide to Great Instrumentalists* (New York: Facts on File, 1982).

Harris, Robert, *What to Listen for in Mozart* (New York: Simon and Schuster, 1991).

Heston, Charlton, "Just a Song," *National Review*, Volume XLIV (August 17, 1992), pp. 37, 53.

Lejeune, Anthony, "No More Enchanted Evenings," *National Review*, Volume XLV (March 29, 1993), pp. 62-64.

Lipman, Samuel, *Arguing for Music, Arguing for Culture: Essays* (Boston, MA: Godine Publishers, Inc., 1990).

Lipman, Samuel, "Does the Piano Have a Future?," *Commentary*, Volume 88 (December, 1989), pp. 48-53.

Lipman, Samuel, *The House of Music: Art in an Era of Institutions* (Boston, MA: Godine Publishers, 1984).

Lipman, Samuel, *Music After Modernism* (New York: Basic Books, 1979).

Lipman, Samuel, "Where the New Music Went Wrong," *Commentary*, Volume 90 (December, 1990), pp. 51-54.

Osborne, Richard, ed., *Conversations With Von Karajan* (New York: Harper & Row, 1990).

Page, Tim, *Music From the Road: Views and Reviews 1978 - 1991* (New York: Oxford University Press, 1992).

Pattison, Robert, *The Triumph of Vulgarity: Rock Music in the Mirror of Romanticism* (New York: Oxford University Press, 1987).

Teachout, Terry, "Rap and Racism," *Commentary*, Volume 89 (March, 1990), pp. 60-61.

Tovey, Sir Donald Francis, *Essays in Musical Analysis: Chamber Music* (New York: Oxford University Press, 1989).

Youngren, William H., "Bashing Toscanini," *Commentary*, Volume 85 (April, 1988), pp. 58-62.

Organizations

American Music Center 30 W. 26th Street, Suite 1001, New York, NY 10010-2011, (212)-366-5260. Publications: *AMC Membership Directory, AMC Newsletter, New Music Repertory Directory*. Seeks to encourage the creation, performance, and recognition of contemporary American music.

Country Music Association One Music Circle South, Nashville, TN 37203, (615)-244-2840. Publication: *Close-Up*. Seeks to promote and publicize country music.

Country Music Foundation 4 Music Square, E., Nashville, TN 37203, (615)-256-1639. Publication: *Journal of Country Music*. To preserve the history of country music and encourage scholarly research in the field of country music and related areas.

Lincoln Center for the Performing Arts 70 Lincoln Center Plaza, New York, NY 10023, (212)-875-5000. Publication: *Calendar of Events.* Cultural center in New York City to sustain, encourage, and promote musical and performing arts.

Parents' Music Resource Center 1500 Arlington Blvd., #130, Arlington, VA 22209, (703)-527-9466. Publication: *Record.* Works for "ethical boundaries" in the production of recorded music; specifically works to alert parents and children to lyrics describing explicit sex, violence, substance abuse, and the occult.

Songwriters Guild of America 276 Fifth Avenue, Room 306, New York, NY 10001, (212)-686-6820. Publication: *Songwriters Guild of America - News.* Professional organization of songwriters.

NARCOTICS
(see also **Marijuana**)

Books and Articles

Adams, James Ring, "Losing the Drug War: Drugs, Banks, and Florida
      Politics," *The American Spectator*, Volume 21 (September, 1988), pp. 20-24.
Adams, James Ring, "Medellin's New Generation," *The American Spectator*,
      Volume 24 (December, 1991), pp. 22-25.
Adelson, Joseph, "Drugs and Youth," *Commentary*, Volume 87 (May, 1989), pp.
      24-28.
Anderson, Gary M. and Tollison, Robert D., "The War on Drugs as Antitrust
      Regulation," *The Cato Journal*, Volume 10 (Winter, 1991), pp. 691-701.
Alexander, Bruce, "Snow Job: Cocaine's Hazards and Addictive Power Have
      Been Greatly Exaggerated," *Reason*, Volume 22 (December, 1990), pp. 29-
      34.
Argostegui, Martin, "Castro's Scapegoat," *National Review*, Volume LIV
      (December 28, 1992), pp. 33-35.
Benjamin, Daniel K. and Miller, Roger LeRoy, *Undoing Drugs: Beyond
      Legalization* (New York: Basic Books, 1991).
Boaz, David, et al., "America After Prohibition: The Next Debate Over Drug
      Legalization: How Would It Work?," *Reason*, Volume 20 (October, 1988),
      pp. 22-29.
Boaz, David, *The Crisis in Drug Prohibition* (Washington, DC: The Cato
      Institute, 1990).
Brock, David, "The World of Narco-Terrorism," *The American Spectator*,
      Volume 22 (June, 1989), pp. 24-28.

Buechler, Mark, "Why Not Ban Falling in Love?," *Reason*, Volume 19 (March, 1988), pp. 28-31.

Dennis, Richard J., "Life After Legalization: Scenes From a Post-War America," *Reason*, Volume 23 (February, 1992), pp. 34-39.

Gazzaniga, Michael S., "The Federal Drugstore," *National Review*, Volume XLII (February 5, 1990), pp. 34-41.

Gazzaniga, Michael S., "Just the Facts, Fellas," *National Review*, Volume XLII (April 1, 1990), pp. 44-59.

Gold, Mark S., "Legalize Drugs: Just Say Never," *National Review*, Volume XLII (April 1, 1990), pp. 42-43.

Jacobs, James B., "Imagining Drug Legalization," *The Public Interest*, Number 101 (Fall, 1990), pp. 28-42.

Kaplan, John, "Taking Drugs Seriously," *The Public Interest*, Number 92 (Summer, 1988), pp. 32-50.

Mano, D. Keith, "Legalize Drugs," *National Review*, Volume XLII (May 28, 1990), pp. 49-52.

Nadelmann, Ethan A., "The Case for Legalization," *The Public Interest*, Number 92 (Summer, 1988), pp. 3-31.

Reuter, Peter, "Can the Borders Be Sealed?," *The Public Interest*, Number 92 (Summer, 1988), pp. 51-65.

Smith, Philip, "The Soldiers' Story: People in the Trenches Speak Out Against the War on Drugs," *Reason*, Volume 20 (August/September, 1988), pp. 31-33.

Trebach, Arnold S., *The Great Drug War: And Radical Proposals that Could Make America Safe Again* (New York: Macmillan, 1987).

Trebach, Arnold S. and Zeese, Kevin B., eds., *Drug Prohibition and the Conscience of Nations* (Washington, DC: Drug Policy Foundation, 1990).

van den Haag, Ernest, "Never, Again," *National Review*, Volume XLII (April 1, 1990), pp. 43-44.

NATIONAL PARKS

Books and Articles

Baden, John A., "Sylvan Socialism: The U.S. Forest Service," *Chronicles*, Volume 14 (August, 1990), pp. 23-26.

Chase, Alston, *Playing God in Yellowstone: The Destruction of America's First National Park* (San Diego, CA: Harcourt Brace Jovanovich, 1986).

Morrison, Micah, "The Yellowstone Scam," *The American Spectator*, Volume 22 (August, 1989), pp. 17-20.

Morrison, Micah, "While Yellowstone Burned," *The American Spectator*, Volume 21 (November, 1988), pp. 18-22.

Organization

National Recreation and Parks Association 1800 Silas Dean Highway, #1, Rocky Hill, CT 06067, (203)-721-1055. Publication: *APRS National Resource Directory*. Professional organization; conducts research and educational sessions; maintains library.

NATIONAL SECURITY
(see also **Foreign Policy (U.S.)**)

Books and Articles

Bohi, Douglas R., "Thinking Through Energy Security Issues," *The American Enterprise*, Volume 2 (September/October, 1991), pp. 32-35.

Bryen, Steven and Ledeen, Michael, "Breaching Export Controls: A Dumb Policy in a Dangerous World," *The American Enterprise*, Volume 2 (July/August, 1991), pp. 64-72.

Kapstein, Ethan B., "Losing Control: National Security and the Global Economy," *The National Interest*, Number 18 (Winter, 1989/90), pp. 85-90.

Triplett, William C. II, "Crimes Against the Alliance: The Toshiba-Kongsberg Export Violations," *Policy Review*, Number 44 (Spring, 1988), pp. 8-13.

Organizations

American Defense Institute 1055 North Fairfax Street, 2nd Floor, Alexandria, VA 22313, (703)-519-7000. Publications: *ADI News, POW/MIA News*. Purpose is to educate young Americans on current issues of national defense. Seeks to inform the American people of the threat to freedom and the need for a strong national defense.

Center for Strategic and International Studies 1800 K Street, NW, Suite 400, Washington, DC 20006, (202)-887-0200. Publications: *The Washington Quarterly, Washington Papers, Panel Reports*. A public policy research institute that provides policymakers with a strategic perspective on issues relating to international economics, politics, security and business. Committed to serving the common interests of the United States and other countries around the world that support representative government and the rule of law.

Center for Security Policy 1250 24th Street, NW, Suite 600, Washington, DC 20037, (202)-466-0515. Publication: *Newsletter*. Policy information network focusing on international security policy issues. Provides information to members of legislative and executive branches of government, the media, and the general public.

Council for Inter-American Security 1700 K Street, NW, Suite 650, Washington, DC 20036, (202)-393-6622. Publication: *West Watch: A Report on the Americas and the World.* Purpose is to broaden cross-cultural understanding and cooperation among non-Marxist, political, academic, and private sector leaders throughout the Americas; to promote U.S. policies conducive to freedom and security of the Western Hemisphere.

George C. Marshall Institute 1730 M Street, NW, #502, Washington, DC 20036, (202)-296-9655.

The Hoover Institution Stanford University, Stanford, CA 94305-6010, (415)-723-1687. A public policy research center devoted to advanced study on domestic public policy and international affairs. Has one of the world's largest archives and most complete libraries devoted to the economic, social and political changes of the the twentieth century.

Hudson Institute Herman Kahn Center, 5395 Emerson Way, P.O. Box 26-919, Indianapolis, IN 46226, (317)-545-1000. Publications: *Hudson Institute Briefing, Hudson Institute Opinion, Hudson Institute Report.* Studies public policy issues in areas of national security, international and domestic economics, education and employment, energy and technology, and future studies.

Institute for Foreign Policy Analysis 675 Massachusetts Avenue, 10th Floor, Cambridge, MA 02139, (617)-492-2116.

International Security Council 2401 Pennsylvania Avenue, NW, Suite 604, Washington, DC 20037, (202)-828-0802. Publication: *Global Affairs.* Objective is to raise public awareness of the geopolitical struggle between the U.S. and Soviet Union.

National Defense Council Foundation 1220 King Street, Suite #1, Alexandria, VA 22314, (703)-836-3443. Publication: *Newsletter.* Conducts studies on low-intensity conflict and research on drug trafficking.

National Strategy Information Center 140 East 56th Street, #5-H, New York, NY 10022, (212)-838-2912.

United States Global Strategy Council 1800 K Street, NW, Suite 1102, Washington, DC 20006, (202)-466-6029.

United States Strategic Institute P.O. Box 15618, Kenmore Station, Boston, MA 02215, (617)-353-8700. Publications: *Strategic Review, Monograph Series, USSI Reports Series.* "To provide a forum in which members of the broad policy community can contribute to informed debate and improved understanding of the complex problems of strategy and national defense as they affect the interests of the U.S. and its allies."

NATIONAL SERVICE

Books and Articles

Buckley, William F., Jr., *Gratitude: Reflections on What We Owe to Our Country* (New York: Random House, 1990).

Evers, Williamson M., *National Service: Pro and Con* (Stanford, CA: Hoover Institution Press, 1990).

Wildavsky, Ben, "Mandatory Voluntarism: Is There Harm in Having to Do Good?," *The American Enterprise*, Volume 2 (September/October, 1991), pp. 64-71.

NATIONAL SOCIALISM
(see **Nazism**)

NATURAL LAW

Books and Articles

Aragones, Jay J., "Beyond Bork and Brennan: Should Catholic Law Schools Teach Natural Law?," *Crisis*, Volume 8 (November, 1990), pp. 20-24.

Arkes, Hadley, *Beyond the Constitution* (Princeton, NJ: Princeton University Press, 1990).

Ball, William Bentley, "The Tempting of Robert Bork: What's a Constitution Without Natural Law?," *Crisis*, Volume 8 (June, 1990), pp. 28-32.

Hittinger, Russell, *A Critique of the New Natural Law Theory* (Notre Dame, IN: University of Notre Dame Press, 1989).

Hittinger, Russell, "The Recovery of Natural Law and the 'Common Morality,'" *This World*, Number 18 (Summer, 1987), pp. 62-74.

Jaffa, Harry V., "Of Men, Hogs, and Law," *National Review*, Volume XLIV (February 3, 1992), pp. 40-41.

van den Haag, Ernest, "Not Above the Law," *National Review*, Volume XLIII (October 7, 1991), pp. 35-36.

Stanlis, Peter J., *Edmund Burke and the Natural Law* (Lafayette, LA: Huntington House, 1986).

Weinreb, Lloyd, *Natural Law and Justice* (Cambridge, MA: Harvard University Press, 1987).

Organizations

Natural Law Society c/o Prof. Virginia Black, Philosophy and Religious Studies Department, Pace University, Pleasantville, NY 10570-2799, (914)-773-3309. Publication: *Cumulative Index*. Seeks to maintain ongoing debate between those who believe in natural law and those who don't; maintains library and biographical archive.

NAVY
(see Military (U.S.))

NAZISM

Books and Articles

Fest, Joachim, *The Face of the Third Reich: Portraits of the Nazi Leadership* (New York: Random House, 1977).
Hohne, Heinz, *The Order of the Death's Head: The Story of Hitler's S.S.* (New York: Coward-McCann, 1969).
Karetnikova, Inga and Golomstock, Igor, "Totalitarian Culture: The Encounter in Paris," *National Review*, Volume XXXVIII (May 9, 1986), pp. 42-45.
Lilla, Mark, "What Heidegger Wrought," *Commentary*, Volume 89 (January, 1990), pp. 41-51.
Methvim, Eugene, "Hitler and Stalin - Twentieth Century Superkillers," *National Review*, Volume XXXVII (May 31, 1985), pp. 22-29.
Speer, Albert, *Inside the Third Reich: Memoirs* (New York: Macmillan, 1970).

NICARAGUA

Books and Articles

Abrams, Elliott, "Who Won Nicaragua?," *Commentary*, Volume 92 (July, 1991), pp. 24-27.
Christian, Shirley, *Nicaragua: Revolution in the Family* (New York: Random House, 1985).
Cruz, Arturo J., Jr., "Anatomy of an Execution," *Commentary*, Volume 88 (November, 1989), pp. 54-56.
Cruz, Arturo J., Jr. and Falcoff, Mark, "Who Won Nicaragua?," *Commentary*, Volume 89 (May, 1990), pp. 31-38.
Evans-Pritchard, Ambrose, "Nicaragua's Killing Fields," *National Review*, Volume XLIII (April 29, 1991), pp. 38-44.

Evans-Pritchard, Ambrose, "Will the Sandinistas Give Up Power?," *National Review*, Volume XLII (April 1, 1990), pp. 36-38, 59.

Moore, Gary, "Educating the New Nicaragua," *This World*, Number 14 (Spring/Summer, 1986), pp. 12-25.

Moore, Gary, "Reporting Nicaragua," *The National Interest*, Number 4 (Summer, 1986), pp. 79-87.

Muravchik, Joshua, *News Coverage of the Sandinista Revolution* (Washington, DC: American Enterprise Institute for Public Policy Research, 1988).

O'Rourke, P. J., "Mood Swings in Nicaragua," *The American Spectator*, Volume 23 (May, 1990), pp. 18-21.

Weiner, Lauren, "Violinistas," *The American Spectator*, Volume 23 (December, 1990), pp. 21-23.

NORTH ATLANTIC TREATY ORGANIZATION (NATO)

Books and Articles

Bandow, Doug, "What Next for NATO: Get the Superpowers Out of Europe," *Reason*, Volume 20 (April, 1989), pp. 32-36.

Bell, Coral, "Why Russia Should Join NATO," *The National Interest*, Number 22 (Winter, 1990/91), pp. 37-47.

Codevilla, Angelo, "American Soldiers in Europe: Hostages to Fortune," *The National Interest*, Number 8 (Summer, 1987), pp. 89-93.

Coffey, John W., "American Soldiers in Europe: A Bulwark of Freedom," *The National Interest*, Number 8 (Summer, 1987), pp. 83-89.

Gray, Colin S., "NATO: Time to Call It a Day?," *The National Interest*, Number 10 (Winter, 1987/88), pp. 13-26.

Joffe, Josef, *The Limited Partnership: Europe, the United States, and the Burdens of Alliance* (New York: Ballinger Publishing Company, 1987).

Layne, Christopher, "Continental Divide: Time to Disengage in Europe," *The National Interest*, Number 13, (Fall, 1988), pp. 13-27.

Snyder, Jed C., "NATO: What Now?," *The American Enterprise*, Volume 2 (September/October, 1991), pp. 73-79.

Snyder, Jed C., "The Rights and Wrongs of Mr. Layne," *The National Interest*, Number 13 (Fall, 1988), pp. 28-35.

NUCLEAR ENERGY

Books and Articles

Caufield, Catherine, *Multiple Exposures: Chronicles of the Radiation Age* (New York: Harper & Row, 1989).

Cohen, Bernard L., "King Coal and the Meltdown Myth," *National Review*, Volume XXXIII (June 12, 1981), pp. 667-669.

Isaac, Rael Jean, "Games Anti-Nukes Play," *The American Spectator*, Volume 18 (November, 1985), pp. 12-16.

Lilienthal, David, *Atomic Energy: A New Start* (New York: Harper & Row, 1980).

McCracken, Samuel, "Two Years Later, Most Systems Go!," *National Review*, Volume XXXIII (March 20, 1981), pp. 278-281.

McCracken, Samuel, *The War Against the Atom* (New York: Basic Books, 1982).

Mallove, Eugene F., *Fire from Ice: Searching for the Truth Behind the Cold Fusion Furor* (New York: John Wiley and Sons, 1991).

Stelzer, Irwin M., "A Nuclear Power Revival: Blight or Blessing?," *The American Enterprise*, Volume 2 (November/ December, 1991), pp. 38-45.

Organizations

Americans for Nuclear Energy 2525 Wilson Blvd., Arlington, VA 22201, (703)-528-4430. Publication: *Nuclear Advocate*. Promotes nuclear energy.

Fusion Power Associates Two Professional Drive, Suite 248 Gaithersburg, MD 20879, (301)-258-0545. Publications: *Fusion Power Associates - Executive Newsletter, What's News in Fusion.* Seeks to promote and increase public awareness of fusion power and its potential; conducts research and maintains Fusion Information Network.

NUCLEAR PROLIFERATION

Books and Articles

Clancy, Tom and Seitz, Russell, "Five Minutes Past Midnight - And Welcome to the Age of Nuclear Proliferation," *The National Interest*, Number 26 (Winter, 1991/92), pp. 3-12.

Frankel, Benjamin, "Explosive Matter: Nuclear Proliferation Policy," *The American Enterprise*, Volume 1 (March/April, 1990), pp. 8-10.

NUCLEAR WAR

Books and Articles

Adelson, Joseph, "The Nuclear Bubble," *Commentary*, Volume 90 (November, 1990), pp. 39-44.

Kahn, Herman, *Thinking About the Unthinkable in the 1980s* (New York: Simon & Schuster, 1984).

Levin, Michael, "Philosophers Discover the Bomb," *National Review*, Volume XXXIX (December 4, 1987), pp. 34-39.

Seitz, Russell, "In from the Cold: 'Nuclear Winter' Melts Down," *The National Interest*, Number 5 (Fall, 1986), pp. 3-17.

Seitz, Russell, "Spirits of the Air," *National Review*, Volume XLII (April 1, 1990), pp. 46-47.

Sparks, Brad, "The Scandal of Nuclear Winter," *National Review*, Volume XXXVII (November 15, 1985), pp. 28-38.

Wohlstetter, Albert, "Swords Without Shields," *The National Interest*, Number 8 (Summer, 1987), pp. 31-57.

NUCLEAR WEAPONS

Books and Articles

Cohen, Sam, *The Truth About the Neutron Bomb: The Inventor of the Bomb Speaks Out* (New York: William Morrow, 1983).

Isaac, Rael Jean, "The Nuclear Test Ban Hoax," *The American Spectator*, Volume 20 (May, 1987), pp. 21-26.

Martino, Joseph P., *A Fighting Chance: The Moral Use of Nuclear Weapons* (San Francisco, CA: Ignatius Press, 1988).

Organizations

United States Arms Control and Disarmament Agency 320 Twenty-first Street, NW, Washington, DC 20451, (202)-247-8677. Publications: *World Military Expenditures, Documents on Disarmament, Arms Control and Disarmament Agreements.* Formulates and implements arms control and disarmament policies that will promote the national security of the U.S.; areas of responsiblity include: strategic nuclear weapons, conventional force reductions, chemical weapons, international arms trade, and prevention of the proliferation of nuclear weaponry.

OIL INDUSTRY

Books and Articles

Yergin, Daniel, *The Prize: The Epic Quest for Oil, Money, and Power* (New York: Simon & Schuster, 1991).

Organizations

American Petroleum Institute 1220 L Street, NW, Washington, DC 20005, (202)-682-8000. Publications: *Directory, Publications and Materials.* Seeks to maintain cooperation between government and industry on all matters of national concern; fosters foreign and domestic trade in American petroleum products; promotes the interests of the petroleum industry; encourages the study of the arts and sciences connected with the petroleum industry.

OLD AGE

Books and Articles

Hiss, Beth B. and Markson, Elizabeth W., eds., *Growing Old in America: New Perspectives on Old Age* (New Brunswick, NJ: Transaction Books, 1985). Warshawsky, Mark J., "Retiree Health Benefits: Promises Uncertain?," *The American Enterprise*, Volume 2 (July/August, 1991), pp. 57-63.

OPERA

Organizations

Lincoln Center for the Performing Arts 140 West 65th Street, New York, NY 10023, (212)-877-1800. Cultural center dedicated to promoting musical and performing arts; maintains library.

ORGANIZATIONS

Organizations

Society for Nonprofit Organizations 6314 Odana Road, Suite 1, Madison, WI 53719, (608)-274-9777. Publications: *National Directory of Service and Product Providers to Nonprofit Organizations, Nonprofit World: The National Nonprofit Leadership and Management Journal, Resource Center Catalog.* Purpose is to provide a forum for the exchange of information, knowledge, and ideas on strengthening and increasing productivity within nonprofit organizations and among their leaders.

ORGANIZED CRIME

Books and Articles

Capeci, Jerry and Mustain, Gene, *Mob Star: The Story of John Gotti* (New York: Watts, Franklin, Inc., 1988).

Delattre, Edwin J., "New Faces of Organized Crime," *The American Enterprise*, Volume 1 (May/June, 1990), pp. 38-45.

English, T. J., *The Westies: Inside the Hell's Kitchen Irish Mob* (New York: G.P. Putnam's Sons, 1990).

Kurins, Andris and O'Brien, Joseph F., *Boss of Bosses: The Fall of the Godfather: The FBI and Paul Castellano* (New York: Simon and Schuster, 1991).

McMenamin, Michael, "Cleaning Up the Teamsters," *Reason*, Volume 21 (May, 1989), pp. 26-31.

Pileggi, Nicholas, *Wiseguy: Life in a Mafia Family* (New York: Simon & Schuster, 1985).

Pistone, Joseph D., *Donnie Brasco: My Undercover Life in the Mafia*, With Richard Woodley. (New York: New American Library, 1987).

Posner, Gerald, *Warlords of Crime: Chinese Secret Societies - The New Mafia* (New York: McGraw-Hill, 1989).

Sterling, Claire, *Octopus: The Long Reach of the International Sicilian Mafia* (New York: W. W. Norton, 1990).

Sterling, Claire, *The Time of the Assassins* (New York: Holt, Rinehart & Winston, 1983).

PATENTS

Books and Articles

Merges, Robert, "What Should Be Patentable?," *The American Enterprise*, Volume 2 (March/April, 1991), pp. 13-15.

Organizations

Affiliated Inventors Foundation 2132 East Bijou Street, Colorado Springs, CO 80909-5950, (719)-635-1234. Publications: *Invention News, Invention Digest*. Offers assistance to independent inventors; provides low-cost or free patent attorney and consulting services.

American Intellectual Property Law Association 2001 Jefferson Davis Highway, Suite 203, Arlington, VA 22202, (703)-415-0780. Publications: *AIPLA Bulletin, AIPLA Quarterly Journal*. To aid in the operation and improvement of U.S. patent, trademark, and copyright systems, including the laws by which they are governed and rules and regulations under which federal agencies administer those laws.

PEACE CORPS

Books and Articles

Edwards, Elizabeth, "Shangri-La Revisited: Conservatives in the Peace Corps," *Policy Review*, Number 47 (Winter, 1989), pp. 70-73.

PENTAGON
(see **Military (U.S.)**)

PERFORMING ARTS
(see **Music, Theater**)

PHARMACEUTICALS

Books and Articles

Calfee, John E., "FDA Regulation: Moving Toward a Black Market in Information," *The American Enterprise*, Volume 3 (March/April, 1992), pp. 34-41.

Larson, Elizabeth, "Unequal Treatments," *Reason*, Volume 23 (April, 1992), pp. 48-50.

Moore, William J. and Newman, Robert J., "Drug Restrictions and Medicaid Costs," *The American Enterprise*, Volume 1 (September/October, 1990), pp. 76-78.

Rubin, Paul H., "What the FDA Doesn't Want You to Know," *The American Enterprise*, Volume 2 (May/June, 1991), pp. 18-20.

PHILANTHROPY

Books and Articles

Adelson, Joseph, "The Psychology of Altruism," *Commentary*, Volume 86 (November, 1988), pp. 40-44.

Bennett, James T., *Patterns of Corporate Philanthropy: Ideas, Advocacy, and the Corporation* (Washington, DC: Capital Research Center, 1990).

Carlson, Tucker, "Holy Dolers: The Secular Lessons of Mormon Charity," *Policy Review*, Number 59 (Winter, 1992), pp. 25-31.

DiLorenzo, Thomas J. and Bennett, James T., *Unfair Competition: The Profits of Nonprofits* (Lanham, MD: Hamilton Press, 1988).

Olasky, Marvin, *The Tragedy of American Compassion* (Washington, DC: Regnery Gateway, 1992).

Poole, William T., "How Big Business Bankrolls the Left," *National Review*, Volume XLI (March 10, 1989), pp. 34-37.

Wuthnow, Robert, ed., *Faith and Philanthropy in America: Exploring the Role of Religion in America's Voluntary Sector* (San Francisco, CA: Jossey-Bass, 1990).

PHILOSOPHY

Books and Articles

Brown, Harold O. J., "Regression and Renewal: The Prophecies of Pitirim Sorokin," *Chronicles*, Volume 16 (January, 1992), pp. 26-28.

Clark, Stephen R. L., "The Spiritual Meaning of Philosophy," *Chronicles*, Volume 13 (September, 1989), pp. 14-19.

Fleming, Thomas, "Flies Trapped in Honey," *Chronicles*, Volume 16 (January, 1992), pp. 10-13.

Fortin, Ernest, "Between the Lines: Was Leo Strauss a Secret Enemy of Truth?," *Crisis*, Volume 7 (December, 1989), pp. 19-26.

Gray, John, *Liberalisms: Essays in Political Philosophy* (New York: Routledge, Chapman and Hall, 1989).

Hayek, Friedrich, *The Constitution of Liberty* (Chicago, IL: University of Chicago Press, 1978).

Hook, Sidney, *The Hero in History: A Study in Limitations and Possibility* (Boston, MA: Beacon Press, 1955).

Johnson, Paul, *Intellectuals* (New York: Harper & Row, 1988).

Levy, David, *Political Order: Philosophical Anthropology, Modernity, and the Challenge of Ideology* (Baton Rouge, LA: Louisiana State University Press, 1988).

Lilla, Mark, "What Heidegger Wrought," *Commentary*, Volume 89 (January, 1990), pp. 41-51.

MacIntyre, Alasdair, *Whose Justice? Which Rationality?* (Notre Dame, IN: Notre Dame University Press, 1988).

MacIntyre, Alasdair, *Three Rival Versions of Moral Enquiry: Encyclopedia, Genealogy, and Tradition* (Notre Dame, IN: University of Notre Dame Press, 1990).

McCoy, Charles N. R., *On the Intelligibility of Political Philosophy*, James V. Schall, ed. (Washington, DC: Catholic University of America Press, 1989).

Mead, Walter B., "Christianity and the Modern Political Order: The Question of Functionality," *Modern Age*, Volume 32 (Spring, 1988), pp. 122-130.

Molnar, Thomas, "Selling Heidegger Short," *Chronicles*, Volume 12 (June, 1988), pp. 34-36.

Ortega y Gasset, Jose, *Man and Crisis* (New York: W. W. Norton, 1958).

Pangle, Thomas L., *The Enobling of Democracy: The Challenge of the Postmodern Age* (Baltimore, MD: Johns Hopkins University Press, 1992).

Pangle, Thomas, L., ed., *The Rebirth of Classical Political Rationalism: An Introduction to the Thought of Leo Strauss* (Chicago, IL: University of Chicago Press, 1989).

Popper, Karl, *The Poverty of Historicism* (New York: Routledge, Chapman & Hall, 1988).

Strauss, Leo., *The Spirit of Modern Republicanism: The Moral Vision of the American Founders and the Philosophy of Locke,* Thomas L. Pangle, ed. (Chicago, IL: University of Chicago Press, 1988).

Ryn, Claes G., "Political Philosophy and the Unwritten Constitution," *Modern Age*, Volume 34 (Summer, 1992), pp. 303-309.

Schall, James V., *Reason, Revelation, and the Foundations of Political Philosophy* (Baton Rouge, LA: Louisiana State University Press, 1987).

Scruton, Roger, *The Philosopher on Dover Beach: Essays* (New York: St. Martin's Press, 1990).

Strauss, Leo and Cropsey, Joseph, eds., *History of Political Philosophy*, 3rd ed. (Chicago, IL: University of Chicago Press, 1987).

Organizations

The Claremont Institute for the Study of Statesmanship and Political Philosophy 250 West 1st Street, #330, Claremont, CA 91711, (909)-621-5831. Publication: *Principles, National Review West.* Non-partisan foundation dedicated to recovering America's first principles and the institutions that proceed from them.

Institute for Humane Studies George Mason University, 4400 University Drive, Fairfax, VA 22030, (703)-323-1055.

Intercollegiate Studies Institute 14 South Bryn Mawr Avenue, Bryn Mawr, PA 19010, (215)-525-7501. Publications: *Modern Age, Intercollegiate Review: A Journal of Scholarship and Opinion, Continuity: A Journal of History, The Political Science Reviewer.* Seeks to develop an understanding of "the conservative philosophy of individual liberty, limited government, free-market economics, the right of private property, and the spiritual and moral underpinnings of this philosophy,"; promotes sound scholarship to this end.

Social Philosophy and Policy Center Bowling Green State University, Bowling Green, OH 43403, (419)-372-2536.

PHYSICS

Organizations

American Institute of Physics 335 East 45th Street, New York, NY 10017, (212)-661-9404. Publication: *AIP History of Physics Newsletter*. Seeks to spread knowledge of physics; provides information about physics education to students and schools; maintains the Neils Bohr Library of History of Physics and biographical archives.

PLAYS
(see **Theater**)

POETRY
(see also **Authors**)

Books and Articles

Epstein, Joseph, "Who Killed Poetry?," *Commentary*, Volume 86 (August, 1988), pp. 13-20.
Kermode, Frank, *An Appetite for Poetry* (Cambridge, MA: Harvard University Press, 1989).
Nims, John Fredrick, ed., *The Harper Anthology of Poetry* (New York: Harper & Row, 1981).
Ricks, Christopher, *The Force of Poetry* (New York: Oxford University Press, 1987).

POLAND

Books and Articles

Toranska, Teresa, *"Them": Stalin's Polish Puppets* (New York: Harper & Row, 1987).
Zawodny, Janusz K., *Death in the Forest: The Story of the Katyn Forest Massacre* (Notre Dame, IN: University of Notre Dame Press, 1962).

POLICE

Books and Articles

Baker, Mark, *Cops: Their Lives in Their Own Words* (New York: Simon and Schuster, 1985).

Conlon, Edward, "Down in the Hole: Six Weeks with the Police in New York's Subway Tunnels," *The American Spectator*, Volume 25 (May, 1992), pp. 29-41.

Greenberg, Reuben M., "Less Bang-Bang for the Buck: The Market Approach to Crime Control," *Policy Review*, Number 59 (Winter, 1992), pp. 56-60.

Meese, Edwin, III and Carrico, Bob, "Taking Back the Streets: Police Methods That Work," *Policy Review*, Number 54 (Fall, 1990), pp. 22-30.

Simon, David, *Homicide: A Year on the Killing Streets* (New York: Ballantine Books, 1991).

Organizations

The Fraternal Order of Police 2100 Gardiner Lane, Louisville, KY 40205-2900, (502)-451-2700. Publications: *National FOP Journal*. Service organization of full-time law enforcement officers.

POLITICAL CORRECTNESS

Books and Articles

Bethell, Tom, "Totem and Taboo at Stanford," *National Review*, Volume XXXIX (October 9, 1987), pp. 42-50.

Bethell, Tom, "Tulane and the Big Government Campus," *The American Spectator*, Volume 24 (May, 1991), pp. 9-11.

Bryden, David P., "It Ain't What They Teach, It's the Way That They Teach It," *The Public Interest*, Number 103 (Spring, 1991), pp. 38-53.

Coleman, James S., "A Quiet Threat to Academic Freedom," *National Review*, Volume XLIII (March 18, 1991), pp. 28-34.

D'Souza, Dinesh, *Illiberal Education: The Politics of Race and Sex on Campus* (New York: The Free Press, 1991).

D'Souza, Dinesh, "'PC' So Far," *Commentary*, Volume 92 (October, 1991), pp. 44-46.

Ferguson, Tim W., "Benetton U," *The American Spectator*, Volume 25 (January, 1992), pp. 49-51.

Finn, Chester E., Jr., "The Campus: 'An Island of Repression in a Sea of Freedom,'" *Commentary*, Volume 88 (September, 1989), pp. 17-23.

Frum, David, "Campus Counterrevolution," *The American Spectator*, Volume 24 (May, 1991), pp. 12-14.

Gallagher, Margaret Anne, "A Tyranny of Pity," *National Review*, Volume XXXVIII (September 26, 1986), pp. 28-32.

Hentoff, Nat, "The New Jacobins: Will the Terror of Political Correctness Spread from the Campus to the 'Real World'?," *Reason*, Volume 23 (November, 1991), pp. 30-33.

Iannone, Carol, "PC and the Ellis Affair," *Commentary*, Volume 92 (July, 1991), p. 52-54.

Kesler, Charles, "Shanty Time," *National Review*, Volume XXXVIII (September 6, 1986), pp. 33-36.

Mandelstamm, Allan B., "McCarthy's Ghost: Reminiscences of a Politically Incorrect Professor," *Crisis*, Volume 9 (September, 1991), pp. 14-18.

Norden, Edward, "A Month in Paradise," *The American Spectator*, Volume 25 (April, 1992), pp. 32-46.

Roche, John P., "Above the Law?," *National Review*, Volume XLIII (October 21, 1991), pp. 33-36.

Roche, John P., "The New Left Vigilantes," *National Review*, Volume XLI (December 8, 1989), pp. 34-35.

Seligman, Daniel, "How to Be Politically Correct," *Commentary*, Volume 93 January, 1992), pp. 53-54.

Sykes, Chales J., *A Nation of Victims* (New York: St. Martins, 1992).

Teachout, Terry, "Dead Center: The Myth of the Middle," *National Review*, Volume XLIV (November 2, 1992), pp. 53-55.

Tyrrell, R. Emmett, "A Bizarre Province," *The American Spectator*, Volume 24 (November, 1991), pp. 16-18.

Tyrrell, R. Emmett, "PC People," *The American Spectator*, Volume 24 (May, 1991), pp. 8-9.

Organizations

Accuracy in Academia 1275 K Street, NW, Suite 1150, Washington, DC 20005, (202)-789-4076. Publications: *The Campus Report, Academic License: The War on Academic Freedom*. Seeks accurate use of facts and historical information on college and university campuses.

Young America's Foundation 110 Elden Street, Suite A, Herndon, VA 22070 (703)-318-9608. Publications: *Libertas, Campus Leader, Continuity*. Service organization for politically conservative high school and college students; committed to bringing balance to college campuses.

POLITICS

Books and Articles

Barone, Michael and Ujifusa, Grant, *The Almanac of American Politics* (Washington, DC: National Journal, annual).

Bedard, Paul, "They'd Rather Be Hunting," *National Review*, Volume XLIV (November 30, 1992), pp. 34-37.

Bell, Jeffrey, *Populism and Elitism: Political Combat in the Age of Democracy* (Washington, DC: Regnery Gateway, 1992).

Garment, Suzanne, *Scandal: The Culture of Mistrust in American Politics* (New York: Times Books, 1991).

Hunter, James Davidson, *Culture Wars: The Struggle to Define America* (New York: Basic Books, 1991).

Inhaber, Herbert, "Of NIMBYs, LULUs, and NIMTOOs," *The Public Interest*, Number 107 (Spring, 1992), pp. 52-64.

Kirk, Russell, "Will American Caesars Arise?," *Modern Age*, Volume 32 (Summer, 1989), pp. 208-214.

McClay, Wilfred, "Religion in Politics; Politics in Religion," *Commentary*, Volume 86 (October, 1988), pp. 43-49.

Mayer, William G., "The Shifting Sands of Public Opinion: Is Liberalism Back?," *The Public Interest*, Number 107 (Spring, 1992), pp. 3-17.

O'Sullivan, John, "The Goofy Politics of George Bush," *National Review*, Volume XLIV (February 3, 1992), pp. 26-35.

O'Sullivan, John, "Why Bush Lost," *National Review*, Volume XLIV (November 30, 1992), pp. 30-34.

Rector, Robert and Sanera, Michael, eds., *Steering the Elephant: How Washington Works* (New York: Universe Books, 1987).

Schneider, William, "Off with Their Heads!: Public Resentment of Professionalism in Politics," *The American Enterprise*, Volume 3 (July/August, 1992), pp. 29-37.

Zoll, Donald Atwell, "On Political Leadership," *Modern Age*, Volume 32 (Summer, 1989), pp. 215-223.

Organizations

Leadership Institute 8001 Braddock Road, Suite 502, Springfield, VA 22151 (703)-321-8580. Publications: *Building Leadership, Leadership Training Service Directory*. Seeks to prepare conservatives for employment in Congress and other public policy organizations.

National Conservative Political Action Committee 618 Alfred Street, Alexandria, VA 22314-4002, (703)-684-1800. Political conservatives seeking to replace liberal politicians with conservatives in office.

POLLUTION
(see **Environment, Sanitation**)

POPULATION

Books and Articles

Bailey, Ronald, "Raining in Their Hearts," *National Review*, Volume XLII (December 3, 1990), pp. 32-36.

Bethell, Tom, "Imperialism and the Pill," *National Review*, Volume XXXVIII (March 14, 1986), pp. 38-40.

Fleming, Thomas, "America, from Republic to Ant Farm," *Chronicles*, Volume 15 (October, 1991), pp. 14-17.

Fumento, Michael, "The Profits of Doom: How to Achieve Fame and Fortune by Being Spectacularly Wrong," *Crisis*, Volume 9 (February, 1991), pp. 14-18.

Kasun, Jacqueline, "A Nation of Davids: Population Control and the Environment," *Chronicles*, Volume 15 (October, 1991), pp. 23-24.

Kasun, Jacqueline, *The War Against Population: The Economics and Ideology of Population Control* (San Francisco, CA: Ignatius Press, 1988).

Moore, Stephen, "So Much for 'Scarce Resources,'" *The Public Interest*, Number 106 (Winter, 1992), pp. 97-107.

Percival, Ray, "Malthus and His Ghost," *National Review*, Volume XLI (August 18, 1989), pp. 30-33.

Shaw, Peter, "Apocalypse Again," *Commentary*, Volume 87 (April, 1989), pp. 50-52.

Simon, Julian, "The Unreported Revolution in Population Economics," *The Public Interest*, Number 101 (Fall, 1990), pp. 89-100.

Simon, Julian, *The Ultimate Resource* (Princeton, NJ: Princeton University Press, 1982).

Simon, Julian, *Population Matters* (New Brunswick, NJ: Transaction Books, 1990).

Skerry, Peter, "The Census Wars," *The Public Interest*, Number 106 (Winter, 1992), pp. 17-31.

Smithson, Charles and Maurice, Charles, *The Doomsday Myth: 10,000 Years of Economic Crisis* (Stanford, CA: Hoover Institution Press, 1984).

Wattenberg, Ben, *The Birth Dearth* (New York: Pharos Books, 1987).

Zinsmeister, Karl, "Supply-Side Demography," *The National Interest*, Number 19 (Spring, 1990), pp. 68-75.

Organizations

Bureau of the Census Customer Services, U.S. Department of Commerce, Washington, DC 20233, (301)-763-4100. Provides population statistics.

PORNOGRAPHY

Books and Articles

van den Haag, Ernest, "Thinking About Rape," *The American Spectator*,
    Volume 25 (April, 1992), pp. 56-57.

Organizations

Morality in Media 475 Riverside Drive, Suite 1901, New York, NY 10115, (212)-870-3222. Publications: *Morality in Media Newsletter, Obscenity Law Bulletin*.
People concerned about the sale of pornography to the young.

National Coalition Against Pornography 800 Compton Road, Suite 9224,
Cincinnati, OH 45231, (513)-521-6227. Seeks to unite and assist religious and
civic groups and individuals who wish to eliminate what the group considers
obscenity and pornography.

POSTAL SERVICE

Books and Articles

Adie, Douglas, *Monopoly Mail: Privatizing the U.S. Postal Service* (New
    Brunswick, NJ: Transaction Books, 1988).
Bandow, Doug, "Private Cures for Postal Ills," *Reason*, Volume 20 (December,
    1988), pp. 24-27.
Crutcher, John, "Yes, Postmaster General," *Reason*, Volume 20 (December,
    1988), pp. 20-23.
Lochhead, Carolyn, "The Superior Mail: Nothing Boosts the Prospects of
    Private Mail Delivery Like Postal Service Ineptitude and a 22% Rate Hike,"
    Reason, Volume 23 (May, 1991), pp. 32-35.

POVERTY

Books and Articles

DiIulio, John J., Jr., "The Underclass: The Impact of Inner-City Crime," *The
    Public Interest*, Number 96 (Summer, 1989), pp. 28-46.
Eberstadt, Nick, "Economic and Material Poverty in the U.S.," *The Public
    Interest*, Number 90 (Winter, 1988), pp. 50-65.
Friedman, Fred, "Ladders of Opportunity: Why Some Groups Succeed Faster,"
    Crisis, Volume 10 (February, 1992), pp. 22-28.

Kilberg, William J., "How We Pay People: Changing Compensation: More to Our Benefits?," *The American Enterprise*, Volume 1 (September/October, 1990), pp. 25-33.

Kosters, Marvin H., "Be Cool, Stay in School," *The American Enterprise*, Volume 1 (March/April, 1990), pp. 60-67.

Kosters, Marvin H., "The Measure of Measures," *The American Enterprise*, Volume 2 (January/February, 1991), pp. 58-65.

Kosters, Marvin H. and Ross, Murray N., "A Shrinking Middle Class?," *The Public Interest*, Number 90 (Winter, 1988), pp. 3-27.

Magnet, Myron, "Rebels With a Cause," *National Review*, Volume XLV (March 15, 1993), pp. 46-50.

Mead, Lawrence M., "The New Politics of the New Poverty," *The Public Interest*, Number 103 (Spring, 1991), pp. 3-20.

Moynihan, Daniel Patrick, "The Underclass: Toward a Post-Industrial Social Policy," *The Public Interest*, Number 96 (Summer, 1989), pp. 16-27.

Murray, Charles, "White Welfare, White Families, White Trash," *National Review*, Volume XXXVIII (March 28, 1986), pp. 30-34.

Sawhill, Isabel V., "The Underclass: An Overview," *The Public Interest*, Number 96 (Summer, 1989), pp. 3-15.

Scanlan, James P., "The Perils of Provocative Statistics," *The Public Interest*, Number 102 (Winter, 1991), pp. 3-14.

Schwartz, Joel, "The Moral Environment of the Poor," *The Public Interest*, Number 103 (Spring, 1991), pp. 21-37.

Sowell, Thomas, *Markets and Minorities* (New York: Basic Books, 1981).

Stein, Herbert, "The Middle Class Blues," *The American Enterprise*, Volume 3 (March/April, 1992), pp. 5-9.

Vinovskis, Maris A., "Teenage Pregnancy and the Underclass," *The Public Interest*, Number 93 (Fall, 1988), pp. 87-96.

Zinsmeister, Karl, "Is Poverty the Problem? Why We Need More Intact Families and Fewer Transfer Programs," *Crisis*, Volume 7 (July/August, 1989), pp. 28-32.

POW/MIA

Organizations

National League of Families of American Prisoners and Missing in Southeast Asia 1001 Connecticut Avenue, NW, Suite 219, Washington, DC 20036, (202)-223-6846. Publications: *Annual Report, Newsletter*. Family members of American servicemen who are missing and/or prisoners in Southeast Asia as a result of the Vietnam War.

PRESIDENCY

Books and Articles

Crovitz, L. Gordon and Rabkin, Jeremy A., eds., *The Fettered Presidency: Legal Constraints on the Executive Branch* (Washington, DC: American Enterprise Institute for Public Policy Research, 1989).

Crovitz, L. Gordon, "How Ronald Reagan Weakened the Presidency," *Commentary*, Volume 86 (September, 1988), pp. 25-29.

Eastland, Terry, *Energy in the Executive: The Case for the Strong Presidency* (New York: The Free Press, 1992).

Lehman, John, *Making War: The 200-Year-Old Battle Between the President and Congress Over How Ameica Goes to War* (New York: Charles Scribners Sons, 1993).

Mansfield, Harvey C., Jr., *Taming the Prince: The Necessary Contradictions of Modern Executive Power* (New York: The Free Press, 1989).

Sidak, J. Gregory and Smith, Thomas A., "The Veto Power: How Free Is the President's Hand?," *The American Enterprise*, Volume 2 (March/April, 1991), pp. 59-64.

PRIMARIES
(see **Elections, Electoral Reform**)

PRISON

Books and Articles

Abell, Richard B., "Beyond Willie Horton: The Battle of the Prison Bulge," *Policy Review*, Number 47 (Winter, 1989), pp. 32-35.

DiIulio, John J., "What's Wrong with Private Prisons," *The Public Interest*, Number 92 (Summer, 1988), pp. 66-83.

Earley, Pete, *The Hot House: Life Inside Leavenworth Prison* (New York: Bantam Books, 1992).

Eckerd, Jack, "Responsibility, Love, and Privatization: A Businessman's Guide to Criminal Rehabilitation," *Policy Review*, Number 45 (Summer, 1988), pp. 52-55.

Logan, Charles H., *Private Prisons: Cons and Pros* (New York: Oxford University Press, 1990).

Methvin, Eugene H., "Highest Court Cost," *National Review*, Volume XLIV (March 16, 1992), pp. 36-38.

Prout, Curtis and Ross, Robert, *Care and Punishment: The Dilemmas of Prison Medicine* (Pittsburgh, PA: University of Pittsburgh Press, 1988).

PRIVACY

Books and Articles

Jaffa, Harry V. and Sobran, Joseph, "A Right to Privacy?," *National Review*, Volume XLI (March 24, 1989), pp. 51-52.
Sullum, Jacob, "Secrets for Sale: Do Strangers with Computers Know Too Much About You?," *Reason*, Volume 23 (April, 1992), pp. 28-35.

PRIVATE SCHOOLS
(see **Education (Lower)**)

PRIVATIZATION

Books and Articles

DiIulio, John J., Jr., "What's Wrong With Private Prisons," *The Public Interest*, Number 92 (Summer, 1988), pp. 66-83.
Eckerd, Jack, "Responsibility, Love, and Privatization: A Businessman's Guide to Criminal Rehabilitation," *Policy Review*, Number 45 (Summer, 1988), pp. 52-55.
Fitzgerald, Randall, *When Government Goes Private: Successful Alternatives to Public Services* (New York: Universe Books, 1988).
Logan, Charles H., *Private Prisons: Cons and Pros* (New York: Oxford University Press, 1990).
Poole, Robert W., Jr., "Stocks Populi: Privatization Can Win Bipartisan Support," *Policy Review*, Number 46 (Fall, 1988), pp. 24-29.
Prout, Curtis and Ross, Robert, *Care and Punishment: The Dilemmas of Prison Medicine* (Pittsburgh, PA: University of Pittsburgh Press, 1989).

Organizations

Foundation for Research on Economics and the Environment 4900 25th Avenue, NE, Suite 201, Seattle, WA 98105, (206)-548-1776; or, during the summer months: 502 South 19th Street, #35, Bozeman, MT 59715, (406)-585-1776.

Privatization Council, Inc. 1101 Connecticut Avenue, NW, Suite 700, Washington, DC 20036, (202)-857-1142. Publications: *Compendium of Privatization Laws, Privatization Review*. Purpose is to inform the public about the benefits of private ownership, operation, and management of public services and projects.

Shadow Privatization Commission Reason Foundation, 3415 South Sepulveda Boulevard, Suite 400, Los Angeles, CA 90034, (310)-391-2245.

PROPERTY RIGHTS

Books and Articles

Bethell, Tom, "Property and Justice," *The American Enterprise*, Volume 2 (November/December, 1991), pp. 23-26.

Bethell, Tom, "The Forgotten Right of Privacy," *National Review*, Volume XL (July 8, 1988), pp. 36-38, 53.

Bethell, Tom, "How to Start a Revolution Without Really Trying," *National Review*, Volume XXXVII (November 15, 1985), pp. 40-42, 61.

Epstein, Richard, *Takings: Private Property and the Power of Eminent Domain* (Cambridge, MA: Harvard University Press, 1985).

Fortin, Ernest L., "Free Markets Have Their Limits: Two Cheers for Capitalism," *Crisis*, Volume 10 (July/August, 1992), pp. 20-25.

Inhaber, Herbert, "Of LULUs, NIMBYs, and NIMTOOs," *The Public Interest*, Number 107 (Spring, 1992), pp. 52-64.

Langbein, John H., "The Inheritance Revolution," *The Public Interest*, Number 102 (Winter, 1991), pp. 15-31.

Pejovich, Svetozar, *The Economics of Property Rights: Towards a Theory of Comparative Systems* (Boston, MA: Kluwer Academic Publishers, 1990).

Smith, Fred L. and Kushner, Kathy H., "Good Fences Make Good Neighbors," *National Review*, Volume XLII (April 1, 1990), pp. 31-33, 59.

Organizations

Northwest Legal Foundation 557 Roy Street, #100, Seattle, WA 98109, (206)-283-0503. Public interest law firm dedicated to promoting responsible exercise of government authority and safeguarding individual rights and freedoms guaranteed by the federal and state constitutions. Provides legal representation on issues involving governmental actions or laws which have a significant public impact.

Pacific Legal Foundation 2700 Gateway Oaks Drive, #200, Sacramento, CA 95833, (916)-641-8888. Publications: *At Issue, In Perspective, Achieving a Balanced Environmental Policy*. Litigates nationally on behalf of personal freedoms, free enterprise, private property rights, and a balanced approach to environmental considerations.

PROTECTIONISM
(see also **International Trade**)

Books and Articles

Brimelow, Peter, "Before You Bet Against the Market ...," *Chronicles*, Volume 14 (January, 1990), pp. 16-18.

Cregan, John P., ed., *America Asleep: The Free Trade Syndrome and the Global Economic Challenge* (Washington, DC: The United States Industrial Council Educational Foundation, 1992).

Frantz, Douglas and Collins, Catherine, *Selling Out: How We Are Letting Japan Buy Our Land, Our Industries, Our Financial Institutions, and Our Future* (Chicago, IL: Contemporary Books, 1989).

Friedman, George and LeBard, Meredith, *The Coming War with Japan* (New York: St. Martin's Press, 1991).

Goodrich, Tucker, "Iacocca Broke," *National Review*, Volume XLII (December 3, 1990), pp. 44-45.

Harrigan, Anthony, et al., eds., *Putting America First: A Conservative Trade Alternative* (Washington, DC: United States Industrial Council Educational Foundation, 1987).

Hawkins, William R., "Free Trade Is No Free Lunch," *National Review*, Volume XXXIX (August 28, 1987), pp. 38-39.

Hawkins, William R., "Neomercantilism: Is There a Case for Tariffs?," With Comments by J. K. Galbraith and Milton Friedman, *National Review*, Volume XXXVI (April 6, 1984), pp. 25-45.

Hawkins, William R., "Whose Wealth of Whose Nation? The Case Against Unfettered Trade," *Chronicles*, Volume 14 (January, 1990), pp. 19-21.

Schlosstein, Steven, *Trade War: Greed, Power, and Industrial Policy on Opposite Sides of the Pacific* (New York: Congdon and Weed, 1984).

Stelzer, Irwin M., "The New Protectionism," *National Review*, Volume XLIV (March 16, 1992), pp. 30-34.

Tumlir, Jan, *Protectionism: Trade Policy in Democratic Societies* (Washington, DC: American Enterprise Institute for Public Policy Research, 1985).

PROTESTANTISM

Books and Articles

Brookhiser, Richard, "Are There Episcopalians in Foxholes?," *National Review*, Volume XLIII (July 29, 1991), pp. 24-28.

Brookhiser, Richard, *The Way of the WASP: How It Made America, and How It Can Save It, So to Speak* (New York: The Free Press, 1991).

Hunter, James Davison, "American Protestantism: Sorting Out the Present, Looking Toward the Future," *This World*, Number 17 (Spring, 1987), pp. 53-76.

Martin, David, "Speaking in Latin Tongues," *National Review*, Volume XLI (September 29, 1989), pp. 30-35.

Martin, David, *Tongues of Fire: The Explosion of Protestantism in Latin America* (Cambridge, MA: Basil Blackwell, 1990).

Novak, Michael, "Father of Neoconservatives," *National Review*, Volume XLIV (May 11, 1992), pp. 39-42.

Stoll, David, *Is Latin America Turning Protestant? The Politics of Evangelical Growth* (Berkeley, CA: University of California Press, 1990).

Organizations

American Baptist Historical Society 1106 S. Goodman Street, Rochester, NY 14620, (716)-473-1740. Publications: *American Baptist Quarterly, The Associate, Primary Source*. Promotes the study of Baptist history and theology.

Concordia Historical Institute 801 DeMun Avenue, St. Louis, MO 63105, (314)-721-5934. Publication: *Concordia Historical Institute Quarterly*. Serves as information bureau and research center on all phases of Lutheranism in America.

Evangelical Christian Publishers Association 3225 South Hardy Drive, Suite 101, Tempe, AZ 85282, (602)-966-3998. Publications: *Footprints, Handbook*. Companies that publish Christian religious literature. Conducts annual sales and operation survey and a series of educational seminars.

Lutheran Educational Conference of North America 122 C Street, NW, Suite 300, Washington, DC 20001, (202)-783-7505. Publications: *Lutheran Educational Conference of North America - Papers and Proceedings, Lutheran Higher Education Directory*. Provides forum for Lutheran institutions of higher education, boards, organizations, and individuals to discuss issues concerning Lutheran higher education.

Presbyterian Historical Society 425 Lombard Street, Philadelphia, PA 19147, (215)-627-1852. Publication: *American Presbyterians: Journal of Presbyterian History*. Maintains library and archives; preserves the written history of American Presbyterianism.

Rose Hill Forum House of Studies P.O. Box 3126, Aiken, SC 29802, (803)-641-1614. House of studies in the Anglican tradition; holds conferences and retreats for those who would like to study the Christian heritage in an environment free from skepticism and cynicism of many academic classrooms.

Southern Baptist Convention, Christian Life Commission 901 Commerce Street, #550, Nashville, TN 37203, (615)-244-2495; 400 North Capitol Street, NW, Suite

594, Washington, DC 20001, (202)-638-3223. Publications: *Light, Salt.* The CLC is the ethics, public policy and religious liberty agency of the SBC.

PSYCHIATRY

Books and Articles

Adelson, Joseph, "The Nuclear Bubble," *Commentary*, Volume 90 (November, 1990), pp. 39-44.

Anchell, Melvin, "Psychoanalysis vs. Sex Education," *National Review*, Volume XXXVIII (June 20, 1986), pp. 33-38, 60-61.

Isaac, Rael Jean and Armat, Virginia C., *Madness in the Streets: How Psychiatry and the Law Abandoned the Mentally Ill* (New York: The Free Press, 1990).

Szasz, Thomas, "Psychiatry in the Age of AIDS," *Reason*, Volume 21 (December, 1989), pp. 31-34.

Szasz, Thomas, "Whose Competence?," *National Review*, Volume XLI (September 15, 1989), pp. 38, 60.

Torrey, E. Fuller, *Freudian Fraud: The Malignant Effect of Freud's Theory on American Thought and Culture* (New York: Harper Collins, 1992).

Torrey, E. Fuller, "The Mental-Health Mess," *National Review*, Volume XLIV (December 28, 1992), pp. 22-25.

Torrey, E. Fuller, *Nowhere to Go: The Tragic Odyssey of the Homeless Mentally Ill* (New York: Harper & Row, 1989).

Wood, Garth, *The Myth of Neurosis: Overcoming the Illness Excuse* (New York: Harper & Row, 1986).

Zilbergeld, Bernie, *The Shrinking of America: Myths of Psychological Change* (Boston, MA: Little, Brown, 1983).

PSYCHOLOGY

Books and Articles

Adelson, Joseph, "The Psychology of Altruism," *Commentary*, Volume 86 (November, 1988), pp. 40-44.

Angres, Ronald, "Who, Really, Was Bruno Bettelheim?," *Commentary*, Volume 90 (October, 1990), pp. 26-30.

Browning, Don S., *Religious Thought and the Modern Psychologies: A Critical Conversation in the Theology of Culture* (Minneapolis, MN: Fortress Press, 1987).

Burke, Thomas, ed., *Man and Mind: A Christian Theory of Personality* (Hillsdale, MI: Hillsdale College Press, 1987).

Gazzaniga, Michael, *The Social Brain: Discovering the Networks of the Mind* (New York: Basic Books, 1985).

Harrigan, Anthony, "The Private Worlds of Mind," *Chronicles*, Volume 15 (September, 1991), pp. 26-29.

Katz, Jack, *Seductions of Crime: Moral and Sensual Attractions in Doing Evil* (New York: Basic Books, 1988).

Kristol, Elizabeth, "Declarations of Codependence," *The American Spectator*, Volume 27 (June, 1990), pp. 21-23.

Lynn, Richard, "What Makes People Rich?," *National Review*, Volume XLIII (September 9, 1991), pp. 30-33.

Roth, Byron M., "Social Psychology's 'Racism,'" *The Public Interest*, Number 98 (Winter, 1990), pp. 26-36.

Vitz, Paul C., *Sigmund Freud's Christian Unconscious* (New York: Guilford Press, 1988).

PUBLIC RELATIONS
(see **Advertising**)

PUBLIC SCHOOLS
(see **Education (Lower)**)

PUBLISHING

Books and Articles

Coyne, John R., "Henry Regnery: A Public Private Man," *National Review*, Volume XLI (June 16, 1989), pp. 40-42.

Dalton, Katherine, "Books and Book Reviewing, or Why All Press Is Good Press," *Chronicles*, Volume 13 (January, 1989), pp. 20-23.

Garrett, George, "Publishing is ...," *Chronicles*, Volume 13 (January, 1989), pp. 12-15.

Greer, Jane, "Don't Quit Your Job to Raise a Litmag," *Chronicles*, Volume 13 (January, 1989), pp. 26-28.

Kopff, E. Christian, "Publishers and Sinners," *Chronicles*, Volume 13 (January, 1989), pp. 16-18.

McGonigle, Thomas, "The World of the Small Press," *Chronicles*, Volume 13 (January, 1989), pp. 49-51.

QUOTAS
(see **Affirmative Action**)

RACISM

Books and Articles

Brimelow, Peter, "Racism at Work?," *National Review*, Volume XLV (April 12, 1993), p. 42.

Efron, Edith, "Native Son: Why a Black Supreme Court Nominee Has No Rights White Men Need Respect," *Reason*, Volume 23 (February, 1992), pp. 23-32.

Puddington, Arch, "Is White Racism the Problem?," *Commentary*, Volume 94 (July, 1992), pp. 31-36.

Scanlan, James P., "Illusions of Job Segregation," *The Public Interest*, Number 93 (Fall, 1988), pp. 54-69.

Schuman, Howard, et al., *Racial Attitudes in America: Trends and Interpretations* (Cambridge, MA: Harvard University Press, 1985).

Sowell, Thomas, *The Economics and Politics of Race: An International Perspective* (New York: William Morrow, 1983).

RADIO

Books and Articles

Morris, Geoffrey, "Talk of the Town," *National Review*, Volume XLIII (July 29, 1991), pp. 37, 53.

Roberts, James C., "The Power of Talk Radio," *The American Enterprise*, Volume 2 (May/June, 1991), pp. 56-61.

Organizations

Radio Free Europe/Radio Liberty 1201 Connecticut Avenue, NW, Suite 1100, Washington, DC 20036, (202)-457-6900. Publications: *Radio Free Europe Research Report, Radio Liberty Research Bulletin, RFE Background Reports and Situation Reports, RFE Press Survey, RFE Monitoring Transcripty.* Provides daily broadcasts to Eastern Europe and the Commonwealth of Independent States; research documentation is available by subscription; operates reference library.

RAILROADS

Organizations

National Railroad Historical Society P.O. Box 58153, Philadelphia, PA 19102-8153, (215)-557-6606. Publication: *National Railway Bulletin.* Preserves historical information on railroad subjects; conducts research; maintains library and photo archive.

Free Congress Foundation 717 Second Street, NE, Washington, DC 20002, (202)-546-3004. Publication: *The New Electric Railway Journal.* Quarterly seeks to promote electric railways as a major element in a solution to our nation's urban transportation problems, but to do so in ways that ensure the taxpayer gets maximum benefits from public monies used to support mass transit.

REAGANISM

Books and Articles

Adelman, Kenneth L., et al., "Where We Succeeded, Where We Failed: Lessons from Reagan Officials for the Next Conservative Presidency," *Policy Review*, Number 43 (Winter, 1988), pp. 44-57.

Ambrose, Stephen E., et al., "How Great Was Ronald Reagan? Our 40th President's Place in History," *Policy Review*, Number 46 (Fall, 1988), pp. 30-37.

Anderson, Martin, *Revolution* (San Diego, CA: Harcourt Brace Jovanovich, 1988).

Archer, Bill, "'Who's the Fairest of Them All?' The Truth About the '80s," *Policy Review*, Number 57 (Summer, 1991), pp. 67-73.

Bartley, Robert L., "How Reaganomics Made the World Work," *National Review*, Volume XLI (April 21, 1989), pp. 30-34.

Bartley, Robert L., *The Seven Fat Years: And How to Do It Again* (New York: The Free Press, 1992).

Baucom, Donald R., "Hail to the Chiefs: The Untold History of Reagan's SDI Decision," *Policy Review*, Number 53 (Summer, 1990), pp. 66-73.

Bennett, William J., *The De-Valuing of America: The Fight for Our Culture and Our Children* (New York: Summit Books, 1992).

Bernstein, Peter L., "Savings - and Investment and Other Myths," *The Public Interest*, Number 107 (Spring, 1992), pp. 87-94.

Brookes, Warren T., "The Silent Boom," *The American Spectator*, Volume 21 (August, 1988), pp. 16-19.

Brookhiser, Richard, *The Outside Story: How Democrats and Republicans Re-Elected Reagan* (New York: Doubleday, 1986).

Cannon, Lou, *Reagan* (New York: Putnam, 1982).

Crovitz, L. Gordon, "How Ronald Reagan Weakened the Presidency," *Commentary*, Volume 86 (September, 1988), pp. 25-29.

Daxon, Thomas E., "Shrinking Mortgage: Ronald Reagan Was a Friend to Future Taxpayers," *Policy Review*, Number 47 (Winter, 1989), pp. 68-69.

Detlefsen, Robert, *Civil Rights Under Reagan* (San Francisco, CA: Institute for Contemporary Studies Press, 1991).

Eastland, Terry, "Reagan Justice: Combating Excess, Strengthening the Rule of Law," *Policy Review*, Number 46 (Fall, 1988), p. 16-23.

Eastland, Terry, "Wanted: Energy in the Executive," *The American Spectator*, Volume 21 (November, 1988), pp. 14-16.

Fried, Charles, *Order and Law: Arguing the Revolution - A Firsthand Account* (New York: Simon & Schuster, 1991).

"From Carter to Bush: Are You Better Off Than You Were 15 Years Ago?," *Policy Review*, Number 61 (Summer, 1992), pp. 86-88.

Gaffney, Frank J., Jr., "A Policy Abandoned: How the Reagan Administration Formulated, Implemented, and Retreated from Its Arms Control Policy," *The National Interest*, Number 11 (Spring, 1988), pp. 43-52.

Haskins, Ron and Brown, Hank, "A Billion Here, a Billion There: Social Spending Under Ronald Reagan," *Policy Review*, Number 49 (Summer, 1989), pp. 22-28.

Jones, Charles O., *The Reagan Legacy: Promise and Performance* (Chatham, NJ: Chatham House, 1988).

Kirkpatrick, Jeane J., et al., "The American 80's: Disaster or Triumph? A Symposium," *Commentary*, Volume 90 (September, 1990), pp. 13-52.

Lindsey, Lawrence, *The Growth Experiment: How Tax Policy Is Transforming the U.S. Economy* (New York: Basic Books, 1990).

McGurn, William, "Lose One for the Gipper: Reagan's Presidency Has Stood the Test of History, but Will He Survive the Resentment of Historians?," *Crisis*, Volume 9 (June, 1991), pp. 31-34.

McKenzie, Richard B., "Was It a Decade of Greed?," *The Public Interest*, Number 106 (Winter, 1992), pp. 91-96.

Meiners, Roger E. and Yandle, Bruce, eds., *Regulation and the Reagan Era: Politics, Bureaucracy, and the Public Interest* (New York: Holmes and Meier, 1989).

Menges, Constantine, *Inside the National Security Council: The True Story of the Making and Unmaking of Reagan's Foreign Policy* (New York: Simon & Schuster, 1988).

Moore, Stephen, "Reaganomics in Reverse," *National Review*, Volume XLIII (February 25, 1991), pp. 43-44.

Niskanen, William A., *Reaganomics: An Insider's Account of the Policies and the People* (New York: Oxford University Press, 1988).

Perkins, Joseph, "Boom Time for Black America: The Middle Class Is Surging Under Reagan," *Policy Review*, Number 45 (Summer, 1988), pp. 26-28.

O'Sullivan, John, "Is the Heroic Age of Conservatism Over?," *National Review*, Volume XLIII (January 28, 1991), pp. 32-37.

Reagan, Ronald, *Abortion and the Conscience of the Nation* (Nashville, TN: Thomas Nelson Publishers, 1984).

Reagan, Ronald, *An American Life: The Autobiography* (New York: Simon & Schuster, 1990).

Reagan, Ronald, "The Great Rejuvenator: The Best of Ronald Reagan's Speeches," *Policy Review*, Number 46 (Fall, 1988), pp. 38-43.

Reagan, Ronald, *Speaking My Mind: Selected Speeches* (New York: Simon & Schuster, 1989).

Richman, Sheldon L., "Free Not to Choose: How the Bush and Reagan Administrations Subverted the 'Choice in Education' Movement," *Chronicles*, Volume 14 (March, 1990), pp. 48-50.

Roberts, Paul Craig, "Reaganomics and the Crash: The Fallacious Attack on the Twin Towers of Debt," *Policy Review*, Number 43 (Winter, 1988), pp. 38-42.

Rubenstein, Ed, "Decade of Greed?," *National Review*, Volume XLII (December 31, 1990), pp. 37-38.

Rubenstein, Ed, et al., "The Real Reagan Record," *National Review*, Volume XLIV (August 31, 1992), pp. 25-62.

Stubblebine, William Craig and Willett, Thomas, D., eds., *Reaganomics: A Midterm Report* (San Francisco, CA: Institute for Contemporary Studies, 1983).

Thatcher, Margaret, "Reagan's Leadership, America's Recovery," *National Review*, Volume XL (December 30, 1988), pp. 22-24.

Troy, Daniel E., "A Difference of Opinion: Reagan/Bush Judges vs. Their Predecessors," *Policy Review*, Number 61 (Summer, 1992), pp. 27-33.

Weidenbaum, Murray, *Rendezvous With Reality: The American Economy After Reagan* (New York: Basic Books, 1988).

Weinberger, Caspar, *Fighting for Peace: Seven Critical Years in the Pentagon* (New York: Warner Books, 1990).

Wildavsky, Aaron, "The Triumph of Ronald Reagan," *The National Interest*, Number 14 (Winter, 1988/89), pp. 3-9.

Wolfe, Tom, et al., "The Reagan Legacy," *National Review*, Volume XL (August 5, 1988), pp. 35-38.

Zycher, Benjamin, "Debt, Lies and Reaganomics," *National Review*, Volume XLIV (December 14, 1992), pp. 41-43.

Organizations

Ronald Reagan Presidential Library and Center for Public Affairs 40 Presidential Drive, Simi Valley, CA 93065, (805)-522-8511.

REAPPORTIONMENT

Books and Articles

Butler, David and Cain, Bruce E., "Redrawing District Lines: What's Going on and What's at Stake," *The American Enterprise*, Volume 2 (July/August, 1991), pp. 29-39.

RECESSION
(see **Economic Theories**)

REDISTRICTING
(see **Reapportionment**)

REFUGEES

Books and Articles

Aron, Leon, "The Russians Are Coming: Millions of Soviet Refugees Will Be
Fleeing to the West," *Policy Review*, Number 58 (Fall, 1991), pp. 44-49.
Moore, Stephen, "Flee Market: More Refugees at Lower Cost," *Policy Review*,
Number 52 (Spring, 1990), pp. 64-68.

REGULATION
(see also **Economic Theories, Privatization**)

Books and Articles

Adler, Jonathan H., "Quayle's Hush-Hushed Council," *National Review*,
Volume XLIV (November 2, 1992), p. 28.
Brookes, Warren T., "America Dragged Down," *National Review*, Volume XLII
(October 15, 1990), pp. 34-43.
Calfee, John E., "FDA Regulation: Moving Toward a Black Market in
Information," *The American Enterprise*, Volume 3 (March/April, 1992), pp.
34-41.
Crandall, Robert W., "What Makes Deregulation Happen?," *The American
Enterprise*, Volume 3 (March/April, 1992), pp. 12-14.
Fleming, Thomas, "The Facts of Life," *Chronicles*, Volume 14 (October, 1990),
pp. 12-15.
Gattuso, James L., "Clear the Runways: Ending Congestion and Delays,"
Reason, Volume 20 (February, 1989), pp. 31-32.
Gladwell, Malcolm, "Risk, Regulation, and Biotechnology," *The American
Spectator*, Volume 22 (January, 1989), pp. 21-24.
Hahn, Robert W., and Hopkins, Thomas D., "Regulation/Deregulation:
Looking Backward, Looking Forward," *The American Enterprise*, Volume 3
(July/August, 1992), pp. 70-79.
Horner, Constance, "Beyond Mr. Gradgrind: The Case for Deregulating the
Public Sector," *Policy Review*, Number 44 (Spring, 1988), pp. 34-38.

Kahn, Alfred E., "Surprises, but Few Regrets: A Conversation with Alfred E. Kahn," With Robert W. Poole, Jr., *Reason*, Volume 20 (February, 1989), pp. 35-39.

McChesney, Fred, "Antitrust and Regulation: Chicago's Contradictory Views," *The Cato Journal*, Volume 10 (Winter, 1991), pp. 775-798.

Marshall, Jonathan, "Risky Business," *Reason*, Volume 24 (August/September, 1992), pp. 52-53.

Meiners, Roger E. and Yandle, Bruce, eds., *Regulation and the Reagan Era: Politics, Bureaucracy, and the Public Interest* (New York: Holmes and Meier, 1989).

Miller, James C., III and Mink, Phillip, "The Ink of the Octopus: An Agenda for Deregulation," *Policy Review*, Number 61 (Summer, 1992), pp. 4-12.

Miniter, Richard, "Muddy Waters: The Quagmire of Wetlands Regulation," *Policy Review*, Number 56 (Spring, 1991), pp. 70-77.

Person, Lawrence, "Super Saver: $100 Billion and a Whole Lot of Time," *Reason*, Volume 20 (February, 1989), p. 30.

Poole, Robert W., Jr., "Deregulation: Finishing the Jobs," *National Review*, Volume XLIV (November 2, 1992), pp. 25-29.

Poole, Robert W., Jr., "Onward and Upward: Free the Airports," *Reason*, Volume 20 (February, 1989), pp. 33-35.

Rabkin, Jeremy, *Judicial Compulsions: How Public Law Distorts Public Policy* (New York: Basic Books, 1989).

Rabkin, Jeremy, "Micromanaging the Administrative Agencies," *The Public Interest*, Number 100 (Summer, 1990), pp. 116-130.

Rubin, Paul H., "The Economics of Regulating Deception," *The Cato Journal*, Volume 10 (Winter, 1991), pp. 667-690.

Samuel, Peter, "Green Grows the Downturn, O!," *National Review*, Volume XLIII (December 2, 1991), pp. 38-40.

Samuel, Peter, "Over and Out: The Drama Behind Airline Deregulation," *Reason*, Volume 20 (February, 1989), pp. 27-29.

Samuel, Peter, "Who Will Regulate the Regulators?," *National Review*, Volume XLIV (November 2, 1992), pp. 38-42.

Sidak, J. Gregory, "Broadcast News," *The American Enterprise*, Volume 3 (March/April, 1992), pp. 71-75.

Stelzer, Irwin M., "Save Us from the Re-regulators," *The American Spectator*, Volume 22 (February, 1989), pp. 25-26.

Stelzer, Irwin M., "Two Styles of Regulatory Reform," *The American Enterprise*, Volume 1 (March/April, 1990), pp. 70-77.

Weidenbaum, Murray, "Return of the 'R' Word: The Regulatory Assault on the Economy," *Policy Review*, Number 59 (Winter, 1992), pp. 40-43.

Organizations

American Enterprise Institute for Public Policy Research 1150 17th Street, NW, Washington, DC 20036, (202)-862-5800. Publications: *The American*

Enterprise, Regulation: A Journal on Government and Society. Provides conservative-leaning studies on a range of foreign and domestic issues.

Center for Individual Rights 1300 19th Street, NW, Suite 260, Washington, DC 20036, (202)-833-8400. Public interest law firm which litigates academic freedom and constitutional and regulatory issues. Seeks to limit the growth and size of government.

Competitive Enterprise Institute 233 Pennsyvania Avenue, SE, Suite 200, Washington, DC 20003, (202)-547-1010.

Foundation for Research on Economics and the Environment 4900 25th Avenue, NE, Suite 201, Seattle, WA 98105, (206)-548-1776; during the summer months: 502 South 19th Street, #35, Bozeman, MT 59715, (406)-585-1776.

RELIGION

Books and Articles

Adler, Mortimer J., *Truth in Religion: The Plurality of Religions and the Unity of Truth* (New York: Macmillan, 1990).

Amos, Gary T., *Defending the Declaration: How the Bible Influenced the Writing of the Declaration of Independence* (Brentwood, TN: Wolgemuth and Hyatt, 1990).

Berger, Peter L., "The First Freedom," *Commentary*, Volume 86 (December, 1988), pp. 64-67.

Dalin, David G., "Will Herberg in Retrospect," *Commentary*, Volume 86 (July, 1988), pp. 38-43.

Finn, James, ed., *Global Economics and Religion* (New Brunswick, NJ: Transaction Books, 1983).

Fleming, Thomas, "Peace on Earth Among Men of Good Will," *Chronicles*, Volume 14 (February, 1990), pp. 12-14.

Fowler, Robert Booth, *Unconventional Partners: Religion and Liberal Culture in the United States* (Grand Rapids, MI: William Eerdmans, 1989).

Hand, W. Brevard, "Humanism a Religion?," *This World*, Number 17 (Spring, 1987), pp. 110-114.

Herberg, Will, *Protestant - Catholic - Jew* (Chicago, IL: University of Chicago Press, 1983).

Hitchcock, James, *What Is Secular Humanism? Why Humanism Became Secular and How It Is Changing Our World* (Ann Arbor, MI: Servant Books, 1982).

Hunter, James Davidson, "'America's Fourth Faith': A Sociological Perspective on Secular Humanism," *This World*, Number 19 (Fall, 1987), pp. 101-110.

Johnson, Paul, "Idols of Destruction: Is There a Substitute For God?," *Crisis*, Volume 9 (June, 1991), pp. 24-30.

Johnston, George Sim, "Baby Boom Spirituality: How Well Does Religion Go with White Wine and Brie?," *Crisis*, Volume 9 (February, 1991), pp. 32-36.

Kristol, Irving, "Christmas, Christians, and Jews," *National Review*, Volume XL (December 30, 1988), pp. 26-27, 56.

Lefever, Ernest W., "Backward, Christian Soldiers!: The Politics of the World Council of Churches," *The National Interest*, Number 14 (Winter, 1988/89), pp. 72-82.

McClay, Wilfred, "Religion in Politics; Politics in Religion," *Commentary*, Volume 86 (October, 1988), pp. 43-49.

Martin, David, "What Makes People Good?," *National Review*, Volume XLIII (September 9, 1991), pp. 25-30.

Morrow, Kevin, "The Politics of Christian Elites," *Crisis*, Volume 7 (July/August, 1989), pp. 45-47.

Nelson, Robert H., "Unoriginal Sin: The Judeo-Christian Roots of Ecotheology," *Policy Review*, Number 53 (Summer, 1990), pp. 52-59.

Neuhaus, Richard John, *The Naked Public Square: Religion and Democracy in America* (Grand Rapids, MI: William Eerdmans, 1984).

Novak, Michael, *Belief and Unbelief: A Philosophy of Self-Knowledge* (Lanham, MD: University Press of America, 1986).

Pelikan, Jaroslav, *The Melody of Theology: A Philosophical Dictionary* (Cambridge, MA: Harvard University Press, 1988).

Pelikan, Jaroslav, ed., *The World Treasury of Modern Religious Thought* (Boston, MA: Little, Brown, 1990).

Reichley, James, *Religion in American Public Life* (Washington, DC: The Brookings Institution, 1985).

Schlossberg, Herbert, *Idols for Destruction: Christian Faith and Its Confrontation with American Society* (Nashville, TN: Thomas Nelson Publishers, 1983).

Tanner, Stephen L., "Religion and Critical Theory," *Chronicles*, Volume 14 (July, 1990), pp. 51-53.

Turner, James, *Without God, Without Creed: The Origins of Unbelief in America* (Baltimore, MD: Johns Hopkins University Press, 1985).

Organizations

Acton Institute for the Study of Religion and Liberty 161 Ottawa, NW, Grand Rapids, MI 49503, (616)-454-3080. Publications: *Religion & Liberty, R&L Notes*. Advocates a society that combines religious, civil and free market liberties, placing a high value on education and religion. Seeks to advance liberty's progress by working with religious and business leaders and students to promote a society that respects religious pluralism, individual liberties, voluntary exchanges in free and open markets, and a limited government.

Institute on Religion and Democracy 1331 H Street, NW, Suite 900, Washington, DC 20005, (202)-393-3200. Publications: *Briefing Paper, Religion and Democracy, The Religion and Economics Report*. Concerned with the tendency of certain denominations to support left-wing and Marxist regimes and movements; demands accountability of church groups for aid rendered for political purposes.

Rutherford Institute P.O. Box 7482, Charlottesville, VA 22906-7482, (804)-978-3888. Publications: *Rutherford Institute Action Newsletter, Rutherford Journal*. Provides free legal services to those whose right to freedom of religion is being encroached upon by government; concerned with family values, the right to school prayer, protection of the unborn.

REPUBLICAN PARTY

Books and Articles

Devine, Donald, "A Federalist Agenda: Some Advice for the Republicans," *Chronicles*, Volume 14 (May, 1990), pp. 21-24.

Fredenburg, Michael, "Party Without a Cause," *National Review*, Volume XLIV (February 17, 1992), pp. 36-39.

Garris, Eric, "Libertarians Belong in the GOP," *Reason*, Volume 20 (March, 1989), pp. 27-28.

McGurn, William, "Abortion and the GOP," *National Review*, Volume XLV (March 15, 1993), pp. 51-54.

Richardson, Heather S., "What Next?," *National Review*, Volume XLV (February 15, 1993), pp. 38-39.

Rollins, Edward J., "Junk Bond," *National Review*, Volume XLV (March 1, 1993), pp. 41-44.

Rusher, William A., "Forward, March!," *National Review*, Volume XLV (February 15, 1993), pp. 37-42.

Organizations

Republican National Committee 310 South Street, SE, Washington, DC 20003, (202)-863-8500.

RESEARCH AND DEVELOPMENT

Books and Articles

Gazzaniga, Michael S., "Saving Science and Saving Money," *National Review*, Volume XXXV (March 18, 1983), p. 322.

Martino, Joseph P., "Political Science: Pork Invades the Lab," *Reason*, Volume 20 (March, 1989), pp. 32-35.

Organizations

Council on Research and Technology 1735 New York Avenue, NW, Suite 500, Washington, DC 20006, (202)-628-1700. Seeks to establish a national research and development policy to ensure American technological competitiveness in the global economy; supports tax incentives for companies with strong R&D programs.

REVENUE SHARING
(see **Federalism**)

REVOLUTIONARY WAR
(see **War of Independence**)

RIGHT TO WORK

Books and Articles

Larson, Reed, "Harry Beck's Earthquake: The Coming Dues-Payers' Revolt Against Organized Labor," *Policy Review*, Number 49 (Summer, 1989), pp. 74-76.

Organizations

Center on National Labor Policy 8001 Forbes Place, Suite 101 B, Springfield, VA 22151, (703)-321-9180. Publications: *Insider's Report, News.* Protects employers, employees, and consumers who have been denied their civil rights through the excesses of union and government power, including illegal public employee strikes; promotes free enterprise in U.S. labor policy; offers free legal services; monitors the National Labor Relations Board.

National Right to Work Committee 8001 Braddock Road, Springfield, VA 22160 (703)-321-9820. Publications: *Insiders Report, National Right to Work Newsletter.* Promotes the idea that all have a right to employment without being compelled to join a union; lobbies; conducts research and educational programs.

National Right to Work Legal Defense and Education Foundation 8001 Braddock Road, Springfield, VA 22160, (703)-321-8510. Publication: *Foundation Action.* Opposes compulsory union membership; provides legal aid in the following types of cases, among others: misuse of compulsory union dues for political or ideological reasons, violations of the merit principle in public employment, and abuses of compulsory union hiring hall "referral" systems.

SANITATION

Books and Articles

Bovard, James, "A Hazardous Waste: What Else Can You Call Environmental Regulations that Prevent Recycling, Discourage Cleanups, and Stifle Improvements in Waste Management," *Reason*, Volume 21 (November, 1989), pp. 32-35.

Postrel, Virginia I. and Scarlett, Lynn, "Talking Trash: There's a Solution to America's Garbage Problem, but It Isn't What You Think," *Reason*, Volume 23 (August/September, 1991), pp. 22-31.

Starr, Roger, "Waste Disposal: A Miracle of Immaculate Consumption," *The Public Interest*, Number 105 (Fall, 1991), pp. 17-29.

Organizations

Coalition for Responsible Waste Incineration 1333 Connecticut Avenue, NW, Suite 1200, Washington, DC 20036, (202)-775-98-69. Publication: *CRWI Information Kit*. Promotes responsible incineration of industrial wastes as part of an overall waste management strategy.

National Solid Wastes Management Association 1730 Rhode Island Avenue, NW, Suite 1000, Washington, DC 20036, (202)-659-4613. Publication: *Waste Age: The Authoritative Voice of Waste Systems and Technology*. Maintains speakers' bureau; compiles statistics; conducts research programs; sponsors competitions; presents awards.

SCHOOL CHOICE

Books and Articles

Ball, G. Carl, et al., "In Search of Educational Excellence: Business Leaders Discuss School Choice and Accountability," *Policy Review*, Number 54 (Fall, 1990), pp. 54-59.

Chubb, John E. and Moe, Terry M., *Politics, Markets, and America's Schools* (Washington, DC: Brookings Institution, 1989).

Finn, Chester E., Jr., "Razing the Liberal Plantation: The Choice Backlash," *National Review*, Volume XLI (November 10, 1989), pp. 30-32.

Finn, Chester E., Jr., *We Must Take Charge: Our Schools and Our Future* (New York: The Free Press, 1991).

Glenn, Charles L., "Controlled Choice in Massachusetts' Public Schools," *The Public Interest*, Number 103 (Spring, 1991), pp. 88-105.

Gwartney, James D., "A Positive Proposal to Improve Our Schools," *The Cato Journal*, Volume 10 (Spring/Summer, 1990), pp. 159-173.

Hood, John, "Choice Challenges: Opposition to Public School Choice Is Fading, but Daunting Obstacles Await Those Who Support More Substantive Reforms," *Reason*, Volume 23 (October, 1991), pp. 43-49.

Hood, John, "Strength in Diversity," *Reason*, Volume 22 (January, 1991), pp. 28-34.

Lieberman, Myron, *Privatization and Educational Choice* (New York: St. Martin's Press, 1989).

Lieberman, Myron, *Public School Choice: Current Issues and Future Prospects* (Lancaster, PA: Technomic, 1990).

Miller, John J., "Whose Choice?," *National Review*, Volume XLIV (December 14, 1992), pp. 44-45.

Myers, William and Schwartz, Michael, "State of Choice: Minnesota Leads the Nation in Public School Options," *Policy Review*, Number 54 (Fall, 1990), pp. 67-69.

Quade, Quentin L., "A Public School Monopoly: A Pro-Choice Education Agenda," *Crisis*, Volume 10 (April, 1992), pp. 37-39.

Richman, Sheldon L., "Not Free to Choose: How the Bush and Reagan Administrations Subverted the 'Choice in Education' Movement," *Chronicles*, Volume 14 (March, 1990), pp. 48-50.

Tucker, Jeffrey A., "Evils of Choice," *National Review*, Volume XLV (March 1, 1993), pp. 44-46.

West, Edwin G., "Open Enrollment: A Vehicle for Market Competition in Schooling?," *The Cato Journal*, Volume 9 (Spring/Summer, 1989), pp. 253-262.

West, Edwin G., "Restoring Family Autonomy in Education," *Chronicles*, Volume 14 (October, 1990), pp. 16-21.

Organizations

National Association for Legal Support of Alternative Schools P.O. Box 2823, Santa Fe, NM 87504, (505)-471-6928. Publication: *National Association for the Legal Support of Alternative Schools - Tidbits*. National information and legal service center designed to research, coordinate, and support legal actions involving nonpublic educational alternatives.

SCIENCE

Books and Articles

Bruce, Robert V., *The Launching of Modern American Science, 1846 - 1876* (New York: Knopf, 1987).

Dyson, Freeman, *Eros to Gaia* (New York: Pantheon Books, 1992).

Finn, Chester E., Jr., "The Science of Bad Science," *The American Spectator*, Volume 22 (August, 1989), pp. 34-35.

Goldberg, Steven, "Feminism Against Science," *National Review*, Volume XLIII (November 18, 1991), pp. 30-33.

Regis, Ed, *Great Mambo Chicken and the Transhuman Condition: Science Slightly over the Edge* (Reading, MA: Addison-Wesley, 1990).

Organizations

Access Research Network P.O. Box 38069, Colorado Springs, CO 80937-8069, (719)-633-1772. Answers laymen's questions on science, technology and society.

American Council on Science & Health 1995 Broadway, 2nd Floor, New York, NY 10023-5860, (212)-362-7044. Publications: *Media Updates, Priorities: For Long Life and Good Health*. Provides consumers with balanced evaluations of food, chemicals, the environment, and health issues.

SECOND AMENDMENT RIGHTS
(see **Gun Control**)

SELECTIVE SERVICE

Books and Articles

Armstrong, Bill, "The Senator's View," *National Review*, Volume XXXIII (March 6, 1981), pp. 215-217.

Gold, Philip, *Evasions: The American Way of Military Service* (New York: Paragon House, 1986).

Rehyansky, Joseph A., "The Major's View," *National Review*, Volume XXXIII (March 6, 1981), pp. 217-221.

SENATE
(see **Congress**)

SEXUAL REVOLUTION

Books and Articles

Anchell, Melvin, "Psychoanalysis vs. Sex Education," *National Review*, Volume XXXVIII (June 20, 1986), pp. 33-38, 60-61.

Bennett, William J., "Why Johnny Can't Abstain," *National Review*, Volume XXXIX (July 3, 1987), pp. 36-38, 56.

Furstenberg, Frank, Jr., et al., "The Teenage Marriage Controversy," *The Public Interest*, Number 90 (Winter, 1988), pp. 121-132.

Gallagher, Maggie, *Enemies of Eros: How the Sexual Revolution Is Killing Family, Marriage, and Sex and What We Can Do About It* (Chicago, IL: Bonus Books, 1989).

Gilder, George, *Men and Marriage* (Gretna, LA: Pelican Publishing Co., 1985).

Gilder, George, *Sexual Suicide* (New York: Quadrangle Books, 1973).

Hale, John P., "Sex Ed, Up to Date," *National Review*, Volume XLIV (May 25, 1992), pp. 31-33.

Kasun, Jacqueline, "Our Erogenous Zones: The Bizarre World of Sex Education," *Crisis*, Volume 6 (March, 1988), pp. 28-34.

McConnell, Margaret Liu, "Living with *Roe v. Wade*," *Commentary*, Volume 90 (November, 1990), pp. 34-38.

Reisman, Judith, et al., *Kinsey, Sex, and Fraud: The Indoctrination of a People* (Lafayette, LA: Huntington House, 1990).

Schwartz, Michael, "Sex as Apple Pie," *National Review*, Volume XL (June 10, 1988), pp. 39-40, 57.

Scruton, Roger, *Sexual Desire: A Moral Philosophy of the Erotic* (New York: The Free Press, 1986).

Vinovskis, Maris A., "Teenage Pregnancy and the Underclass," *The Public Interest*, Number 93 (Fall, 1988), pp. 87-96.

SEXUALLY TRANSMITTED DISEASES
(see **Acquired Immune Deficiency Syndrome, Sexual Revolution**)

SHAKESPEARE

Books and Articles

Booth, Stephen, *King Lear, Macbeth, Indefinition, and Tragedy* (New Haven, CT: Yale University Press, 1983).

Heston, Charlton and Sobran, Joseph, "Touch Swords," *National Review*, Volume XLIII (June 10, 1991), pp. 34-35, 53.

Ogburn, Charlton, *The Mysterious William Shakespeare: The Myth and the Reality* (New York: Dodd, Mead, 1984).

Sobran, Joseph, "Bard Thou Never Wert," *National Review*, Volume XLIII (April 29, 1991), pp. 44-46.
Sobran, Joseph, "Shakespeare's Tragic Flaw: What's Missing from the Bard's Moral Universe," *Crisis*, Volume 9 (October, 1991), pp. 26-29.

Organizations

Shakespeare Association of America Department of English, Southern Methodist University, Dallas, TX 75275, (214)-692-2946. Publications: *Bulletin, Directory of Members.* The association seeks to forward research, criticism, teaching, and production of Shakespearean and other Renaissance drama.

Shakespeare Data Bank 1217 Ashland Avenue, Evanston, IL 60202, (708)-475-7550. Scholar associates united to compile a Shakespearean data bank to enhance the studying, teaching, producing, directing, acting, understanding, and appreciation of William Shakespeare and his works.

Shakespeare Oxford Society Box 16254, Baltimore, MD 21210, (513)-381-5001. Publication: *Newsletter.* Attempts to verify evidence bearing on the authorship of works attributed to Shakespeare, particularly evidence indicating that Edward de Vere, the 17th Earl of Oxford, was the true author.

SLAVERY

Books and Articles

Brooks, Amanda Lee, "The Uses of History," *National Review*, Volume XLII (May 14, 1990), pp. 36-40.
Davis, David Brion, *The Problem of Slavery in the Age of Revolution, 1770 - 1823* (Ithaca, NY: Cornell University Press, 1975).
Fogel, Robert William, *Without Consent or Contract: The Rise and Fall of American Slavery* (New York: Norton, 1989).
Goldwin, Robert A. and Kaufman, Art, eds., *Slavery and Its Consequences: The Constitution, Equality, and Race* (Washington, DC: American Enterprise Institute for Public Policy Research, 1988).
Tise, Larry E., *Proslavery: A History of the Defense of Slavery in America, 1701-1840* (Athens, GA: University of Georgia Press, 1987).

SMOKING
(see **Tobacco**)

SOCIAL SCIENCE

Books and Articles

Finn, Chester E., Jr., "The Social Studies Debacle," *The American Spectator*,
Volume 21 (May, 1988), pp. 35-36.
Fussell, Paul, *Class: A Guide Through the American Status System* (New York:
Marboro Books, 1990).
Hunter, James Davidson, "'America's Fourth Faith': A Sociological Perspective on
Secular Humanism," *This World*, Number 19 (Fall, 1987), pp. 101-110.

SOCIAL SECURITY

Books and Articles

Ferrara, Peter J., "March Toward Freedom," *National Review*, Volume XLII
(July 9, 1990), pp. 38-40.
Hunter, Lawrence A., et al., "The Hoax on You: How Much Are You
Overpaying for Social Security?," *Policy Review*, Number 51 (Winter, 1990),
pp. 62-63.
Weaver, Carolyn L., "Reassessing Federal Disability Insurance," *The Public
Interest*, Number 106 (Winter, 1992), pp. 108-121.

SOCIAL WORK
(see **Welfare**)

SOCIALISM

Books and Articles

Bastiat, Frederic, *The Law* (Irvington-on-Hudson, NY: The Foundation for
Economic Education, 1961).
Codevilla, Angelo, "Is Olaf Palme the Wave of the Future?," *Commentary*,
Volume 89 (March, 1990), pp. 26-32.
Crozier, Brian and Seldon, Arthur, *Socialism: The Grand Delusion* (New York:
Universe Books, 1986.)
De Jasay, Anthony, "After Socialism, What?," *National Review*, Volume XLIII
(May 27, 1991), pp. 25-29.
Gray, John, "The Anti-Socialists," *National Review*, Volume XLII (July 23,
1990), pp. 26-29.

Gray, John, "The End of History - Or of Liberalism?," *National Review*, Volume XLI (October 27, 1989), pp. 33-35.

Gray, John, "The Road From Serfdom: F. A. Hayek, R.I.P.," *National Review*, Volume XLIV (April 27, 1992), pp. 32-37.

Hart, Jeffrey, "The New York Intellectuals and the Socialist Legacy," *National Review*, Volume XXXIX (September 11, 1987), pp. 58-64.

Hayek, F. A., *The Fatal Conceit: The Errors of Socialism* (Chicago, IL: University of Chicago Press, 1988).

Hook, Sidney, *Out of Step: An Unquiet Life in the Twentieth Century* (New York: Harper & Row, 1987).

Horowitz, David, "Socialism: Guilty as Charged," *Commentary*, Volume 90 (December, 1990), pp. 17-24.

Lipset, Seymour Martin, "The Death of the Third Way: Everywhere but Here, That Is," *The National Interest*, Number 20 (Summer, 1990), pp. 25-37.

Panichas, George A., et al., "On the Future of Socialism: A Symposium," *Modern Age*, Volume 34 (Fall, 1991), pp. 2-59.

Stein, Herbert and Lipset, Seymour Martin, "An Exchange: Herbert Stein on 'The Third Way' with a Response by Seymour Martin Lipset," *The National Interest*, Number 21 (Fall, 1990), pp. 109-115.

Tismaneanu, Vladimir, *The Crisis of Marxist Ideology in Eastern Europe* (New York: Routledge, Chapman and Hall, 1988).

Urena, Enrique, *Capitalism or Socialism? An Economic Critique for Christians* (Chicago, IL: Franciscan Herald Press, 1988).

Watson, George, "Forty-Niners: Marx, Engels, and Harrod's," *Chronicles*, Volume 12 (June, 1988), pp. 27-30.

Wheelersburg, Robert P., "The Swedish Model Rejected," *This World*, Number 27 (Winter, 1992), pp. 64-75.

THE SOUTH

Books and Articles

Anderson, Don, "Reviving Self-Rule: Ward Government in the South," *Chronicles*, Volume 14 (March, 1990), pp. 14-17.

Black, Earl and Black, Merle, *The Vital South: How Presidents Are Elected* (Cambridge, MA: Harvard University Press, 1992).

Bradford, M. E., *Against the Barbarians and Other Reflections on Familiar Themes* (Columbia, MO: University of Missouri Press, 1992).

Bradford, M. E., *The Reactionary Imperative: Essays Literary and Political* (Peru, IL: Sherwood Sugden, 1990).

Bradford, M. E., *Remembering Who We Are: Observations of a Southern Conservative* (Athens, GA: University of Georgia Press, 1985).

Brooks, Cleanth, *The Language of the American South* (Athens, GA: University of Georgia Press, 1985).

Frady, Marshall, *Southerners: A Journalist's Odyssey* (New York: New American Library, 1980).

Heilman, Robert B., *The Southern Connection* (Baton Rouge, LA: Louisiana State University Press, 1991).

Hobson, Fred, *The Southern Writer in the Postmodern World* (Athens, GA: University of Georgia Press, 1991).

Hobson, Fred, *Tell About the South: The Southern Rage to Explain* (Baton Rouge, LA: Louisiana State University Press, 1983).

Kirby, Jack Temple, *Media-Made Dixie: The South in the American Imagination* (Baton Rouge, LA: Louisiana State University Press, 1978).

Kirby, Jack Temple, *Rural Worlds Lost: The American South 1920 - 1960* (Baton Rouge, LA: Louisiana State University Press, 1987).

Lytle, Andrew N., *From Eden to Babylon: The Social and Political Essays of Andrew Nelson Lytle* (Washington, DC: Regnery Gateway, 1990).

Lytle, Andrew N., *Southerners and Europeans: Essays in a Time of Disorder* (Baton Rouge, LA: Louisiana State University Press, 1988).

McWhiney, Grady and Jamieson, Perry D., *Attack and Die: Civil War Military Tactics and the Southern Heritage* (Tuscaloosa, AL: University of Alabama Press, 1982).

McWhiney, Grady, *Cracker Culture: Celtic Ways in the Old South* (Tuscaloosa, AL: University of Alabama Press, 1989).

Montgomery, Marion, *Possum, and Other Receipts for the Recovery of "Southern" Being* (Atlanta, GA: University of Georgia Press, 1987).

Owsley, Harriet Chappell, *Frank Lawrence Owsley: Historian of the Old South* (Nashville, TN: Vanderbilt University Press, 1990).

Percy, Walker, *Signposts in a Strange Land* (New York: Farrar, Straus and Giroux, 1991).

Reed, John Shelton, *Southern Folk, Plain and Fancy: Native White Social Types* (Athens, GA: University of Georgia Press, 1986).

Reed, John Shelton, *Whistling Dixie: Dispatches From the South* (Columbia, MO: University of Missouri Press, 1990).

Regnery, Henry, "Richard Weaver: A Southern Agrarian at the University of Chicago," *Modern Age*, Volume 32 (Spring, 1988), pp. 102-112.

Tate, J. O., "Conserve What?," *National Review*, Volume XXXVI (January 27, 1984), pp. 48-52.

Weaver, Richard M., *The Southern Essays of Richard M. Weaver* (Indianapolis, IN: Liberty Press, 1987).

Weaver, Richard M., *The Southern Tradition at Bay: A History of Postbellum Thought*, George M. Curtis, III and James J. Thompson, Jr., eds., (New Rochelle, NY: Arlington House, 1968).

Wilson, Clyde N., *Carolina Cavalier: The Life and Mind of James Johnston Pettigrew* (Athens, GA: University of Georgia Press, 1990).

SOUTH AFRICA

Books and Articles

Adams, James, *The Unnatural Alliance* (New York: Quartet Books, 1984).

Becker, Jillian, "Nadine Gordimer's Politics," *Commentary*, Volume 93 (February, 1992), pp. 51-54.

Campbell, Keith, *ANC: Soviet Task Force?* (London: Institute for the Study of Terrorism, 1987).

Clark, Andrew, "Quiet Revolution: South Africa's Blacks Are Realizing Their Economic Power. Can Apartheid Survive?," *Reason*, Volume 21 (July, 1989), pp. 16-23.

Horowitz, Donald L., *A Democratic South Africa? Constitutional Engineering in a Divided Society* (Berkeley, CA: University of California Press, 1991).

Kaempfer, William H. and Lowenberg, Anton D., "Sanctioning South Africa: The Politics Behind the Policies," *The Cato Journal*, Volume 8 (Winter, 1989), pp. 713-727.

Muravchik, Joshua, "Mandela in America," *Commentary*, Volume 90 (October, 1990), pp. 11-18.

Raditsa, Leo, *Prisoners of a Dream: The South African Mirage. Historical Essay on the Denton Hearings* (Annapolis, MD: Prince George Street Press, 1989).

Raditsa, Leo, "You Say You Want a Revolution?," *Chronicles*, Volume 13 (June, 1989), pp. 19-21.

Roberts, David, Jr., "The ANC in Its Own Words," *Commentary*, Volume 86 (July, 1988), pp. 31-37.

Rusher, William, *A Short Course on South Africa* (New York: Communications Distribution, 1987).

Vale, Colin, "After Apartheid: An Interview with F. W. de Klerk," *National Review*, Volume XLII (October 15, 1990), pp. 57-64.

Williams, Walter, *South Africa's War Against Capitalism* (New York: Praeger Publishers, 1989).

SOUTH AMERICA
(see **Latin America**)

SOVIET MILITARY

Books and Articles

Baxter, William, *Soviet Airland Battle Tactics* (Novato, CA: Presidio Press, 1980).

Erickson, John, et al., *Soviet Ground Forces: An Operational Assessment* (Boulder, CO: Westview Press, 1986).

Isby, David, *Ten Million Bayonets: Inside the Armies of the Soviet Union* (New York: Arms and Armour Press, 1988).

Isby, David, *Weapons and Tactics of the Soviet Army* (Alexandria, VA: Jane's Information Group, 1988).

Luttwak, Edward N., *The Grand Strategy of the Soviet Union* (New York: St. Martin's Press, 1983).

Moynahan, Brian, *Claws of the Bear: The History of the Red Army from the Revolution to the Present* (Boston, MA: Houghton Mifflin, 1989).

Seaton, Albert and Seaton, Joan, *The Soviet Army: 1918 to the Present* (New York: New American Library, 1986).

Vigor, P. H., *Soviet Blitzkrieg Theory* (New York: St. Martin's Press, 1983).

SOVIET UNION
(see Commonwealth of Independent States)

SPACE EXPLORATION

Books and Articles

Daniel, J. Anthony, "Capital Takes to Space," *The American Spectator*, Volume 21 (October, 1988), pp. 14-16.

Heppenheimer, T. A., "Beyond Tommorrowland: Realistic, Useful Alternatives to NASA's Grandiose Space Station," *Reason*, Volume 23 (May, 1991), pp. 40-44.

Jastrow, Robert, *Journey to the Stars: Space Exploration - Tomorrow and Beyond* (New York: Bantam Books, 1989).

McDougall, Walter, *The Heavens and the Earth: A Political History of the Space Age* (New York: Basic Books, 1985).

Mallon, Thomas, "By the Late Morning's Light," *The American Spectator*, Volume 21 (December, 1988), pp. 26-29.

Organizations

National Space Society 922 Pennsylvania Avenue, SE, Washington, DC 20003, (202)-543-1900. Publication: *Ad Astra*. Individuals dedicated "to convincing our nation and its leadership of the critical need for a growing progressive American technology for which a strong space program provides the thrust and momentum."

Space Studies Institute P.O. Box 82, Princeton, NJ 08542, (609)-921-0377. Publication: *SSI Update*. Promotes space manufacturing research and human exploration of space.

SPAIN

Books and Articles

Fusi, Juan Pablo, *Franco: A Biography,* Felipe Fernandez-Armesto, trans. (New York: Harper & Row, 1987).
Hughes, Robert, *Barcelona* (New York: Knopf, 1992).
Orwell, George, *Homage to Catalonia* (San Diego, CA: Harcourt Brace Jovanovich, 1969).

SPECIAL PROSECUTOR

Books and Articles

Abrams, Elliot, *Undue Process: A Story of How Political Differences Are Turned Into Crimes* (New York: The Free Press, 1992).
Eastland, Terry, *Ethics, Politics, and the Independent Counsel: Executive Power, Executive Vice 1789 - 1989* (Washington, DC: National Legal Center for the Public Interest, 1989).
Eastland, Terry, "Impeachment by Other Means," *Commentary*, Volume 88 (August, 1989), pp. 40-44.
Eastland, Terry, "The Independent Counsel Regime," *The Public Interest*, Number 100 (Summer, 1990), pp. 68-80.
Rabkin, Jeremy, "Politics by Independent Counsel," *The American Spectator*, Volume 20 (May, 1987), pp. 14-15.

SPORTS

Books and Articles

Giamatti, A. Bartlett, *Take Time for Paradise: Americans and Their Games* (New York: Summit Books, 1989).
Novak, Michael, *The Joy of Sports: End Zones, Bases, Baskets, Balls, and the Consecration of the American Spirit* (Lanham, MD: Madison Books, 1988).
Williamson, Chilton, "Blood at Eastertide," *Chronicles*, Volume 16 (April, 1992), pp. 21-25.

STALINISM

Books and Articles

Carynnyk, Marco, "The Killing Fields of Kiev," *Commentary*, Volume 90 (October, 1990), pp. 19-25.

Conquest, Robert, *The Great Terror: A Reassessment* (New York: Oxford University Press, 1990).

Conquest, Robert, *The Great Terror: Stalin's Purge of the Thirties* (New York: Macmillan, 1968).

Conquest, Robert, *The Harvest of Sorrow: Soviet Collectivization and the Terror-Famine* (New York: Oxford University Press, 1986).

Conquest, Robert, *Kolyma: The Arctic Death Camps* (New York: Viking Press, 1978).

Conquest, Robert, *The Nation Killers: The Soviet Deportation of Nationalities* (New York: Macmillan, 1970).

Conquest, Robert, *Stalin: Breaker of Nations* (New York: Viking, 1991).

Conquest, Robert, *Stalin and the Kirov Murder* (New York: Oxford University Press, 1989).

Dolot, Miron, *Execution by Hunger: The Hidden Holocaust* (New York: Norton, 1985).

Herling, Gustav, *A World Apart: The Journal of a Gulag Survivor* (New York: Arbor House, 1986).

Laqueur, Walter, *Stalin: The Glastnost Revelations* (New York: Scribner's, 1990).

Methvin, Eugene, "Hitler and Stalin - Twentieth Century Superkillers," *National Review*, Volume XXXVII (May 31, 1985), pp. 22-29.

Methvin, Eugene H., "The Unquiet Ghosts of Stalin's Victims," *National Review*, Volume XLI (September 1, 1989), pp. 24-25, 52.

O'Neill, William L., *A Better World: The Great Schism - Stalinism and the American Intellectuals* (New York: Simon & Schuster, 1982).

Paluch, Peter, "Spiking the Ukrainian Famine, Again," *National Review*, Volume XXXVIII (April 11, 1986), pp. 33-39.

Puddington, Arch, "Denying the Terror Famine," *National Review*, Volume XLIV (May 25, 1992), pp. 33-36.

Tolstoy, Nikolai, *Stalin's Secret War* (London: J. Cape, 1981).

Tucker, Robert C., *Stalin in Power: The Revolution From Above, 1929 - 1941* (New York: Norton, 1990).

Ulam, Adam, *Stalin: The Man and His Era* (New York: Viking Press, 1973).

Watson, George, "Conversation in Warsaw," *Chronicles*, Volume 14 (August, 1990), pp. 57-58.

Zawodny, Janusz K., *Death in the Forest: The Story of the Katyn Forest Massacre* (Notre Dame, IN: University of Notre Dame Press, 1962).

STATE/REGIONAL CONSERVATISM

Organizations

American Legislative Exchange Council 214 Massachusetts Avenue, NE, Suite 240, Washington, DC 20002, (202)-547-4646. Publications: *FYI, State Factor.* Supports the preservation of individual liberties, American values and institutions, free enterprise, private property rights, and limited government through reduced reliance on the federal government; calls for a greater role to be played by the states. Maintains research department and compiles statistics.

Beacon Hill Institute for Public Policy Research Suffolk University, 8 Ashburton Place, Boston, MA 02180, (617)-573-8750. Publication: *BHI Faxsheet.* Uses free market model to analyze public policy issues that affect Massachusetts.

California Public Policy Foundation P.O. Box 56671, Sherman Oaks, CA 91413-1671, (818)-501-7730. Publication: *California Political Review.* Educational Foundation.

Capitol Research Center 727 15th Street, NW, 8th Floor, Washington, DC 20005, (202)-737-5677. Publications: *Organizational Trends, Alternatives in Philanthropy, Philanthropy, Culture and Society.* Provides grantmakers with information on which public policy, special interest and traditional charitable organizations promote the principles of free enterprise, individual initiative and responsibility, and limited government.

Capitol Resource Institute 4825 J Street, Suite 100, Sacramento, CA 95819, (916)-731-5200. Publications: *Capitol Contacts, California Citizen, Talking Points.* Public policy organization that focuses on issues affecting the family.

Cascade Policy Institute 813 South Alder, Suite 707, Portland, OR 97205, (503)-242-0900. Publication: *Cascade News.* Oregon-based free market think tank. Seeks to find voluntary, market-oriented answers to state's public policy questions.

Center for the American Experiment 2342 Plaza VII, 45 South 7th Street, Minneapolis, MN 55403, (612)-338-3605. Publication: *American Experiment.* Non-partisan, tax-exempt, public policy and educational institution which brings conservative and alternative ideas to bear on the most difficult issues facing Minnesota and the nation.

The Claremont Institute's Golden State Center for Policy Studies 2012 H Street, Suite 101, Sacramento, CA 95814, (916)-446-7924. State-level think tank that focuses on California-specific issues, including state fiscal policy, state education reform, health care reform, welfare and social services reform, and immigration reform at the state level.

Council of State Governments P.O. Box 11910, 3572 Iron Works Pike, Lexington, KY 40578, (606)-231-1939. Publications: *Backgrounders, Book of the States, Journal of State Government, State Administrative Officials Classified by Functions, State Elective Officials and the Legislatures, State Government News, State Government Research Checklist, State Legislative Leadership Committees and Staff.* Joint agency of all state governments. Works to strengthen state government.

Delaware Public Policy Institute 1201 North Orange Street, 2nd Floor, P.O. Box 671, Wilmington, DE 19899, (302)-655-7221. Seeks practical free-market solutions for Delaware's public policy issues.

Empire Foundation for Policy Research 130 Washington Avenue, 1st Floor, Albany, NY 12201, (518)-432-4444. A think tank that seeks to devise proposals and plans to make New York government more·accountable and more efficient.

Evergreen Freedom Foundation P.O. Box 552, Olympia, WA 98507, (206)-357-5614. Publications: *Newsletter, Policy Highlighters.* Research and public policy organization that focuses on state-level issues such as land-use, taxes, education reform, health care reform, welfare reform and the budget.

Georgia Public Policy Foundation 2900 Chamblee-Tucker Road, Suite 6, Atlanta, GA 30341-4128, (404)-455-7600. Publication: *The Georgia Policy Review.* Non-partisan, non-profit research foundation that focuses on state-level public policy issues from a perspective of limited government, free enterprise and individual liberty.

Barry Goldwater Institute for Public Policy Research 201 North Central Avenue, Concourse Level, Phoenix, AZ 85004, (602)-256-7018. Focuses on offering market-based solutions to public policy problems at the state level. Agenda includes education and health care reform, privatization, and regulatory reform.

The Heartland Institute 634 South Wabash Avenue, 2nd Floor, Chicago, IL 60605, (312)-427-3060. Publication: *Intellectual Ammunition.* Research organization that seeks free-market solutions to a number of public policy issues, including health care, environmental regulations, taxes and education. The Institute has branches in several states.

The Heartland Institute - Illinois 634 South Wabash Avenue, 2nd Floor, Chicago, IL 60605, (312)-427-3060.

The Heartland Institute - Michigan 2525 Penobscot Building, Detroit, MI 48226, (313)-961-1950.

The Heartland Institute - Missouri 2458 Old Dorsett Road, Suite 230, St. Louis, MO 63043, (314)-344-1100.

The Heartland Institute - Ohio 14805 Detroit Avenue, Cleveland, OH 44107, (216)-221-1233.

The Heartland Institute - Wisconsin 924 East Juneau Avenue, #215, Milwaukee, WI 53202, (414)-347-1807.

Independence Institute 14142 Denver West Parkway, Suite 101, Golden, CO 80401, (303)-279-6536. Publications: *Independence Institute Paper, Independence Bulletin.* Free market think tank that serves Colorado and the Western states. Issues that receive Institute's primary focus are taxes, schools, health care, and the environment.

Indiana Policy Review Foundation 320 North Meridian Street, #615, Indianapolis, IN 46204, (317)-236-7360. Publication: *Indiana Policy Review.* Seeks to marshall the best research on governmental, economic and educational issues at the state and municipal level by exalting the truths of the Declaration of Independence, especially those concerning the interrelated freedoms of religion, enterprise and speech; emphasizing the primacy of the individual in solving public concerns; and recognizing that the equality of opportunity is sacrificed in pursuit of equality of results.

James Madison Institute of Policy Studies 2010 Delta Boulevard, P.O. Box 13894, Tallahasse, Florida 32303, (904)-386-3131. Publication: *The Madison Messenger.* Florida-based think tank dedicated to economic freedom, limited government, federalism, traditional values, and individual responsibility.

John Locke Foundation 6512 Six Forks Road, Suite 203B, Raleigh, NC 27615, (919)-847-2690. Publications: *The Carolina Journal, The Locke Letter.* Free-market, limited-government think tank established to study state and local issues, primarily education and economic issues.

The Mackinac Center 119 Ashman Street, P.O. Box 568, Midland, MI 48640, (517)-631-0900. Publication: *Newsletter.* Non-partisan research and educational organization devoted to analyzing Michigan economics from a free market perspective.

The Pioneer Institute for Public Policy Research 21 Custom House Street, #801, Boston, MA 02110, (617)-261-9755. Publication: *Pioneer Papers.* Non-profit, non-partisan public policy research institute dedicated to examining pressing issues facing Massachusetts and changing the state's intellectual climate. Uses entrepreneurial, private sector and free-market principles to force effective public policy.

Public Affairs Research Institute of New Jersey 212 Carnegie Center, #100, Princeton, NJ 08540, (609)-452-0220. Non-profit, non-partisan policy analysis organization dealing with New Jersey state public policy issues.

Resource Institute of Oklahoma 28 Northwest 7th Street, Oklahoma City, OK 73102, (405)-239-6700. Research and education organization seeking to educate Oklahomans on public policy as it impacts the family.

South Carolina Policy Council 1518 Washington Street, Columbia, SC 29201, (803)-779-5022. Publications: *The Policy Council News, Capital Comments, Policy Council Issues Papers.* State-based public policy research and education foundation whose mission is to promote limited government, lower taxes and government accountability in the Palmetto State.

Texas Public Policy Foundation P.O. Box 17447, San Antonio, TX 78217, (512)-829-7138. Publications: *Policy Issue Papers, Newsletter.* Non-partisan, non-profit public policy research center dedicated to influencing the public policy debate in Texas by providing sound research analysis, new ideas and policy directions on state issues. Aim is to enhance the freedom and quality of life for all Texans by promoting limited government, individual responsibility, market economics, educational excellence and traditional values.

Washington Institute for Policy Studies 223 105th Avenue, NE, #202, Bellevue, WA 98004, (206)-454-3057. Non-partisan, non-profit research organization founded to support state, local and national policies based on limited government, individual freedom, free enterprise and more accountability for how tax dollars are spent.

Washington Research Council 906 South Columbia Street, Suite 350, Olympia, WA 98501, (206)-357-6643. Publication: *The WRC Notebook.* Non-profit, public policy research organization that studies state and local government in Washington. Specializes in fiscal affairs and tax and spending issues. Seeks free-market solutions to public policy problems.

Wisconsin Policy Research Institute 3107 North Shepard Avenue, Milwaukee, WI 53211, (414)-963-0600. Publications: *WPRI Reports, Wisconsin Update.* A non-profit institute established to study public policy issues affecting Wisconsin, focusing on education, welfare and social services, criminal justice, taxes and spending, and economic development.

Yankee Institute for Public Policy Studies 117 New London Turnpike, Glastonbury, CT 06033, (203)-633-8188. Non-partisan, non-profit educational and research group focusing on policy issues that affect Connecticut. Primary issues of concern are taxes, government spending, privatization and education.

STOCK MARKET
(see **Wall Street**)

STRATEGIC DEFENSE INITIATIVE

Books and Articles

Baucom, Donald R., "Hail to the Chiefs: The Untold History of Reagan's SDI Decision," *Policy Review*, Number 53 (Summer, 1990), pp. 66-73.

Chalfont, Alun, *Star Wars: Suicide or Survival?* (Boston, MA: Little, Brown, 1986).

Codevilla, Angelo, "A Question of Patriot-ism: Why Isn't America Building Missile Defenses Today?," *Policy Review*, Number 56 (Spring, 1991), pp. 16-21.

Codevilla, Angelo, "Who Killed SDI?," *National Review*, Volume XLV (May 10, 1993), pp. 40-43.

Jastrow, Robert, *How to Make Nuclear Weapons Obsolete* (Boston, MA: Little, Brown, 1985).

McDougall, Walter, *The Heavens and the Earth: A Political History of the Space Age* (New York: Basic Books, 1985).

Spring, Baker, "MAD Dogs and Congressmen: Arguments Against SDI Are Impotent and Obsolete," *Policy Review*, Number 58 (Fall, 1991), pp. 79-81.

The Technical Panel on Missile Defense of the George C. Marshall Institute, "SDI: Making America Secure," *National Review*, Volume XL (April 1, 1988), pp. 36-45.

Weigel, George, "Breaking the Doctrinal Gridlock: Common Security and the Strategic Defense Initiative," *This World*, Number 16 (Winter, 1987), pp. 3-22.

Wohlstetter, Albert, "Swords Without Shields," *The National Interest*, Number 8 (Summer, 1987), pp. 31-57.

Organizations

George C. Marshall Institute 1730 M Street, NW, #502, Washington, DC 20036, (202)-296-9655.

High Frontier 2800 Shirlington Road, Suite 405 A, Arlington, VA 22206, (703)-671-4111. Publications: *High Frontier: A Strategy for National Survival, A Defense That Defends: Blocking Nuclear Attacks.* Advocates the use of outer space for non-nuclear commercial and military purposes.

SUPREME COURT

Books and Articles

Bork, Robert H., "An End to Political Judging?," *National Review*, Volume XLII (December 31, 1990), pp. 30-32.

Bork, Robert H., "Beside the Law," *National Review*, Volume XLIV (October 19, 1992), pp. 38-44.

Brock, David, *The Real Anita Hill: The Inventing of the Woman of the Year* (New York: The Free Press, 1993).

Cord, Robert L., "Church, State, and the Rehnquist Court," *National Review*, Volume XLIV (August 17, 1992), pp. 35-37.

Douglas, Jack D., "The (Politically) Supreme Court," *Chronicles*, Volume 12 (March, 1988), pp. 8-11.

Eastland, Terry, "Deconstructing David Souter," *National Review*, Volume XLII (December 3, 1990), pp. 37-39.

Eastland, Terry, "Hill's Rats," *The American Spectator*, Volume 25 (July, 1992), pp. 48-51.

Eastland, Terry, "While Justice Sleeps," *National Review*, Volume XLI (April 21, 1989), pp. 24-26.

Efron, Edith, "Native Son: Why a Black Supreme Court Nominee Has No Rights White Men Need Respect," *Reason*, Volume 23 (February, 1992), pp. 23-32.

Fried, Charles, *Order and Law: Arguing the Reagan Revolution - A Firsthand Account* (New York: Simon & Schuster, 1991).

Garment, Suzanne, "The War Against Robert H. Bork," *Commentary*, Volume 85 (January, 1988), pp. 17-26.

Garment, Suzanne, "Why Anita Hill Lost," *Commentary*, Volume 93 (January, 1992), pp. 26-35.

McGuigan, Patrick B. and Weyrich, Dawn M., *Ninth Justice: The Fight for Bork* (Washington, DC: Regnery Gateway, 1990).

McGurn, William, "The Trials of Clarence Thomas," *National Review*, Volume XLIII (August 12, 1991), pp. 36-40.

Puddington, Arch, "Clarence Thomas and the Blacks," *Commentary*, Volume 93 (February, 1992), pp. 28-33.

Rehnquist, William H., *The Supreme Court: How It Was, How It Is* (New York: William Morrow, 1987).

Wildavsky, Aaron, "Robert Bork and the Crime of Inequality," *The Public Interest*, Number 98 (Winter, 1990), pp. 98-117.

TAXATION

Books and Articles

Adams, James Ring, "Is the Tax Revolt Dead?," *National Review*, Volume XXXVII (September 6, 1985), pp. 28-36.

Anderson, Martin, et al., "The Great American Tax Debate: A Symposium," *Policy Review*, Number 56 (Spring, 1991), pp. 53-59.

Archer, Bill, "Who's the Fairest of Them All? The Truth About the '80s," *Policy Review*, Number 57 (Summer, 1991), pp. 67-73.

Carlson, Allan, "A Pro-Family Income Tax," *The Public Interest*, Number 94 (Winter, 1989), pp. 69-76.

Daxon, Thomas E., "Shrinking Mortgage: Ronald Reagan Was a Friend to Future Taxpayers," *Policy Review*, Number 47 (Winter, 1989), pp. 68-69.

Gray, Arthur, Jr. and Laffer, Arthur, "Debt and Taxes," *National Review*, Volume XLI (September 1, 1989), pp. 38-39.

Hall, Robert E. and Rabushka, Alvin, *Low Tax, Simple Tax, Flat Tax* (New York: McGraw-Hill, 1983).

Hodge, Scott A., "Pork Chop: Budget Questions for Your Congressman," *Policy Review*, Number 58 (Fall, 1991), pp. 58-59.

Kudlow, Lawrence A., "No New Tax Cuts," *National Review*, Volume XLIV (March 2, 1992), pp. 38-41.

Kudlow, Lawrence A., "VAT Attacks," *National Review*, Volume XLV (May 24, 1993), pp. 40-43.

Langbein, John H., "The Inheritance Revolution," *The Public Interest*, Number 102 (Winter, 1991), pp. 15-31.

Lindsey, Lawrence, "The Surplus of '99," *National Review*, Volume XLII (April 30, 1990), pp. 34-36.

Lindsey, Lawrence, *The Growth Experiment: How Tax Policy Is Transforming the U.S. Economy* (New York: Basic Books, 1990).

Mackay, Robert J. and Mix, Phoebe A., "Uncertain Futures: The Tax Treatment of Hedging," *The American Enterprise*, Volume 3 (May/June, 1992), pp. 67-71.

Mitchell, Daniel J., "Anatomy of a Phony Story," *National Review*, Volume XLIV (September 14, 1992), pp. 52-53.

Mitchell, Daniel J., "Bush's Rasputin," *National Review*, Volume XLIV (December 28, 1992), pp. 29-31.

Moore, Stephen, "Read Our Lips: The Tax Revolt Lives," *Reason*, Volume 24 (June, 1992), pp. 40-45.

Payne, James L., "Unhappy Returns: The $600-Billion Tax Ripoff," *Policy Review*, Number 59 (Winter, 1992), pp. 18-24.

Roberts, Paul Craig, "Economic Dominoes," *National Review*, Volume XLIV (November 30, 1992), pp. 37-42.

Stein, Herbert, "Tax Policy and Recessions: From Herbert Hoover to George Bush," *The American Enterprise*, Volume 3 (January/February, 1992), pp. 6-11.

Steuerle, C. Eugene, "Tax Policy in the 1990s," *The American Enterprise*, Volume 1 (May/June, 1990), pp. 46-51.

Yandle, Bruce, "Taxation, Political Action, and Superfund," *The Cato Journal*, Volume 8 (Winter, 1989), pp. 751-764.

Organizations

Americans for Tax Reform 1302 Connecticut Avenue, NW Suite 440, Washington, DC 20036, (202)-785-0266. Publication: *Memos*. Sponsors the Pledge Coalition, a covenant made by incumbents and other candidates for national office who promise to oppose all income tax increases.

Institute for Research on the Economics of Taxation 1331 Pennsylvania Avenue, NW, Suite 515, Washington, DC 20004, (202)-347-9570.

National Tax-Limitation Committee 151 North Sunrise Avenue, Suite 901, Roseville, CA 95661, (916)-786-9400. Publications: *Tax Limitation News, Tax Watch*. Campaigns for federal and state constitutional amendments which would limit government spending and taxation.

National Taxpayers Union 325 Pennsylvania Avenue, SE, Washington, DC 20003, (202)-543-1300. Publications: *Dollars and Sense, Tax Savings Report, Cut Local Taxes, Congressional Spending Analysis, Taxpayer's Action Guide*. Seeks to: reduce government spending, cut taxes, protect the rights of taxpayers.

TEACHERS

Books and Articles

Alexander, Dan C., Jr., *Who's Ruining Our Schools? The Case Against the NEA Teachers Union* (Washington, DC: Save Our Schools Research and Education Foundation, 1986).

Barzun, Jacques, *Begin Here: The Forgotten Conditions of Teaching and Learning* (Chicago, IL: University of Chicago Press, 1991).

Brooks, David, "Forget the Fire, Just Keep Teaching," *National Review*, Volume XXXVII (December 13, 1985), pp. 24-29.

Damerell, Reginald G., *Education's Smoking Gun: How Teachers Colleges Have Destroyed Education in America* (New York: Freundlich Books, 1985).

Kramer, Rita and Kramer, Yale, "Eastside Story," *The American Spectator*, Volume 22 (August, 1989), pp. 21-24.

Kramer, Rita, *Ed School Follies: The Miseducation of America's Teachers*
(New York: The Free Press, 1991).

Mitchell, Richard, *The Graves of Academe* (New York: Simon & Schuster, 1987).

Sachar, Emily, *Shut Up and Let the Lady Teach: A Teacher's Year in a Public
School* (New York: Poseidon Press, 1991).

Wooster, Martin Morse, "Control Freaks: How Progressives and Efficiency
Experts Abolished School-Based Management," *Reason*, Volume 24 (May,
1992), pp. 33-35.

Organizations

Concerned Educators Against Forced Unionism 8001 Braddock Road, Suite 500
Springfield, VA 22160, (703)-321-8519. Publications: *Concerned Educators
Against Forced Unionism - Insiders Report, News.* Educational professionals
whose objective is to ensure that educational personnel have the right to accept or
reject representation by a labor union.

TECHNOLOGY

Books and Articles

Beltz, Cynthia A., "How to Lose the Race: Industrial Policy and the Lessons of
HDTV," *The American Enterprise*, Volume 2 (May/June, 1991), pp. 22-27.

Bryen, Steven and Ledeen, Michael, "Breaching Export Controls: A Dumb
Policy in a Dangerous World," *The American Enterprise*, Volume 2
(July/August, 1991), pp. 64-72.

Ellul, Jacques, *The Tecnological Bluff* (Grand Rapids, MI: William Eerdmans,
1990).

Gilder, George, *Microcosm: The Quantum Revolution in Economics and
Technology* (New York: Simon & Schuster, 1990).

Hardison, O. B., *Disappearing Through the Skylight: Culture and Technology in
the Twentieth Century* (New York: Viking, 1989).

Harrison, Frank R., III, "Values, Epistemology, and High-Tech," *Modern Age*,
Volume 32 (Summer, 1989), pp. 231-237.

Hawke, David Freeman, *Nuts and Bolts of the Past: A History of American
Technology, 1776 - 1860* (New York: Harper & Row, 1989).

Kirkwood, R. Cort, "Inside the Red-Trade Lobby," *National Review*, Volume XL
(April 29, 1988), pp. 35-40.

McKenzie, Richard B., "Capital Flight: The Hidden Power of Technology to
Shrink Big Government," *Reason*, Volume 20 (March, 1989), pp. 22-26.

McWilliams, Peter, *The Personal Computer Book* (Los Angeles, CA: Prelude
Press, 1990).

Melvern, Linda, et al., *Techno-Bandits* (Boston, MA: Houghton, Mifflin, 1984).

Molnar, Thomas, "Technology and the Ethical Imperative," *Chronicles,* Volume 12 (February, 1988), pp. 14-15.
Nelson, Richard R., *High Technology Policies: A Five-Nation Comparison* (Washington, DC: American Enterprise Institute for Public Policy Research, 1984).

Organizations

Access Research Network P.O. Box 38069, Colorado Springs, CO 80937-8069, (719)-633-1772. Answers laymen's questions on science, technology, and society.

Electronic Industries Association 2001 Pennsylvania Avenue, NW, Suite 1100 Washington, DC 20006, (202)-457-4900. Publication: *EIA Publications Index.* Trade organization representing manufacturers of electronic parts, tubes, and solid state components; radio, television, and video systems; audio equipment; government electronic systems; and industrial and communications electronic products.

Semiconductor Industry Association 4300 Stevens Creek Boulevard, Suite 271 San Jose, CA 95129, (408)-246-2711. Publications: *Circuit, Semiconductor Industry Association - Yearbook and Directory.* Companies that produce semiconductor products such as discrete components, integrated circuits, and microprocessors.

TELECOMMUNICATIONS
(see **Communications**)

TELEVISION

Books and Articles

Arkes, Hadley, "Moral Obtuseness in America," *National Review,* Volume XLI (June 16, 1989), pp. 33-36.
Buckley, William F., Jr., *On the Firing Line: The Public Life of Our Public Figures* (New York: Random House, 1989).
Donlan, Thomas G., "The Sharper Image: I Want My HDTV," *Reason,* Volume 23 (June, 1991), pp. 40-45.
Lichter, S. Robert, et al., *Watching America: What Television Tells Us About Our Lives* (New York: Prentice Hall, 1991).
Lindberg, Tod and Arkes, Hadley, "The World According to Moyers," *National Review,* Volume XLI (March 10, 1989), pp. 22-25.

Oliver, Charles, "Beyond Big Bird: PBS Is a Relic in an Age of TV Choice," *Reason*, Volume 23 (June, 1991), pp. 32-37.
Ozersky, Josh, "Nick at Nite, TV, and You," *Chronicles*, Volume 15 (April, 1991), pp. 21-25.

Organizations

Academy of Television Arts and Sciences 5220 Lankershim Boulevard, North Hollywood, CA 91601, (818)-754-2800. Publications: *Debut, Emmy Directory, Emmy Magazine*. Advances the arts and sciences of television through services to the industry in education, preservation of television programs, and information and community relations; fosters creative leadership in the television industry.

American Family Association P.O. Drawer and Federal Box 2440, Tupelo, MS 38803, (601)-844-5036. Publication: *AFA Journal*. Fosters "the biblical ethic of decency in American society with a primary emphasis on television."

Media Action Research Center 475 Riverside Drive, Suite 1901, New York, NY 10115, (212)-865-6690. Publication: *Media and Values*. Seeks to bring about what the group sees as positive changes in the content and style of television.

TERM LIMITS

Books and Articles

Coyne, James K. and Fund, John H., *Cleaning House: America's Campaign for Term Limits* (Washington, DC: Regnery Gateway, 1992).
Erickson, S. C., "A Bulwark Against Faction: James Madison's Case for Term Limits," *Policy Review*, Number 63 (Winter, 1993), pp. 76-78.
Eastland, Terry, "The Limits of Term Limits," *Commentary*, Volume 95 (Fall, 1993), pp. 53-55.
Mason, David M., ed., *Term Limits: Sweeping the States?* (Washington, DC: Heritage Foundation, 1991).
Will, George F., *Restoration: Congress, Term Limits, and the Recovery of Deliberative Democracy* (New York: Free Press, 1992).
Will, George F., *The Wedge: A Case for Term Limits for Congress* (New York: Free Press, 1992).

Organizations

Americans Back in Charge 1873 South Bellaire, Suite 1700, Denver, CO 80222, (303)-758-7343.

Term Limits Legal Institute 900 2nd Street NE, Suite 200A, Washington, DC 20002, (202)-371-0450.

US Term Limits 666 11th Street, NW, Suite 840, Washington, DC 20001, (202)-393-6440. A non-partisan group working to limit the terms of congressional, state and local elected officials.

TERRORISM

Books and Articles

Alexander, Edward, "Professor of Terror," *Commentary*, Volume 88 (August, 1989), pp. 49-50.

Brock, David, "The World of Narco-terrorism," *The American Spectator*, Volume 22 (June, 1989), pp. 24-28.

Copeland, Miles, "Confrontations of the Third Kind," *National Review*, Volume XXXVI (July 27, 1984), pp. 28-29, 53.

Dobson, Christopher and Payne, Ronald, *Counterattack: The West's Battle Against the Terrorists* (New York: Facts on File, 1982).

el-Khazen, Farid, "The Rise and Fall of the PLO," *The National Interest*, Number 10 (Winter, 1987/88), pp. 39-47.

Feith, Douglas J., "Law in the Service of Terror - The Strange Case of the Additional Protocol," *The National Interest*, Number 1 (Fall, 1985), pp. 36-47.

Gerson, Allan, "Terrorism and Turtle Bay," *The National Interest*, Number 11 (Spring, 1988), pp. 95-99.

Kirkpatrick, Jeane J., "How the PLO Was Legitimized," *Commentary*, Volume 88 (July, 1989), pp. 21-28.

Kupperman, Robert H., et al., "Terrorism - What Should We Do? A Symposium," *This World*, Number 12 (Fall, 1985), pp. 31-84.

Pipes, Daniel, "PLO, Inc.," *The American Spectator*, Volume 24 (February, 1991), pp. 27-28.

Pipes, Daniel, "Terrorism: The Syrian Connection," *The National Interest*, Number 15 (Spring, 1989), pp. 15-28.

Pisano, Vittorfranco S., *The Dynamics of Subversion and Violence in Contemporary Italy* (Stanford, CA: Hoover Institution Press, 1987).

Schoenberg, Harris Okun, *A Mandate for Terror: The United Nations and the PLO* (New York: Shapolsky Publishers, Inc., 1988).

Seger, Karl, *The Antiterrorism Handbook: A Practical Guide to Counteraction Planning and Operations for Individuals, Corporations, and Government* (Novato, CA: Presidio Press, 1990).

Shackley, Theodore G., et al., *You're the Target: Coping with Terror and Crime* (Alexandria, VA: New World Publishing, 1989).

Shultz, Richard H., Jr., *The Soviet Union and Revolutionary Warfare: Principles, Practices, and Regional Comparisons* (Stanford, CA: Hoover Institution Press, 1989).

Sterling, Claire, *The Terror Network: The Secret War of International Terrorism* (New York: Reader's Digest Press, 1981).

Sterling, Claire, *The Time of the Assassins* (Fort Worth, TX: Holt, Rinehart & Winston, 1987).

Taheri, Amir, *Holy Terror: Inside the World of Islamic Terrorism* (Bethesda, MD: Adler and Adler, 1987).

Organizations

National Defense Council Foundation 1220 King Street, Suite #1, Alexandria, VA 22314, (703)-836-3443. Publication: *Newsletter*. Studies terrorism and low-intensity conflict; conducts research on drug trafficking, including narco-terrorism.

TEST-BAN TREATY

Books and Articles

Isaac, Rael Jean, "The Nuclear Test Ban Hoax," *The American Spectator*, Volume 20 (May, 1987), pp. 21-26.

TEXTBOOKS

Books and Articles

Bethell, Tom, "Socialism by the Textbook," *National Review*, Volume XLI (October 13, 1989), pp. 36-38.

Hand, W. Brevard, "Humanism a Religion?," *This World*, Number 17 (Spring, 1987), pp. 110-114.

Vitz, Paul C., *Censorship: Evidence of Bias in Our Children's Textbooks* (Ann Arbor, MI: Servant Books, 1986).

Organizations

Educational Research Analysts P.O. Box 7518, Longview, TX 75607-7518, (903)-753-5993. Publications: *The MEL GABLER'S Newsletter, Textbooks on Trial, What Are They Teaching Our Children?, Are Textbooks Harming Our Children?* Reviews and analyzes public school textbooks in order to reveal those that conflict with traditional values, including "censorship" of the Judeo-Christian ethic, free-enterprise economics, strict construction of the Constitution, and creationism.

THEATER

Books and Articles

Aeschliman, M. D., "The Violent Bear It Away," *National Review*, Volume XXXVI (May 18, 1984), pp. 44-47.

Cronin, Mari, "The Economics of the New York Theater," *Chronicles*, Volume 14 (February, 1990), pp. 49-50.

Lejeune, Anthony, "No More Enchanted Evenings," *National Review*, Volume XLV (March 29, 1993), pp. 62-64.

Tookey, Christopher, "The Charge of the Angry Brigade," *National Review*, Volume XLI (November 24, 1989), pp. 41-44.

Organizations

Lincoln Center for the Performing Arts 70 Lincoln Center Plaza, New York, NY 10023, (212)-875-5000. Publication: *Lincoln Center for the Performing Arts - Calendar of Events*. Cultural center in New York City to sustain, encourage, and promote musical and performing arts.

THIRD WORLD

Books and Articles

Bauer, P. T., *The Development Frontier: Essays in Applied Economics* (Cambridge, MA: Harvard University Press, 1991).

Bauer, P. T., *Dissent on Development: Studies & Debates in Development Economics* (Cambridge, MA: Harvard University Press, 1972).

Bauer, P. T., *Economic Analysis & Policy in Underdeveloped Countries* (Duke University Commonwealth-Studies Center Publication: Number 4. Westport, CT: Greenwood, 1982).

Bauer, P. T., *Equality, the Third World, and Economic Delusion* (Cambridge, MA: Harvard University Press, 1981).

Bauer, P. T. *Reality and Rhetoric: Studies in the Economics of Development* (Cambridge, MA: Harvard University Press, 1984).

Bruckner, Pascal, *The Tears of the White Man: Compassion as Contempt* (New York: The Free Press, 1986).

de Soto, Hernando, *The Other Path: The Invisible Revolution in the Third World* (New York: Harper & Row, 1989).

Eberstadt, Nicholas, "Is Third World Debt Killing Children? UNworthy Conclusions About the Consequences of Debt," *The American Enterprise*, Volume 1 (November/December, 1990), pp. 56-63.

Harries, Owen, "Lower Case: The Third World, R.I.P.," *The National Interest*, Number 26 (Winter 1991/92), pp. 109-112.

Krauss, Melvyn B., *Development Without Aid: Growth, Poverty, and Government* (New York: The New Press, 1982).

Lamm, Richard D., "The New Wealth of Nations," *Chronicles*, Volume 15 (October, 1991), pp. 25-27.

McGurn, William, "A Banana Republic Baedeker," *The American Spectator*, Volume 22 (March, 1989), pp. 16-18.

O'Neil, Daniel J., "Edmund Burke, Karl Marx, and the Contemporary Third World," *Modern Age*, Volume 34 (Summer, 1992), pp. 349-358.

Plattner, Marc F., "Thinking About the 'North-South Gap,'" *This World*, Number 7 (Winter, 1984), pp. 20-30.

Rangel, Carlos, *Third World Ideology and Western Reality: Manufacturing Political Myth* (New Brunswick, NJ: Transaction Books, 1986).

Rubin, Barry, *Modern Dictators: Third World Coup-Makers, Strongmen, and Populist Tyrants* (New York: McGraw-Hill, 1987).

Ryrie, William, "The Mature Society: Capitalism and the Third World," *Crisis*, Volume 10 (July/August, 1992), pp. 25-32.

Stelzer, Irwin M., "Nagging Debtors," *The American Spectator*, Volume 21 (October, 1988), pp. 30-31.

Stelzer, Irwin M., "Third World Deadbeats," *The American Spectator*, Volume 22 (April, 1989), pp. 34-35.

Thompson, W. Scott, *The Third World: Premises of U.S. Policy* (San Francisco, CA: Institute for Contemporary Studies, 1978).

TOBACCO

Books and Articles

Caldwell, Christopher, "Smoke Gets in Your Eyes," *The American Spectator*, Volume 25 (May, 1992), pp. 25-28.

Goodin, Robert E., *No Smoking: The Ethical Issues* (Chicago, IL: University of Chicago Press, 1989).

King, Florence, "I'd Rather Smoke than Kiss," *National Review*, Volume XLII (July 9, 1990), pp. 32-36.

Lee, Dwight R., "Government v. Coase: The Case of Smoking," *The Cato Journal*, Volume 11 (Spring/Summer, 1991), pp. 151-164.

Machan, Tibor R., "Dr. Koop on Life, Liberty, and a 'Smoke-Free' America," *Chronicles*, Volume 13 (June, 1989), pp. 50-51.

Sullum, Jacob, "Smoke and Mirrors," *Reason*, Volume 22 (February, 1991), **pp.** 28-33.

Organizations

Council for Tobacco Research - U.S.A. 900 Third Avenue, New York, NY 10022, (212)-421-8885. Sponsors program of research into questions of tobacco use and health, organized by representatives of tobacco manufacturers, growers, and warehousemen.

Smoker's Rights Alliance 20 E. Main Street, Suite 710, Mesa, AZ 85201, (602)-461-8882. Publication: *Smoke Signals.* Individuals interested in preserving the right to smoke without unnecessary interference by government.

Tobacco Institute 1875 I Street, NW, Suite 800, Washington, DC 20006, (202)-457-4800. Publications: *Tax Burden on Tobacco, Tobacco Industry Profile.* Promote better public understanding of the tobacco industry and its place in the nation's economy; compiles and reports information on tobacco.

Tobacco Merchants Association of United States 231 Clarksville Road, Suite 6, Lawrenceville, NJ 08648, (609)-275-4900. Publications: *Leaf Bulletin, TMA International Report, TMA Issues Monitor, Tobacco Barometer, Legislative Bulletin, Tobacco Trade Barometer, Trademark Report, Tobacco Tax Guide.* Manufacturers of tobacco products, leaf dealers, suppliers, distributors, and others related to the tobacco industry.

TOURISM
(see **Travel**)

TOXIC WASTE
(see **Environment, Sanitation**)

TRANSPORTATION
(see also **Airlines, Highways, Railroads**)

Books and Articles

Conlon, Edward, "Down in the Hole: Six Weeks with the Police in New York's Subway Tunnels," *The American Spectator*, Volume 25 (May, 1992), pp. 29-41.

Dwyer, Jim, *Subway Lives: 24 Hours in the Life of the New York City Subway* (New York: Crown, 1991).

Gordon, Peter and Richardson, Harry, "Notes from Underground: The Failure of Urban Mass Transit," *The Public Interest*, Number 94 (Winter, 1989), pp. 77-86.

Gordon, Peter and Richardson, Harry, "You Can't Get There from Here: 19th-Century Transit Plans Won't Solve 21st-Century Traffic Problems," *Reason*, Volume 21 (August/September, 1989), pp. 34-37.

Ramsey, James B., "Selling the New York Subways," *National Review*, Volume XXXV (February 4, 1983), pp. 112-16.

Semmens, John and Kresich, Dianne, "Razing Arizona: How Phoenix Taxpayers Derailed an $8-Billion Transit System," *Policy Review*, Number 54 (Fall, 1990), pp. 62-66.

Organizations

American Bus Association 1015 15th Street, NW, Suite 250, Washington, DC 20005, (202)-842-1645. Publications: *Bus Operator, Destinations, Motorcoach Marketer, SCAN Newsletter, Transit Times Newsletter, Travel SCAN Newsletter*. Seeks to improve bus service, to stimulate the establishment of bus terminals and connecting schedules, and to develop and promote increased bus utilization in travel and tourism.

American Public Transit Association 1201 New York Avenue, NW, Suite 400, Washington, DC 20005, (202)-898-4000. Publications: *APTA Directory, Passenger Transport: The Weekly Newspaper of the Transit Industry, Transit Fact Book*. Maintains biographical archives, hall of fame, and 20,000 volumes on urban transportation and related fields.

Transportation Research Board 2101 Constitution Avenue, NW, Washington, DC 20418, (202)-334-2934. Publications: *Highway Safety Literature, HRIS Abstracts, TR News*. Encourages research and provides a national clearinghouse and correlation service for research activities and information on transportation technology.

TRAVEL

Books and Articles

Fleming, Thomas, "Travelers' Tales," *Chronicles*, Volume 12 (November, 1988), pp. 6-8.

Fussell, Paul, ed., *The Norton Book of Travel* (New York: Norton, 1987).

McGurn, William, "A Banana Republic Baedeker," *The American Spectator*, Volume 22 (March, 1989), pp. 16-18.

Organizations

International Airline Passengers Association P.O. Box 870188, Dallas, TX 75287-0188, (214)-404-9980. Publications: *International Flight Log and Travel Directory, International Member Benefits Directory, Magazine, Newsletter.* Purposes are to provide all types of services for individuals who travel a great deal and to represent the frequent flyer in matters of safety, comfort, convenience, and economy.

Travel Industry Association of America Two Lafayette Center, 1133 21st Street, NW, 8th Floor, Washington, DC 20036, (202)-293-1433. Publications: *Annual Report, International Travel News Directory, Newsline, Travel Industry Association of America Directory of Membership and Services, Contact USA.* Seeks to stimulate growth of domestic and international travel.

TREATIES

Books and Articles

Beichman, Arnold, *The Long Pretense: Soviet Treaty Diplomacy from Lenin to Gorbachev* (New Brunswick, NJ: Transaction Books, 1991).

TRUCKING INDUSTRY

Organizations

American Trucking Associations 2200 Mill Road, Alexandria, VA 22314, (703)-838-1700. Operates Motor Carrier Advisory Service, a guide to federal and state regulations; provides quarterly financial and operating statistics service. Offers comprehensive accounting service for all sizes of carriers.

UNEMPLOYMENT
(see **Employment**)

UNION OF SOVIET SOCIALIST REPUBLICS
(see **Commonwealth of Independent States**)

UNIONS
(see **Labor Unions**)

UNITED KINGDOM

Books and Articles

Barnett, Correlli, *The Pride and the Fall: The Dream and the Illusion of Britain as a Great Nation* (New York: The Free Press, 1987).

Gilbert, Martin, *Churchill: A Life* (New York: Henry Holt & Company, 1991).

Harris, Robin, "The Next Stage of Thatcherism," *National Review*, Volume XLIII (January 28, 1991), pp. 42-43.

Horne, Alistair, *Harold Macmillan, Volume One, 1894 - 1956* (New York: Viking, 1989).

Johnson, Paul, *A History of the English People* (New York: Perennial Library, 1985).

Lejeune, Anthony, "Catch the Falling Pound," *National Review*, Volume XLIV (November 2, 1992), pp. 21-22.

Letwin, Shirley Robin, *The Anatomy of Thatcherism* (New Brunswick, NJ: Transaction Books, 1993).

Mount, Ferdinand, "Thatcher's Decade," *The National Interest*, Number 14 (Winter, 1988/89), pp. 10-20.

O'Sullivan, John, "Britain: Under the Iron (High) Heel?," *Commentary*, Volume 88 (September, 1989), pp. 47-52.

O'Sullivan, John, "Is the Heroic Age of Conservatism Over?," *National Review*, Volume XLIII (January 28, 1991), pp. 32-37.

Reagan, Ronald, et al., "Margaret Thatcher and the Revival of the West," *National Review*, Volume XLI (May 19, 1989), pp. 21-25.

Stelzer, Irwin M., "What Thatcher Wrought," *The Public Interest*, Number 107 (Spring, 1992), pp. 18-51.

Walters, Alan, *Britain's Economic Renaissance: Margaret Thatcher's Reforms, 1979 - 1984* (New York: Oxford University Press, 1986).

Warren, Spencer, "The Lady's Not for Turning: The Domestic Triumphs of Margaret Thatcher," *Policy Review*, Number 60 (Spring, 1992), pp. 62-69.

UNITED NATIONS

Books and Articles

Bethell, Tom, "The Last Best Hope at Forty," *National Review*, Volume XXXVII (May 31, 1985), pp. 33-35.

Conrad, John P. and van den Haag, Ernest, *The UN: In or Out? A Debate Between Ernest van den Haag and John P. Conrad* (New York: Plenum Press, 1987).

Eberstadt, Nicholas, "Is Third World Debt Killing Children? UNworthy Conclusions About the Consequences of Debt," *The American Enterprise*, Volume 1 (November/December, 1990), pp. 56-63.

Gerson, Allan, "International Law in the New Era," *The American Enterprise*, Volume 1 (November/December, 1990), pp. 64-69.

Gerson, Allan, *The Kirkpatrick Mission: Diplomacy Without Apology. America at the United Nations, 1981-1985* (New York: The Free Press, 1991).

Gerson, Allan, "Terrorism and Turtle Bay," *The National Interest*, Number 11 (Spring, 1988), pp. 95-99.

Keyes, Alan L., "Fixing the U.N.," *The National Interest*, Number 4 (Summer, 1986), pp. 12-23.

Kirkpatrick, Jeane J., *Legitimacy and Force: State Papers and Current Perspectives, Vol. I: Political and Moral Dimensions, Vol. II: National and International Dimensions* (New Brunswick, NJ: Transaction Books, 1987).

Lengyel, Peter, *International Social Science: The UNESCO Experience* (New Brunswick, NJ: Transaction Books, 1986).

Mallon, Thomas, "The People Next Door," *The American Spectator*, Volume 22 (December, 1989), pp. 22-26.

Schoenberg, Harris Okun, *A Mandate for Terror: The United Nations and the PLO* (New York: Shapolsky Publishers, 1988).

Sorzano, Jose S., "The U.N.: 40 Years, 40 Facts," *The National Interest*, Number 2 (Winter, 1986), pp. 112-115.

Williamson, Richard S., "Agencies of Change," *The American Enterprise*, Volume 1 (November/December, 1990), pp. 70-74.

U.S. CIVIL WAR

Books and Articles

Boritt, Gabor S., ed., *Why the Confederacy Lost* (New York: Oxford University Press, 1992).

Burns, Ken, et al., *The Civil War: An Illustrated History* (New York: Knopf, 1990).

Davis, Burke, *Gray Fox: Robert E. Lee and the Civil War* (New York: Crown Publishers, 1988).

Davis, Burke, *Jeb Stuart: The Last Cavalier* (New York: Crown Publishers, 1988).

Davis, Burke, *Sherman's March* (New York: Random House, 1980).

Davis, Burke, *They Called Him Stonewall: A Life of Lt. General T. J. Jackson, C.S.A.* (New York: Crown Publishers, 1988).

Davis, Burke, *To Appomattox: Nine April Days, 1865* (Philadelphia, PA: Eastern Acorn Press, 1989).

Davis, George B., et al., *The Official Military Atlas of the Civil War* (New York: Fairfax Press, 1983).

Fleming, Thomas, "The Civil War and American Destiny," *National Review*, Volume XXXIX (November 6, 1987), pp. 48-53.

Fleming, Thomas, "Lincoln's Tragic Heroism," *National Review*, Volume XLI (December 8, 1989), pp. 38-40.

Foote, Shelby, *The Civil War: A Narrative: Fort Sumter to Perryville*. Vol. 1. (New York: Random House, 1958).

Foote, Shelby, *The Civil War: A Narrative: Fredericksburg to Meridian*. Vol. 2. (New York: Random House, 1963).

Foote, Shelby, *The Civil War: A Narrative: Red River to Appomattox*. Vol. 3. (New York: Random House, 1974).

Freeman, Douglas Southall, *Lee's Lieutenants: A Study in Command*, 3 vols. (New York: Scribner's, 1986).

Gragg, Rod, *The Illustrated Confederate Reader* (New York: Harper and Row, 1989).

Hagerman, Edward, *The American Civil War and the Origins of Modern Warfare: Ideas, Organization, and Field Command* (Bloomington, IN: Indiana University Press, 1992).

Jaffa, Harry V., "Lincoln's Character Assassins," *National Review*, Volume XLII (January 22, 1990), pp. 34-38.

Jones, Archer, *Civil War Command and Strategy: The Process of Victory and Defeat* (New York: The Free Press, 1992).

Linderman, Gerald F., *Embattled Courage: The Experience of Combat in the American Civil War* (New York: Free Press, 1987).

Luvaas, Jay, *The Military Legacy of the Civil War: The European Inheritance* (Chicago, IL: University of Chicago Press, 1959).

McFeely, William S., *Grant: A Biography* (New York: Norton, 1981).

McPherson, James M., *Battle Cry of Freedom: The Civil War Era* (New York: Oxford University Press, 1988).

McWhiney, Grady and Jamieson, Perry D., *Attack and Die: Civil War Military Tactics and the Southern Heritage* (Tuscaloosa, AL: University of Alabama Press, 1982).

Mitchell, Reid, *Civil War Soldiers: Their Expectations and Their Experiences* (New York: Viking, 1988).

Pfanz, Harry W., *Gettysburg - The Second Day* (Chapel Hill, NC: University of North Carolina Press, 1987).

Royster, Charles, *The Destructive War: William Tecumseh Sherman, Stonewall Jackson, and the Americans* (New York: Knopf, 1991).

Scott, Robert Garth, *Into the Wilderness with the Army of the Potomac* (Bloomington, IN: Indiana University Press, 1985).

Sears, Stephen W., *Landscape Turned Red: The Battle of Antietam* (New York: Ticknor and Fields, 1983).

Sears, Stephen W., *To the Gates of Richmond: The Peninsula Campaign* (Boston, MA: Ticknor & Fields, 1992).

Seay, Davin, "Battlefield Tour," *National Review*, Volume XXXVII (July 26, 1985), pp. 33-37.

Sword, Wiley, *Embrace an Angry Wind: The Confederacy's Last Hurrah: Spring Hill, Franklin, and Nashville* (New York: Harper Collins, 1992).

Sword, Wiley, *Shiloh: Bloody April* (Philadelphia, PA: Eastern Acorn Press, 1983).

Wheeler, Richard, *Lee's Terrible Swift Sword: Antietam, Fredericksburg, Chancellorsville: An Eyewitness History* (New York: Harper Collins, 1992).

Wheeler, Richard, *Sword over Richmond: An Eyewitness History of McClellan's Peninsula Campaign* (New York: Harper and Row, 1986).

Wheeler, Richard, *Witness to Gettysburg* (New York: Harper and Row, 1987).

Organizations

Civil War Round Table Associates P.O. Box 7388, Little Rock, AR 72217, (501)-225-3996. Publications: *Civil War Round Table Digest, Roster CWRT's and Related Organizations, CWRT Organization Guide*. Preserves Civil War historical sites; develops local roundtables.

Civil War Society P.O. Box 770, Berryville, VA 22611, (703)-955-1176. Publication: *Civil War: The Magazine of the Civil War Society*. Students, educators, reenactors, and others interested in the history of the U.S. Civil War.

The Museum of the Confederacy 1201 E. Clay Street, Richmond, VA 23219, (804)-649-1861. Publication: *Museum of the Confederacy - Journal*. Authors, educators, students, and others interested in the study of Confederate history and culture.

Robert E. Lee Memorial Association Stratford Hall Plantation, Stratford, VA 22558, (804)-493-8038. Publications: *Newsletter, Stratford Journal, Stratford Summer Journal, Growing Up in the 1850s: The Journal of Agnes Lee, The Story of Lee*. Seeks to restore, preserve, and maintain Stratford Hall Plantation as a living memorial to General Robert E. Lee and to honor other famous men who lived there.

Ulysses S. Grant Association Morris Library, Southern Illinois University, Carbondale, IL 62901, (618)-453-2773. For general dissemination of information about Ulysses S. Grant.

U.S. FOREIGN POLICY

Books and Articles

Abrams, Elliott, "Can Democracy Drive Foreign Policy?," *National Review*, Volume XLIV (May 11, 1992), pp. 25-28.

Abrams, Elliott, "Good-bye to the New World Order," *National Review*, Volume XLIV (November 30, 1992), pp. 42-44.

Barrett, William, et al., "Human Rights and American Foreign Policy: A Symposium," *Commentary*, Volume 72 (November, 1981), pp. 25-63.

Bartley, Robert L., "A Win-Win Game," *The National Interest*, Number 21 (Fall, 1990), pp. 26-28.

Benedict, Ruth Sarles, "The America First Committee: The Anti-War Warriors," *Chronicles*, Volume 15 (December, 1991), pp. 23-24.

Brock, David, "Mr. Symms Goes to Jamba: A Kind Word for Congress in Foreign Policy," *Policy Review*, Number 59 (Winter, 1992), pp. 32-39.

Brock, David, "The Prince Metternichs of Congress," *The American Spectator*, Volume 23 (February, 1990), pp. 22-27.

Buchanan, Patrick J., "America First - and Second, and Third," *The National Interest*, Number 19 (Spring, 1990), pp. 77-82.

Burnham, James, *Containment or Liberation? An Inquiry into the Aims of United States Foreign Policy* (New York: John Day, 1952).

Carlson, Allan C., "Foreign Policy, 'The American Way', and the Passing of the Post-War Consensus," *This World*, Number 5 (Spring/Summer, 1983), pp. 18-54.

Carpenter, Ted Galen, "An Independent Course," *The National Interest*, Number 21 (Fall, 1990), pp. 28-31.

Cohen, Eliot A., "The Future of Force and American Strategy," *The National Interest*, Number 21 (Fall, 1990), pp. 3-15.

Cole, Wayne S., "The America First Committee: What Might Have Been," *Chronicles*, Volume 15 (December, 1991), pp. 20-22.

Coleman, Peter, *The Liberal Conspiracy: The Congress for Cultural Freedom and the Struggle for the Mind of Postwar Europe* (New York: The Free Press, 1989).

Crovitz, L. Gordon, "Micromanaging Foreign Policy," *The Public Interest*, Number 100 (Summer, 1990), pp. 102-115.

Crozier, Brian, "The Forlorn Cause," *National Review*, Volume XLV (February 1, 1993), pp. 50-53.

Doenecke, Justus D., "The America First Committee: Origins and Outcome," *Chronicles*, Volume 15 (December, 1991), pp. 16-19.

Doenecke, Justus D., *In Danger Undaunted: The Anti-Interventionist Movement of 1940 - 41 as Revealed in the Papers of the America First Committee* (Stanford, CA: Hoover Institution Press, 1990).

Fleming, Thomas, "America First: 1941 - 1991," *Chronicles*, Volume 15 (December, 1991), pp. 12-14.

Fleming, Thomas, "Banana Republicans," *Chronicles*, Volume 14 (January, 1990), pp. 12-14.

Fleming, Thomas, "Further Reflections on Violence," *Chronicles*, Volume 14 (November, 1990), pp. 12-15.

Francis, Samuel, "Principalities and Powers," *Chronicles*, Volume 15 (December, 1991), pp. 9-11.

Friedberg, Aaron L., "The Making of American National Strategy, 1948 - 1988," *The National Interest*, Number 11 (Spring, 1988), pp. 65-75.

Gershman, Carl, "Freedom Remains the Touchstone," *The National Interest*, Number 19 (Spring, 1990), pp. 83-86.

Glazer, Nathan, "A Time for Modesty," *The National Interest*, Number 21 (Fall, 1990), pp. 31-35.

Gray, Colin S., *War, Peace, and Victory: Strategy and Statecraft for the Next Century* (New York: Simon & Schuster, 1990).

Gray, John, "Backward into the Future," *National Review*, Volume XLV (March 29, 1993), pp. 27-32.

Haass, Richard N., "Dealing with Friendly Tyrants," *The National Interest*, Number 15 (Spring, 1989), pp. 40-48.

Harries, Owen, "'Exporting Democracy' - and Getting It Wrong," *The National Interest*, Number 13 (Fall, 1988), pp. 3-12.

Holbrooke, Richard, et al., "Are We Moving Toward a New Foreign Policy Consensus?," *The National Interest*, Number 4 (Summer, 1986), pp. 3-11.

Holmes, Kim R., et al., "Making the World Safe for America: The Heritage 'Blueprint' and Its Critics," *Policy Review*, Number 61 (Summer, 1992), pp. 50-69.

Joffe, Josef, "Entangled Forever," *The National Interest*, Number 21 (Fall, 1990), pp. 35-40.

Johnson, Paul, "Wanted: A New Imperialism," *National Review*, Volume XLIV (December 14, 1992), pp. 28-34.

Kedourie, Elie, "Iraq: The Mystery of American Policy," *Commentary*, Volume 91 (June, 1991), pp. 15-19.

Kirkpatrick, Jeane J., "A Normal Country in a Normal Time," *The National Interest*, Number 21 (Fall, 1990), pp. 40-44.

Krauthammer, Charles, "Isolationism: A Riposte," *The National Interest*, Number 2 (Winter, 1985/1986), pp. 115-118.

Krauthammer, Charles, "Universal Dominion: Toward a Unipolar World," *The National Interest*, Number 18 (Winter, 1989/90), pp. 46-49.

Kristol, Irving, "Defining Our National Interest," *The National Interest*, Number 21 (Fall, 1990), pp. 16-25.

Kristol, Irving, "Foreign Policy in an Age of Ideology," *The National Interest*, Number 1 (Fall, 1985), pp. 6-15.

Lagon, Mark P. and Lind, Michael, "American Way: The Enduring Interests of U.S. Foreign Policy," *Policy Review*, Number 57 (Summer, 1991), pp. 38-44.

Ledeen, Michael, "The Second Democratic Revolution," *The American Spectator*, Volume 23 (October, 1990), pp. 19-22.

Lefever, Ernest W., *Ethics and United States Foreign Policy* (Lanham, MD: University Press of America, 1986).

Liggio, Leonard P., "The America First Committee: Redskins and Palefaces," *Chronicles*, Volume 15 (December, 1991), pp. 25-26.

Luttwak, Edward N., "Do We Need a New Grand Strategy?," *The National Interest*, Number 15 (Spring, 1989), pp. 3-14.

Menges, Constantine C., "That Old Summit Magic," *National Review*, Volume XL (June 24, 1988), pp. 37-40.

O'Sullivan, John, "James Burnham and the New World Order," *National Review*, Volume XLII (November 5, 1990), pp. 34-50.

Pappas, Theodore, "The New World Order: Just Another Form of Cultural Amnesia," *Chronicles*, Volume 15 (September, 1991), pp. 23-25.

Pines, Burton Yale, "A Primer for Conservatives," *The National Interest*, Number 23 (Spring, 1991), pp. 61-68.

Pipes, Richard, *Survival Is Not Enough: Soviet Realities and America's Future* (New York: Simon & Schuster, 1985).

Podhoretz, Norman, "Enter the Peace Party," *Commentary*, Volume 91 (January, 1991), pp. 17-21.

Roche, John P., "Ain't Gonna Study (Cold) War No More," *National Review*, Volume XLII (March 19, 1990), pp. 27-28.

Rodman, Peter W., "The Imperial Congress," *The National Interest*, Number 1 (Fall, 1985), pp. 26-35.

Rodman, Peter, "Intervention and its Discontents," *National Review*, Volume XLV (March 29, 1993), pp. 28-29.

Rothbard, Murray N., "Foreign Policy for the Post-Cold War World," *Chronicles*, Volume 14 (May, 1990), pp. 16-20.

Saveth, Edward N., "Suicide of an Elite," *Commentary*, Volume 92 (August, 1991), pp. 44-47.

Snyder, Jed C., "Must the U.S. Disengage?," *National Review*, Volume XLIV (November 16, 1992), pp. 29-33.

Tarcov, Nathan, "If This Long War Is Over," *The National Interest*, Number 18 (Winter, 1989/90), pp. 50-53.

Tucker, Robert W., "Exemplar or Crusader? Reflections on America's Role," *The National Interest*, Number 5 (Fall, 1986), pp. 64-75.

Tucker, Robert W., "Isolation and Intervention," *The National Interest*, Number 1 (Fall, 1985), pp. 16-25.

Vlahos, Michael, "Look Homeward," *The National Interest*, Number 20 (Summer, 1990), pp. 49-53.

Wallop, Malcolm, "The Ultimate High Ground," *The National Interest*, Number 21 (Fall, 1990), pp. 47-51.

Wattenberg, Ben J., "Neo-Manifest Destinarianism," *The National Interest*, Number 21 (Fall, 1990), pp. 51-54.

Weigel, George, "The National Interest and the National Purpose: From Policy Debate to Moral Argument," *This World*, Number 19 (Fall, 1987), pp. 79-100.

Weigel, George, "On the Road to Isolationism?," *Commentary*, Volume 93 (January, 1992), pp. 36-42.

Weinberger, Caspar, *Fighting for Peace: Seven Critical Years in the Pentagon* (New York: Warner Books, 1990).
Weyrich, Paul M., "A Populist Policy," *The National Interest*, Number 21 (Fall, 1990), pp. 54-57.
Worsthorne, Peregrine, "Not Too Much Zeal, Please," *The National Interest*, Number 21 (Fall, 1990), pp. 57-61.

Organizations

Center for International Relations 5702 Newington Road, Bethesda, MD 20816, (301)-229-4843. Washington-based think tank which networks with like-minded public policy organizations in other regions of the world.

Center for Security Policy 1250 24th Street, NW, Suite 875, Washington, DC 20037, (202)-466-0515. Publication: *Newsletter*. Policy information network focusing on international security policy issues. Provides information to members of the legislative and executive branches of government, the media, and the general public.

Center for Strategic and International Studies 1800 K Street, NW, Suite 400, Washington, DC 20006, (202)-887-0200. Publications: *The Washington Quarterly, Washington Papers, Panel Reports.* A public policy research institute that provides policymakers with a strategic perspective on issues relating to international economics, politics, security and business. Committed to serving the common interests of the United States and other countries around the world that support representative government and the rule of law.

Ethics and Public Policy Center 1015 15th Street, NW, #900, Washington, DC 20005, (202)-682-1200. Publication: *Newsletter*. Attempts to clarify the relationship "between political necessity and moral principle,"; focuses on the role of organized religion in the public policy arena.

Foreign Policy Research Institute 3615 Chestnut Street, Philadelphia, PA 19104, (215)-382-0685. Publication: *Orbis: A Journal of World Affairs*. Seeks to disseminate scholarly research affecting the national interests of the U.S.; by serving as spur for the exchange of ideas, the Institute consciously attempts to influence the climate in which policy is made.

The Hoover Institution Stanford University, Stanford, CA 94305-6010, (415)-723-1687. A public policy research center devoted to advanced study on domestic public policy and international affairs. Has one of the world's largest archives and most complete libraries devoted to the economic, social and political changes of the the twentieth century.

Institute for Foreign Policy Analysis 675 Massachusetts Avenue, 10th Floor, Cambridge, MA 02139, (617)-492-2116.

International Security Council 2401 Pennsylvania Avenue, Suite 604, Washington, DC 20037, (202)-828-0802. Publication: *Global Affairs*. Objective is to raise public awareness of the geopolitical struggle between the U.S. and the Soviet Union.

National Center for Public Policy Research 1776 K Street, NW, Washington DC 20006, (202)-429-7360. Publications: *Newsletter, A Letter From Central America, Catholic Study Council - Bulletin*. Educates public about policy issues, with focus on foreign affairs; Afghanistan and Central America are areas of particular expertise.

National Defense Council Foundation 1220 King Street, Suite #1, Alexandria, VA 22314, (703)-836-3443. Publication: *Newsletter*. Studies low-intensity conflict and terrorism.

U.S. Global Strategy Council 1800 K Street, NW, Suite 1102, Washington, DC 20006, (202)-466-6029.

UNIVERSITIES

Books and Articles

Bethell, Tom, "Tulane and the Big Government Campus," *The American Spectator*, Volume 24 (May, 1991), pp. 9-11.

Bunzel, John H., "Affirmative-Action Admissions: How It 'Works' at UC Berkeley," *The Public Interest*, Number 93 (Fall, 1988), pp. 111-129.

Bunzel, John H., "Black and White at Stanford," *The Public Interest*, Number 105 (Fall, 1991), pp. 61-77.

Bunzel, John H., "Exclusive Opportunities," *The American Enterprise*, Volume 1 (March/April, 1990), pp. 47-51.

Daniels, Edmund D. and Weiss, Michael David, "'Equality' Over Quality," *Reason*, Volume 23 (July, 1991), pp. 44-45.

Ferguson, Tim W., "Benetton U," *The American Spectator*, Volume 25 (January, 1992), pp. 49-51.

Frum, David, "Campus Counterrevolution," *The American Spectator*, Volume 24 (May, 1991), pp. 12-14.

Horner, Charles, et al., *The Common Sense Guide to American Colleges 1991 - 1992* (Lanham, MD: Madison Books/ University Press of America, 1991).

Miner, Brad and Sykes, Charles, *The National Review College Guide: America's 50 Top Liberal Arts Schools* (New York: National Review Books, 1991).

Morris, Stephen J., "Ho Chi Minh, Pol Pot, and Cornell," *The National Interest*, Number 16 (Summer, 1989), pp. 49-62.

Norden, Edward, "A Month in Paradise," *The American Spectator*, Volume 25 (April, 1992), pp. 32-46.

Platt, Michael, "Thomas Aquinas and America: How One College Might Strengthen the Souls of Youth and Reinvigorate the Republic," *Crisis*, Volume 9 (July/August, 1991), pp. 21-25, 42.

Short, Thomas, "A 'New Racism' on Campus," *Commentary*, Volume 86 (August, 1988), pp. 46-50.

Sowell, Thomas, *Choosing a College* (New York: Harper & Row, 1989).

URBAN AFFAIRS

Books and Articles

Anderson, Lorrin, "Guilt and Gasoline," *National Review*, Volume XLIV (June 8, 1992), pp. 35-37.

Bray, Thomas, "Reading America the Riot Act: The Kerner Report and Its Culture of Violence," *Policy Review*, Number 43 (Winter, 1988), pp. 32-36.

Coyle, Dennis, "The Balkans by the Bay," *The Public Interest*, Number 91 (Spring, 1988), pp. 67-78.

Foster, Sarah E., "Invasion of the City Snatchers," *Reason*, Volume 19 (January, 1988), pp. 22-29.

Frieden, Bernard J., "The Downtown Job Puzzle," *The Public Interest*, Number 97 (Fall, 1989), pp. 71-86.

Hall, Peter, *Cities of Tomorrow: An Intellectual History of Urban Planning and Design in the Twentieth Century* (New York: Basil Blackwell, 1988).

Keyes, Alan, "Restoring Community," *National Review*, Volume XLIV (June 8, 1992), pp. 38-41.

Methvin, Eugene H., "How to Hold a Riot," *National Review*, Volume XLIV (June 8, 1992), pp. 32-35.

Moore, Stephen, "Big-Town Blues," *National Review*, Volume XLIV (October 5, 1992), pp. 52-54.

Morris, Charles R., *The Cost of Good Intentions: New York City and the Liberal Experiment, 1960 - 1965* (New York: Norton, 1980).

Murray, Charles, "Causes, Root Causes, and Cures," *National Review*, Volume XLIV (June 8, 1992), pp. 30-32.

Norman, Geoffrey, "The Hustle and Hypocrisy of Andrew Young's Atlanta," *The American Spectator*, Volume 21 (June, 1988), pp. 23-27.

Skogan, Wesley, *Disorder and Decline: Crime and the Spiral of Decay in American Neighborhoods* (New York: The Free Press, 1990).

Starr, Roger, *The Rise and Fall of New York City* (New York: Basic Books, 1985).

Valiunas, Algis, "Black and White Mischief in Chicago," *The American Spectator*, Volume 21 (October, 1988), pp. 21-25.

Organizations

Manhattan Institute for Policy Research 52 Vanderbilt Avenue, New York, NY 10017, (212)-599-7000. Publication: *City Journal*. Purpose is to assist scholars, government officials and the public in obtaining a better understanding of economic processes and the effect of government programs on the economic situation.

UTILITIES

Organizations

Edison Electric Institute 701 Pennsylvania Avenue, NW, Washington, DC 20004, (202)-508-5000. Publications: *Electrical Reports, Rate Book, Statistical Reports, Statistical Yearbook, Electric Power Surveys*. Investor-owned electric utility companies operating in the U.S.

Institute of Public Utilities 113 Olds Hall, Michigan State University, East Lansing, MI 48824-1047, (517)-355-1876. Privately-owned utility companies. Facilitates discussion of problems currently faced by public utility industry.

VETERANS

Organizations

American Legion c/o Public Relations Division, 700 N. Pennsylvania Street, P.O. Box 1055, Indianapolis, IN 46204, (317)-635-8411. Publications: *The American Legion Magazine, The American Legion Dispatch*. Honorably discharged wartime veterans, both male and female.

VIETNAM
(see also **Vietnam War**)

Books and Articles

LeBoutillier, John, *Vietnam Now: A Case for Normalizing Relations with Hanoi* (New York: Praeger Publishers, 1989).

McGurn, William, "The Scandal of the Boat People," *Commentary*, Volume 89 (January, 1990), pp. 36-40.

Pham, Huy Ty, "The Fall of Hanoi," *National Review*, Volume XLIII (February 11, 1991), pp. 40-43.

VIETNAM WAR

Books and Articles

Anderson, Charles R., *The Grunts* (Novato, CA: Presidio Press, 1976).

Billingsley, K. L., "A Vietnam Memorial: The National Council of Churches in Indochina," *This World*, Number 23 (Fall, 1988), pp. 25-39.

Bosiljevac, T. L., *Seals: UDT/SEAL Operations in Vietnam* (Boulder, CO: Paladin Press, 1990).

Broughton, Jack, *Going Downtown: The War Against Hanoi and Washington* (New York: Orion Books, 1988).

Broughton, Jack, *Thud Ridge* (Philadelphia, PA: J. B. Lippincott Co., 1969).

Brown, Dale and Matthews, Lloyd J., eds., *Assessing the Vietnam War: A Collection from the Journal of the U.S. Army War College* (McLean, VA: Pergamon-Brassey's, 1987).

Carhart, Tom, *The Offering* (New York: William Morrow, 1987).

Chanoff, David and van Toai, Doan, *Portrait of the Enemy* (New York: Random House, 1986).

Currey, Cecil B. ("Cincinnatus"), *Self-Destruction: The Disintegration and Decay of the United States Army During the Vietnam Era* (New York: Norton, 1981).

Davidson, Phillip B., *Vietnam at War: The History, 1946 - 1975* (Novato, CA: Presidio Press, 1988).

Krepinevich, Andrew, *The Army and Vietnam* (Baltimore, MD: Johns Hopkins University Press, 1986).

Lanning, Michael Lee and Stubbe, Ray William, *Inside Force Recon: Recon Marines in Vietnam* (New York: Ivy Books, 1989).

Lewy, Guenter, *America in Vietnam* (New York: Oxford University Press, 1978).

McDonough, James R., *Platoon Leader* (Novato, CA: Presidio Press, 1985).

Moore, Harold G. and Galloway, Joseph L., *Ia Drang: The Battle that Changed the War in Vietnam* (New York: Random House, 1992).

Morris, Stephen J., "Ho Chi Minh, Pol Pot, and Cornell," *The National Interest*, Number 16 (Summer, 1989), pp. 49-62.

Nichols, John B. and Tillman, Barrett, *On Yankee Station: The Naval Air War Over Vietnam* (Annapolis, MD: Naval Institute Press, 1987).

Owens, Mackubin T., "Vietnam and the Just-War Tradition," *This World*, Number 7 (Winter, 1984), pp. 43-65.

Palmer, Bruce, Jr., *The 25-Year War: America's Military Role in Vietnam* (Lexington, KY: University Press of Kentucky, 1984).

Podhoretz, Norman, *Why We Were in Vietnam* (New York: Simon & Schuster, 1982).

Roche, John P., "Indochina Revisited: The Demise of Liberalism and Internationalism," *National Review*, Volume XXXVII (May 3, 1985), pp. 26-44.

Stanton, Shelby L., *The Rise and Fall of an American Army: U.S. Ground Forces in Vietnam, 1965 - 1973* (Novato, California: Presidio Press, 1985).

Stockdale, James Bond, "The Bull's-Eye of Disaster," *Chronicles*, Volume 13 (August, 1989), pp. 14-20.

Stockdale, James Bond, "Tragedy, Comedy, and Modern Times," *Chronicles*, Volume 14 (November, 1990), pp. 22-26.

Summers, Harry G., "Conservatives, Containment, and Vietnam," *The American Spectator*, Volume 21 (June, 1988), pp. 28-30.

Summers, Harry G., *On Strategy: A Critical Analysis of the Vietnam War* (Novato, CA: Presidio Press, 1982).

Winters, Francis X., "They Shoot Allies, Don't They?," *National Review*, Volume XL (November 25, 1988), pp. 34-37.

VOUCHERS
(see **School Choice**)

VOLUNTEERISM
(see **National Service**)

WALL STREET

Books and Articles

Bandow, Doug, "Insider Trading - Where's the Crime?," *National Review*, Volume XLII (April 16, 1990), pp. 37-38.

Crovitz, L. Gordon, "Michael Milken and His Enemies," *National Review*, Volume XLII (October 1, 1990), pp. 23-27.

Friedman, Milton, "1929 and 1987: The Differences," *National Review*, Volume XXXIX (November 20, 1987), p. 50.

Grundfest, Joseph A., "Financial Scandals in the United States and Japan," *The American Enterprise*, Volume 3 (May/June, 1992), pp. 34-45.

Laws, Margaret, "The Insider Story," *National Review*, Volume XLII (May 28, 1990), pp. 33-35.

Lewis, Michael, *Liar's Poker: Rising Through the Wreckage on Wall Street* (New York: Norton, 1989).

Manne, Henry G. and Ribstein, Larry E., "The SEC v. the American Shareholder," *National Review*, Volume XL (November 25, 1988), pp. 26-29.

McMenamin, Michael, "Witchhunt," *Reason*, Volume 20 (October, 1988), pp. 34-40.

Mysak, Joe, "The Beauty of Municipal Bonds," *The American Spectator*, Volume 22 (June, 1989), pp. 18-20.

Pound, John, "Proxy Contests: The SEC Rewrites the Rules," *The American Enterprise*, Volume 2 (September/October, 1991), pp. 56-63.

Stelzer, Irwin M., "The SEC vs. Drexel Burnham Milken," *The American Spectator*, Volume 21 (November, 1988), pp. 33-34.

Stelzer, Irwin M., "The Truth About Takeovers," *The American Spectator*, Volume 20 (June, 1987), pp. 14-15.

Wanniski, Jude, "Insider Reporting," *National Review*, Volume XLIII (December 2, 1991), pp. 26-31.

WAR

Books and Articles

Aron, Raymond, *The Century of Total War* (Boston, MA: The Beacon Press, 1955).

Aron, Raymond, *Clausewitz: Philosopher of War* (Englewood Cliffs, NJ: Prentice-Hall, 1985).

Bolger, Daniel, *Americans at War, 1975 - 1986: An Era of Violent Peace* (Novato, CA: Presidio Press, 1988).

Carver, Michael, *War Since 1945* (New York: G. P. Putnam's Sons, 1981).

Codevilla, Angelo, "Magnificent, but Was It War?," *Commentary*, Volume 93 (April, 1992), pp. 15-20.

Cohen, Eliot A. and Gooch, John, *Military Misfortunes: The Anatomy of Failure in War* (New York: The Free Press, 1990).

Cowley, Robert, *Experience of War: An Anthology of Articles from MHQ: The Quarterly Journal of Military History* (New York: Norton, 1992).

Diagram Group, *Weapons: An International Encyclopedia From 5000 B.C. to 2000 A.D.* (New York: St. Martin's Press, 1990).

Duffy, Christopher, *The Military Experience in the Age of Reason* (New York: Atheneum, 1988).

Dunnigan, James F., *How to Make War: A Comprehensive Guide to Modern Warfare* (New York: William Morrow, 1982).

Dupuy, Trevor N., "How the War Was Won," *National Review*, Volume XLIII (April 1, 1991), pp. 29-31.

Ellis, John, *The Social History of the Machine Gun* (London: Croom Helm, 1987).

Ethell, Jeffrey and Price, Alfred, *Air War South Atlantic* (New York: Macmillan, 1983).

Farwell, Byron, *Eminent Victorian Soldiers: Seekers of Glory* (New York: Norton, 1986).

Foss, Christopher F. and Miller, David, *Modern Land Combat* (New York: Portland House, 1987).

Goldich, Robert L., "The Strategic Importance of Mass," *The National Interest*, Number 6 (Winter, 1986/87), pp. 66-74.

Gray, Colin S., *The Leverage of Sea Power: The Strategic Advantage of Navies in Major Wars* (New York: The Free Press, 1992).

Griffith, Paddy, *Forward into Battle: Fighting Tactics From Waterloo to Vietnam* (Chichester, England: Anthony Bird Publications, 1981).

Griffith, Paddy, *The Ultimate Weaponry: The Most Lethal Conventional Firepower in the World* (New York: St. Martin's Press, 1991).

Hagerman, Edward, *The American Civil War and the Origins of Modern Warfare: Ideas, Organization, and Field Command* (Bloomington, IN: Indiana University Press, 1992).

Hastings, Max, ed., *The Oxford Book of Military Anecdotes* (New York: Oxford University Press, 1986).

Holmes, Richard, *Acts of War: The Behavior of Men in Battle* (New York: The Free Press, 1986).

Holmes, Richard, *Firing Line* (London: Jonathan Cape, 1985).

Howard, Michael, *The Lessons of History* (New Haven, CT: Yale University Press, 1991).

Keegan, John, *The Face of Battle* (New York: Dorset Press, 1976).

Keegan, John, *The Mask of Command* (New York: Viking Press, 1987).

Keegan, John, *The Price of Admiralty: The Evolution of Naval Warfare* (New York: Viking Press, 1989).

Luttwak, Edward N., *The Pentagon and the Art of War: The Question of Military Reform* (New York: Simon & Schuster, 1984).

Luttwak, Edward N., *Strategy: The Logic of War and Peace* (Cambridge, MA: Harvard University Press, 1987).

Luttwak, Edward N., *Strategy and Politics: Collected Essays* (New Brunswick, NJ: Transaction Books, 1980).

Luttwak, Edward N., *Strategy and History: Collected Essays,* Vol. II. (New Brunswick, NJ: Transaction Books, 1985).

Luttwak, Edward N., "Victory Through Air Power," *Commentary*, Volume 92 (August, 1991), pp. 27-30.

Macksey, Kenneth and Woodhouse, William, *The Penguin Encyclopedia of Modern Warfare: From the Crimean War to the Present Day* (New York: Viking Press, 1991).

Macksey, Kenneth, *Tank Versus Tank: The Illustrated Story of Armored Battlefield Conflict in the Twentieth Century* (New York: Crescent Books, 1991).

Martin, Laurence, *NATO and the Defense of the West: An Analysis of America's First Line of Defense* (New York: Holt Rinehart and Winston, 1985).

Miller, Chris and Miller, David, *Modern Naval Combat* (New York: Crescent Books, 1986).

Millett, Allan R. and Williamson, Murray, "Lessons of War," *The National Interest*, Number 14 (Winter, 1988/89), pp. 83-95.

Millett, Allan R. and Williamson, Murray, eds., *Military Effectiveness, Vol. I: The First World War, Vol. II: The Interwar Period, Vol. III: The Second World War* (Winchester, MA: Unwin Hyman, Inc., 1988).

Moore, John E. and Compton-Hall, Richard, *Submarine Warfare: Today and Tomorrow* (Bethesda, MD: Adler and Adler, 1986).

Price, Alfred, *Air Battle Central Europe* (New York: The Free Press, 1986).

Rodger, N. A. M., *The Wooden World: An Anatomy of the Georgian Navy* (Annapolis, MD: Naval Institute Press, 1986).

Seabury, Paul and Codevilla, Angelo, *War: Ends and Means* (New York: Basic Books, 1989).

Van Creveld, Martin, *Technology and War: From 2000 B.C. to the Present* (New York: The Free Press, 1989).

Veale, F. J. P., *Advance to Barbarism: The Development of Total Warfare from Sarajevo to Hiroshima* (New York: Devin-Adair, 1968).

Vigor, P. H., *Soviet Blitzkrieg Theory* (New York: St. Martin's Press, 1983).

Weigley, Russell F., *The Age of Battles: The Quest for Decisive Warfare From Breitenfeld to Waterloo* (Bloomington, IN: University of Indiana Press, 1991).

Organizations

Scipio Society of Naval and Military History 15 Ridge Road, Cold Spring Harbor, NY 11724, (516)-367-6691. Publications: *Directory, The Grenade.* Scholars and amateur historians interested in naval and military history.

WAR OF INDEPENDENCE

Books and Articles

Ketchum, Richard M., *Decisive Day: The Battle for Bunker Hill* (Garden City, NY: Doubleday, 1991).

Langguth, A. J., *Patriots: The Men Who Started the American Revolution* (New York: Simon and Schuster, 1988).

Stokesbury, James L., *A Short History of the American Revolution* (New York: William Morrow, 1991).

Tucker, Robert W. and Hendrickson, David C., *The Fall of the First British Empire: Origins of the War of American Independence* (Baltimore, MD: Johns Hopkins University Press, 1982).

Wallace, Willard M., *Appeal to Arms: A Military History of the American Revolution* (New York: Harper and Brothers, 1951).

Woods, W. J., *Battles of the Revolutionary War 1775 - 1781* (Chapel Hill, NC: Algonquin Books of Chapel Hill, 1990).

WATER PROJECTS

Books and Articles

Elliot, Michael, "The Global Politics of Water," *The American Enterprise*, Volume 2 (September/October, 1991), pp. 27-31.

Hayward, Steven, "Muddy Waters," *Reason*, Volume 23 (July, 1991), pp. 46-47.

Reisner, Marc, *Cadillac Desert: The American West and Its Disappearing Water* (New York: Viking, 1987).

WELFARE

Books and Articles

Butler, Stuart, "Razing the Liberal Plantation: A Conservative War on Poverty," *National Review*, Volume XLI (November 10, 1989), pp. 27-30.

Eberstadt, Nicholas, "Is Illegitimacy a Public-Health Hazard?," *National Review*, Volume XL (December 30, 1988), pp. 36-39.

Frum, David, "A Poorhouse Divided," *The American Spectator*, Volume 24 (February, 1991), pp. 16-18.

Graham, George G., "WIC: A Food Program that Fails," *The Public Interest*, Number 103 (Spring, 1991), pp. 66-75.

Hopkins, Kevin, "A New Deal for America's Poor: Abolish Welfare, Guarantee Jobs," *Policy Review*, Number 45 (Summer, 1988), pp. 70-73.

Kilberg, William J., "How We Pay People: Changing Compensation: More to Our Benefits?," *The American Enterprise*, Volume 1 (September/October, 1990), pp. 25-33.

Mead, Lawrence M., "The Democrats' Dilemma," *Commentary*, Volume 93 (January, 1992), pp. 43-47.

Mead, Lawrence M., "Jobs for the Welfare Poor: Work Requirements Can Overcome the Barriers," *Policy Review*, Number 43 (Winter, 1988), pp. 60-69.

Mead, Lawrence M., "The New Welfare Debate," *Commentary*, Volume 85 (March, 1988), pp. 44-52.

Moynihan, Daniel Patrick, "How the Great Society 'Destroyed the American Family,'" *The Public Interest*, Number 108 (Summer, 1992), pp. 53-64.

Moynihan, Daniel Patrick, "The Underclass: Toward a Post-Industrial Social Policy," *The Public Interest*, Number 96 (Summer, 1989), pp. 16-27.

Murray, Charles, "How to Lie with Statistics," *National Review*, Volume XXXVIII (February 28, 1986), pp. 39-41.

Murray, Charles, "The Legacy of the 60s," *Commentary*, Volume 94 (July, 1992), pp. 23-30.

Murray Charles, *Losing Ground: American Social Policy 1950 - 1980* (New York: Basic Books, 1984).

Murray, Charles, "White Welfare, White Families, White Trash," *National Review*, Volume XXXVIII (March 28, 1986), pp. 30-34.

Novak, Michael, et al., *The New Consensus on Family and Welfare: A Community of Self-Reliance* (Washington, DC: American Enterprise Institute for Public Policy Research, 1987).

Olasky, Marvin, "Beyond the Stingy Welfare State: What We Can Learn from the Compassion of the 19th Century," *Policy Review*, Number 54 (Fall, 1990), pp. 2-14.

Rector, Robert, "Requiem for the War on Poverty: Rethinking Welfare After the L.A. Riots," *Policy Review*, Number 61 (Summer, 1992), pp. 40-46.

Tucker, William, "Our Homestead Plan for the Poor," *The American Spectator*, Volume 21 (July, 1988), pp. 25-28.

Tullock, Gordon, *The Economics of Income Redistribution* (Norwell, MA: Kluwer Nijhoff Publishers, 1983).

Tullock, Gordon, *Welfare for the Well-to-Do* (Dallas, TX: Fisher Institute, 1983).

THE WEST

Books and Articles

Bradford, M. E., "A View From the Top of the Ridge: On the Literature of the American West," *Chronicles*, Volume 13 (February, 1989), pp. 43-47.

Bredahl, A. Carl., "Inscribing the American Frontier," *Chronicles*, Volume 15 (November, 1991), pp. 26-30.

Faulk, Odie B., "Epitaph for Tombstone," *Chronicles*, Volume 13 (February, 1989), pp. 8-10.

Lamm, Richard D. and McCarthy, Michael, *The Angry West: A Vulnerable Land and Its Future* (Boston, MA: Houghton Mifflin, 1982).

Lamm, Richard D., "Decline of the West: A Western View on the Fall of American Civilization," *Chronicles*, Volume 13 (February, 1989), pp. 16-19.

McNamee, Gregory, "Plundered Province: The American West as Literary Region," *Chronicles*, Volume 15 (November, 1991), pp. 46-48.

Reisner, Marc, *Cadillac Desert: The American West and Its Disappearing Water* (New York: Viking, 1987).

Turner, Frederick Jackson, *The Turner Thesis Concerning the Role of the Frontier in American History* (Boston, MA: D.C. Heath and Co., 1956).

Wiley, Peter and Gottlieb, Robert, *Empires in the Sun: The Rise of the New American West* (New York: Putnam, 1982).

Williamson, Chilton, Jr., "Big Little House in American Literature," *Chronicles*, Volume 15 (November, 1991), pp. 20-25.

Williamson, Chilton, Jr., "The Cow in the Trail," *Chronicles*, Volume 13 (November, 1989), pp. 12-14.

Williamson, Chilton, Jr., *Roughnecking It: Life in the Overthrust* (New York: Simon & Schuster, 1982).

Williamson, Chilton, Jr., "Western Is as Western Does," *Chronicles*, Volume 15 (November, 1991), pp. 12-13.

Organizations

National Cowboy Hall of Fame and Western Heritage Center 1700 N.E. 63rd Street, Oklahoma City, OK 73111, (405)-478-2250. Publication: *Persimmon Hill*. Persons interested in preserving the heritage of the American West and in honoring the pioneers who developed the West.

WESTERN CIVILIZATION/HERITAGE

Books and Articles

Barzun, Jacques, *The Culture We Deserve,* Arthur Krystal, ed. (Middletown, CT: Wesleyan University Press, 1989).

Barzun, Jacques, *The House of Intellect* (New York: Harper and Brothers, 1959).

Bradford, M. E., et al., "The State of the Humanities: A Symposium," *Modern Age*, Volume 34 (Winter, 1992), pp. 98-167.

Congdon, Tim, "Is Europe on the Road to Serfdom?," *National Review*, Volume XLII (September 17, 1990), pp. 40-43.

Dawson, Christopher, *The Making of Europe* (New York: New American Library, 1956).

Dawson, Christopher, *Religion and the Rise of Western Culture* (Garden City, NY: Doubleday/Image, 1958).

Fleming, Thomas, "Revolution and Tradition in the Humanities Curriculum," *Chronicles*, Volume 14 (September, 1990), pp. 13-16.

Gottfried, Paul, "Academics, Therapists, and the German Connection," *Chronicles*, Volume 14 (September, 1990), pp. 21-23.

Grant, Michael, *The Founders of the Western World: A History of Greece and Rome* (New York: Scribner's, 1991).

Johnston, J. F., Jr., "Decadence Revisited," *Modern Age*, Volume 33 (Spring, 1990), pp. 23-32.

Kagan, Donald, "An Address to the Class of 1944," *Commentary*, Volume 91 (January, 1991), pp. 47-49.

Molnar, Thomas, "The Teaching of Humanities and Other Trivia," *Chronicles*, Volume 14 (September, 1990), pp. 24-25.

Neusner, Jacob, "Can Humanity Forget What It Knows?," *Chronicles*, Volume 15 (September, 1991), pp. 19-22.

Roberts, J. M., *Triumph of the West* (Boston, MA: Little, Brown, 1987).

Schram, Glenn N., "Western Civilization in the Light of the Philosophy of History," *Modern Age*, Volume 33 (Fall, 1990), pp. 249-258.

Stockdale, James Bond, "Learning Goodness: Why Western Civ Is the Best Refuge in Adversity," *Chronicles*, Volume 12 (July, 1988), pp. 9-12.

Tarnas, Richard, *The Passion of the Western Mind: Understanding the Ideas That Have Shaped Our World View* (New York: Crown, 1991).

Wegierski, Mark, "Some Thoughts on the Ancient East and Modern West," *This World*, Number 27 (Winter, 1992), pp. 81-92.

WESTERN EUROPE

Books and Articles

Krauss, Melvyn, *How NATO Weakens the West* (New York: Simon & Schuster, 1986).

WOMEN

Books and Articles

Amiel, Barbara, "Feminism Hits Middle Age," *National Review*, Volume XLI (November 24, 1989), pp. 23-25, 58-59.

Barlow, Janet Scott, "Still Crazy After All These Years," *Chronicles*, Volume 12 (July, 1988), pp. 6-8.

Burleigh, Anne Husted, "After the Revolution: Can the 'Nineties Girl' Be Happy?," *Crisis*, Volume 8 (December, 1990), pp. 18-25.

Caplan, Gerald, "Battered Wives, Battered Justice," *National Review*, Volume XLIII (February 25, 1991), pp. 39-43.

Davidson, Nicholas, *The Failure of Feminism* (New York: Prometheus Books, 1988).

Davidson, Nicholas, "The Myths of Feminism," *National Review*, Volume XLI (May 19, 1989), pp. 44-46.

Davidson, Nicholas, "Who is Pete Schaub?," *Chronicles*, Volume 13 (January, 1989), pp. 46-48.

Donnelly, Elaine, "What Did You Do in the Gulf, Mommy?," *National Review*, Volume XLIII (November 18, 1991), pp. 41-44.

Finn, Chester E., Jr., "Biased Against Everyone," *The American Spectator*, Volume 25 (June, 1992), p. 37.

Fitzpatrick, Donna R., "The Third Stage: A Successful Career Woman Asks: Has Feminism Helped Me or Hurt Me?," *Crisis*, Volume 6 (May, 1988), pp. 25-29.

Frohnen, Bruce, "Mother Knows Best," *Chronicles*, Volume 13 (November, 1989), pp. 50-52.

Gallagher, Maggie, *Enemies of Eros: How the Sexual Revolution Is Killing Family, Marriage, and Sex and What Can We Do About It* (Chicago, IL: Bonus Books, 1990).

Gilbert, Neil, "The Phantom Epidemic of Sexual Assault," *The Public Interest*, Number 103 (Spring, 1991), pp. 54-65.

Gilder, George, "Still Seeking a Glass Slipper," *National Review*, Volume XLIV (December 14, 1992), pp. 38-41.

Goldberg, Steven, "Feminism Against Science," *National Review*, Volume XLIII (November 18, 1991), pp. 30-33.

Grenier, Richard, "Killer Bimbos," *Commentary*, Volume 92 (September, 1991), pp. 50-52.

Gustin, Kimberly J., "Women's Studies, A Major Error: Our Campus Scout Reports From the Front," *Crisis*, Volume 9 (January, 1991), pp. 31-33.

Gutmann, Stephanie, "It Sounds Like I Raped You: How Date-Rape 'Education' Fosters Confusion, Undermines Personal Responsibility, and Trivializes Sexual Violence," *Reason*, Volume 22 (July, 1990), pp. 22-27.

Hazen, Helen, *Endless Rapture: Rape, Romance, and the Female Imagination* (New York: Scribner's, 1983).

Iannone, Carol, "Analyzing a Feminist Whine," *The American Spectator*, Volume 21 (May, 1988), pp. 30-31.

Iannone, Carol, "Feminism vs. Literature," *Commentary*, Volume 86 (July, 1988), pp. 49-53.

Kersten, Katherine, "What Do Women Want? A Conservative Feminist Manifesto," *Policy Review*, Number 56 (Spring, 1991), pp. 4-15.

Kramer, Rita, "Are Girls Shortchanged at School?," *Commentary*, Volume 93 (June, 1992), pp. 48-49.

Lerner, Robert, and Rothman, Stanley, "Newspeak, Feminist-Style," *Commentary*, Volume 89 (April, 1990), pp. 54-56.

Letwin, Shirley Robin, "Law and the Unreasonable Woman," *National Review*, Volume XLIII (November 18, 1991), pp. 34-36.

Levin, Michael, *Feminism and Freedom* (New Brunswick, NJ: Transaction Books, 1988).

McDonnell, Thomas P., "Emily and the Feminists," *Chronicles*, Volume 12 (July, 1988), pp. 12-14.

Minogue, Kenneth, "The Goddess That Failed," *National Review*, Volume XLIII (November 18, 1991), pp. 46-48.

Mitchell, Brian, *Weak Link: The Feminization of the American Military* (Washington, DC: Regnery Gateway, 1989).

Mitchell, Brian, "Women in Arms: What Happened in Panama," *Chronicles*, Volume 14 (May, 1990), pp. 54-55.

Morgenson, Gretchen, "May I Have the Pleasure ...," *National Review*, Volume XLIII (November 18, 1991), pp. 36-41.

Munson, Naomi, "Harassment Blues," *Commentary*, Volume 93 (February, 1992), pp. 49-51.

Neely, James C., *Gender: The Myth of Equality* (New York: Simon & Schuster, 1983).

Norden, Edward, "Right Behind You, Scarlett!," *The American Spectator*, Volume 24 (August, 1991), pp. 14-16.

Oddie, William, "The Goddess Squad," *National Review*, Volume XLIII (November 18, 1991), pp. 44-46.

O'Neill, June, "Women and Wages," *The American Enterprise*, Volume 1 (November/December, 1990), pp. 25-33.

Paul, Ellen Frankel, *Equity and Gender: The Comparable Worth Debate* (New Brunswick, NJ: Transaction Books, 1989).

Podhoretz, Norman, "Rape in Feminist Eyes," *Commentary*, Volume 92 (October, 1991), pp. 29-35.

Scanlan, James P., "Illusions of Job Segregation," *The Public Interest*, Number 93 (Fall, 1988), pp. 54-69.

Shalit, Ruth, "Radical Exhibitionists: When Rape Victims Become Actors in Campus Political Theater, Someone Inevitably Gets Hurt," *Reason*, Volume 24 (July, 1992), pp. 36-41.

Steele, Betty, *The Feminist Takeover: Patriarchy to Matriarchy in Two Decades* (Gaithersburg, MD: Human Life International, 1992).

Stein, Sara Bonnett, *Girls and Boys: The Limits of Non-sexist Childrearing* (New York: Scribner's, 1984).

Tate, J. O., "Don't Get Your Knickers in a Twist," *National Review*, Volume XXXVII (November 15, 1985), pp. 48-54.

Weiss, Michael, "Crimes of the Head: Feminist Legal Theory Is Creating a Government Not of Laws but of Women," *Reason*, Volume 23 (January, 1992), pp. 29-33.

Wisse, Ruth R., "Living with Women's Lib," *Commentary*, Volume 86 (August, 1988), pp. 40-45.

van den Haag, Ernest, "Thinking About Rape," *The American Spectator*, Volume 25 (April, 1992), pp. 56-57.

Zagano, Phyllis, "In Whose Image? - Feminist Theory at the Crossroads," *This World*, Number 15 (Fall, 1986), pp. 78-86.

Organizations

Concerned Women for America 370 L'Enfant Promenade, SW, Suite 800, Washington, DC 20024, (202)-488-7000. Publication: *The Family Voice*. Seeks to preserve traditional family values and protect the rights of the family.

Eagle Forum P.O. Box 618, Alton. IL 62002, (618)-462-5415. Publication: *Phyllis Schlafly Report*. Opposes Equal Rights Amendment; very supportive of the traditional family; concerned with the decline of traditional morality.

Mothers at Home 8310A Old Courthouse Road, Vienna, VA 22182, (703)-827-5903, (800)-783-4MOM. Publication: *Welcome Home*. Dedicated to the support of mothers who choose to stay at home to raise their families.

WORKFORCE

Books and Articles

Burtless, Gary, *A Future of Lousy Jobs? The Changing Structure of U.S. Wages*
(Washington, DC: The Brookings Institution, 1990).
Weaver, Carolyn, "Vocational Rehabilitation Reform: Holding Out a Hand?,"
The American Enterprise, Volume 2 (July/August, 1991), pp. 20-23.

Organizations

ESOP Association 1100 17th Street, NW, Suite 1207, Washington, DC 20036, (202)-293-2971. Publications: *ESOP Association Directory, ESOP Report and Profile, ESOP Survey, How the ESOP Really Works, Structuring Leveraged ESOP Transactions*. Acts as national information clearinghouse for the press and public interested in the concept of employee ownership.

National Center on Education and the Economy 39 State Street, Suite 500, Rochester, NY 14614, (716)-546-7620. Publications: *A Nation Prepared: Teachers for the 21st Century, Redesigning America's Schools: The Public Speaks, To Secure Our Future*. Seeks to draw public attention to the link between economic growth and the skills and abilities of the people who contribute to that growth.

WORLD BANK
(see **Banking/Banks, Foreign Aid, International Economy**)

WORLD WAR I

Books and Articles

Blunden, Edmund, *Undertones of War* (New York: Harvest/Harcourt Brace and World, 1965).

Chapman, Guy, *A Passionate Prodigality* (New York: Holt Rinehart and Winston, 1966).

Editors of American Heritage, *The American Heritage History of World War I* (Scranton, PA: American Heritage Press, 1964).

Eksteins, Modris, *The Rites of Spring: The Great War and the Birth of the Modern Age* (Boston, MA: Houghton Mifflin, 1989).

Ellis, John, *Eye-Deep in Hell: Trench Warfare in World War I* (New York: Pantheon Books, 1976).

Farrar-Hockley, Anthony, *Death of an Army: The First Battle of Ypres, 1914, in which the British Regular Army Was Destroyed* (New York: William Morrow, 1968).

Farwell, Byron, *The Great War in Africa, 1914 - 1918* (New York: Norton, 1986).

Fussell, Paul, ed., *Siegfried Sassoon's Long Journey: Selections from the Sherston Memoirs* (New York: Oxford University Press, 1983).

Graves, Robert, *Good-bye to All That: An Autobiography* (London: Jonathan Cape, 1929).

Hart, B. H. Liddell, *The Real War: 1914 - 1918* (Boston, MA: Little, Brown, 1930).

Hynes, Samuel, *A War Imagined: The First World War and English Culture* (New York: Atheneum, 1991).

Horne, Alistair, *The Price of Glory: Verdun 1916* (New York: St. Martin's Press, 1962).

Macdonald, Lyn, *Somme* (London: Michael Joseph, 1983).

Massie, Robert K., *Dreadnought: Britain, Germany, and the Coming of the Great War* (New York: Random House, 1991).

Middlebrook, Martin, *The First Day on the Somme: 1 July, 1916* (New York: W. W. Norton, 1972).

Richards, Frank, *Old Soldiers Never Die* (New York: Berkley Medallion, 1966).

Sassoon, Siegfried, *Diaries, 1915 - 1918*, Rupert Hart-Davis, ed. (London: Faber and Faber, 1983).

Shermer, David, *World War I* (London: Octopus Books, 1975).

Terraine, John, *The Great War, 1914 - 1918: A Pictorial History* (London: Hutchinson and Co., 1965).

Vaughan, Edwin Campion, *Some Desperate Glory: The World War I Diary of a British Officer, 1917* (New York: Henry Holt, 1988).

Wolff, Leon, *In Flanders Fields: The 1917 Campaign* (New York: Time Incorporated, 1958).

WORLD WAR II

Books and Articles

Allen, Louis, *Burma: The Longest War, 1941-1945* (New York: St. Martin's, 1985).

Barnett, Correlli, *The Desert Generals* (New York: Viking Press, 1961).

Barnett, Correlli, *Engage the Enemy More Closely: The Royal Navy in the Second World War* (New York: Norton, 1991).

Barnett, Correlli, ed., *Hitler's Generals: Authoritative Portraits of the Men Who Waged Hitler's War* (New York: Quill Books, 1991).

Baudot, Marcel, et al., eds., *The Historical Encyclopedia of World War II*, Jesse Dilson, trans. (New York: Facts on File, 1989).

Breur, William B., *Retaking the Philippines: America's Return to Corregidor, Manila, and Bataan: October 1944 - March 1945* (New York: St. Martin's Press, 1986).

Casey, William, *The Secret War Against Hitler* (Washington, DC: Regnery Gateway, 1988).

Cave Brown, Anthony, *Bodyguard of Lies* (New York: Harper & Row, 1975).

Clark, Alan, *Barbarossa: The Russian-German Conflict, 1941-1945* (New York: William Morrow, 1965).

Connolly, Cyril, ed., *The Golden Horizon* (New York: University Books, 1955).

Craig, William, *Enemy at the Gates: The Battle for Stalingrad* (New York: Reader's Digest Press/E.P. Dutton, 1973).

Deighton, Len, *Blitzkrieg: From the Rise of Hitler to the Fall of Dunkirk* (New York: Ballantine Books, 1977).

D'Este, Carlo, *Bitter Victory: The Battle for Sicily, 1943* (New York: E.P. Dutton, 1988).

D'Este, Carlo, *Decision in Normandy* (New York: E.P. Dutton, 1983).

D'Este, Carlo, *Fatal Decision: Anzio and the Battle for Rome* (New York: Harper Collins, 1991).

D'Este, Carlo, *World War II in the Mediterranean, 1942 - 1945* (Chapel Hill, NC: Algonquin Books of Chapel Hill, 1990).

Duffy, Christopher, *Red Storm on the Reich: The Soviet March on Germany, 1945* (New York: Atheneum, 1991).

Eisenhower, John S. D., *The Bitter Woods* (New York: G. P. Putnam's Sons, 1969).

Ellis, John, *Brute Force: Allied Strategy and Tactics in the Second World War* (New York: Viking, 1991).

Ellis, John, *The Sharp End of War: The Fighting Man in World War II* (New York: Scribner's, 1980).

Elstob, Peter, *Battle of the Reichswald* (New York: Ballantine Books, 1970).

Fahey, James J., *Pacific War Diary, 1942 - 1945* (Boston, MA: Houghton Mifflin, 1992).

Falk, Stanley, *Liberation of the Philippines* (New York: Ballantine Books, 1971).

Frank, Benis M., *Okinawa: Touchstone to Victory* (New York: Ballantine Books, 1970).

Frank, Richard B., *Guadalcanal: The Definitive Account of the Landmark Battle* (New York: Random House, 1990).

Frankland, Noble, *Bomber Offensive: The Devastation of Europe* (New York: Ballantine Books, 1970).

Fussell, Paul, *Wartime: Understanding and Behavior in the Second World War* (New York: Oxford University Press, 1989).

Galland, Adolf, *The First and the Last: The Rise and Fall of the German Fighter Forces, 1938 - 1945* (New York: Henry Holt, 1954).

Gelb, Norman, *Desperate Venture: The Story of Operation Torch, the Allied Invasion of North Africa* (New York: William Morrow, 1992).

Gelb, Norman, *Dunkirk: The Complete Story of the First Step in the Defeat of Hitler* (New York: William Morrow, 1989).

Gilbert, Martin, *The Second World War: A Complete History* (New York: Henry Holt, 1989).

Gilbert, Martin, *Winston Churchill: The Road to Victory, 1941 - 1945* (Boston, MA: Houghton Mifflin, 1986).

Graham, Dominick and Bidwell, Shelford, *Tug of War: The Battle for Italy 1943 - 1945* (New York: St. Martin's, 1986).

Hart, B. H. Liddell, *The German Generals Talk* (New York: William Morrow, 1948).

Hastings, Max, *Das Reich: Resistance and the March of the Second SS Panzer Division Through France* (New York: Holt Rinehart and Winston, 1981).

Hastings, Max, *Overlord: D-Day and the Battle for Normandy* (New York: Simon & Schuster, 1984).

Hughes, Terry and Costello, John, *The Battle for the Atlantic* (New York: The Dial Press/James Wade, 1977).

Jukes, Geoffrey, *The Defense of Moscow* (New York: Ballantine Books, 1970).

Jukes, Geoffrey, *Kursk: The Clash of Armour* (New York: Ballantine Books, 1969).

Keegan, John, *The Second World War* (New York: Viking, 1990).

Keegan, John, *Six Armies in Normandy: From D-Day to the Liberation of Paris* (New York: Viking, 1982).

Kennedy, Paul, *Pacific Onslaught: 7th Dec. 1941/7th Feb. 1943* (New York: Ballantine Books, 1972).

Kennedy, Paul, *Pacific Victory* (New York: Ballantine Books, 1973).

Lawton, Manny, *Some Survived: An Epic Account of Japanese Captivity During World War II* (Chapel Hill, NC: Algonquin Books of Chapel Hill, 1985).

Lucas, James, *War on the Eastern Front, 1941 - 1945: The General Soldier in Russia* (New York: Stein and Day, 1980).

MacDonald, Charles B., *Company Commander* (New York: Bantam Books, 1978).

MacDonald, Charles B., *The Mighty Endeavor: The American Armed Forces in Europe Theater in World War II* (New York: Oxford University Press, 1969).

Nisbet, Robert, *Roosevelt and Stalin: The Failed Courtship* (Washington, DC: Regnery Gateway, 1988).

Overy, R. J., *The Air War, 1939 - 1945* (New York: Stein and Day, 1981).

Read, Anthony and Fisher, David, *The Deadly Embrace: Hitler, Stalin, and the Nazi-Soviet Pact, 1939 - 1941* (New York: Norton, 1988).

Roscoe, Theodore, *United States Submarine Operations in World War II* (Annapolis, MD: United States Naval Institute, 1949).

Ross, Bill D., *Peleliu, Tragic Triumph: The Untold Story of the Pacific War's Forgotten Battle* (New York: Random House, 1991).

Sajer, Guy, *The Forgotten Soldier* (New York: Harper & Row, 1971).

Seaton, Albert, *The Battle for Moscow* (New York: Stein and Day, 1971).

Seaton, Albert, *The German Army, 1933 - 1945* (New York: St. Martin's Press, 1982).

Shaw, Henry I., Jr., *Tarawa: A Legend Is Born* (New York: Ballantine Books, 1969).

Thompson, R. W., *Battle for the Rhine* (New York: Ballantine Books, 1959).

Trotter, William R., *A Frozen Hell: The Russo-Finnish Winter War of 1939 - 40* (Chapel Hill, NC: Algonquin Books of Chapel Hill, 1991).

Vader, John, *New Guinea: The Tide Is Stemmed* (New York: Ballantine Books, 1971).

Van Der Vat, Dan, *The Pacific Campaign, World War II: The US-Japanese Naval War, 1941 - 1945* (New York: Simon & Schuster, 1991).

Whitting, Charles, *Battle of the Ruhr Pocket* (New York: Ballantine Books, 1970).

Willmott, H. P., *The Great Crusade: A New Complete History of the Second World War* (New York: The Free Press, 1989).

Wilmot, Chester, *The Struggle for Europe* (New York: Harper and Brothers, 1952).

Ziemke, Earl F. and Bauer, Magna E., *Moscow to Stalingrad: Decision in the East* (New York: Military Heritage Press, 1988).

Ziemke, Earl F., *Stalingrad to Berlin: The German Defeat in the East* (New York: Military Heritage Press, 1985).

WRITING
(see **Grammar**)

YACHTING
(see **Boating**)

YOUTH
(see also **Children**)

Books and Articles

Furstenberg, Frank, Jr., et al., "The Teenage Marriage Controversy," *The Public Interest*, Number 90 (Winter, 1988), pp. 121-132.

Grigg, William, "Scouting and Sin: The Case Against the Boy Scouts," *Chronicles*, Volume 16 (January, 1992), pp. 44-46.

Lerman, Robert I. and Pouncy, Hillard, "The Compelling Case for Youth Apprenticeships," *The Public Interest*, Number 101 (Fall, 1990), pp. 62-77.

Organizations

Boy Scouts of America 1325 West Walnut Hill Lane, P.O. Box 152079, Irving, TX 75015, (214)-580-2000. Publications: *Boys' Life, Boy Scouts of America - Annual Report to Congress, Exploring Magazine: The Journal for Explorers, Scouting Magazine: A Family Magazine.* Educational program geared toward the character development, citizenship training, and mental and physical fitness of boys and young adults.

Girl Scouts of the U.S.A. 420 Fifth Avenue, New York, NY 10018-2702, (212)-852-8000. Publications: *Annual Environmental Scanning Report, Girl Scout Leader: For Adults in Girl Scouting, Girl Scouts of the U.S.A. - Annual Report, GSUSA News.* Helps girls develop as happy, resourceful individuals willing to share their abilities as citizens in their homes, their communities, their country and the world. Promotes ethical code through the Girl Scout Promise and Law.

National Catholic Committee on Scouting c/o Boy Scouts of America, 1325 West Walnut Hill Lane, P.O. Box 152079-2079, Irving, TX 75015-2079, (214)-580-2109. Publication: *National Catholic Committee on Scouting - Newsletter.* Functions on national and diocesan levels to advise national and local Boy Scouts of America councils on principles and practices of the Catholic Church as they apply to the Scout units in Catholic parishes.

National Traditionalist Caucus P.O. Box 971, General Post Office, New York, NY 10116, (212)-685-4689. Publication: *EXCALIBUR.* Conservative youth organization concerned with the political education of high school, junior high school, and college students.

Students for America 3509 Haworth Drive, Suite 200, Raleigh, NC 27609, (919)-782-0213. Publications: *Free Voice, Newsletter.* Politically conservative students united to develop programs to advance conservative principles and Judeo-Christian values on American college campuses.

Third Generation c/o Heritage Foundation, 214 Massachusetts Avenue, NE, Washington, DC 20002, (202)-546-4400. Conservative individuals and political activists under 35 years of age.

Young Americans for Freedom 4501 Daly Drive, Suite 101, Chantilly, VA 22021. Publications: *Dialogue on Liberty, New Guard, YAF in the News.* Nonpartisan, political youth (up to age 39). Seeks to promote a conservative philosophy of free enterprise and strong national defense.

Young America's Foundation 110 Elden Street, Suite A, Herndon, VA 22070, (703)-318-9608. Publications: *Libertas, Campus Leader, Continuity.* Service organization for politically conservative high school and college students; committed to bringing balance to college campuses.

APPENDIX A

STATES
(Governors' Offices and State Tourism Bureaus)

ALABAMA Governor's Office, State Capitol, Montgomery, AL 36130, (205)-261-2500. Alabama Bureau of Tourism and Travel, 532 South Perry Street, Montgomery, AL 36104-4616, (205)-242-4169.

ALASKA Governor's Office, Box A, Juneau, AK 99811, (907)-465-3500. Alaska Division of Tourism, 333 Willoughby Avenue, Juneau, AK 99811-0001, (907)-465-2010.

ARIZONA Governor's Office, State Capitol, West Wing, Phoenix, AZ 85007, (602)-542-4331. Arizona Office of Tourism, 1100 West Washington Street, Phoenix, AZ 85007-2939, (602)-542-3618.

ARKANSAS Governor's Office, State Capitol, Little Rock, AR 72201, (501)-682-2345. Arkansas Division of Parks and Tourism, 1 Capitol Mall, Little Rock, AR 72201-1087, (501)-682-7777.

CALIFORNIA Governor's Office, State Capitol Building, Sacramento, CA 95814, (916)-445-2815. California Office of Tourism, 1121 L Street, Suite 103, Sacramento, CA 95814-3926, (916)-322-2881.

COLORADO Governor's Office, 136 State Capitol, Denver, CO 80203, (303)-866-2471. Colorado Tourism Board, 1625 Broadway, Suite 1700, Denver, CO 80202-4734, (303)-592-5410.

CONNECTICUT Governor's Office, State Capitol, 210 Capitol Avenue, Hartford, CT 06106, (203)-566-4840. Connecticut Tourism Division, 865 Brook Street, Rocky Hill, CT 06067-3405, (203)-258-4286.

DELAWARE Governor's Office, Legislative Hall, Dover, DE 19901, (302)-736-4101. Delaware Tourism Office, 99 Kings Highway, Dover, DE 19901-3816, (302)-739-4271.

DISTRICT OF COLUMBIA Delegate's Office, 2135 Rayburn House Office Building, Washington, DC 20515, (202)-225-8050. Capitol Reservations, 1730 Rhode Island Avenue, NW, Suite 302, Washington, DC 20036-3101, (202)-452-1270.

FLORIDA Governor's Office, The Capitol, Tallahassee, FL 32301, (904)-488-2272. Florida Division of Tourism, 107 West Gaines Street, Room 505, Tallahassee, FL 32399-2000, (904)-487-0162.

GEORGIA Governor's Office, 203 State Capitol, Atlanta, GA 30334, (404)-656-1776. Georgia Department of Industry, Trade and Tourism, 285 Peachtree Center Avenue, NE, Marquis Tower II, Suite 1000, Atlanta, GA 30303-1505, (404)-656-3553.

HAWAII Governor's Office, State Capitol, Executive Chambers, Honolulu, HI 96813, (808)-548-5420. Hawaii Department of Business, Economic Development and Tourism, 737 Bishop Street, Grosvenor Center, Mauka Tower, Suite 1900, Honolulu, HI 96813-0000, (808)-548-7700.

IDAHO Governor's Office, State House, Boise, ID 83720, (208)-334-2100. Idaho Tourism Division, 700 West State Street, 2nd Floor, Boise, ID 83720-0001, (208)-334-2017.

ILLINOIS Governor's Office, State Capitol Building, Room 207, Springfield, IL 62706, (217)-782-6830. Illinois Tourist Informational Center, 310 South Michigan, Chicago, IL 60604-4287, (312)-793-2094.

INDIANA Governor's Office, 206 State House, Indianapolis, IN 46204, (317)-232-4567. Indiana Department of Commerce, Tourism and Film Development Division, 1 North Capitol Avenue, Suite 700, Indianapolis, IN 46204-2026, (317)-232-8860.

IOWA Governor's Office, State Capitol, Des Moines, IA 50319, (515)-281-5211. Iowa Division of Tourism, 200 East Grand Avenue, Des Moines, IA 50309-1827, (515)-281-3100.

KANSAS Governor's Office, State Capitol, 2nd Floor, Topeka, KS 66612, (913)-296-3232. Kansas Division of Travel and Tourism, 400 Southwest 8th Street, 5th Floor, Topeka, KS 66603-0000, (913)-296-2009.

KENTUCKY Governor's Office, State Capitol, Frankfort, KY 40601, (502)-564-2611. Kentucky Department of Travel Development, Capitol Plaza Tower, 22nd Floor, Frankfort, KY 40601, (502)-564-4930.

LOUISIANA Governor's Office, State Capitol, Baton Rouge, LA 70804, (504)-342-7015. Louisiana Office of Tourism, 900 Riverside Street, North, Baton Rouge, LA 70802-5236, (504)-342-8119.

MAINE Governor's Office, State House, Station 1, Augusta, ME 04333, (207)-289-3531. Maine Division of Tourism, 189 State Street, Augusta, ME 04333-0001, (207)-289-5710.

MARYLAND Governor's Office, State House, Annapolis, MD 21404, (301)-974-3901. Maryland Office of Tourist Development, 217 East Redwood Street, 9th Floor, Baltimore, MD 21202-3316, (301)-333-6611.

MASSACHUSETTS Governor's Office, State House, Room 360, Boston, MA 02133, (617)-727-3600. Massachusetts Office of Travel and Tourism, 100 Cambridge Street, 13th Floor, Boston, MA 02202-0001, (617)-727-3205.

MICHIGAN Governor's Office, Capitol Building, Lansing, MI 48909, (517)-373-3400. Michigan Travel Bureau, 333 South Capitol Avenue, Suite F, Lansing, MI 48933-2022, (517)-373-0670.

MINNESOTA Governor's Office, 130 State Capitol Building, Aurora Avenue, St. Paul, MN 55155, (612)-296-3391. Minnesota Office of Tourism, 375 Jackson Street, Suite 250, St. Paul, MN 55101-1810, (612)-296-5029.

MISSISSIPPI Governor's Office, P.O. Box 139, Jackson, MS 39205, (601)-359-3100. Mississippi Tourism Division, 550 High Street, Suite 1200, Jackson, MS 32901-1113, (601)-359-3297.

MISSOURI Governor's Office, P.O. Box 720, Jefferson City, MO 65102, (314)-751-3222. Missouri Division of Tourism, 301 West High Street, Jefferson City, MO 65102-0000, (314)-751-4133.

MONTANA Governor's Office, Helena, MT 59620, (406)-444-3111. Montana Promotion Division, 1424 9th Avenue, Helena, MT 59601-4503, (406)-444-2654.

NEBRASKA Governor's Office, State Capitol Building, Room 2316, Lincoln, NE 68509, (402)-471-2244. Nebraska Travel and Tourism Division, Department of Economic Development, 301 Centennial Mall, South, Lincoln, NE 68508-2529, (402)-471-3794.

NEVADA Governor's Office, Executive Chambers, Capitol Building, Carson City, NV 89710, (702)-885-5670. Nevada Commission on Tourism, 5151 South Carson Street, Carson City, NV 89710-0000, (702)-687-4322.

NEW HAMPSHIRE Governor's Office, State House, Concord, NH 03301, (603)-271-2121. New Hampshire Office of Vacation Travel, 105 Loudon Road, Concord, NH 03301-5601, (603)-271-2666.

NEW JERSEY Governor's Office, State House, 125 West State Street, CN-001, Trenton, NJ 08625, (609)-292-6000. New Jersey Division of Travel and Tourism, 20 West State Street, Trenton, NJ 08625-0001, (609)-292-2470.

NEW MEXICO Governor's Office, State Capitol, Room 417, Santa Fe, NM 87503, (505)-827-3000. New Mexico Tourism and Travel Division, 1100 St. Francis Drive, Santa Fe, NM 87503-0001, (505)-827-0291.

NEW YORK Governor's Office, Executive Chamber, State Capitol, Albany, NY 12224, (518)-474-8390. New York Division of Tourism, 1 Commerce Plaza, Albany, NY 12245-0001, (518)-473-0715.

NORTH CAROLINA Governor's Office, State Capitol, Raleigh, NC 27611, (919)-733-4240. North Carolina Travel and Tourism Division, 430 North Salisbury Street, Raleigh, NC 27603-6651, (919)-733-4171.

NORTH DAKOTA Governor's Office, State Capitol, Bismarck, ND 58505, (701)-224-2200. North Dakota Tourism and Promotion, 604 East Boulevard Avenue, Liberty Memorial Building, Bismarck, ND 58505-0000, (701)-224-2525.

OHIO Governor's Office, State House, Columbus, OH 43266-0601, (614)-466-3555. Ohio Division of Travel and Tourism, 77 South High Street, Columbus, OH 43266-0001, (614)-466-8844.

OKLAHOMA Governor's Office, State Capitol Building, Room 212, Oklahoma City, OK 73105, (405)-521-2342. Oklahoma Tourism and Recreation Department, 500 Will Rogers Building, Oklahoma City, OK 73105-4402, (405)-521-2413.

OREGON Governor's Office, State Capitol, Room 254, Salem, OR 97310, (503)-378-3111. Oregon Tourism Division, 775 Summer Street, NE, Salem, OR 97310-0001, (503)-373-1200.

PENNSYLVANIA Governor's Office, 225 Main Capitol Building, Harrisburg, PA 17120, (717)-787-2500. Pennsylvania Bureau of Travel Marketing, 453 Forum Building, Harrisburg, PA 17120-0001, (717)-787-5453.

RHODE ISLAND Governor's Office, 222 State House, Providence, RI 02903, (401)-277-2080. Rhode Island Tourism and Promotion Division, 7 Jackson Walkway, Providence, RI 02903-3622, (401)-277-2601.

SOUTH CAROLINA Governor's Office, P.O. Box 11369, The State House, Columbia, SC 29211, (803)-734-9818. South Carolina Division of Tourism, 1205 Pendleton Street, Columbia, SC 29201-3731, (803)-734-0135.

SOUTH DAKOTA Governor's Office, State Capitol Building, Pierre, SD 57501, (605)-773-3212. South Dakota Tourism Division, Capitol Lake Plaza, Pierre, SD 57501-3369, (605)-773-3301.

TENNESSEE Governor's Office, State Capitol, Nashville, TN 37219, (615)-741-2001. Tennessee Department of Tourist Development, 320 6th Avenue, North, Nashville, TN 37219-5605, (615)-741-2159.

TEXAS Governor's Office, State Capitol, P.O. Box 12428, Austin, TX 78711, (512)-463-2000. Texas Tourist Division, 816 Congress Avenue, Suite 1200, Austin, TX 78701-2443, (512)-472-5059.

UTAH Governor's Office, 210 State Capitol, Salt Lake City, UT 84114, (801)-538-1000. Utah Travel Council, Council Hall, Capitol Hill, Salt Lake City, UT 84114-0000, (801)-538-1030.

VERMONT Governor's Office, 109 State Street, 5th Floor, Montpelier, VT 05602, (802)-828-3333. Vermont Travel Division, 134 State Street, Montpelier, VT 05602-2707, (802)-828-3236.

VIRGINIA Governor's Office, State Capitol, Richmond, VA 23219, (804)-786-2211. Virginia Division of Tourism, 1021 East Cary Street, 14th Floor, Richmond, VA 23219-4000, (804)-786-2051.

WASHINGTON Governor's Office, Office of the Governor, Olympia, WA 98504, (206)-753-6780. Washington Tourism Development Division, General Administration Building, Olympia, WA 98504-0001, (206)-753-5600.

WEST VIRGINIA Governor's Office, State Capitol, Charleston, WV 25305, (304)-340-1600. West Virginia Tourism and Parks Division, 2101 Washington Street East, Charleston, WV 25305-0001, (304)-348-2200.

WISCONSIN Governor's Office, State Capitol, 115 East State Capitol, Madison, WI 53702, (608)-266-1212. Wisconsin Tourism Development, 123 West Washington Avenue, 6th Floor, Madison, WI 53702-0001, (608)-266-2147.

WYOMING Governor's Office, State Capitol Building, Cheyenne, WY 82002, (307)-777-7434. Wyoming Tourism and Marketing Division, IH-25 & College Drive, Cheyenne, WY 82002-0001, (307)-777-7777.

APPENDIX B

CONSERVATIVE PUBLICATIONS

The American Enterprise 1150 17th Street, NW, Washington, DC 20036, (202)-862-5800.

The American Spectator P.O. Box 549, Arlington, VA 22216-0549, (703)-243-3733.

The Cato Journal Cato Institute, 224 Second Street, SE, Washington, DC 20003, (202)-546-0200.

Chronicles 934 North Main Street, Rockford, IL 61103, (815)-964-5054.

Commentary 165 East 56th Street, New York, NY 10022, (212)-751-4000.

Conservative Chronicle Box 29, Hampton, IA 50441, (515)-456-2585.

Crisis 1511 K Street, NW, Suite 525, Washington, DC 20005, (202)-347-7411.

Human Events 422 First Street, SE, Washington, DC 20003, (202)-546-0856.

Modern Age Intercollegiate Studies Institute, Inc., 14 S. Bryn Mawr Avenue, Bryn Mawr, PA 19010-3275, (215)-525-3315.

The National Interest 1112 16th Street, NW, Suite 540, Washington, DC 20036, (202)-467-4884.

National Review 150 East 35th Street, New York, NY 10016, (212)-679-7330.

Policy Review 214 Massachusetts Avenue, NE, Washington, DC 20002-4999, (202)-546-4400.

The Public Interest 1112 16th Street, NW, Suite 530, Washington, DC 20036, (202)-785-8555.

Reason 3415 S. Sepulveda Blvd., Suite 400, Los Angeles, CA 90034, (310)-391-2245.

This World Elizabethtown College Institute for Business and Society, Elizabethtown, PA 17022, (717)-361-1000 (x1312).